GOTHIC FOR GIRLS

GOTHIC FOR GIRLS
MISTY™ AND BRITISH COMICS

JULIA ROUND

FOREWORD BY MEL GIBSON

University Press of Mississippi / Jackson

The University Press of Mississippi is the scholarly publishing agency of
the Mississippi Institutions of Higher Learning: Alcorn State University,
Delta State University, Jackson State University, Mississippi State University,
Mississippi University for Women, Mississippi Valley State University,
University of Mississippi, and University of Southern Mississippi.

www.upress.state.ms.us

Designed by Peter D. Halverson

The University Press of Mississippi is a member of the Association of University Presses.

Page ii: Cover of *Misty* #27. Misty designed and drawn by Shirley Bellwood, image manipulated and colored by Jack Cunningham/Ted Andrews for the comic book cover. Reproduced with permission of Misty™ Rebellion Publishing IP Ltd.; copyright © Rebellion Publishing IP Ltd., all rights reserved.

Copyright © 2019 by University Press of Mississippi
All rights reserved

First printing 2019
∞

Library of Congress Cataloging-in-Publication Data available

LCCN 2019020040
ISBN 9781496824455 (hardcover)
ISBN 9781496824462 (paperback)
ISBN 9781496824479 (epub single)
ISBN 9781496824486 (epub institutional)
ISBN 9781496824493 (pdf single)
ISBN 9781496824509 (pdf institutional)

British Library Cataloging-in-Publication Data available

For Dana, our Child of the Mists

CONTENTS

	Foreword by Dr. Mel Gibson	xii
	Acknowledgments	xv
	Introduction	3
1.	The Rise and Fall of British Girls' Comics	14
2.	Anonymous Authors	35
3.	Astonishing Artists	60
4.	Visceral Visuals	83
5.	Shocking Stories	94
6.	Horror and Gothic in the 1970s	108
7.	Our Friend of the Mists	127
8.	A Taxonomy of Terror	151
9.	Terror, Horror, and Female Gothic	187
10.	Deep Cuts: Gothic Concepts and Identities	208
11.	Surface Reflections: Gothic Symbols, Settings, and Archetypes	226
12.	Gothic for Girls	246
13.	Make *Misty* for Me	264
14.	Leaving These Misty Isles	282
	Reflections	294
	Notes	297
	References	304
	Index	325

Figure 0.1. "The Haunting of Julia Round." Art by Letty Wilson, written by Julia Round. Produced by Inkpot Studios.

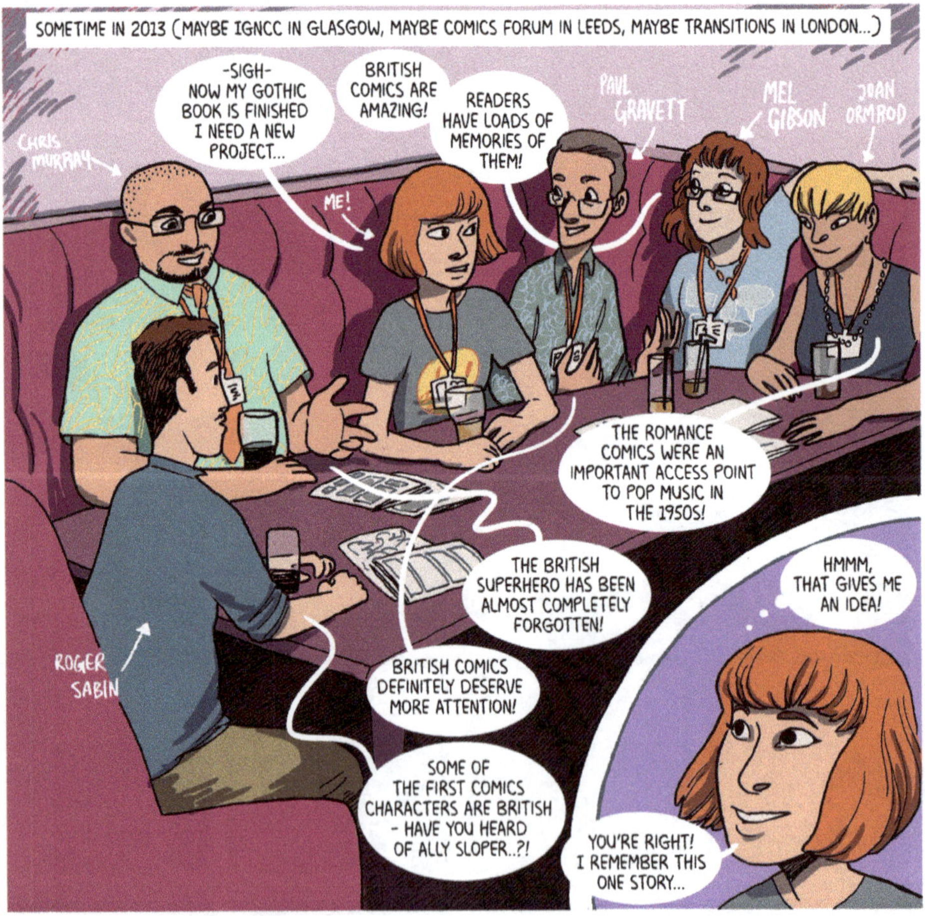

FOREWORD

Mel Gibson

The story of the British girls' comic was, for a long time, a lost history (or perhaps "herstory"). Often innovative, girls' comics were perceived as lesser fare by many, in part because they were aimed at girls, a group whose engagement with popular culture was something that was frequently spoken of disparagingly. All the same, beginning in the 1950s, these genuinely popular weekly anthology comics, some circulating more than 800,000 a week, engaged a number of generations of predominantly female readers before fading away completely in the first decade of the twenty-first century.

This book engages specifically with one of those comics, *Misty*, a title filled with narratives of mystery and terror. In exploring both the popularity of a specific comic and why it ended, Julia Round adds nuance to our understanding of the demise of the genre, which may have come about for a number of reasons—including problematic (one might say monstrous) management practices that failed to value both creators and child audiences, changing media landscapes, and shifting notions of childhood.

Further, and linking comic, genre, and history, one can argue that the disappearance of these comics was particularly horrific given that they were created by some of the most significant comics writers in Britain, working with talented artists from both Britain and Europe. This book is partly dedicated to exploring who created *Misty*, at times an act of detection as well as cooperation with others interested in the field, given that the publishers tended not to reveal the names of artists or writers. Julia has additionally managed to contact numerous people involved in creating the comic, particularly from the editorial team, adding another layer to the analysis through the inclusion of interview material.

Despite the negative views of girls' comics, they offered a huge range of stories, including complex and challenging ones alongside short and simple ones, across many genres. These texts offered various pleasures, including that of being scared, pleasures always enhanced by the wait for the next episode. As always with serial and other fictions, being able to engage with prediction and anticipation drew readers in, and talking about what they had read often cemented their relationship with both peers and comics culture. In a sense, this book is an extension of such conversations, albeit in an adult and largely academic context.

Since the genre ended, both fans and academics have worked to increase awareness of these texts and their significance. The idea of celebrating popular culture for girls, and exploring what girls have done with the popular culture offered to them, has increasingly appeared in work across a range of academic disciplines and engaged with a number of approaches, from work on audiences and memory, like my own, to textual analysis of narratives on specific themes. This book adds another contribution in analyzing content, production, and audience, and it also aims to think through why comics for young people, especially girls, have been largely, as yet, neglected.

For many readers and researchers, the touchstones within this genre include *Bunty* from DC Thomson, the longest-lived of the titles, best known for the school story "The Four Marys"; *Girl* from Hulton Press, seen as significant, in part, because of its high production values; and *Jackie*, also from DC Thomson, which engaged with the world of popular culture, contributing to an aspirational girls' culture for both teens and younger readers. *Misty* was also one of these touchstone comics, to the extent that a long-running campaign has existed to get the comic back in print, a goal that has recently been realized in the form of several edited collections (including new work inspired by the original comic). Whilst comparatively short-lived, *Misty* has become a rallying point for readers interested in "spooky" stories and horror in comics, as well as innovation in terms of form and narrative.

Misty was not the only comic to create weird narratives, of course. *Spellbound*, *Jinty*, and *Diana*, among others, also engaged with ghost stories, tales of retribution, dreadful twists of fate, magical objects, dark fairy tales, and horrible and mysterious happenings. What *Misty* did that made it distinctive is something that Julia Round explores here by analyzing the comic. The way that the team engaged with readers, both through letter pages and by responding to direct feedback on stories, is given attention, too. Further, the author has developed a complementary set of materials, including a searchable database, which covers stories, themes, and creators. This database acts not only as a companion to this book but also as a stimulus, it is to be hoped, to further research.

In addition to contextualizing *Misty* in the world of comics, the author offers some thoughts that place it in the wider context of horror across film, books and television in the 1970s. The links between this comic and fairy tales and children's books are also considered. Further, this book explores how *Misty* relates to issues within both cultural and literary studies, including, perhaps most significantly, Gothic scholarship and the concept of Gothic for Girls.

Finally, the author also adds a highly personal aspect to this book in the introduction, through her memory of one particular story in the comic, the impact that it had on her as a child, and the way that memory continued into adulthood. One might consider it a story suitable for inclusion in a new *Misty* anthology, perhaps titled "The Haunting of Julia Round."[1] Tracking down this persistent childhood memory provided the impetus for this major piece of research, and in discussing the emotional impact of her rediscovery of this narrative, Julia Round also shows the power of texts from childhood.

ACKNOWLEDGMENTS

This book has been a labor of love, and I owe an enormous debt of gratitude to many people: Ted Andrews, David Baillie, María Barrera Castell, Bournemouth University and the Centre for the Study of Journalism, Culture and Community, the Comics UK forum members, Jack Cunningham, Paul Fisher Davies, Anne Digby, Brenda Ellis, Helen Fay, Blas Gallego, David Gesalí, the "Get MISTY Back in Print!" group members, Mel Gibson, Kelvin Gosnell, Lee Grice, John Harnett, Frances Hawkhead, Hans Holm, Shaun Kimber, Catriona Laird, Chris Lillyman, Chris Lloyd, Terry Magee, Daniel McGachey, Jean-Matthieu Méon, Pat Mills, Isidre Monés, Chris Murray, Greg O'Neill, Joan Ormrod, John Packard, Wilf Prigmore, Rebellion Publishing, Keith Richardson, David Roach, Mark "Spreadsheet" Round, my parents Alan and Val Round, Roger Sabin, John Sanders, Jenni Scott, Basil and Sue Sellwood, Ben Smith, Bronwen Thomas, and Letty Wilson.

GOTHIC FOR GIRLS

INTRODUCTION

Once upon a time there was a girl who was not very pretty. She was given a magic mirror and told it would make her beautiful if she followed its instructions correctly. And it worked! But as she got more lovely, she also became mean and vain, and one day she did something wrong with the instructions, and when she woke up the next day and looked in her mirror, her beautiful face was shattered and warped.

How would you like to wake up every day . . . like this?

This was my memory of a story in a comic that I read as a child and have never, ever forgotten. I think I found it at a church hall jumble sale. I would have been eight or nine, as I also remember reading a magazine article the same day about a horror film called *A Nightmare on Elm Street* (1984, released in the United Kingdom on July 12, 1985).

I read this story and was transfixed by its final panel, with its threatening narration and close-up image of the girl's ruined face—like bad plastic surgery or a melted candle. I didn't sleep that night. I told my parents it was because of the Freddy Krueger article (I don't know why; perhaps I was already learning to think of comics as something childish). But it wasn't. The final image and sentence of that story stayed with me.

Although I threw the comic away and (temporarily) banned myself from anything horror based, I never forgot that story. Years later, I would periodically find myself searching for it online, using phrases such as "mirror girls horror comic story wake up like this" that produced lots of possibilities from multiple titles (*Jinty*, *Girl*, *Spellbound*, *Misty*, and *June* were all contenders) but no results. Then one day a chance conversation about girls' comics and horror reminded me of it again. I still didn't know the title of the comic, but somehow I felt sure it was *Misty*, which I had other memories of from doctors' and dentists' waiting rooms and jumble sales. I was looking for a new direction for my research into Gothic after my first book, so I decided this would be my next project, and made numerous trips to the British Library to read the entire series.

It seemed uncanny but serendipitous that the story was in the last binder I read (which had been unavailable on my first visit). I'd had a few false alarms before, as a surprising number of *Misty* stories dealt with mirrors, and my summary was pretty vague, but as soon as the tale began, I knew this was The One. I felt physically sick and excited as I turned the pages, and it was all there, exactly as I remembered it, even the final narrated line, which I had carried with me almost verbatim for over thirty years. To say this was an emotional moment would be pretty insufficient.

The story is "Mirror . . . Mirror" (art by Isidre Monés, writer unknown), published in *Misty* #37 on October 14, 1978.[1] It marks the starting point for all my research and has been in my head for so long I'm sure I've overemphasized its impact on the average reader. But once I started researching *Misty*, I discovered many other stories that also hit and haunted me. I found so much to explore here: the comic's alluring host with her poetic words, its dramatic tales of horrifying fates and karmic justice, and its incredible artwork and striking layouts. I wanted to tell everybody about this comic that continued to surprise me more than thirty years later, and found myself summarizing *Misty*'s most shudder-making stories to anyone who would listen—a surprising number of people.[2] I discovered an online community of people who felt exactly the same way about our beloved *Misty*, but also realized that, like many girls' comics, it had been almost completely forgotten by the world at large (at least until interest began to rise again with Rebellion's purchase of the copyright). I talked girls' comics with Joan Ormrod and Mel Gibson (to whom I am indebted for her kind foreword to this book) and became certain that *Misty* was an important part of this forgotten genre's history. Thanks to Paul Gravett, I was introduced to the British comics legend Pat Mills and was inspired by his generosity and enthusiasm. Paul also invited me to interview *Misty*'s legendary cover artist Shirley Bellwood, though sadly, owing to her health, I was unable to do so. Pat put me in touch with David Roach, who shared his encyclopedic knowledge of Spanish comics artists with me, and through them both I managed to track down the surviving *Misty* editorial team: Wilf Prigmore, Jack Cunningham, and Ted Andrews, and even some of the Spanish artists who contributed to the comic. Before I knew it, nearly four years had passed, and I had become completely immersed in archival, cultural, and critical research based on *Misty*. Thus what started out as a personal mission to revisit some childhood memories and perhaps write an article or two developing my previous research around Gothic and comics became a fully fledged book project that has easily been the most rewarding and entertaining I have undertaken to date. It has also enabled me to share much more of my supporting research than ever before, as many of my notes are published on my website at www.juliaround.com/misty, which also now includes a searchable database of all the *Misty* stories, summaries, creators, and origins, along with some of the interviews that I conducted for this project.

This book is the first full-length critical study of any individual British girls' comic. It contains a wealth of primary research taken from archival visits, creator interviews, and online discussions with past readers and reveals a great deal about the hidden history and production practices of the comics industry in this country. Many of the writers, artists, editors, and associates interviewed here have never previously spoken about their work for British comics. Their recollections give a fascinating picture of how the industry operated—one that is in danger of being entirely lost owing to a lack of records and the ephemeral nature of these publications. It has been a joy to be able to identify and name the creators of these stories and to finally credit them for their work. Alongside this, the book offers extensive close analysis of the content and themes of *Misty*. Having a corpus of manageable size has allowed me to perform quantitative and qualitative analysis of the comic's entire content, accurately reflecting and preserving this information for future generations, as for many years the comics themselves were not considered collectible or worth storing. The statistical analysis and close reading I have done also explores *Misty*'s use and manipulation of Gothic themes, and so this book also develops an existing body of Gothic critical theory. By synthesizing and reflecting on this, I offer suggestions for a new and undertheorized subgenre: Gothic for Girls.

Over the last few decades, Gothic themes have gained in prominence within children's literature, forming more than a "publishing trend." Writing in 2001, Reynolds et al. (2001, 1) claim that horror has "spectacularly dominated children's publishing" for the preceding two decades, aimed at readers as young as six or seven. Critics now acknowledge that "the children's Gothic no longer seems marginal" (A. Jackson 2017, 1), and children's literature appears as "a particularly dark tradition" in some texts (Spooner 2017, 184). Alongside this sits a highly popular subgenre of young adult literature dealing with supernatural and Gothic themes. James (2009, 116) points out that "young adult readers, poised between childhood and adulthood, have proven especially receptive to the Gothic's themes of liminality, monstrosity, transgression, romance, and sexuality" (see also M. Smith and Moruzi 2018). Crawford (2014) also traces a historical lineage from early Romance and Gothic to the rise of the paranormal romance in the 1970s and its movement into young adult fiction in the 1990s. As such, my arguments have great potential impact on how we might better understand and create literature and periodicals for children and young adults, particularly when these draw on genres such as horror, mystery, and Gothic.

Before diving into the dark and approaching *Misty* as a Gothic text, it seems important to define some of these terms and offer a working definition of Gothic itself. But straightaway we find difficulties here, as Gothic is constantly changing to suit its time. Even if we leave aside its origins and focus only on the literary tradition of the past 250 years, how can novels as far apart as Horace Walpole's *The Castle of Otranto* (1764) and Tom Baker's *The Boy Who Kicked Pigs* (1999) be reconciled under a single label? One is a supernatural melodrama in a medieval vein, whose hyperbolic dialogue and hysterical characters uncover an ancient curse; the other is a blackly humorous parody of a children's tale that ends in mass death and visceral violence. In historical, philosophical, formal, generic, and cultural terms, they are far apart, but both nonetheless fall under the label of "Gothic."

Gothic motifs and themes have also changed as the literary genre developed: Botting (1996) identifies a historical turn from external to internal, where the object of terror is no longer cast out or banished but instead identified within ourselves. While haunted landscapes remain, the urban and suburban now sit in counterpoint to the ancient castle: Count Dracula is at his most terrifying in London, not Transylvania, and suburban madness replaces the archaic setting in American Gothic. Characters and archetypes have also changed: monsters become sympathetic heroes, and Auerbach (1995) traces the many ways in which our vampires have increasingly come to reflect our social concerns and ourselves. Similarly, over the past century, we have seen the zombie change from a living slave to a cannibalistic corpse, and then back again to an infected living person.

Gothic also invites a wide range of different critical approaches from different times and disciplines. Early historical studies and surveys (Summers, Birkhead, Varma) initially gave way to psychoanalytic readings, leading on to textual, aesthetic, structural, cultural, ideological, gendered, (and many more!) models. In the main, rather than considering Gothic as a historically limited genre, many critics today view it as an overarching mode of cultural production, of the type identified in Frye's *Anatomy of Criticism* (1957). Conceiving Gothic in this way places it alongside Frye's other categories of the mythic, romantic, high mimetic, low mimetic, and ironic: as a mode of creation that produces different genres at different times. Punter famously states that "Gothic is the paradigm of all fiction, all textuality" (1998, 1). He also describes Gothic as an "ur form," claiming that, rather than predicting fears and anxieties, it is an adaptable and "capacious vessel into which all kinds of content can be poured" (Punter 2013a, 692). Mighall (1999, xxv) also claims that "Gothic is a process, not an essence; a rhetoric rather than a store of universal symbols," and that established institutions, texts, and ideas have Gothic "thrust upon them." Anne Williams (1995) too sees Gothic as something larger than a literary genre: describing it as a poetic tradition or way of writing. Miles (2002, 4) calls it a "discursive site," and Khair (2014, 223) names it similarly "as a literary discourse ...defined against discourses of order, reason, balance and moderation." Other critics go still further: Jones (2009, 2010) argues that Gothic is much more than a genre or mode, instead defining it as a "habitus." The habitus is Bourdieu's concept of a "system of internalised structures [and] schemes of perception" (1984, 86) that categorizes existence and structures the behavior of different social groups. In Jones's parsing, Gothic shapes the way we understand and respond to reality (and literature) through its resonances with our everyday lives and cultural groups.

These elevations of Gothic connect it with Romance, validating critical interest and placing Gothic within a familiar cultural history of revolt against the Enlightenment (Baldick and Mighall 2012). Cultural materialist perspectives also situate Gothic in this manner: as a type of writing or thought that comes in response to social trauma (Punter 1980, 14) or maybe even expresses desires for cataclysm and upheaval (Warwick 2007). Gothic thus takes on different forms at different times (from, say, the Enlightenment to the millennium and Y2K panic). While Baldick and Mighall (2012) attack these definitions as simplistic and tautological, they do serve as a description (if not an analysis) of what Gothic does. It articulates fears and Others and enables responses to them—although the assumption that Gothic reflects rather than creates such demons is problematic.

Baldick and Mighall continue to expose the contradictions in a view of Gothic as subversive or reactionary, pointing out that the same texts can be read as "tamely humanitarian: they credibly encourage respect for women's property rights, and they imply that rape, arbitrary imprisonment, and torture are, on the whole, a bad thing" (2012, 285). Subsequent critics such as Crawford (2014) have exposed the divergence possible in interpretations of Gothic texts. So it seems that Gothic can be read as both rebellious and conservative and can thus also be claimed as ambivalent. *Misty*'s combination of transgressive characters and aspirational heroines, together with magical rewards and extreme punishments, offers a good example of this tension.

Alongside Gothics that are traumatic, sublime, and Romantic, Spooner (2017) also draws attention to popular contemporary forms of Gothic that seem celebratory or playful, arguing that these examples of "happy Gothic" may draw on aesthetic over affect but also carry political weight. In contrast to Jameson's (2000, 289) description of Gothic as a "boring and exhausted paradigm," Spooner (2017, 6) claims its new forms as "Post-Millennial Gothic"—taking in lighthearted and celebratory aspects and positioning Gothic, like postmodernism, as both a continuation and break with the previous century. She argues that Gothic aesthetics (rather than thematics) dominate in contemporary versions, while recognizing that the borders between these categories can be blurred. Buckley (2018, 57) also validates Gothic aesthetic, suggesting that "critics should not so readily dismiss the "trappings" of Gothic fiction in order to plunge into its psychic depths." Baddeley (2002) similarly privileges the superficial and stylized elements of Gothic by merging these with action, arguing that the contemporary Goth lifestyle is an "aesthetic" that simultaneously constitutes a "lived commentary" on social, political and cultural issues (Martin 2002; Carrington 2011). These numerous Gothics are acknowledged in Sowerby's (2012, 35) statement that "'Gothic' has proved to be a truly protean term."

So Gothic is multiple and mutable, ranging from parody to pain, and can appear as affect, aesthetic, or practice. Identifying it becomes difficult without resorting to a "tiresome catalogue of motifs" (G. Williams 2014, 413) or "Gothic shopping list" (Spooner 2017, 53). The best definitions are those that are flexible enough to be applied across centuries and media, such as Hogle's (2002) "Gothic matrix" (an antiquated space, a hidden secret, a physical or psychological haunting, and an oscillation between reality and the supernatural), or Baldick's combination of "a fearful sense of inheritance in time with a claustrophobic sense of enclosure in space" (1992, xix). However, in their flexibility, such definitions can also tend toward vagueness. As Baldick and Mighall (2012, 273) also note: "Gothic criticism has done little to define the nature of Gothic except by the broadest kind of negation: the Gothic is cast as the opposite of Enlightenment reason, as it is the opposite of bourgeois literary realism." Piatti-Farnell and Beville (2014, 1) concur that although Gothic has found embodiment in various media and activities, it "has yet to find a coherent definition." Sedgwick (1986, 3) points out that "'Gothic' has not been the most supple or useful of critical adjectives"; Germanà (2013, 13) claims that it "typically resist[s] definition"; and Moers also suggests that the meaning of Gothic "is not so easily stated except that it has to do with fear" ([1976] 1978, 90).

Critics who name Gothic a literature of fear are in good company; H. P. Lovecraft opens his discussion in "Supernatural Horror in Literature" by claiming that "the oldest and strongest emotion of mankind is fear, and the oldest and strongest kind of fear is fear of the unknown" (1927, 41) and that this fear forms the basis for "the weirdly horrible tale" as a literary form. Gross defines Gothic literature as a "literature where fear is the motivating and sustaining emotion" (1989, 1). Punter's landmark critical study of "Gothic fictions" is titled "The Literature of Terror" (1980). But fear is subjective (what scares one may not scare another) and thus vague. My students assure me that *The Castle of Otranto* no longer inspires fear—but it is certainly still a Gothic novel. For this reason, many scholars try to draw divisions between the different forms that fear can take, and the opposing qualities of their definitions often echo the paradoxes already noted within Gothic. James Beattie (1783, 615) first distinguishes horror by its physical effects, as it "make[s] the blood seem to run cold." Ann Radcliffe then famously separates terror and horror, claiming that "terror and horror are so far opposite, that the first expands the soul, and awakens the faculties to a high degree of life; the other contracts, freezes, and nearly annihilates them" (1826, 5). Lovecraft too breaks down fear, dividing it into archaic, pre-psychoanalytic fear and "mere" physical fear or repulsion (1927). Subsequent critics and creators from Devendra Varma (1957) to Stephen King (1981) have continued to explore this famous distinction between terror (the obscure, unseen) and horror (the shown atrocity). Wheatley (2006) looks at literature, television, and radio to suggest that Gothic anthologies are built around two distinct types of tale: the understated ghost story (Radcliffe's "terror") and the effects-driven supernatural horror. Hume (1969) points out that the two types work in opposing ways: terror-Gothic uses the sublime feeling of fear to attract the reader and thus avoids repulsion, whereas horror-Gothic relies on psychological realism to compel the reader, even into repugnance. In general, scholars agree on these categories, although some critics diverge (Twitchell 1985). Townshend (2016, 37) asserts that "terror is the writing of sublimity, horror the literature of sensation," and Wisker (2005, 149) points out that "horror [in contrast to Gothic] is more likely to be or to threaten to be violent and evoke disgust and/or terror." However, both critics also note that the two types cross and blur at points. Wisker (2005, 8) claims that "horror uses many [Gothic] formulae," and Townshend (2016, 25) also notes that both "horror and terror are subsumed under the broader category of the 'Gothic'" in *The Castle of Otranto* (1765).

These definitions of Gothic, horror, and terror all refer primarily to a fearful reaction, but to analyze literature without surveying reader response requires textual criteria. To this end, Heiland (2004) suggests that we should not look for fear exclusively in the reading experience but instead hunt for signs of its textual presence, for example, in the scenarios or characters offered. Both horror and terror seem well suited to the comics medium. Stylized art and staccato panels lend themselves well to the grotesque image or a horrifying reveal. The medium also exploits terror's imaginative potential, as pivotal moments can be obscured or omitted between panels, and the reader is required to recognize, interpret, or even create the story events. *Misty*'s covers and stories exploit both of these types of fear in lexis and image, as I will show.

In my book *Gothic in Comics and Graphic Novels* (2014a), I argued for a critical approach to comics that drew on three main Gothic themes: haunting, encryption, and excess, at both an aesthetic and affective level. I carry these ideas forward into this book, in which I use the term "Gothic" in its widest sense. Gothic is a mode of creation (both literary and cultural) that draws on fear and is both disturbing and appealing. It is an affective and structural paradox: simultaneously giving us too much information (the *super*natural, the unreal) and too little (the hidden, unseen, unknown). It is built on confrontations between opposing ideas and contains an inner conflict characterized by ambivalence and uncertainty. It inverts, distorts, and obscures. It is transgressive and seductive. Its common tropes (which are both aesthetic and affective) include temporal or spatial haunting, a reliance on hidden meaning (the crypt), and a sense of excess beyond control. Within Gothic I recognize the distinctions that Radcliffe et al. have drawn between terror (the threatening, obscured, and unknown) and horror (the shocking, grotesque, and obscene). Alongside these terms, I also recognize horror as a cinematic and literary genre that privileges this second type of fear: a genre that shocks, disturbs, and confronts.

I also use associated terms such as "mystery" and "uncanny" in the following discussion. Mystery appears frequently, as this was how comics like *Misty* and *Spellbound* identified themselves. Etymologically from the Latin *mysterium* (a secret thing), mystery refers to literature that centers on a puzzling scenario or has an outcome that is impossible to explain or rationalize. As such it strongly connotes the supernatural and Gothic. Alongside this, I also use the term "uncanny," as mystery often arises from everyday objects or scenarios with weird or offbeat elements. I draw this Gothic notion from the work of Sigmund Freud: *das unheimlich*, the familiar made strange. Ambivalence is another key idea that informs both of these terms: in common usage, ambivalence is the state of having mixed feelings or contradictory ideas about something, and has been described as "central to the Gothic" (Edwards 2013, 4).

By exploring the construction and reception of Gothic tropes, themes, and terms in girls' comics like *Misty*, I want to demonstrate the power and impact of Gothic in all its forms and cast some light on its continued presence and appeal. I hope this book gives some sense of the import and value that can be found in girls' stories, and that it conveys some of the intensity and mystery of *Misty*. I've tried to give the uninitiated a sense of what this comic was about, as well as illuminate its themes and ideas for readers already familiar with it, and to use this analysis to reflect on bigger issues within literary and cultural studies, particularly relating to gender and Gothic.

Chapter 1, "The Rise and Fall of British Girls' Comics," provides context and background to the study. It tells the story of *Misty*'s creation and situates it within the wider picture of British girls' comics in the late twentieth century. It draws on archival research and analysis of predecessor titles and also reviews and summarizes the critical work published on the genre to date. Chapter 2, "Anonymous Authors," continues to reveal *Misty*'s hidden history. It explains the weekly process of putting the comic together, giving detailed information on its editorial team and its script fees and practices and identifying a number of the *Misty* writers. In particular, it reflects on the comic's framing and marketing as a "mystery paper" rather than "horror comic" and responds to gendered claims about its creators and contributors. This chapter also includes the previously unseen script for "The Banana King," a Pat Mills story that would become "Red

Knee—White Terror!" (*Misty* #1, with art by John Richardson), and analyzes the script alongside the published version to demonstrate how the *Misty* tales were shaped around mystery and terror rather than outright horror. Chapter 3, "Astonishing Artists," then offers a complementary analysis of *Misty*'s artistic production. It explores the process of designing and printing the comic and identifies the artists who worked on it. In particular, it explains the background to the extensive use of Spanish artists in British comics and the links between the two countries and their comics publishing.

The next two chapters discuss *Misty* more closely. Chapter 4, "Visceral Visuals," explores the comic's artistry and layout in more detail, using close analysis of a randomized sample of ten issues to discuss the dynamic "big visuals" used in its pages. It concludes that *Misty*'s stories consistently play with aesthetic and medium by using dramatic layouts and nonstandard paneling. This is seldom linked to specific narratological moments and so is perhaps best read as reflecting the overall sense that the stories carry: playing with reality and conveying uncontainedness and transgression. Chapter 5, "Shocking Stories," identifies the various types of story included in the comic, noting that there are clear differences between its serials, single stories, and comedy series, and exploring their use of Gothic heroines, cautionary tales, and the whimsical macabre.

Themes of transgression are the subject of chapter 6, "Horror and Gothic in the 1970s," which considers some of the possible influences on *Misty*, drawing links with other comics as well as a wider tradition of horror across multiple media in 1970s Britain. This exploration of the surrounding atmosphere of cultural horror then leads into a discussion of Misty herself in chapter 7, "Our Friend of the Mists." This summarizes the appearance of host characters in British and American comics, contextualizing Misty's role as host and guide. It proceeds to analyze the Gothic language and imagery used in her inside-cover welcomes to each issue and draws attention to key tropes that emerge, including mystery, nature, history, and the body. Gothic themes such as these are then carried forward into chapter 8, which sets out a typology of the different *Misty* stories. This "Taxonomy of Terror" discusses the typical themes of the *Misty* tales, using qualitative and quantitative research into the entire corpus of 443 stories.[3] This chapter reflects on various claims about *Misty*'s content and applies Pat Mills's girls' comics formulas to its stories. It then suggests an alternative approach developed from my analysis of plot summaries to produce an inductive list of common plot tropes (such as external magic, internal power, backfiring actions, and more). It relates these tropes to established Gothic themes and concludes that although the fare of Misty was not as consistently negative as readers might remember, it was perhaps more shocking due to inconsistency with moral "rules."

Chapter 9, "Terror, Horror, and Female Gothic," draws on the previous chapter and the earlier discussion to explore how terror and horror are used in *Misty*, focusing on its covers, visuals, and story content. These theoretical ideas are then developed further with reference to the Female Gothic, a contested term with variable meaning. The chapter summarizes the evolution of Female Gothic scholarship and arrives at a working definition. It notes the Female Gothic's focus on the problems of female experience and use of feminine or domestic symbols, and its simultaneous mobilization of rebellion/transgression and morality/conservatism. Chapter 10, "Deep Cuts," then examines the presence of Female Gothic concepts and identity positions in *Misty*. It focuses on the abject, the grotesque, and the uncanny and discusses the ways in which they are informed by transgression and transformation. It argues that *Misty*'s use of the supernatural often twists these themes into metaphors for the experiences of a female teenage audience: for example, through grotesque bodies, uncontrolled growth, and the exclusion of male characters. It demonstrates that the *Misty* serials in particular are often set in an uncanny atmosphere of mystery and provide a space for uncertainties about family figures and patriarchal authority to be explored. Outcomes are uncertain, and the options available to the protagonists frequently comment on the limitations placed on women. Chapter 11, "Surface Reflections," then examines the use of Gothic symbols, settings, and archetypes in the context of gender. It pays particular attention to the use of the double, the Other, and associated symbols such as mirrors and masks, arguing that these devices are used to explore the limits of female identity and to interrogate issues of control and change. It also analyzes the settings of the *Misty* stories, demonstrating that they often contain an intrusion of the past into the present, creating the "Gothic cusp," which manifests as an uncanny feeling of dislocation. The chapter concludes by exploring the treatment of Gothic archetypes (focusing particularly on witches, vampires, and ghosts) and reveals that such characters appear less than might be expected, and are frequently handled subversively or sympathetically.

Chapter 12, "Gothic for Girls," then uses these analyses to construct the conventions of this subgenre and reflect on its development and position within children's literature. It surveys existing work on childhood and Gothic, with a particular focus on the fairy tale and the cautionary tale as subgenres of children's literature. It argues that *Misty* combines Female Gothic tropes with fairy-tale markers to create stories that bring together adult and child concerns. The chapter concludes by relating *Misty* to some contemporary examples of dark fairy tales and offering a working definition of Gothic for Girls. Elements of this definition include an isolated or trapped female protagonist in an abstract world that juxtaposes the mundane and supernatural, a narrative awakening to magical potential that is often driven by fear and particularly terror, the use of feminine symbols and fairy-tale sins as catalysts, and the weight placed on personal responsibility and self-control or self-acceptance.

The book concludes by extending these ideas to readers, as chapter 13 then explores the cry of "Make *Misty* for Me" by examining the comic's letters page, which reveals an active, empowered, and diverse audience. Few critics have analyzed comics letters pages in any depth, and this chapter discusses what self-image the "Write to Misty" page constructs for the comic and its readers. It frames its findings with scholarship on female audiences and their periodical publications and uses this work to reflect on their consistency with the dominant discourses of Gothic and horror, the reputation and readership of British girls' comics, and the uses made of comics letters pages more generally. Finally, the comic's demise and Misty's dwindling appearances in *Tammy* are the focus of chapter 14, "Leaving These Misty Isles," which considers the material produced after the comic's original run ended and the memories of its readers. It discusses the possible reasons for the comic's termination and looks more closely at the process of merging *Misty* into *Tammy*, demonstrating how Misty's role was significantly altered and weakened. It examines the material included in the annuals and reprints and summarizes the postmillennial reemergence of *Misty* in fan websites, tribute publications, and reprinted and new material from Egmont and Rebellion. My concluding remarks ("Reflections") then expand on the significance of my definition of Gothic for Girls and consider what *Misty* can tell us about current approaches to critical theory, gender studies, and comics studies.

Producing this book has been a peculiarly Gothic process of exploring, uncovering, and decrypting. I can't imagine that anyone else will ever enjoy it as much as I have, but if (in traditional fairy-tale style) I had three wishes, I know what they would be. First, that the book provides useful new material for readers already interested in the lost history of British girls' comics. Second, that it might introduce some new readers to this disregarded genre—and maybe even to the joys of comics more generally. And third, that it helps to increase the visibility of an often-marginalized audience and develop our understanding of the range and complexity of Gothic literature.

Now settle down to read with me, and I hope that these shudder-making speculations will touch you with the terror that can come from the turn of a page.
  Your friend,
  Julia

CHAPTER 1

THE RISE AND FALL OF BRITISH GIRLS' COMICS

Misty was first published on February 4, 1978, by International Publishing Corporation (IPC), announcing itself as "No. 1 of a great mystery paper for girls!" It would run weekly for 101 issues before merging with *Tammy* in January 1980,[1] and it also produced three holiday specials (1978, 1979, 1980), six annuals (1979–86), and eight issues of reprints called *The Best of Misty Monthly* (1986). More recently Egmont released two versions of a *Misty* reprint collection (2009, 2012), before selling the rights to Rebellion, who have to date published two reprinted collections (2016, 2017) and a combined *Scream! & Misty* Halloween special of new material (2017).[2] While the newer *Misty* collections are in print and available to buy, the older publications are harder to find, although some can be read online.[3]

Misty appeared at the end of three decades during which British girls' comics had dramatically flourished and then dwindled. This chapter gives a brief critical history of this period, tracing the rise of British girls' comics in the 1950s and their market dominance in the next decades, before the demise of the market and the merging of numerous titles in the 1970s and 1980s. I demonstrate how *Misty* and its predecessor *Spellbound* (DC Thomson, 1976–78) grew out of a wider thematic and stylistic evolution of girls' comics, led by the competition between two main publishers, DC Thomson and Fleetway/IPC, which produced a diverse range of titles with clear and distinct identities. I then show how the industry's ultimate collapse was due to abandoning this vision, driven by a combination of technological, capitalist, and conservative influences.

Girls' comics are the "forgotten herstory" of the British industry. Despite being created by some of Europe's top talent and being arguably stronger in plot, characterization, quality, and visuals than many of the boys' equivalents, the genre has attracted little critical attention to date, and toward the end of the twentieth century, it received little care to boot. Anecdotal stories abound of old girls' comics being used literally to mop the floor of workshops or given away for free in the car parks outside comics conventions; and of original artwork (including an unpublished Bellwood piece of Misty) being rescued from a studio where it was being used as a cutting board.[4] Dealers destroyed the copies that they came across, considering them to have no value (Gibson 2015, 23), as there was no interest from the 1990s collectors' market (Sabin 1996). Mel Gibson says that when she began her research there were no archives containing girls' comics to work with (2015, 21), and the impossibility of accessing the texts themselves led to her instead collecting the oral histories of female comics readers. Martin Barker also notes the difficulties and expense of obtaining these comics (1989, vii).

Roger Sabin calls it a "sad fact" that girls' comics do not feature in more general histories of the medium (1996, 81), explaining that although comics made enormous strides between the 1930s and 1960s, the assumption was that most were being read by boys aged eight to twelve. But given the rise and proliferation of girls' comics from the 1950s onward, it is unclear quite why the genre has been overlooked and mistreated for so long, although the difficulties of finding resources and perhaps also a devaluing of young and female audiences and their artifacts are likely factors. Even when comics began to garner serious scholarly attention, the academy remained mostly uninterested in girls' titles. A number of scholars have published articles and books on British girls' magazines and comics, but these most commonly focus on the romance genre or subsume comics into a wider discussion of girlhood or targeted publishing. At this time, no single volume dedicated to the textual analysis of British girls' comics exists.[5]

Scholarship on girls' periodicals and magazines shows that although gender, class, race, and age all structure the experience of girlhood, these media play a pivotal role, as they both set and respond to readers' desires and social trends. Critics such as Tinkler (1995), Schrøder (2000), and Tebbutt (2016) thus consider girls' magazines as cultural artifacts that reinforce particular visions of femininity. In general, they draw attention to the contradictory impulses that underlie such magazines, which must tread a line between reader engagement and social norms, often resulting in restrictive and demeaning female roles. For example, Tinkler (1995) explores the way in which British magazines and story papers addressed and depicted girlhood between 1920 and 1950. She gives extensive historical context of the opportunities and restrictions placed on girls in these decades and draws on close analysis of the magazines' letters pages, features, and stories to argue that they construct the experience of girlhood around key themes such as femininity, occupation, and relationships. She demonstrates that the magazines sought to address readers' interests and desires while simultaneously avoiding any direct challenge to patriarchal interests, often leading to complex negotiations of ideology and paradoxical treatments of the female body, behavior, appearance, and so forth. Similarly, Tebbutt (2016) examines the way in which British youth and its culture/s have transformed over the last two centuries, moving from being a mass group primarily defined by its role in production to a collection of subgroups and niche markets defined through consumption habits. She concludes that although industrialization, urbanization, modern democracy, and new ideas have transformed youth culture, the roots of ignoring, controlling, and marginalizing particular groups and practices go deep, and we need to keep asking how disenfranchised groups such as young female readers can be empowered. In particular Tebbutt draws attention to magazine reading and "bedroom culture" as examples of the private domestic space of a teenage girl, which is largely ignored in scholarship when compared to the public space of men (176). Although these studies shed light on an under-researched area, they often focus on the way in which traditional assumptions and restrictions are sustained by these publications (see, e.g., Tebbutt 2016, 160).

Many other studies of female periodicals discuss gossip or fashion magazines, either exclusively or as part of wider feminist research, and the majority do not have positive things to say (Friedan 1963; Tuchman et al. 1978; Winship 1987; Wolf 1991; Damon-Moore 1994). Critics such as Hermes (1995, 149) note this critical "denigration of women's magazines," although there has been a move in more recent studies (Gibson 2010; H. Wood 2016) to address the traditional discourse of concern that surrounds women's magazines. This later research explores the interpretative uses that women make of their reading, or their rhetorical contributions to newspapers and periodicals, rather than making value judgments about perceived content.

When comics scholarship has turned its attention to girls' comics, it has often followed this negative trend. Alderson (1968) views girls' comics as commodities that offer amorality, anti-intellectualism, rejection of complexity, daydreamy escapism, and a "debased" usage of the word and concept of love. Sharpe (1976) critiques their use of stereotypes within her wider study of the role models and stereotypes available to girls through media and lifestyle. McRobbie's (1978a, 1978b, 1981) semiological analysis identifies four codes (romance, fashion and beauty, pop, and personal and domestic life) that transmit clear messages of acceptability in these fields. Chapman (2011, 111) argues that girls' comics construct a "socially approved model of adolescent femininity." They are perceived as tools of oppression, in which female protagonists are positioned as victims and girlhood is constructed in accordance with femininity and passivity (see also Cadogan and Craig 1976; Walkerdine 1984; McRobbie 1991).

However, notable scholars such as Gibson and Barker offer alternative readings that critique the idea of a singular ideology being put across by such a wide range of titles and reframe their characters and themes. Barker reviews and discredits a number of classic readings of girls' romance comics (using *Jackie* as a case study). He points out that these readings are "almost all hostile" (1989, 139) and make the fundamental mistake of assuming that these comics form a unity. This assumed unity is both internal (i.e., claims that there is a coherent unified message made up of the individual stories, the editorial, letters page, and other features) and also external (i.e., claims that girls' comics all carry the same priorities and there is no difference between the range of comics published over the last thirty years). Barker dismisses the arguments of Alderson, Sharpe and McRobbie, concluding that they all "start from unsatisfactory theories of influence and ideology" (159).

Extending Hermes' approach, Gibson's work creates a "readers' history" of British comics, combining oral histories from readers with textual analysis. She identifies the ways in which British comics publishers trod a fine line between adventure and propriety, and argues against the assumptions made by Chapman et al. Gibson's research redefines the characters and story tropes of these comics by shedding light on how they appeared in audience understandings. For example, readers saw "victim heroines" as "survivors," and Gibson identifies their different attitudes and personalities while also noting that "important feminine qualities" such as humility and "not showing off" (2010, 127) underpin their narratives. These critical models acknowledge British comics' differences and contradictory underlying drives. They inform much of my following analysis of *Misty*, which explores the paradoxes they identify through a Gothic lens. In this I also draw on critics such as Crawford (2014), who demonstrates the active agency of female readers of contemporary Gothic, whose interpretations of texts such as *Twilight* are at odds with "objective" critical readings.

Taking this more nuanced view of girls' comics between the 1950s and 1980s demonstrates that these titles go far beyond reinforcing stereotypes of heterosexual romance and fashion. These comics were a boom industry, and by the end of the 1950s at least fifty different titles were being published in the United Kingdom, with more emerging in the 1960s and 1970s. At their peak, the girls' comics outsold the boys' and were read voraciously by readers of both genders. Pat Mills (2012) gives approximate sales figures on launch as follows: *Tammy*, 250,000 copies per week; *2000AD*, 220,000 copies per week; and *Misty*, 170,000 copies a week. Sabin points out that these comics were sites of innovation, some of which "reshaped the medium forever" (1996, 81). Chapman comments that "girls' comics have often been regarded as superior in storytelling and characterization: they afford greater prominence to character motivation and they do not rely on direct action as the resolution to all problems" (2011, 110). The writer John Wagner (2016) also compares the genres, claiming that the boys' comics "paled in comparison to the stories in *Judy*, *Mandy* and especially *Bunty*—clever, meaty, affecting." Barker describes

Mills's and Wagner's work for the IPC girls' comics as "their forte . . . taut, frightening stories" (1989, 17).

Before the comics boom of the 1950s, girls had been reading text story papers for some years. Tinkler points toward a wide readership for schoolgirl papers, citing previous critics such as Jenkinson (1940), Trease (1948), Jephcott (1942, 1948), and Fenwick (1953). Jenkinson (1940) also claims that a quarter of girls' reading ranged beyond this and was devoted to boys' "bloods" (Chapman 2011). Despite their popularity, the girls' papers were the first to fall to paper shortages during World War II, and Chapman notes that only two survived when the war ended in 1945: *Girls' Crystal* and *The Girl's Own Paper*. After years of this slim fare, the girls' comics boom began in earnest when Amalgamated Press revamped and relaunched their old text-based story paper *School Friend* (a casualty of the war) in May 1950 as a picture-strip paper (Amalgamated, then IPC, 1950–65). Anne Digby (2017), writer for *School Friend, Girl, Tammy, Jinty*, and other titles, explains: "*School Friend* was the first UK weekly paper ever to publish stories for girls in picture strip form. It sold a million copies a week in its first few years and led directly to rival companies coming into the girls' market for the first time—Hulton Press with *Girl* [in 1951] and DC Thomson with *Bunty* [in 1958]." *Girl* (1951–64) was the sister paper to Hulton Press's *Eagle* and was shortly followed by *Girls' Crystal*, reconfigured as a comic and released by Amalgamated Press from 1953 until 1963, when it merged with *School Friend*. The anthology structure and combination of one-off stories and serials that characterize British girls' comics may be because these earliest titles were reworked versions of older prose story papers. They were also continually known as "story papers" in an act of elitism designed to appeal to a wider female audience; *Misty*'s first editor, Wilf Prigmore (2017b), explains: "Girls were always a bit more sophisticated than boys so they were always called story papers for girls, not comics."

Chapman examines the rhetoric around the launch of these titles and concludes that it was driven by commercial ambition. The success of the revived *School Friend* and the visible female readership for titles such as *Eagle* meant that publishers saw a new market here. The titles were incredibly popular straightaway: Chapman also cites Fenwick's (1953) study of schoolgirl reading habits, which revealed that 94 percent of fourteen- and fifteen-year-old girls read comics, and within this number nearly 60 percent read *School Friend* and 38 percent read *Girl*. However, the content of these comics was generally conservative and conventional. Chapman (2011, 112) reads *School Friend*'s stories and themes as reflective of prewar Britain and its values and (as the title suggests) largely set in the safe, sealed space of the school story. Its characters are resolutely middle- or upper-middle-class, and story plots and outcomes are ideologically conservative and based on fixed social relations. *Girl* (despite its strong moral and Christian overtones) offers more diverse fare, with discordant characters arriving to disrupt the status quo of a class or community, and some protofeminist stories in its dramatizations of historical figures or significant women in history. Its tales often use exclusive private-school settings and middle-class adventuresses, and although career girl protagonists also feature, most are in gender-approved occupations such as nurses, air hostesses, or ballet dancers.

The "second wave" of girls' comics began in 1958 when DC Thomson published *Bunty* (1958–2001), the longest running of all the girls' comics, spanning forty-three years and 2,249 issues. *Bunty* was a direct reaction to the staid, safe, middle-class titles, with a "cheap and cheerful" look (Sabin 1996, 82) aimed at a working-class audience (Gibson 2003, 91). Rather than cozy school communities or secret societies, *Bunty* protagonists were often outsiders. The dramatic tension frequently came from a sense of exclusion or inability to fit in, and Chapman notes that the stories often included a heavy dose of psychological cruelty. My own analysis of early girls' comics supports this observation. For example, *Bunty* #1 (January 18, 1958) contains stories such as "Orphan of the Circus" ("Lili was born and bred in the circus. It was her life. Then, one day, tragedy struck") and "Molly in Lonely Wood" ("The story of poor crippled Molly and her animal friends"). While Molly's story takes a positive turn as she helps a writer research her book, Lili's mother dies early on, and the cruel circus owner schemes against her. The trend continues with stories such as "Lonesome Lucy" and "Elvirita," a Spanish orphan (December 20, 1958). Other titles have a similar theme, printing stories such as "Cherry and the Children" (*School Friend*, 1963), "The Courage of Little Sister" (*Diana* #1, February 23, 1963), "The Girls of Hard Luck Hall" (*Diana* #6, March 30, 1963), "Mandy the Thirteenth" (*Diana* #127, July 24, 1965), and "No Love for Jenny" (*Diana* #141, October 30, 1985). These stories typically deal with unlucky or victimized protagonists, such as the orphans Betty and Pam, whose guardians are trying to prevent Betty from marrying and leaving them ("The Courage of Little Sister"). Spooky and mystery stories also feature, such as "The Phantom Ballerina" (*School Friend*, March 5, 1960), "Jane and the Ghostly Hound" (*School Friend*, May 21, 1960), and "The Hunted Ballerina" (*Diana* #141, October 30, 1965). The other girls' comics followed suit and also looked to other media for inspiration: after the movie release of *Day of the Triffids* (1963), the story was serialized in *Girl* (January 11, 1964), with art by Leo Davy.

Bunty was followed by numerous imitators and competitors, such as *Judy* (DC Thomson, 1960–91), *Diana* (DC Thomson, 1963–76), and *Mandy* (DC Thomson, 1967–91), which all ran for decades. In particular *Diana* had its share of hard-luck and spooky stories, alongside science fiction ("The Fabulous Four") and horror ("The Man in Black"). The late 1950s and early 1960s also brought a new wave of romance comics such as *Marilyn* (Amalgamated,

1955–65), *Valentine* (Amalgamated, 1957–74), *Roxy* (Amalgamated, 1958–63), *Mirabelle* (Pearson, 1956–77), and *Romeo* (DC Thomson, 1957–74). *Jackie* followed (DC Thomson, 1964–93) and by the early 1970s was selling over a million copies per issue (Sabin 1996, 84). It built on the norms established by the romance comics and provided a stepping-stone to women's magazines. Sabin and Chapman attribute *Jackie*'s popularity to the British cultural revolution and the emergence of young adults as a distinct consumer group. The romance boom began to die in the mid-1960s, however, and throughout the 1970s comics sales declined steadily across the board. This hit girls' comics in particular, perhaps due to the rise of women's magazines, other media (such as affordable children's paperbacks), and a cultural landscape and values that were swiftly changing.

As the foregoing discussion shows, Amalgamated Press and DC Thomson were engaged in a back-and-forth that would continue under various guises over the following decades. DC Thomson's history is simple: created in 1905 through a merger with competitor Leng, it has remained a family-run company in Dundee ever since. By contrast, Amalgamated Press and many other firms would be combined to later become IPC. In 1958 Cecil Harmsworth King (chairman of the newspaper group informally known as "the Mirror Group") bought Amalgamated Press and in 1959 was appointed its chairman, changing its name to Fleetway Publications (named after its headquarters, Fleetway House, in Farringdon Street, London). Fleetway took over other companies such as Odhams in 1961 (which had already absorbed Hulton Press in 1959) and went on to purchase publishers such as George Newnes. By 1963 King's publishing holdings included four national newspapers, one hundred national magazines, and more than two hundred trade and technical publications. No significant management changes were made at the point of acquisition, but in 1963 he incorporated all these subsidiaries under the holding company International Publishing Corporation. A management group was set up in 1965, and in 1968 IPC was reorganized into six divisions, one of which (IPC Magazines) included the "Juveniles Group," which contained the comics.

IPC remained in direct competition with DC Thomson, as can be seen from the company's makeup and publishing history. In 1968 John Sanders was appointed to the position of publisher (a similar role to managing director) at IPC and set about attacking the existing comics market. This was dominated by DC Thomson, whose front-runners, *Bunty*, *Judy*, and *Diana*, had "virtually unassailable sales," against which IPC had only *School Friend*, which was feeling "ancient" by this point (Sanders 2018a). There was no way that IPC could beat DC Thomson with lower costs (DC Thomson did not recognize unions, paid low rates, and thus had minimal overheads), so Sanders focused on story quality. He wanted to modernize the girls' comics to "embrace" the modern world—recognizing "bent policemen and antsy schoolmasters, and dreadful family problems," and hired John Purdie (a former DC Thomson editor living in London) as managing editor. The duo would go on to work together for eighteen years, and in due course Purdie became assistant editorial director of all the IPC comics and finally assistant managing director. Sanders (2018a) describes him as "just brilliant creatively. In the history of twentieth century ephemera John Purdie was unsurpassed."

Sanders and Purdie engaged a number of writers and artists whose creative genius took the comics market in a new direction, which Sanders (2018a) summarizes as follows:

> We agreed we needed to make little girls cry. We needed stories that broke their hearts, because we thought that was what they wanted. . . . Typical story line: Sonia wants to dance. She has enormous talent. But she has recently broken her leg and it's slow healing. Her dad is a drunk and her mum is spaced out, leaving Sonia to look after her five brothers and sisters. Her ballet teacher is saying, "If only, Sonia, you had a normal home life . . ." Sonia grits her teeth during the day, dries her tears under the bedclothes at night. She is preparing to enter a ballet contest, determined to win when, in the last frame, there's a knock at the door. It's a cop. Will she come down to the police station because her young brother has just been arrested for shoplifting . . .
>
> This kind of "cry with me" story was new for girls fifty years ago and it worked.

Within three years, IPC had half the market and was averaging five million sales a week against DC Thomson's five million. This occurred in the first three months of 1971, when UK comic sales exceeded ten million copies a week for the first time ever (Sanders 2018a).

As well as taking a substantial share of their market, IPC also headhunted DC Thomson's staff. Many of the IPC staff working on the juvenile titles came from DC Thomson (including John Purdie, Gerry Finley-Day, John Wagner, Pat Mills, Malcolm Shaw, Jack Cunningham, and Joe Collins), attracted by the greater freedom and happier atmosphere that IPC offered. Wilf Prigmore (2016a) confirms: "IPC was a lot freer, there was quite a good atmosphere there, there was a pub directly opposite, and a lot of time was spent in there and a lot of ideas were probably hatched in the pub." Art editor Chris Lloyd (2018) agrees that "the work was interesting, but the social side was even more interesting—it was one big party." The introduction of new blood into IPC and the competition with DC Thomson no doubt increased the ambition being thrown into new titles, and it was a time of high energy: Mills (2016a) stresses that the "youngish people from DC Thomson had a different outlook to the regime and IPC and arguably even within DC Thomson themselves, and so that's the kind of energy that was pouring into girls' comics in the early '70s." Describing IPC as "a rival company" to DC Thomson, Prigmore continues: "The early comics were not imitations, but set up specifically to rival *Bunty* and *Judy* and the others.... Then of course you started getting your own slightly different feel to the IPC ones." Managing editor Gil Page also emphasizes the way in which this competition structured IPC's output: "Something was always being worked on at Fleetway, just in case the powers-that-be had to combat a title launched by our great rivals in Dundee, DC Thomson.... They used to dictate our launch patterns and when we promoted, as well as determining our cover prices" (McDonald 2018, 11–13).

The back-and-forth can also be seen in the comics themselves, across all genres. *Eagle* had dominated the boys' market since its launch (1950), until DC Thomson brought out a number of new titles, of which *Victor* (1961) and *Hornet* (1963) had the most impact. When DC Thomson's *Warlord* (1974) came out, it rewrote the rules for boys' action titles, bringing in longer stories and dramatic layouts. IPC responded to its military themes and gritty action with *Battle Picture Weekly* in 1975 and the now-notorious *Action* in 1976, and DC Thomson hit back with *Bullet* in 1976. For the girls, *School Friend* (1950) competed with *Girl* (1951), and the romance comics also battled it out as *Marilyn* (1955) and *Valentine* (1957) fought against DC Thomson's *Romeo* (1957) and *Jackie* (1964). DC Thomson's *Bunty* (1958) was another game changer, offering a dramatic take on the now-stale school formula, until IPC responded by taking the genre to the next level.

Chapman cites *Tammy* (IPC, 1971–84) as launching this next "new wave" of girls' comics, followed by *Jinty* a few years later (IPC, 1974–81), which borrowed heavily from its pioneering sister and from established titles such as *June* (IPC, 1961–74). This was the "dark wave" or "third wave" of which *Misty* would become a part in 1978. John Purdie (managing director of IPC Magazines and deputy editorial director of the Juveniles Group) assembled a young team to work on *Tammy*, led by editor Gerry Finley-Day, who would be followed by Wilf Prigmore. Like *Bunty*, *Tammy* was aimed at a working-class audience (Mills 2011) and became an "exceptional" comic with "a circulation of something like a quarter of a million per week, maybe even more" (Mills 2011). Pat Mills, then a young freelance writer who had previously worked at DC Thomson on *Romeo*, became a freelance subeditor of *Tammy* and helped Finley-Day fill it to the brim with stories of angst and cruelty, placing protagonists in extreme circumstances and testing them to their limits. *Tammy* also contained "tales of mystery" from its beginning, although these were initially serials (e.g., "The Secret of Trebaran" and "Double for Trouble," *Tammy* #1). The stand-alone "Strange Story" or "Tammy Tale of Mystery" subsequently became a regular feature, adopted from *June and School Friend*.

DC Thomson then released *Spellbound* (1976–78), which prefigures *Misty* in a number of ways. It also builds on the success of the spooky stories in previous comics such as *June and School Friend* (1965–74) and *Diana* (1963–76), particularly as the latter had just ceased publishing when *Spellbound* launched. Announcing itself as "the NEW all mystery story paper for GIRLS" and giving away a free "Mystic Sun" pendant with its first issue, *Spellbound* contained serial stories around supernatural themes, along with its "Spookyspot" letters page, "Zodicat" horoscopes, and a weekly feature of pop stars sharing uncanny experiences or claiming ghostly encounters. The comic was introduced by the "Supercats": the all-girl crew of the spaceship Lynx, who invited readers to join the Supercats Club and had their own serial story in the center pages. They had initially appeared in the *Diana* annuals (1974–77) as "the Fabulous Four."[6] An additional host character, Damian Darke, also introduced weekly "chilling tales" from an old-fashioned gold-bound book.

Surveying the opening ten issues of *Spellbound* reveals stories about Egyptian mummies, racehorses, protagonists unwillingly possessed with strange abilities, threatening witches, and victimized orphans, alongside prose stories (generally ghostly tales written in the first person) and creepy myths and legends. Each issue mixes serial and single stories, and while this structure and content is clearly replicated in *Misty*, there are some stylistic and narrative differences. *Spellbound* sticks quite closely to a grid arrangement for its panels (although the layout uses many circular frames and broken borders), and both dialogue and narrative text are neatly typewritten. It also heads each page with a sentence summarizing or quoting its content (such as "Journey into Danger," "Mysterious Miss Brisson," or "Dad! You can't mean it!"). This, together with the short length of episodes, means that events often seem summarized rather than dramatized. The witches and archetypes that appear are quite stereotypical, such as Aunt Armida in "I Don't Want to Be a Witch!"

The final issue of *Spellbound* (#69) was published on January 14, 1978, and the comic merged into *Debbie* in the following week. DC Thomson subeditor Rhoda Miller (2017b) claims that *Spellbound* ended simply because it fell below the profit line, even though compared to other titles it was still doing relatively well. The timing could not have suited IPC better, as *Misty* #1 was due to launch a few weeks later, on February 4, 1978. However, work on this new mystery paper had begun nearly a year earlier, in 1977. At this time, IPC's Juveniles Group was led by John Sanders (editorial director) and John Purdie (deputy editorial director). Within this group sat the Boys Adventure Group (group editor Bob Bartholomew), the Humour Group (group editor Robert Paynter), the Educational Group (group editor Robert Paynter), the Nurseries Group (managing editor Adrian Vincent), the Young Teens Group (group editor Gaythorne Silvester), and the Girls Adventure Group (group editor Wilfred

Prigmore). Each group had four to six titles, and *Misty* would become part of the Girls Adventure Group along with *Jinty*, *Tammy*, and *Penny* (IPC Directory of Publications and Services, April 1979).

Misty cocreators Pat Mills and Wilf Prigmore both describe the same timeline, which begins with Pat Mills meeting with John Sanders, John Wagner, and (perhaps) John Purdie to pitch an idea for a new girls' comic. The meeting took place in April or May 1977, which Mills (2017c, 2017e) says "is very clear in my mind, as we talked about *Carrie* and then got onto the subject of dental caries." Mills had already had great success with *2000AD* and *Tammy* and proposed "us[ing] my *2000AD* approach on a girls' comic: big visuals and longer, more sophisticated stories with the emphasis on the supernatural and horror. My role models were *Carrie* and *Audrey Rose*, suitably modified for a younger audience" (Mills 2012). The idea was approved, but as *2000AD* had been such a hit, Mills wanted a cut of the profits on the new comic, and this was refused. In turn he rejected Sanders's offer to be its editor (despite the offer being repeated more than once) and also stepped down as editor of *2000AD* in late May 1977 (Mills 2017e).

The mystery-horror comic that became *Misty* was thus passed to Wilf Prigmore, the group editor for Girls Adventure Comics. Prigmore (2017b) explains: "They wanted a new comic, and Pat was called in to come up with the idea. Whatever he said didn't work out, and I was brought in and told 'We want a mystery paper. I remember casting around for something different. I had an idea for a paper called 'Chick' that was rejected." Prigmore was tasked to "come up with some mystery ideas" (2016a) and consulted with Mills on scripts and ideas. Prigmore has been named as *Misty*'s "co-creator" by Mills (2016a), and others agree that he was one of the driving forces behind *Misty*: its art assistant Ted Andrews (2017a) confirms that "through his enthusiasm the whole thing came about."

Neither creator has strong memories of *Spellbound*. Pat Mills (2016a) comments: "I have no recollection of *Spellbound*" and points out that the IPC sales were "so far ahead … we had really trumped DC Thomson," also stressing the time that elapsed between the launch of the two titles. Wilf Prigmore (2017b) also claims, "I really wasn't much aware of it. I was never told 'We want a version of *Spellbound*.' They always spoke about a mystery paper." But the IPC directors would certainly have known of *Spellbound* and wanted a mystery title to compete. Prigmore (2016a) points out that management often had commercial plans and designs that creators weren't aware of, saying, "Things were always going on that you weren't always privy to."

Prigmore got together with writers Pat Mills, Malcolm Shaw, and Bill Harrington to put together some stories and outlines for the new title that would become *Misty*. Mills wanted it to be a horror comic, saying, "I wanted *Misty* to be much scarier and they were toning my stories down" (2017c). Prigmore (2017a) confirms, "The one clear piece of editorial guidance I got from the Two Johnnies (Sanders and Purdie) was: 'We don't want a horror comic!'" During this process, the horror angle was diminished (see chap. 5), and the character of Misty herself was created (see chap. 7) in response to the comic's name.

The comic's title was inspired by the movie *Play Misty for Me* (1971), a psychological horror in which a radio DJ is stalked by an obsessed female fan. The exact circumstances of its creation have been told a few different ways. Pat Mills (2012, 2017d) has claimed credit, saying: "I took the title from the film *Play Misty for Me*," and "I'd seen the film at the cinema and it left a strong impression on me—a female anti-heroine." Although released many years earlier, *Play Misty for Me* was still appearing in some cinemas in 1977 (the Gate Cinema in Notting Hill screened it in May), and its themes of sex and violence certainly make it memorable. Mills (2017d) also points out that "I spend a lot of time thinking up titles, so possibles are always noted down. And then 'Mist' and 'Misty' clearly lend themselves to a comic. I recall mentioning the title to Sanders at our first meeting (with John Wagner) and he could immediately see how the comic would come across." However, John Sanders (2019) says: "I seem to remember the idea of 'Mist' coming out of a discussion we all had on making the girl readers feel a bit creepy.... I think the title was John Purdie's. We were looking for what we wanted in a single word, and 'Misty' was it. I should say that hundreds of words were considered for titles at that time—the old days of a girl's name (Bunty, Judy, Sally) obviously didn't reflect the hidden meaning of the comic."

Wilf Prigmore (2016a) has a different claim to the origin of the comic's name, stating that it didn't emerge until late in the process, after the team had gathered the initial selection of proposed stories for their as-yet-unnamed mystery comic. According to Prigmore, he and John Stenning (subeditor on *Tammy* at the time) visited Mills in Colchester to discuss story ideas and try to find a title or character to hang the comic on. After a lunch, they returned to Pat's home to leaf through dictionaries and other reference books, hoping that something would stick, and Prigmore came across an entry for *Play Misty for Me* in a film reference book. As he recalls: "It was perfect. It was a girl's name, typical of the themes of the comics, and it conjured up all the associations that we wanted. It practically *was* mystery. And it gave us all the associated imagery we could ever need."

In addition to these anecdotes, *Misty*'s art editor Jack Cunningham (2017) has a slightly different perspective: "It didn't have a title to start with. And I don't know where it came from. But I came in one morning and I said to Wilf— 'Misty!' And he said, that's funny, Pat Mills has just said 'Misty' as well. So believe it or not, *Misty* came about in as casual a manner as that."

Although Cunningham doesn't remember what might have sparked the idea ("something I'd heard on the radio or it might have been television . . . I don't know"), my research shows that on Monday, July 4, 1977, ITV launched a season of "For Adults Only" feature films, with *Play Misty for Me* as the first. The "For Adults Only" season received a significant amount of press coverage, as it attracted the attention of Mary Whitehouse, secretary of the National Viewers' and Listeners' Association (see, e.g., "Mrs. Whitehouse urges control of TV X-films," *Times*, Wednesday, June 22, 1977). In addition, the *TV Times* magazine for that week (July 2–8, 1977) has a three-page feature on Clint Eastwood (pp. 57–59) that also mentions the movie. As already noted, the film was still screening semiregularly in London cinemas, and Ray Stevens's cover of the song "Misty" had been released in 1975, reaching number two on the UK Singles Chart. Although ownership of the name cannot be conclusively settled, I personally favor the idea that the title was devised in the summer of 1977, when the movie was foremost in many minds owing to the ITV film season and accompanying publicity.

With the title and content taking shape, a team was put together for the new comic, with Malcolm Shaw penciled in as editor once he had finished wrapping up *New Mirabelle* (which merged into *Pink* on October 22, 1977), and Wilf Prigmore covering the editorial role in the short term before moving back to his position as group editor for the Girls Adventure Group. Shaw (who wrote extensively for *Misty*) then held the editorship of *Misty* for a long time, with Bill Harrington as subeditor, Jack Cunningham as art editor, and Ted Andrews as art assistant. Toward the end of the comic's run, Shaw left IPC to move abroad and was succeeded by Norman Worker as editor, and Bill Harrington is also believed to have edited the later annuals (1981–86).[7]

The final approved dummy of *Misty* was submitted for approval in a presentation folder with the reduced art printed on thick paper—the highest-quality version I have seen of this comic (fig. 1.1). It is hand colored in rough pencil to give a sense of where the four color pages will appear and how they will be used. Only minor changes were made for publication: the serials "Moonchild" and "Paint It Black" switched places, a "These Misty Isles" competition replaced a half-page "Star Days" horoscope, and the page advertising the free gift and introducing the comedy series "Miss T" was moved forward from its original position on the penultimate page. Each subsequent issue of *Misty* followed a similar pattern and was made up of thirty-two pages, consisting of a cover, an inside cover with a poetic letter and full-page picture of Misty herself welcoming the reader, a mix of serial and single stories, one or two pages of letters ("Write to Misty"), one or two pages of horoscopes and advertisements, and intermittent prose stories or features on myths, ghost stories, or legends.

THE RISE AND FALL OF BRITISH GIRLS' COMICS   27

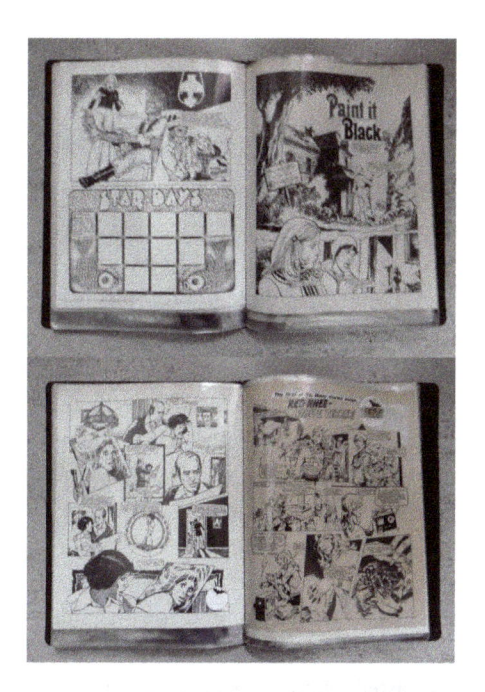

Figure 1.1. Presentation dummy for *Misty* #1. Donated to this project by Wilf Prigmore. *From top left*: Photos of original dummy pages in presentation folder. Scanned cover page with indicative colored pencils. Scanned opening pages showing original typed greeting and overlaid Letraset story titles.

Misty's content was enhanced by dynamic layouts and dramatic art, following Pat Mills's and art editor Doug Church's approach on *2000AD*. In addition, each story or installment ran four pages rather than the usual three, allowing for opening splash pages or large panels and story logos, as the number of panels was still generally the same (on average, twenty-six). Again, this approach follows Mills's work on *2000AD*, which pushed the number of story pages from three to six so that the writers would get paid twice as much (Mills 2017a, 14).

The *Misty* talent is hard to identify, as stories were not credited, and the ledgers are lost to time. Mills's ownership of *Misty* has been well promoted online and in journalistic pieces (e.g., Sweetman 2007a; Freeman n.d.; Mills 2012), but he scripted just five stories. His *2000AD* approach certainly shaped *Misty*'s aesthetic, with longer stories and bigger visuals, replacing *2000AD*'s science fiction theme with the supernatural (Mills 2017a). However, the comic's character and host and its move toward mystery rather than horror seem to have been predominantly led by Prigmore and Shaw. The bulk of the story scripts were provided by editors Malcolm Shaw and Bill Harrington, along with staff and freelance writers such as Alan Davidson, Alison Christie, and doubtless many more.[8] The art came from the United Kingdom and Europe and featured work by Juan Ariza, John Armstrong, Hugo D'Adderio, María Barrera Castell, Mario Capaldi, José Cánovas, Brian Delaney, Eduardo Feito, Blas Gallego, Josép Gual, Carlos Guirado, Ken Houghton, Isidre Monés, Douglas Perry, Jesús Redondo, John Richardson, the Romero brothers, Jaime "Homero" Rumeu, and Peter Wilkes—not to mention regular pieces from Mike Brown, Joe Collins, and Angela Kincaid, who drew "Wendy the Witch," "Miss T," and the "Star Days" sections respectively.[9] Shirley Bellwood created the image of Misty that would appear on the inside cover.

Tales of peril and mystery were not new to girls' comics, but a dark tone and supernatural theme dominate in both *Spellbound* and *Misty*. The stories were directly tailored to give readers what they wanted, based on the voting coupon in each issue and on formulas that had worked in the past. Reader votes were followed religiously: Roach (2016) and Mills (2017a, 80) both confirm that "editors had the most elaborate graph charts, recording the success and failure of individual stories.... It was surprisingly accurate." Mills (2017a) does note that the results were biased in certain ways (e.g., toward action in the boys' titles) and that the system worked less well once a divide between long-term fans and casual readers began to emerge, as older fans would not continue to fill in the coupons. However, in the 1970s, the system worked, producing comics that were based on a flexible formula and direct feedback from their audiences. This perhaps also accounts for the similarities of story types (see chap. 8 for further discussion) that appeared within titles whose framing was quite different.

The free gift that often accompanied a new title was perhaps also responsible for its initial popularity. Here *Misty* excelled (although largely by chance), as it took the step of matching its gifts to its stories.[10] Free gifts were provided by a central promotions department at IPC, and Wilf Prigmore (2016a) remembers the attempts to work the "Lucky Charm Bracelet" given away with *Misty* #1 into the theme of the comic:

> There was a chap whose job it was to go out to Hong Kong and different places in the Far East and pick up gifts as cheaply as possible . . . and he came to me with this horrible blue fish bracelet. I said, "No, no, it's horrible, we can't, what are we going to do with that? It's no good." He said, "Well, it's too late, I've bought them, I've got 250,000," or whatever it was. I thought bloody hell, how am I going to justify this? . . . So I said [to Ted Andrews, the art assistant], "Do something for god's sakes with this horrible blue bracelet." . . . So he came up with a nice little cartoon that ends up with "Oh, it's my lucky day after all. This blue dolphin has brought me *Misty*," and it's an introduction to the comic.

The "Lucky Black Cat Ring" given away with *Misty* #2 is also mentioned in the first installment of "The Cult of the Cat" and then drawn into the story in the issue that accompanied it, which Prigmore (2016a) describes as "one of the few occasions where something could really be closely linked." He also recalls that "cover-mounted free gifts were taped on by hand! The loose insert was a cheaper option" (2017c). This was the format of *Misty*'s final free gift in its third issue, "Your Wheel of Fortune Wallet," which came with extensive instructions spread over the next five issues and a set of picture cards (drawn by Chris Lloyd). However, the cards were not included in some overseas areas, including Ireland, making it quite frustrating. The wallet may have befuddled most readers but is remembered as "a singularly cool free gift," and photos can be found on social media (see, e.g., Great News for All Readers 2018).

The move toward free gifts is, of course, something that now dominates children's comics, particularly ones tied in with a larger entertainment franchise. Rhoda Miller (a subeditor who worked for both DC Thomson and IPC) comments: "I really cannot explain why the comics became less content and more free gifts, except to suggest that research showed children were less inclined to read great screeds of type and preferred more pictorial and less copy. The free gift phenomenon was very much a case of 'The opposition are doing it, so should we'" (2017a). Free gifts aside, though, in general today's children's comics bear little resemblance to their 1970s counterparts. They are often felt to be simply promotional material for toys or movie franchises and are not bought in anything like the numbers seen in the 1970s.[11] What happened and what was to blame? The demise of *Misty* was part of a wider loss of readership that affected British comics (particularly girls' comics) across the board, which had its roots in company policies, the denigration of creators and readers, economic factors, and a loss of clear direction and identity for previously distinct titles.

IPC's corporate structure was absolutely key to the demise. John Sanders (2018b) argues that "half the nation's comics should never have been in the hands of a massive company like IPC anyway because of its corporate structure," pointing out that although IPC had around 150 magazines, including more than forty weekly comics, 60 percent of its revenue came from just four titles: *Woman*, *Woman's Own*, *Woman's Realm*, and *Woman's Weekly*. All of IPC's magazines, with the exception of the comics, gained their profits from at least 50 percent advertising revenue; the rest came from circulation sales revenue. By contrast, Sanders imposed a four-page limit on advertising in the comics, so the revenue base of the Juveniles Group was 95 percent circulation sales and 5 percent advertising. Sanders (2018b) continues: "Big companies don't like an alien beast inside their carefully honed business model; we were tolerated because we made big profits, although no one outside my small management team knew exactly how." This meant that the Juveniles Group was extremely vulnerable to any controversy or complaint that might upset advertisers or result in newsagents threatening not to stock IPC's titles, such as the media outrage over comics such as *Action*. Sanders (2018b) claims that in the 1970s the IPC boys' comics were coming "under constant attack from the media," and this series of "perfect storms" meant that management was quick to abandon titles.

There was no outcry over *Misty*, but it did not make enough profit. As Sanders (2019) explains: "A girls' comic was hemmed in by its cover price. The only way it could survive to find its optimum readership was by putting up the cover price. But that couldn't be done because the opposition's cover prices were already below ours. So a comic was not profitable below a circulation of 200,000 a week, which is ridiculous if you think about it."

Prigmore (2017b) agrees that the fiscal demands of being part of a big company hampered the IPC comics. He describes the IPC Juveniles Group as a "pyramid of power, with accountants on the top and the creatives at the bottom." He explains: "Most comics had a team of four and probably the entire editorial staff of all the comics put together didn't total as much as the team on, for example, *Woman*. So pro-rata the management burden was heavier for us" (2018b). The top-heavy management of the Juveniles Group is evidenced by internal bulletin no. 427 (dated August 8, 1977), which announces the appointment of four new management roles to replace one resignation. These roles (variously named as "publishing managers" or "assistant publishers") went to IPC commercial directors, accountants, or marketing and promotion executives, primarily from its General Magazine Group. Prigmore (2018a) continues: "You can see how top heavy it was with management. I always felt it was like an inverted pyramid with the creatives at the bottom being squashed. Remember, too, all those admin bods had secretaries and offices, expenses etc. No wonder a circulation of 200,000 didn't bring in enough to pay for it all and comics merged and folded."

Pat Mills (2017a) agrees that the company denigrated its creative staff, and it sometimes felt as if the writers and artists were treated as "the enemy," with requests for a fairer deal constantly being ignored. This drive for profit meant that creators sought out more appealing opportunities. Mills (2017a) argues that a lack of rights (ownership, credits) led many to find work elsewhere (France, America), and the writer Anne Digby points toward the move to other media for herself and her husband Alan Davidson. As she explains: "A mass market for children's paperback books opened up in the 1970s, with new imprints like Collins' Armada etc., when hitherto there had only been Puffin. For the first time many more writers could earn a living from writing children's books, with decent advances and the prospect of reprints and royalties if stories proved to be popular."[12]

Publishers also abused their readership, as the merging of titles was a common practice. The British girls' comics catered to all ages and types, from *Twinkle* to *Jackie*, and had a varied aesthetic (from the cheap and cheerful *Bunty* to full-color broadsheets like *Diana*). Mills (2016a) describes the uniting factor as "the old thing that pervades girls' comics all the way through: elitism, and the struggle against it," and also lists a set of different story types that I explore further in chapter 8. But despite the recurrence of many of the same themes or plot catalysts, each title had a different focus and a distinct identity. *Bunty* offered everyday stories; *Tammy* had tortured heroines and a weekly dose of "strange stories"; *Jinty* contained fantasy and science fiction along with dark, cruel stories; and both *Spellbound* and *Misty* told supernatural mystery tales. Despite these distinctions, it was the fate of most of these titles to be merged into each other in pursuit of profit. The prototype *School Friend* merged into *June* in 1965, becoming *June and School Friend* (which then continued successfully for nearly a decade); *Spellbound* merged with *Debbie* in 1978. *Jinty* finally merged with *Tammy* in 1981, having already merged with *Lindy* in 1975 and *Penny* in 1980, while *Tammy* had previously gobbled up *Sally* in 1971, *Sandie* in 1973, and *June* in 1974. *Misty* would merge with *Tammy* in January 1980 after a run of 101 issues.

The merger strategy, known as "hatch, match, and dispatch," was a popular way to bolster sales in a dwindling industry. While some editors viewed it as a way to keep a dying title alive (Gil Page, quoted in McDonald 2018, 14), Pat Mills (2011) describes the merger strategy as "a way of conning the newsagent. . . . It's horrible, accountancy thinking. . . . It treats the readers with utter contempt." New titles always received interest and sold well, but once sales began to fall, every week the distributor would cut the figure. When sales hit a certain low, the publisher would merge the comic with another title so that their combined circulations would be taken into account. Of course, this produced an artificial circulation figure that would not last, and even committed readers quickly drifted from the new combined title, continuing the pattern of falling sales. As reader Winn Payne comments: "Whenever your favourite comic was suddenly combined with another one you knew it was the beginning of the end. ☹ I didn't stick with *Tammy* [after the *Misty* merger] because I thought it was like every other girls' comic and that was why I read *Misty*, because it wasn't ☺" (Moloney 2016). Speaking of *Jinty*, another fan comments: "I remember the feeling of dread. . . . I knew this meant it would disappear after a few months. Heartbroken—it was like a metaphor for the end of my childhood" (Kilpeckhall 2016).

The pursuit of profit needs to be put in context, as comics publishing was quite different in the 1970s than today. Gil Page (McDonald 2018, 13) explains that, apart from launch or promotional periods, everything was sold as "firm sale" (i.e., if copies were unsold, it was the trader's loss, not the publisher's) rather than "sale or return," so sellers would be cautious. Inferior production values and lower cover prices meant that publishers had to sell more to break even, and IPC's prices had to compete with DC Thomson, who "were always cheaper." This meant that even comics that seemed to be doing well could be closed or merged; Page claims that *Misty* closed on a circulation figure of sixty thousand.

The need to bolster sales was also due to the "cost center" policy that IPC introduced in the 1970s (Prigmore 2017b). Every publication or department became its own cost center, and thus each individual issue needed to hit a certain revenue target. Prigmore (2018b) explains: "I tried to argue that *Tammy* as a title could be a cost center, meaning income from Specials (Summer and others), Annuals and syndication would be added but this wasn't how it worked." This practice had a knock-on effect on the production and quality of the titles and the finances of the company overall. As Prigmore (2018b) continues: "As an example, we used to have photos and prints of artwork for colouring processed in our photolab. But when it became a cost center and had to charge enough to cover its overheads it was cheaper for us to pay an outside company to do the work and eventually the photolab was shut. I could never understand the sense of money going out of the company rather than keeping it within. But hey, I'm only a journalist and not an accountant!"

Alongside the drive for profit was a loss of clear direction that also shook the girls' titles. Mills (2016a) claims that talent was pulled quickly from IPC's girls' comics to rescue the boys' ones when the market started to falter in the 1970s. This meant that older editors and writers who did not understand the genre were assigned to titles, such as Norman Worker's appointment as the

Figure 1.2. Fleetway reunion photos at Ye Old Cheshire Cheese, London, ca. 2005. *Left to right*: Peter Wesson (Juveniles Production Dept.), John Fearnley (art assistant, *Tammy*), Derek Pierson (*front*) (art editor, various), John Stenning (*back*) (subeditor, *Tammy*), Jack Cunningham (art editor, *Misty*), Tony Lynch (editor, various humor titles), Ted Andrews (art assistant, *Misty*), Fraser Gray (*front*) (art assistant, *Tiger*), Roy MacAdory (*back*) (artist, *Eagle*), Wilf Prigmore (group editor, Girls Adventure), Kelvin Gosnell (*partially obscured*) (editor, *2000AD*), Paul Ailey (subeditor, various humor titles), Ian Vosper (subeditor, *Tiger*). Photo by Peter Downer (art editor, *Tammy*).

Bottom left to right: Shirley Bellwood (last known photo, taken June 9, 2015; courtesy of Sue Harris, wife of Max Harris, author of *The Unremembered Inn*). Pat Mills (photo used with permission). Malcolm Shaw (photo taken late 1970s, courtesy of Brenda Ellis).

final editor of *Misty*. Worker had previously edited *Sally*, "an ancient comic.... He was of a different generation, he wasn't suitable" (Mills 2011). Mills claims that, shorn of the talent that understood what it was about, *Misty* moved away from creepy mystery and disturbing horror and into more traditional rewrites, which caused its demise. As he characteristically summarizes: "The real truth is the f**kwits won" (Freeman, n.d.).

Finally, the readership for comics was being lured in other directions as the cultural landscape was changing fast. Anne Digby (2017) suggests that "the availability of a wonderful variety of paperback fiction at pocket money prices no doubt contributed to the collapse of the comics industry, not to mention the lure of strong children's drama on TV." Much of this television drama was horror themed (see chap. 6), and alongside this trend, video and computer games were on the rise. Critics such as Chapman also point out that fashions change quickly, and what once felt edgy and exciting quickly became dated as readers moved toward women's magazines and pop culture.

The rise and fall of the British girls' comics industry illustrates that mixing creativity and commerce can produce intense competition that drives innovation and experimentation. However, the priorities and demands of the two are not always compatible, and if the industry does not adapt to its changing cultural context or modify its fiscal expectations, this can hamstring its creative talent and undermine its readership. From today's vantage point, it therefore seems that a combination of technological, capitalist, and conservative forces brought about the quiet end of *Misty* and many other once mighty comics.

CHAPTER 2

ANONYMOUS AUTHORS

It is a travesty that records of the writers and artists who worked on British girls' comics in the 1970s have been so utterly lost. Uncredited and unable to keep originals of their work, most of those still alive have forgotten which stories they worked on, and publishers' ledgers are rarely made available. The next two chapters recover some of this hidden history.[1] I begin this chapter by explaining the weekly process of putting *Misty* together, giving information on script fees and editorial practices. This is complemented by biographical summaries of the writers who worked on *Misty*, taken from interviews that I have made available online. I use this research to reflect on perceptions of the comic's creation and authorship, particularly relating to gender. The chapter concludes by arguing that *Misty*'s redefinition as a mystery title and its problematic relationships with gender and production accord with class-based views of Gothic and horror.

SCRIPT PRACTICES AND PAYMENTS

Although publishers kept ledgers of payment, the artists and writers of the 1970s girls' comics were not allowed to sign their work, and it was common practice to paint out any signature or initials. Credits had once appeared in British comics, for example, in *Eagle* (1950–69) and some romance titles, but by the 1970s this was no longer standard practice, especially at a large company like IPC.[2] This led to many subtle insertions of writer and artist names: for example, the final panel of "Sticks and Stones" (Wilf Prigmore and John Richardson, *Misty* #16) shows a pile of books and newspapers with text such as "Harrington's book rip off" (referring to subeditor Bill Harrington), "Shaw tower block terror" (referencing Malcolm Shaw's "The Sentinels"), and "Cunningham booze shock" (art editor Jack Cunningham). It is unclear whether this is a dig from the artist Richardson (who was described in a letter by Harrington as "difficult to work with" [Fay 2016]) or a joke by the art-editorial team of Jack Cunningham and Ted Andrews. This type of banter was common; Prigmore recalls the character "Tubby Wagner" appearing in *Tammy*'s "Aunt Aggie" story, and "Gosnell's Pie and Mash Shop" appearing in another *Misty* story, which was responded to with "Prigmore's Parlour of Peace" in a *2000AD* tale.[3] The artist John Armstrong in particular managed to mark lots of his pages with his initials. Where spotted, such references would be painted out, but after *2000AD*'s art editor Kevin O'Neill introduced credits, the situation began to change. O'Neill recalls: "We were told British comics had traditionally never had attributions, but IPC were actually scared: if they identified creators, they might lose them to other companies like DC Thomson. I said 'This is bullshit,' stuck credit panels on and told management we were experimenting. They've been there ever since" (Hoad 2015).

Wilf Prigmore brought credits to the IPC girls' comics in 1982 during his time as editor of *Tammy*. "It was a bit revolutionary to have a byline, and I think I must have said at that time, 'Well, look, why is everybody anonymous? If we're doing it for one [*2000AD*], why don't we do it for all?'" (Prigmore 2016a). Credits first appeared in *Tammy* on July 17, 1982, and the last issue to have them was February 11, 1984, by which time Prigmore had ceased to be editor. They were also driven in part by author Anne Digby, who wrote for many girls' comics and had also written a successful series of children's books, the Trebizon school stories. Digby convinced Prigmore that as her school stories were well-known, it would be worth flagging up the author, and also doing this on other stories that were written by the same person, so that the readers could follow writers they liked. Digby's comics story "A Horse Called September"[4] (with art by Eduardo Feito) started in *Tammy* on August 7, 1982, and text and comics adaptations of her Trebizon stories also appeared in *Tammy* the following year.[5] Prigmore (2017b) remembers this as a key part of how the credits started on *Tammy*. However, at the time of *Misty*'s publication, no acknowledgment was given to writers or artists. One suggested reason for this practice is the back-and-forth between IPC and DC Thomson. John Purdie had been a DC Thomson man and had brought many of its staff down to London to work for his rival company, often responding directly to Thomson's output (Prigmore 2017b). I would also suggest that forbidding writers and artists to sign their name diminished any sense of intellectual property and personal ownership, reinforcing that the finished strip was the sole property of the publisher.

In the early 1960s, Fleetway paid in guineas and referred to manuscripts rather than scripts, also banking at Coutts in the Strand. These old-school traditions came from the days of Amalgamated Press and arguably aimed to make the company sound more posh than it actually was (Magee 2017). Fleetway records from *Battle Picture Weekly* comic in 1975 and 1976 show that writers such as Pat Mills, Gerry Finley-Day, and John Wagner were paid between £30 and £38 for a three-page script.[6] Anne Digby (2016) has shared a receipt online dated March 2, 1978, showing that her husband Alan Davidson was paid £51 for a four-page installment (episode 18) of the *Misty* serial "Paint It Black." (This was the only work Alan did for *Misty*, as he was turning his attention to children's books, and he and Anne would leave IPC soon after.)

Converting these values to today's money is difficult, since income can be valued in a number of ways. These include historic standard of living (the food, shelter, and goods that a given amount will buy); labor earnings (relative to those of an average worker); economic status (the relative prestige value of the amount); and economic power (relative to the total output of the economy). However, as a rough guide, a £35 fee in 1975 equates to around £265 (standard of living) or £391 (labor earnings) in 2016 (the economic status and power values are in excess of £500, but because they are freelance fees, we might expect this bump above the average) (measuringworth.com). The perceived value by those who were there is slightly lower: Wilf Prigmore estimates that a three-page script might command a fee of £150 in today's money, and writer Terence Magee estimates similarly in the region of £150 to £200.[7] Magee explains that a three-page script would include twenty-eight "frames" (panels) in the late 1960s and early '70s. In later years, stories were reduced to twenty-one frames, and sometimes even eighteen, to allow the artists room to use their talent. *Misty*, of course, achieved this in a different manner, by allowing four pages for the vast majority of its stories, across an average of twenty-six panels.[8] The scripting practices laid out the script by number of panels, meaning that in general the layout was entirely the artist's domain (Mills 2016a), although the editorial team sometimes marked up the scripts to set out the page breaks and create a punch line for each page (Cunningham 2017).

Magee says that producing this type of script would take him about ten to twelve hours over one and a half days. "This production would include researching in some cases, preparation such as devising what appears in each frame and so forth. I always wrote longhand at first; then the typing at the end was the easy bit. Scripts would always be submitted in meticulous shape (except Gerry Finley-Day, notorious for his messiness. But he was original, imaginative and talented so he was excused)." Magee suggests that an average writer would produce three such scripts per week (although "I'm sure there were some writers a lot faster than me") and so would earn the equivalent of £450 to £600 weekly, although some were more prolific than others. For example, Alison Christie (2015) says that at her height she was writing six stories each week. Anne Digby (2017) describes writing for the comics as "fantastically well paid. . . . I see, via Google, that the average gross weekly wage in 1977 was £78.60p., so Alan's £51 in March 1978 (for a morning's work) was remarkably good. The rewards were even higher in the 1960s when AP's [Amalgamated Press] girls' comics were still booming."

The process of creating *Misty* week by week is somewhat easier to establish from interviews with IPC writers and artists. Stories were selected based on very short initial outlines, particularly if they came from trusted writers. Mills (2016a) describes these initial outlines as follows:

> Maybe a paragraph, "I've come up with this idea for a story, it will be like Stephen King's *Carrie*..." and we would leave it at that. I think what bears this memory of mine out is when I did a story for *Jinty* I very unusually wrote a full outline and I remember distinctly [its editor] Mavis Miller looking at me in horror! She said "What's this?" and I said "It's an outline for the story?!!" and she said "Oh... Thank God, I thought you had written it as a text story at first!," so that gives you an idea of how little we would actually put onto paper.

After the initial brief outline, the writer and subeditors did a lot of work to realize the story, as Wilf Prigmore confirms when describing the scripting practices at IPC. First the editor would consult with the writer on a story summary as Mills describes. The writer would then write the script and send it in. The editorial team reviewed the script before sending it out, either directly to the artist or often to a translator (IPC used an agency in Brussels), with the translated script then being sent on directly to Madrid or Barcelona or somewhere else.

Prigmore (2016a) comments that collaboration with artists abroad "was always fraught with problems.... You couldn't take things for granted and had to spell out exactly what you wanted." He gives examples of colloquialisms that went drastically wrong, such as children literally "blowing raspberries" in a classroom scene, the appearance of a piratical "one-armed bandit" in a bar, and confusion about terms such as "pea souper" for intense fog. He concludes: "So you had to be quite pedantic about what you wanted when sending the scripts out." Alongside this was the more standard editing work, for example, when writers would get carried away and include absurdly long speeches or the like:

> There was a lot of rewriting, and you had to make things really fit into a picture and make the pictures work—you know, you couldn't have ten pictures of two people talking; you had to move that along. So that really was the main part of the subeditors' work. Then, when the artwork came back, checking that you've really got the pictures that you need. And then it went out for lettering. In the early days, it was hand-lettered; there were a few specialists that did that, and then gradually we got the computer or machine-set lettering. And then it would have to be read again, because sometimes people couldn't read any alterations we'd made on the scripts, or there were typos,

and different things. So you'd have to read the balloons when they came back and make sure they were right. And that sort of rounded that off. And then it was adding your bits and pieces: "great news," what's coming next week. And the general producing things: making sure it got away on time, and you had to wrap it all up and deliver it to the printers. (Prigmore 2016a)

With a lead time of around six weeks for each issue, the process was high pressure and sometimes confusing: "I never remembered what day it was. We were living in a different time. And if you do an annual or specials, well, with an annual, you're almost a year in advance" (Prigmore 2016a). *Misty*'s art editor Jack Cunningham (2017) also remembers the juggling that the process required: "You work on the paper that you're doing; you're also looking at the paper that's gone down; you're also looking at what you've got to put in the next paper the week after that, so there's not a great deal of time to think—but you go on as best you can."

THE *MISTY* WRITERS

Pat Mills is the name most often associated with *Misty* and its first creator. He got his first comics job at DC Thomson as "a sort of assistant editor" (2016a) and then went freelance, creating and writing a range of influential and notorious comics. Sometimes described as the "Godfather of British Comics," Mills was a trailblazer who unleashed weeklies such as *Tammy, Jinty, Battle Picture Weekly, Action*, and *2000AD*. After his success with these IPC titles, Mills proposed the initial idea that became *Misty* and was its "consulting editor" for the first few months before moving on (Mills 2016a). He says now that "I wish in a way that I had put my private life second and carried on with *Misty* because I really do believe that *Misty* would have been out there today" (Mills 2016a). However, his vision of *Misty* was very different from that of the IPC management and the comic that it eventually came to be. The team who worked on *Misty* throughout its run do not remember him having any further involvement, and Anne Digby (2017) also states that Mills's "contact with the girls' comics was rather episodic." Rather, his role was characterized by launching creative new titles (often based on controversial new ideas), scripting early installments of lead stories, and then moving on to the next once these were established. In 1976 and 1977 he was heavily involved in launching and editing *2000AD* (he edited the first sixteen progs [issues], finishing in June 1977, after which Kelvin Gosnell took over as editor). In 1978 he continued to write for *2000AD*, including "Judge Dredd" and "Dan Dare," and also devised and launched *Starlord* and scripted ongoing serials such as "Ro-Busters." Of the 443 stories printed in the *Misty* comics and annuals, Mills wrote five: the serials "Moonchild" and "Hush, Hush, Sweet Rachel," and the one-offs "Roots,"[9] "Red Knee—White Terror!" and "Black Sunday," with the majority appearing in its first issue.

Misty's second creator, Wilf Prigmore, joined IPC in 1971 more or less by accident. He was a trainee subjournalist at a local free paper until drastic cutbacks left him out of a job. A friend's father in the Syndication Department of IPC then alerted him to a vacancy in IPC's Competitions Department, which provided the competitions and prizes for all the company's publications. Once there, rather than use the internal mail, Prigmore made it his business to deliver things to the various departments by hand to "see what goes on" (2016a). This meant he was spending time in the Juveniles Group around the time of *Tammy*'s launch and was invited to join its team as *Tammy*'s subeditor a few months later (mid- to late 1971). This brought him into contact with people like Gerry Finley-Day (then *Tammy*'s editor), Pat Mills, and Joe Collins (the creator of *Misty*'s "Miss T"). Prigmore was charged with developing *Misty* out of Pat Mills's original ideas and was responsible for devising the comic's host character and cultivating its mystery tone, also acting as editor for its first few issues. He became group editor for Girls Adventure Comics, then going back to writing and editorial duties on *Tammy* in the early 1980s. He left IPC in 1984 on the back of a NUJ strike, remembering: "They used it to get rid of troublemakers like me. I took my redundancy and went back to journalism" (2017b). As group editor, he had a great influence on IPC's girls' comics and wrote fifteen single stories for *Misty*.

Malcolm Campbell Shaw, *Misty*'s editor, spent his childhood in Paisley in Scotland. He was an only child, with a paranoid schizophrenic mother and a distant father. He attended Glasgow University before changing his focus to journalism and getting a job at DC Thomson and moving to Dundee, a move that changed his politics and taught him his trade. In 1968 he left DC Thomson and moved down to London, surviving on pork pies and pints until he got a job at Fleetway a year or so later, working on titles such as *Romance* and *My Story*. He met his wife Brenda Ellis on October 10, 1970, who describes their meeting as "a bolt of lightning." Brenda remembers him as "a fantastic man" who was "very jolly" despite his ongoing health problems and who "was a very respectful man towards women. . . . I suppose you would call him a feminist." Malcolm was extremely well read and often put a characteristic literary twist in his work: for example, inserting T. S. Eliot poems into his early writing for the romance titles. He is likely the author of *Misty*'s environmental and political stories (see chap. 6), and many of his stories are filled with social commentary, such as the Nazi-occupied Britain of "The Sentinels" or the Marxist overtones of an enslaved Victorian workforce ("End of the Line").

Shaw was never interested in writing for the boys' comics: *Misty*'s genre suited him down to the ground, as his reading tastes lay in science fiction and mystery stories. He took his writing seriously: "He just wanted to write really good-quality stories.... He used to have all these reference books... like *Tales of the British Isles*, *Reader's Digest*, sort of things like spooky stories, legends, and myth, and he referred to lots of these and would mix a lot of these up." Unlike Pat Mills's formula approach (see chap. 8), Malcolm never followed the formulas (B. Ellis 2016).

Mills and Shaw met at Fleetway and worked together to launch *Jinty* in 1974 before it was taken over by Mavis Miller when she left *June*. Shaw was extremely supportive of Miller's editorial work (his wife Brenda Ellis comments, "He really, really rated her. He thought she was absolutely the tops"). He wrote a number of serials for *Jinty*, including "The Robot Who Cried" (1977), a *Pinocchio*-style coming-of-age story about a robot girl who learns what it is to be human. Shaw also edited and contributed a great deal to *New Mirabelle*,[10] which was launched in February 1977 (the same month as *2000AD*). Unfortunately this revamped title only lasted until October 1977, when it merged with *Pink*, leaving him free to devote himself to *Misty*.

The extent of Shaw's writing for *Misty* is lost, but his wife estimates he would have written at least one story for each issue, just for the love of doing so. He has been identified as the author of the serials "The Sentinels," "The Four Faces of Eve," and "End of the Line" and, based on his politics and interest in science fiction, is the likely author of many other stories that combine similar themes. Shaw edited the bulk of the run of *Misty* before giving it up to go freelance and travel with his young family. In 1979 they moved to Castelldefels near Barcelona in Catalonia, Spain, alongside many of the Spanish artists who had worked on the same comics, such as Blas Gallego, José Cánovas, Santiago Hernandez, and Rafael Busom. Shaw and Blas Gallego had become good friends on Gallego's annual trips to London, and he welcomed him to Barcelona. Shaw continued freelance writing for all the girls' titles from Spain, working in the mornings and afternoons, and sending everything in late ("They never got put in the post until the deadline" [B. Ellis 2016]). In 1981 the family moved back to London, and Shaw began developing *BEEB*—a new children's magazine based on BBC TV programs—for Polystyle Publications. Sadly he had suffered from ulcerative colitis since the age of twelve and died of cancer on December 4, 1984, a day before his thirty-eighth birthday. Although Malcolm Shaw wrote for many girls' titles, the *Misty* stories were a perfect fit for his interests and allowed him to push the boundaries of fiction for girls. As Ellis (2016) states: "He was quite proprietorial about *Misty*. He really felt that was such a good comic for girls." Pat Mills (2016a) agrees: "I endlessly bang on about how brilliant Malcolm was. ... Malcolm really cared about what he was doing; he was passionate about it."

Misty's subeditor Bill Harrington was born William Walter Harrington on May 30, 1930. He was a staff writer who had previously written for Fleetway's *Look and Learn* magazine (published 1962–82) and other comics including *Pink* (IPC, 1973–80) and *Tammy* (his story "The Clock and Cluny Jones" was reprinted in the *Misty* Annual 1985). Before this both Mills and Prigmore believe that Harrington was an actor, confirmed by the presence of John Line (*The Brothers*, BBC 1972–76) at his funeral, and Mills (2016a) attributes the "very smooth" dialogue in Harrington's stories to his experience on the stage. Harrington was subeditor for the entire *Misty* run and is credited with writing the serials "The Black Widow" and "The Cult of the Cat" (and presumably also its sequel, "The Nine Lives of Nicola"). Prigmore (2016a) says that Harrington specialized in historical stories, such as "Waifs of the Wigmaker" (*Tammy* #226–37, 1975), commenting: "If you came across similar period play type stories, the chances are it would be a Harrington." Harrington remained at IPC after *Misty* ended and was likely the editor of the *Misty* annuals (Fay 2016), although there is little information about what else he worked on. He wrote a James Bond strip for Scandinavian publishers (Semic Comics) between 1985 and 1988. He died unexpectedly when he was struck by lightning while out walking his dog on Wanstead Flats in June 1989. Prigmore (2017b) remembers him as "a lovely bloke" who perhaps would have appreciated his dramatic exit.

Joe Collins, creator of "Miss T," is often overlooked in discussions of *Misty*, perhaps because his comedy series is such a contrast to the title's other stories. Collins had also come to IPC from DC Thomson and created a number of other comedy strips for different titles, such as "The Kitty Café Cats" (*Girl*), "Snoopa" (*Penny, Jinty and Penny*), and "Edie the Ed's Niece" (*Tammy*). Collins was adept at managing the merger process, combining his characters Edie, Miss T, and Snoopa into "The Crayzees" (*Tammy and Jinty, Tammy and Misty*), which ran until 1984, when it was replaced with another of Collins's comedy strips, "Sadie in Waiting" (*Tammy and Princess*). Prigmore (2016a) describes him as "a good writer and a big part of the comics at the time. . . . He was quite a revelation, a talented bloke." He remembers Collins originally as a writer, who then moved into drawing his own strips. He created Miss T in response to Prigmore's (2017b) suggestion that the comic needed "a friendly witch character." She appears in one way or another in seventy different *Misty* issues, specials, and annuals. Her early appearances take the form of four-panel strips, but in #58 she graduates to a series of full-page adventures, and she also sometimes appears in half-page stories, single-panel gags (or a collection of these), on the inside cover, or just as an illustration on the letters page. She provides much-needed light relief from the dark *Misty* fare, and although not to everybody's taste, she had the overwhelming support of readers when she was criticized in the letters page in late 1979 (see chap. 13).

A typical "Miss T" strip sees her attempting a spell with unexpected and unwanted results: for example, her first appearance in *Misty* #1 is a four-panel strip in which she asks a magic mirror, "Who is the fairest witch of all?" but is told, "I'd have to search long and hard, 'tis true ... to find one uglier than you." The gag is repeated in #3, where she wishes on a magic lamp to be beautiful (the genie admits defeat); and in #89, where an ugly duckling comments, "Boy, I'd hate to have seen *you* as a baby." She is often accompanied by her cat, who comments ironically or sometimes tricks Miss T, for example, throwing a coal bag over her head when she tries to magic up a solar eclipse, explaining, "I hate to see her disappointed" (#6). Miss T is generally the victim in her strips, although occasionally she gets the last laugh: for example, when her broom is mocked by a fellow witch with a skateboard she challenges it to sweep the floor (#38), and gets revenge with her "boomerang pie mix" recipe after receiving a pie in the face (#67).

The names of the other writers who produced *Misty* comics scripts have been lost, and despite interviewing a number of IPC staff, I have been unable to uncover any more. Freelance author Alison Christie (2015) says she contributed stories to *Misty*, but I have found no records of them. Christie began her comics career as a junior subeditor at DC Thomson, working on *Bunty* and writing her first script for the story "Queen of the Gypsies." After moving to work on DC Thomson's nursery titles, she then went freelance, submitting scripts to both DC Thomson and IPC. She wrote some memorable serials, such as "Stefa's Heart of Stone" (*Jinty*) and "Cassie's Coach" (*Tammy*), and also a number of children's books under the name Alison Mary Fitt.

There were doubtless a number of other freelance writers scripting for *Misty*. Even assuming that Shaw and Harrington would between them produce (say) three or four of the six weekly story installments, this leaves nearly half the content unaccounted for.[11] I hope to uncover more of the authorship of *Misty*'s comics strips in the future, but at present this remains unknown.

As well as its comics content, *Misty* also contained frequent text stories, which seem to have been mostly the domain of female writers. One of these was Kitty Punchard (who also wrote under the pseudonym K. Smith), who was born in 1931 in Cornwall and moved to Farnborough in Hampshire in 1968. She was a teacher for most of her career but moved into freelance journalism and writing in the 1970s, becoming a prolific contributor to girls' comics. She wrote mainly for *Misty*, where she was one of the main text story contributors, but also for *Tammy* and *Jinty* and occasionally *Debbie*. Her daughter recalls her mum saying that *Misty* paid the best, but if her story didn't make it into *Misty*, *Debbie* would always take it (Punchard 2016). She was constantly seeking intellectual and creative challenges (winning top prizes in many slogan competitions) and had a strong interest in the otherworldly. She passed away from heart-related problems in August 2014. Her stories for *Misty* remain unidentified.

Other freelance and staff writers also created various elements of *Misty*. The "True Ghost Stories" section began in July 1979 and, although initially anonymous, was credited to Anita Davies in later issues. Writer Maureen Spurgeon also contributed to the comic. She was a journalist and teacher before turning to comics and then children's books; authoring spin-off novels from series such as *The Real Ghostbusters*, *Teenage Mutant Hero Turtles*, and *Count Duckula* in the 1980s and 1990s. She wrote for many comics from the 1960s to the 1980s, such as DC Thomson's *Bunty* and IPC's *Tammy* (including the serial "No Tears for Molly"), and she is thought to have written for *Misty*, although there are no records of her stories. Fondly known as the "White Witch," Spurgeon entertained colleagues with palmistry and other predictions and was "the specialist for any horoscope-type features and stories . . . fortune-telling pieces and lucky charms" (Prigmore 2016b). She wrote the copy to go with *Misty*'s "Wheel of Fortune Wallet" giveaway and may even have devised the wheel itself. Spurgeon was born in London in 1941 and died of cancer on October 30, 2007.

These names are significant, as there has been a tendency to assume that the 1970s British girls' comics were almost entirely written by men. Historically this was also the case; male writers and editors produced all of Amalgamated Press's schoolgirl papers despite creating images of fictional female editors (Tinkler 1995, 69–70). This subterfuge was effective: writing in 1978, Lofts claims that "whilst most of the strips are written by men, they are controlled by young editors of the female variety, who keep pulse on the latest pop stars, fashions and music" (63). When the male control of female papers was recognized, it was rationalized away with claims that men knew what female readers wanted, and were better equipped to deliver it without "mothering" or restricting readers. Lofts's (1978) investigation of male writers' dominance suggests that editors felt women writers were too didactic, and that they already had a large number of established male writers to hand. However, these arguments are unconvincing when we consider that a number of female writers, working for both the male and female papers, were publishing under male pseudonyms.[12] Tinkler points out that apologist studies such as Lofts's (1978) circumnavigate the issue by claiming that the lack of female writers was simply due to a lack of female journalists or the convenience of using established male writers. She instead argues that this lack was created and enabled by the systemic prevention of women's entry to the profession. From this angle, we should also consider critically later statements by writers such as Pat Mills (2016a) that the female IPC staffers were not interested in writing for the girls' comics. Comments from female subeditors at DC Thomson (see, e.g., Miller 2017b) instead suggest that, as well as editing and rewriting the story scripts, the subeditors were expected to write features and interviews and to progress from this role to scripting one's own stories.

The lack of attention paid to female creators of British comics could be due to many things: the absence of published credits, the visibility and vocality of key (male) figures, the disposability of the girls' titles, and the creative links between comics like *Misty* and high-profile boys' titles such as *2000AD*. Some contemporary criticism and scholarship also perpetuate this inequality: in an article celebrating girls' comics, Adi Tantimedh (2014) refers to "writers like Pat Mills, John Wagner and the late Steve Moore" and concludes that Pat Mills wrote "his fair share of the series in *Jinty*." Similarly, Pat Mills (2011) himself makes some quite sweeping claims about the motivation and style of female comics creators, saying that "generally, it was male writers in this field. I think [Anne Digby] is the only woman I can think of who genuinely had a better touch in the way she did this, she wrote far more from the heart, the rest of us were 23-year-old guys killing ourselves laughing as we wrote this stuff, but she wrote from the heart, and it was quite genuine."[13] However, Anne Digby (Alan Davidson's widow) and Brenda Ellis (Malcolm Shaw's widow) have both spoken out against the cynicism Mills claims for the male writers and stressed their husbands' dedication to their work. Malcolm Shaw had a particular interest in science fiction and mystery and threw this into his writing: "He was very creative, and he just wrote what he thought they would enjoy. . . . He wasn't cynical. I'm sure there were some cynical writers [who] did it for a living, and they just churned them out. Whereas Malcolm took it seriously, absolutely seriously" (B. Ellis 2016). Anne Digby (2015) concurs: "How much I agree with Mrs. Shaw that—like her late husband Malcolm—some, at least, of the men who wrote for *Jinty* took their work seriously, writing stories of real quality."

Jenni Scott (2015b) also critiques claims that the writers of girls' comics were entirely male and argues that British comics creators were more diverse in age and gender than has been assumed. She analyzes *Tammy* issues from 1982 and *Girl* in the 1950s and 1960s, both of which included creator credits for a time. These two reference points show that although the majority of writers were indeed male, the split is more even than has been suggested, and she estimates that somewhere between 15 and 40 percent of the stories appearing in each issue were authored by women (this figure is not weighted by number of pages). Scott also draws attention to female writers such as Alison Christie and older male writers such as Len Wenn. At this stage in his career, Wenn was well past the twenty-three-year-old demographic that Mills claims, as were *Misty* subeditor Bill Harrington, its art editor Jack Cunningham, and its final editor Norman Worker. The comments on Scott's (2015b) article also point out that women wrote the majority of the text stories across many titles.

Despite this, those who were there do recall a feeling that IPC had become male dominated by the 1970s. Art editor Jack Cunningham says, "It never really occurred to me, but almost all the writers were male," and although Mavis Miller's name looms large as the well-respected editor of *Jinty*, she was of the older 1950s generation (formerly working on more prestigious magazines such as the *Radio Times*) that was pushed aside at IPC in the 1970s and discarded in a fairly ruthless manner. Wilf Prigmore was promoted to group editor over Miller, and she left IPC in 1984. Writer Terence Magee (2014) points out that "the girls' comics disappeared soon after. Maybe they were shaken up a bit too much."

GOTHIC, CLASS, AND GENDER

The anonymity of creators and the marginalization of female authors in British comics find echoes in Gothic literature. Although Gothic's appeal to female creators and readers is undisputed, the contributions of female writers and the tastes of female audiences have frequently come under fire historically. Early reviews of *Frankenstein* include direct attacks on its author's suspected gender ("The writer of it is, we understand, a female; this is an aggravation of that which is the prevailing fault of the novel" [*British Critic* 1818]) and more implicit denigrations that associate femininity with naivety and inexperience ("We have heard that this work is written by Mr. Shelley; but should be disposed to attribute it to even a less experienced writer than he is . . . the production of a daughter of a celebrated living novelist" (*The Literary Panorama, and National Register* 1818). The characters of Gothic heroines and the tastes of female readers were also undermined and marginalized, as is demonstrated in Austen's satire *Northanger Abbey* (1817) (Priest 2011; Spooner 2017). Although these older scorned Gothics are canonized and accepted today, both scholars point out that the types of Gothic favored by female readers, especially younger audiences, continue to be disparaged amid claims of protecting a tradition perceived as serious and significant. Buckley (2018) draws attention to the numerous critics who are intent on claiming an elite marginal position for Gothic and its themes even though it comes from pulps and mass marketing (noting, e.g., Joshi 2001, 2004; Botting 2008; Beville 2009), and who often sweepingly dismiss feminine Gothic forms to do so (see Botting 2008). As Priest (2011) summarizes: "The Twihards are the new Catherine Morlands."

Haefele-Thomas (2017, 169) argues that "for women writers, often dismissed simply because they are female, writing within a liminal genre like Gothic has enabled them to more honestly and thoroughly critique restrictive social and cultural conventions," such as familial structures, cisgender bodies, and issues based on the intersections of sexuality, race, class, ability, and gender identity. In later chapters, I explore *Misty*'s use of themes such as transformation and transgression in the context of Female Gothic, and chapter 13 demonstrates the active nature of the comic's female readership. However, Gothic's complicated relationships with female creators and consumers also intersect with issues of class and identity that inform British comics.

The elegiac discourse around Gothic (where newer, popular, or parodic works are contrasted unfavorably with older, more serious texts) finds a parallel in IPC's attempts to raise its perceived status (banking at Coutts, commissioning "manuscripts") and its framing of *Misty* as a "mystery story paper" rather than a "horror comic." Pat Mills's original script for a story called "The Banana King," which would become "Red Knee—White Terror!" was instrumental in this decision and is shown here in figure 2.1, along with its published version (fig. 2.2). As originally written, it is a story of building tension, with a malevolent antagonist and a gruesome, detailed spider, which builds to the suggested death of its heroine and ends on a final horrifying image combined with an EC Comics style pun ("A spider that can make you go ... Bananas!"). As published, the story is comparatively toned down: the villain is removed, the spider is revealed as a toy, and the protagonist does not die, although the ending is not entirely reassuring. Nonetheless, the published version sustains the tension of Mills's script, with much of the radio narration and the advance of the spider being used, and although Andrea's scream is perhaps not as hysterical or close-up as Mills desired, the moment dominates the page with the emanata "EEEEAAA" and her shuddering arm, which cuts across the page's center. The first and final images of the spider also contain the sort of convincing, hairy detail that the script requests, and in fact the medium is used to trick the reader here, for if one looks closer, the spider is drawn with much less detail on page 3, as befits a mechanical toy. Comparing the two narratives in this way reveals the subtle changes that were made to reduce the shock value and add a twist ending while retaining the growing tension.

As realized, "Red Knee" largely replaces horror (the startling and repulsive image) with terror (the threat of something unseen or about to happen), a distinction that I discuss further in chapter 9. Although many of the later *Misty* stories would end on a horrifying final image (as noted in chap. 8), the changes made to Mills's script indicate that from the start the vision for the comic was of emotional tension and uncanny intrigue, where everyday settings and characters would be made strange and unfamiliar through the supernatural, rather than outright horror. As Prigmore confirms, "It ['The Banana King'] was really quite a frightening story. That was put forward with some of the ideas and we said, no, no, we're definitely not looking for a horror comic, it's going to be mystery" (Prigmore 2016a).

4

THE BANANA KING. MISTY. P. MILLS.

GENERAL NOTE TO ARTIST: To make this story effective you have got to put a lot of detail into the spider. Bring over how it twitches, writhes its legs, jumps ~~xx~~ about. Some pictures will have to be drawn with just the spider in frame and maybe others taken from exactly the same ~~pixx~~ point of view - same amount of character in each pic... BUT WITH THE SPIDER GETTING CLOSER... and the girl's face becoming increasingly terrified. This type of thing has beeen ~~xuxusxfx~~ successfully done in American comics and if you are unfamiliar with the technique let us know and we will send you some examples. (I've got some , Wilf - if you need them.) For this reason my picture descriptions are just the basis - you must adapt them where you feel it is necessary ~~xuxvexyfxyuu~~. With this kind of story an artist has a stronger creative contribution to make - even adding or ~~xetx~~ deleting a frame - than in an ordinary kinda story. The story will not work if the spider is just a black blob on the page. I suggest the spider could be based on the spider below - a Red Knee - but if you have something better in mind, of course go ahead.

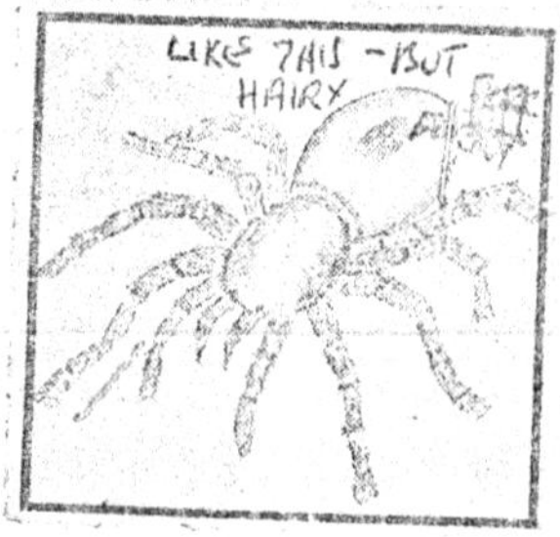

I. Heroine - girl called Andrea - shopping in market. Guy flogging bananas at stall. ~~xofxs~~ Lots ~~fx~~ of women clustering round. Andrea is attracted by his shouting.

PANEL: ANDREA GRAY WAS SHOPPING IN THE MARKET...

BANANA SELLER: ROLL UP, LADIES! GET YOUR BANANAS HERE ... THE FRESHEST IN THE MARKET.

~~Xxvox~~ ANDREA (thinks): BANANAS... YES - I COULD BUY SOME FOR TEA...

2. She goes over and we see that all he sells ~~ib~~ is bananas. There is a sign up "BERTIE WEBB - THE ~~EDXVCXVE~~ BANANA KING" - written in rather spidery lettering. In similar lettering the price: 10p a lb. Coarse looking woman with fag laughs cynically. But he is certainly attracting a lotta people.

/P.T.O.

Figure 2.1. Original script for "The Banana King," by Pat Mills. Donated to this project by Wilf Prigmore.

2. Continued.
   Andrea surprised at price.
   ANDREA: GOSH! YOU'RE SELLING THEM FOR TEN PENCE A POUND... THAT'S EVEN LESS THAN "CHEAPWAYS" SUPERMARKET.

   WOMAN: BLIMEY! YOU MUST BE A HIT BANANAS YERSELF, MR. WEBB - FLOGGIN' 'EM AT THAT PRICE.

3. Head shot of the man... the banana king... and we see now how weird he is.. But still restrained. He smiles a bit evilly. See end of story for further possible character ref

   THE BANANA KING: THEY'RE CHEAP, LADIES - 'COS BANANAS IS ALL I SELL...SEE? I BUY 'EM IN CRATES, STRAIGHT FROM ABROAD. BERTIE WEBB - THE BANANA KING, THAT'S ME!

4. He hands Andrea a bag of bananas and Andrea looks a bit frightened of him.
   THE BANANA KING: COUPLE O' POUNDS FOR YOU, DUCKS? NICE AN' RIPE AN' YELLER. I'M SURE YOU'LL ENJOY 'EM. HEE, HEE!

   ANDREA (thinks): THERE'S SOMETHING A BIT WEIRD ABOUT THE BANANA KING. THAT STRANGE SPIDERY WRITING ON HIS SIGN... AND WHAT AN ODD SMILE...

5. Andrea looks back on the busy scene - a bit puzzled - as she goes to get her bus.

   ANDREA (thinks): COME TO THINK OF IT... I HAVEN'T SEEN HIM ROUND HAMDEN MARKET BEFORE. HE MUST BE NEW. OH, WELL... I'D BETTER HURRY OR I'LL MISS MY BUS.

6. Back home. In the kitchen. She puts her shopping bag down and her ~~put~~ purchases are already down. The bag of bananas is open and is lying on a kitchen surface.

PANEL: BACK HOME—

ANDREA ~~(thinks)~~: MUM'S DOING LATE SHIFT AT THE FACTORY TODAY, SO I'LL GET THE TEA. THESE BANANAS WILL MAKE A NICE DESSERT.

7. She switches on the radio as she busies herself putting other things away.
ANDREA: LET'S SEE WHAT'S ON THE RADIO —
RADIO: THIS IS TONY JACKSON WITH A LOCAL NEWS-FLASH... A WOMAN HAS BEEN ADMITTED TO HAMDEN GENERAL HOSPITAL JUST TWO HOURS AGO — SUFFERING FROM THE BITE OF A POISONOUS SPIDER...

8. Andrea listens a bit worried. The bag of bananas to one side.
RADIO: THE WOMAN IS IN A COMA AT THE MOMENT WITH DOCTORS FIGHTING TO SAVE HER LIFE. THE POISON HAS BEEN IDENTIFIED AS COMING FROM A VENOMOUS SOUTH AMERICAN SPIDER...

ANDREA: HOW AWFUL!

9. ~~Justcxvbg~~ Andrea going towards the bag of bananas.
ANDREA : IF THERE'S ONE THING I CAN'T STAND IT'S SPIDERS. WELL, I'D BETTER GET BUSY WITH (THESE BANANAS FOR) THE TEA...

10. Close shot of spider in bag of bananas... twitching horribly. Plenty of detail nothing else in pic.
NO DIALOGUE.

11. Andrea turns and wipes her brow as the spider crawls out of the banana bag and moves towards her. She doesn't see it.
ANDREA: (THEN) ON SECONDS THOUGHTS—I FEEL ALL HOT AND STICKY AFTER THAT SHOPPING. I'LL HAVE A BATH FIRST...

12. Spider jumps onto her skirt as she leaves the room with the radio.

    RADIO: JUMP AROUND WITH THE POP SOUNDS ON RADEEEEO HAMDEN ... WITH TONEEEE JACKSON...!

13. Andrea now goes up the stairs with the radio. Perhaps we don't see the spider in this pic... so the readers are left wondering... where's it got to?

    RADIO: AND NOW, FOLKS... FLINT-LOCK'S LATEST RECORD...

    ANDREA: OH, SUPER...

14. We now see the spider running up her jumper as she continues up the stairs ...

    ANDREA: HEY... THAT BEAT REALLY GETS YOU GOING...

15. She leans down + turns the taps on in the bathroom. Radio to one side... the spider is now crawling up almost to the top of her jumper.

    RADIO: SOME MORE NEWS ON THE SPIDER HAS JUST COME IN, folks. IT IS BELIEVED TO BE THE RED LEG SPIDER. THE SPIDER DOES NOT LIKE BRITISH WEATHER AND WILL BE LOOKING FOR SOMEWHERE... WARM AND COSEY... TO NEST...

16. Just a very close shot of the spider again at the very top of her jumper.

    VOICE OFF FRAME: CHILDREN ARE WARNED ESPECIALLY – NOT TO GET TOO CLOSE...

17. Andrea takes off her jumper.

    ANDREA: YOU WON'T CATCH ME GOING NEAR SPIDERS...

18. Andrea now in bath. Jumper lying in huddle on the floor. Suggest we may not see spider – although it is on the jumper. Andrea relaxes, closes her eyes.

    ANDREA: MMMM... THAT'S BETTER...

19. The spider crawls off jumper and starts running along the floor.
    Andrea has her eyes closed and is smiling.
    RADIO: (I) I HAVE AN EXPERT IN THE STUDIO WITH ME... PROFESSOR MILLS...
    PROFESSOR, CAN YOU TELL US A BIT MORE ABOUT THIS SPIDER?

    RADIO (2): WELL, TONY... IT'S HAIRY... ABOUT SIX INCHES LONG.. BREEDS
    RAPIDLY AND USUALLY EATS SMALL BIRDS OR MICE...

20. Spider jumps onto the top edge of the bath.
    RADIO: IT'S A CLEVER LITTLE FELLOW... IT CAN LEAP ABOUT THREE FEET IN
    THE AIR...

21. Andrea might now out-stretch her arm (remember to have musical notes or vibration lines from radio where appropriate.) Spider starts to crawl up her arm.
    RADIO (I): SOUNDS HORRIBLE, PROFESSOR. NOW AM I RIGHT IN SAYING THAT
    THERE HAVE BEEN SEVERAL DEATHS THROUGHOUT BRITAIN - CAUSED
    BY THESE SPIDERS WHO HAVE MYSTERIOUSLY GOT HERE FROM ABROAD?

    RADIO (2): I'M AFRAID SO, TONY. IT'S RATHER PUZZLING. YES, THIS SPIDER
    WILL BITE OR SPIT VENOM WHICH CAN PROVE FATAL...

22. Andrea opens her eyes and sees the spider crawling up her arm.
    Starts to look horrified.
    RADIO: BUT REMEMBER, TONY - SOME SPIDERS ARE FRIENDLY. WHY, I HAD A
    PET TARANTULA CALLED "JAKE" WHO WOULD CRAWL ALL OVER ME.
    (ONCE)

23. It crawls up her arm a bit more. Important to build up her expressions of horror gradually - as I have tried to convey with these refs.
    This first one conveys something of her feeling for th

    RADIO: THAT'S ALL VERY WELL, PROFESSOR. BUT WHAT
    WOULD YOU SAY TO SOMEONE WHO HAD THIS SPIDER
    RUNNING UP THEIR ARM RIGHT NOW?

24. It has now climbed onto her ~~si~~ shoulder. I feel the expression in the ~~enclosed~~ *attached* is very near to what is required.

RADIO: I WOULD SAY... DON'T PANIC, TONY...

ANDREA: NO... NO...

25. It crawls ~~××××××××××××××××~~ up her neck towards her hair.

RADIO: JUST RELAX...

ANDREA: IT-IT...W-W-WANTS...TO ...~~××~~ G-GO...ON M-MY...

26. Spider is now on her hair. Depending on how you've built this up ~~w~~ it might be a close shot... or ~~it~~ - maybe more likely - it could be the heroine building up for one almighty scream!
~~××××××××~~ ANDREA: HAIR!!

RADIO: AND IT ~~MAY~~ *might* GO AWAY!

27. Now a really vital pic.... you've got to have her really screaming the house down. With the spider half on her hair, maybe a bit on her fore-head, too. ~~~~ indicates some of the ~~×××××~~ hysteria we need. *very close like this.*

ANDREA: AAAAAAAH!

28. The heroine gets out of the situation – but I feel it spoils the climax if we see her bashing it with a hair-brush here. I feel – keep the tension up here – by showing her radio knocked over – maybe into the bath or on the floor with water splashed about... to suggest strongly that she's snuffed it.

VOICE (from radio): LET'S HOPE THE POLICE FIND OUT MORE ABOUT XXXXX XXXX WHY THESE SPIDERS ARE TURNING UP, TONY. BECAUSE – IF THE BITE DOESN'T PROVE FATAL—IT CAN AFFECT YOUR BRAIN... MAKE YOU DO VERY STRANGE THINGS...

VOICE (from radio): THAT'S TERRIBLE, PROFESSOR!   A SPIDER THAT CAN MAKE YOU GO...

29.   (suggest – if poss. – we can turn over the page to the final shock pics.)

29. Close shot of the Banana king – busy putting spiders in bunches of bananas... spiders on her face and running over his hands. I feel the reference below is pretty hard to beat. Forget the beard and beads and rather long hair... but the pose, the manic look in those eyes is excellent. If the picture could be as large as this – with all that detail... all those lines on the face etc... it could be very effective. Spiders in his hair, too.

VOICE (from off FRAME):

... STARK, STARING MAD!!

(Note to self on ... BANANAS!!)

P.T.O

Figure 2.2. "Red Knee—White Terror!" (*Misty* #1). Art by John Richardson, written by Pat Mills. Reproduced with permission of Misty™ Rebellion Publishing IP Ltd.; copyright © Rebellion Publishing IP Ltd., all rights reserved.

ANONYMOUS AUTHORS

ANONYMOUS AUTHORS 57

AGH! NO... NO!
I WOULD SAY...DON'T PANIC, TONY!
IT-IT... W-WANTS... TO... G-GO...ON M-MY...
HAIR!!
EEEEAAAAA
JUST RELAX...
...AND IT...MIGHT... GO AWAY!
THEN...
WHAT THE-? IT-IT'S A MECHANICAL TOY SPIDER! OH, THAT LITTLE HORROR OF A BROTHER!
HA,HA! FOOLED YOU, EH?
THAT WAS A CRUEL, NASTY THING TO DO, JAMIE! YOU FRIGHTENED THE LIFE OUT OF ME!
OH, I FEEL ALL WEAK. NOW TO FINISH MY BATH IN PEACE...
LET'S HOPE THEY FIND THE LITTLE DEVIL SOON, PROFESSOR!
Chill next week!

The branding of comics like *Misty* and *Spellbound* as "mystery papers" and the changes made to scripts like this can thus be read as a class issue with its roots in fears of populist Gothic fiction. The "story paper" label may have been intended to make the comics sound sophisticated to their young readers, but it perhaps also made these titles more palatable to parents and other gatekeepers by reminding them of the prose story papers of their youth. Similarly, the mystery genre had strong literary connotations in the living memory of older generations, possibly recalling the golden age of British detective fiction in the 1920s and 1930s. By emphasizing intrigue and tension over horror and danger, the girls' comics repositioned themselves as literary and traditional: appropriate material for young female readers. In doing so, they echo some aspects of Gothic. New incarnations of Gothic and their appeal to a female readership have often been decried as frivolous or required reframing as literary and weighty to pass muster, even as its creators (both male and female) exploit Gothic's liminal qualities to write subversively and radically.

CHAPTER 3

ASTONISHING ARTISTS

Identifying comics artwork is an art of detection for fans and critics. Stylistic features such as Ken Houghton's conjoined middle fingers, Brian Delaney's bold lines and blank backgrounds, and John Armstrong's athletic anatomies and smooth, rounded faces become clues in a deductive game played out on numerous forums and blogs.[1] In this chapter, I draw on many such discussions to identify the in-house and freelance artists involved with *Misty* and to analyze their work. I owe a particular debt of gratitude to David Roach's amazing knowledge of Spanish comics artists and his identification of those who contributed to *Misty*.[2] Spanish artists had been used extensively in British comics since the romance titles of the 1950s, and this chapter explores how this arrangement developed through the main publishers and agencies involved. I then identify the artists that appear most frequently in *Misty*, offering brief biographical summaries and analysis of their style and work. The chapter concludes by reflecting on the ways that *Misty*'s aesthetic and image were manipulated to contribute to its ideological repositioning as suitable reading material for young girls.

THE *MISTY* EDITORIAL TEAM

The in-house art team on *Misty* consisted of art editor Jack Cunningham and art assistant Ted Andrews, both of whom held these roles for the comic's entire run. Their role was to produce the comic in the exact form required by the printers, which they did entirely by hand. The art editor was responsible for designing story logos and resizing any elements needed to create the page layouts, for example, to accommodate last-minute demands for advertisement space, which always took priority. The art assistant's (or "bodger") role was to check and edit the artwork as it came in, amending or recoloring pages as needed.

Misty's art editor Jack Cunningham was born on December 17, 1922, in Scotland. He moved down to London from Glasgow around 1955 and took a number of advertising jobs while looking for a job in publishing. Around 1960 he was offered a job by Pat Halls of Newnes and Pearson (*The Strand, Woman's Weekly, Country Life*) on the strength of his art portfolio, and in 1969 the company merged with two others to become part of IPC Magazines. Some of Cunningham's earliest work was on a title called *True Stories*, and he picked up the job as he went along, also working on romance titles such as *Valentine* (1957–74) and, later, on *New Eagle* (1982–94). As *Misty*'s art editor, Cunningham had a "pivotal role" in creating the image of the comic and is described by Prigmore (2018c) as "its third co-creator." Cunningham designed all the story titles and logos and offered direction to the artists by annotating the scripts before they were sent out. When the art was received, Cunningham would resize it and sometimes put figures outside the frames and break it all up bit by bit. He created the moon-and-bat logo that appeared on *Misty*'s cover,[3] and hand-lettered the inside-cover welcome from Misty herself in every issue, which gave greater flexibility to fit the space available, and a more personal air. It also helped develop Misty's character and led to other elements of her mythology such as the Cavern of Dreams and her bat messengers. Cunningham died of a severe stroke on August 5, 2018.

Ted Andrews was born on January 28, 1949, and came to IPC searching for an art opportunity, having previously worked for a private publisher. He was interviewed for freelance work by Jack LeGrand (managing editor of one of the boys' comics groups), and although no freelance work was available, LeGrand offered Andrews a permanent job at £20 per week ("I'd arrived!" [Andrews 2017a]). Some of Andrews's first work was on the IPC Disney comics, and he was art assistant for the entire *Misty* run under Jack Cunningham, who describes him as "a marvel to work with. . . . He was a terrific man" (2017). Andrews describes his role more modestly, saying, "Jack would tell me to do whatever he wanted me to do and I would do it. . . . Mostly getting the artwork finished and ready and retouched. It could be anything, frame by frame. It could be one frame that might need something doing or something added to it, and then I would draw in the style of the artist to make any alterations" (2017b). As well as tidying up and amending the finished artwork as needed (like the scene of "blowing raspberries" also mentioned by Prigmore), Andrews also provided additional graphics. These included the cartoon strip promoting the free gift in *Misty* #1 and illustrations for features such as "No Final Curtains" and "Weird Music" (Annual 1982). Andrews went on to work on the *Sun*'s art desk for eighteen years, also drawing freelance for numerous other British newspapers. He is still a freelance illustrator and cartoonist and promotes his work at http://www.tedart.co.uk.

Misty was produced using letterpress printing, with four colored pages per issue. Prigmore (2016a) explains:

That was one of the few concessions I got: for *Misty* to have some colour, because really I got into all sorts of trouble with management. I kept arguing for a decent publication, decent paper. I said, you know, they've got nice glossy paper abroad and in America, why can't we get away from the horrible letterpress and pretty awful printing? I was always shouted down for that, but the concession I had got was to have four coloured pages: the cover, probably the center spread, and the last page.

Cunningham (2017) concurs with this memory, saying: "Misty had a very tight budget. It wasn't as well backed by management as it could have been. It was never printed on good paper. . . . We were never terribly happy about the cover, it wasn't very good quality paper and the printing wasn't terribly good." But although the team was disappointed with the print and color quality, these elements were often used for good effect. The stories that received coloring often used it to enhance their plot: Prigmore draws attention to "Moodstone" (#1), which reverses the *Wizard of Oz* (1939) tactic as the color slowly drains from the page. Color is also integral to the events of "Terror Wore Blue" (#2), "Green Grow the Riches—O!" (#3), and the serial "The Salamander Girl" (#5–9), which is full of fire and flame. It is similarly well used in "Heaven Is a Hummingbird" (#4), when Lynn's sight is restored as she gazes on a beautiful rainbow, and to emphasize the unnatural transformation of "The Dryad Girl" (#100).

However, it was the extra space for each story, driven by Pat Mills, that really gave both artists and editors the freedom to let *Misty*'s visuals shine in dramatic splash pages and varied panel shapes and sizes. Jack Cunningham (2017) describes the role of editorial in this, in particular focusing on the process of annotating the scripts and manipulating the finished artwork:

> Art was commissioned by someone from the Spanish people. They'd do what they were asked to do; they simply illustrated each scene. But it came back different sizes, so it had to be remodeled to fit the page size. . . . So the first thing I had to do was make a standard size that every artist worked to, and it used to appear as quite simply as square frame, square frame, square frame, and as we got a better idea, we perhaps started off with some figures that were outside of the frame, run the titles across two pages, and that's difficult, and break it all up, bit by bit. Actually, they were quite happy with that, the Spanish artists, because we knew them well, and they had a size to work to and an indication for an opening page and how it should end and that sort of thing. . . . I didn't go through the whole script, of course, but I designed what the opening page should look like and the end page should look like. And then here and there indicate where it would be better to leave a frame open, perhaps. Because it's very static, and very difficult to get any feeling of

movement.... Had it [*Misty*] gone on, because we kept in touch, not with the artists but with the head of the agency, we could have given the artists their head more, because they were very imaginative.

Misty's dramatic layouts are therefore perhaps best described as a collaboration between its editors and artists, with some illustrators presumably having more of a flair for this than others. For example, Isidre Monés (2018) confirms that he devised all his page layouts himself, saying that after his early Warren work, he had "total freedom" and took this as a chance to go "in the opposite direction to the boring arrangement of the so-called European 'clear line.'"[4] The following chapter looks more closely at the use of nonstandard layouts and paneling in *Misty* and the effect these have on its storytelling.

SPANISH COMICS ART AND THE "BIG THREE" STUDIOS

At the time of *Misty*'s production there were three main Spanish art studios: Selecciones Ilustradas, Creaciones Editoriales, and Bardon Art, all of which contributed to *Misty*. There is a misperception that these Spanish artists were used because they were cheap: in fact, they were employed on the basis of their talent. David Roach names them the "Golden Generation" and explores their work more fully in his book *Masters of Spanish Comic Book Art* (2017). As Wilf Prigmore comments: "They had some fantastic artists, of course. They and America had a bit more of a tradition of comics work and being held in some sort of respect.... The Spanish seemed to be particularly good at it, and there were some really good artists there. They certainly filled *2000AD* and *Misty* and a lot of the newer titles over the years." Roach (2016) also draws attention to "the sheer scope of the Spanish artists' work around the world" and stresses: "They weren't used because they were cheap, they were used because they were the best!" Jack Cunningham (2017) agrees: "They were much better than most of the English artists." The original art they produced was the property of the publishers, who, unless it had international appeal for licensing, would reuse it many times in various bodged forms. This recycling should be understood not as part of a shoddy, cut-price approach but rather as determination to get the most out of an expensive piece of good-quality art.

Of the "Big Three" Spanish studios, Selecciones Ilustradas was the most famous and had some of the best talent. Josép Toutain founded the company in 1953 after becoming friends with the artist Francisco Hidalgo and discovering a demand for artists in the French publishing scene. By 1957 Selecciones Ilustradas had a studio in central Barcelona and a roster of around forty artists all aged between fifteen and twenty-one. This young, dynamic company dominated the market, and by the early 1960s, its artists were drawing for every romance comic in the United Kingdom. The company operated like a well-oiled machine: scripts were received, translated, and shared around, and when done, the artist was simply given another. Work was abundant, and artists were paid regularly every fortnight—and at a rate that far exceeded the local market. They produced first-class art for titles in Britain, Germany, France, and Scandinavia. In 1971 Toutain met with publishers in the United States, and the agency's reach expanded still further as its artists became the dominant source of artwork for Warren Publishing (*Eerie, Creepy, Vampirella*). Here they were freed from the genre restrictions of romance comics and encouraged to experiment with dramatic style, texture, and depth, elements that can be seen in their subsequent work on *Misty*. The agency's most prominent *Misty* artists included Isidre Monés Pons, Ramon Escolano, and Jorge Badía Romero.

Although Selecciones Ilustradas was the largest, Creaciones Editoriales (Bruguera) was the first agency to access the European markets in the 1950s. It was founded by the cartoonist Carlos Conti Alcántara in the 1940s and at the end of that decade was bought by Francisco Bruguera, director of the publishing house Editorial Bruguera (with a personal share owned by Bruguera's artistic director Rafael Gonzalez Martinez). Editorial Bruguera was one of the largest publishers of comics in Spain, publishing a range of different titles and genres.[5] It allied with the Belgian agency ALI to represent its artists abroad, first breaking into France and then the United Kingdom in the mid-1950s. Creaciones Editoriales was led by directors José Bielsa and Francisco Ortega and mainly exported to England and Scandinavia. The agency's artists included María Barrera Castell, and many of the artists brought to *Misty* by Blas Gallego were also represented by Creaciones Editoriales, including José Cánovas, the Romero brothers (for a time), and Carlos Freixas (who also provided work through Art Bardon).

Art Bardon (named as an amalgamation of Barcelona and London) was founded by Spanish artist Jordi Macabich and British editor/writer Barry Coker in 1957. Having worked regularly for Creaciones Editoriales, Macabich knew that the British rates of pay were superior and in 1956 decided to take the initiative and visit the London offices of Amalgamated Press, asking for work.[6] He was successful, and the offers kept coming from both Britain and Europe, so after Macabich returned to Barcelona, he asked Barry Coker (a scriptwriter at Amalgamated Press) to act as an agent for him and some friends. Coker liaised with the British publishers, and Bardon Art was born. Described as "not only a transmission belt between the supply and demand of foreign editors and Spanish professionals, but a testing ground . . . and school for many young artists" (Guiral 2010),[7] Bardon rose to dominance in the following decades, representing more than seventy artists at its height in the 1970s and 1980s (Roach 2017), before declining and quietly closing its doors in 2010. Its *Misty* artists included Ramon Escolano, Josép Gual, and Enric Badía Romero.

The competition between these studies was intense, and they treated their staff quite differently. Artists were often enticed away to work for a rival company; Roach (2013, 65) notes that, by the late 1970s, the situation had become so unstable that the three agencies held a summit meeting and thereafter traded artists between themselves. Selecciones Ilustradas was seen as the desirable place to work, with a friendly atmosphere led by Toutain, whereas Creaciones Editoriales was patrician and authoritarian. Creaciones Editoriales and ALI also took a large percentage of their artists' pay, sometimes up to 70 percent of the fee (Roach 2017, 12).

These agencies played a pivotal role in the development and look of the British comics industry. As Martín (1967–68) points out: "Of the whole volume of comic book production made by Spanish artists between 1955 and 1975, at least 40 percent or more of the material created was through the Spanish comics agencies." Guiral (2010, 5) echoes this, stressing that "the history of our comic strip owes space and recognition to Macabich and all of the agents, technicians, scriptwriters and cartoonists; professionals who have worked in silence and with dignity."[8]

The British comics industry placed even more emphasis on the agencies: Roach (2013, 65) describes them as "ubiquitous" and says that until the appearance of *2000AD*, "almost all comic artists worked through agents or agencies and this was particularly true of foreign talent." Agents like Barry Coker (Bardon) and Louis Lorente (Creaciones) would take artists' samples to publishers in giant folders, and good matches would be made for each script. Initially IPC would have closely matched style to story but after some years might have allowed their trusted agents to do this.

Working abroad benefited these artists at a time when comics art was not well regarded in Spain. Guiral confirms that the prices per page were much higher in England. Roach suggests that in the 1950s artists could command 1,000 pesetas a page for their British work (2013, 64), and the rate of pay in 1970s Britain was three times as much as the rest of Europe (2017). For American work, the pay leaped even higher: artists could charge up to 80,000 pesetas for painted covers and the like. Pat Mills (2016a) also suggests there was an additional benefit in the currency exchange rate at this point.

It is hard to establish the 1970s rates of pay, but Roach (2016) suggests around £60 for a page of art. This figure seems in line with the script fees discussed in the previous chapter. A 2012 remittance receipt found in the papers of Shirley Bellwood shows that she was paid £200 for a color illustration for the second installment of "The Ladies of Loxley Hall," published in the *People's Friend* (DC Thomson, 2012). This roughly accords with the perceived value of these fees in today's money. However, depending on the nature of the art (e.g., a full-color painted plate, versus pencil-and-ink pages that would then be colored in house), it is hard to make comparisons.

The Spanish artists defined the look of 1950s romance comics, dominating Fleetway's catalog of titles (such as *Valentine*, *Mirabelle*, *Roxy*, and *Marilyn*), and glamorizing their content. Roach (2017, 15) draws attention to a divide that emerged based on cultural stereotyping, as "The Italian and Argentinian artists were regarded as muscular, almost macho, artists and they were most often given war, historical or adventure strips to draw. By contrast, the Spanish approach was seen as much more stylish and decorative so they tended to be given romance strips." Pat Mills (2016a) recalls that this approach gave the "working class—or ordinary girls, shall we say—reading these stories [what] they wanted: that dreamy, faraway Mills and Boon quality; they didn't want kitchen sink [realism]." Roach also explores the cultural significance of these artists' influence, arguing that their work could even be responsible for the profound changes in female fashions, style, and appearance that took place in 1960s Britain. In 1962 the British look was strongly postwar; however, by 1967 the fashions of Carnaby Street were dominated by large, heavy-lidded eyes, thick mascara, and pouting lips, a style that was considered modern and sleek. Roach suggests that this was an attempt to emulate the 1950s romance comics, drawn by Spanish artists and thus depicting Mediterranean-looking girls with exotic features and dark eyes and coloring (2017, 16). The influence was also reciprocal, as the early artistic liaisons between Britain and France and Spain also helped develop a fresh attitude against a backdrop of Spanish conservatism and Francoism that still hung over the country. Selecciones Ilustradas artist Manel Dominguez recalls the impact that the British music and magazines had on the artists: "The records that we bought on these trips seemed to come almost from a time warp projected into the future. . . . After three months, almost all of us sported those same [Beatles] haircuts. It was the victory of freedom outside the gray mediocrity and self-absorption of the Spain of those years" (quoted in Roach 2017, 11).

THE *MISTY* ARTISTS

The *Misty* artists were scattered, working across many studios, and included a number of people who did not usually work on the girls' comics (such as Puigaget and Guirado, discussed later). Roach (2017, 17) claims that Pat Mills asked Blas Gallego to bring together a group of creators for *Misty*, but in fact Mills (2017e) was not involved. He says this "came later" and points out that there was "nothing remarkable" about using Spanish artists. In fact, the *Misty* artists were headhunted by Wilf Prigmore and Jack Cunningham, who were dispatched on a trip to Barcelona in late 1977 to find artists for their new comic, and Prigmore confirms that Blas Gallego was integral to this process. While Prigmore (2017b) does not remember where the initial contact with the group of Spanish artists who worked on *Misty* came from (saying he was maybe shown their work by agents or that Mills knew it from *2000AD*), on this trip he and Cunningham got in touch with the agents and set themselves up in a hotel in Barcelona for the afternoon. Prigmore describes there being a big feeling of excitement and liberation; Franco had been gone for a while (died November 20, 1975), Catalans were coming out of hiding and able to use their traditional names, the flag was appearing on cars, and so on. The IPC editors got a good turnout and met a lot of artists; most were tired of being ripped off by agents taking 20 percent and wanted to work for the British comics. Prigmore and Cunningham also visited Gallego's home, discussing ideas and leaving some scripts and being told, "I will find you artists." Although Gallego did not act as an agent, he definitely suggested certain names to the *Misty* team and was responsible for particular creators being there, such as José Cánovas (with whom Gallego shared a studio). These artists predominantly worked on the single stories.

While all the artists who worked on *Misty* brought extraordinary talent to their pages, the ones that appear most frequently are shown in table 3.1.

Table 3.1. The artists that appear most frequently in *Misty*. The first column refers to the number of discrete stories that they worked on, and the second gives the number of installments in which their work appeared (many of the serials ran for around ten issues).

Artist	Stories	Episodes
Mario Capaldi	28	100
Joe Collins	1	84
Jaime "Homero" Rumeu	12	81
Brian Delaney	5	65
John Armstrong	28	48
Eduardo Feito	8	48
John Richardson	33	46
Isidre Monés	23	28
Jorge Badía Romero	19	25
María Barrera Castell (Gesalí)	15	24
Juan Ariza	23	23
Carlos Guirado	19	19
Total	214 (48%)	591 (69%)

By far the most dominant artistic presence in the main *Misty* comic strips is Mario Capaldi (1935–2004). Capaldi was a Scottish-born artist whose family originated from Italy. He was born in Glasgow and moved with the family to Middlesbrough in his teens, where he would settle for his adult life. He briefly attended the Glasgow School of Art in the early 1950s and also Middlesbrough's Constantine College in 1959 (at the same time as another future *Misty* artist, John Armstrong), but his parents were not supportive, and he was largely self-taught. His daughter Vanda documents his early life in *Mario: A Biography in Poetry* (Capaldi 2012), emphasizing his dedication to art throughout his life. Reclusive by nature, he worked as a comics artist and illustrator from 1959 to 2003 across numerous titles for many companies (including IPC, DC Thomson, and Marvel UK), and in many different styles and media: oils, watercolor, acrylics, pencils, and inks. He was particularly fond of drawing animals, especially horses. His work for *Misty* was prolific: the six serials "The Sentinels," "Journey into Fear," "The Cats of Carey Street," "Whistle and I'll Come . . . ," "Don't Look Twice," and "Winner Loses All!" and twenty-two single stories, including a number created exclusively for the annuals (the only new material included). Capaldi's art is perfectly balanced and highly expressive, using both clear space and shading to convey mood (see www.mariocapaldiartist.co.uk).

Joe Collins's background is discussed in the previous chapter, where I note the ways in which his comedy series "Miss T" contrasts to the majority of *Misty*'s content. Collins's artistic style on "Miss T" is cartoony and caricaturist, also at odds with the realist or adventure style of many of the other artists. He draws Miss T with a heavy line, and her bulging eyes, tangled, wiry hair, bulbous nose, and warty face should make her a repulsive character. But Miss T exudes innocence and is generally trying to do good (despite unintentional mishaps), making her an appealing heroine. Her battered witch's hat and oversized shoes also contribute to a visual sense of guileless chaos, and the strip enhances this by being heavy on effects: using emanata such as motion lines and sound effects ("Glop," "Burp"). Often these are conceptual rather than sensory or audible (e.g., Vic the Vampire's feelings of "Shame" in fig. 3.1) and also include editorial asides ("Look—no shadow"), which is a common feature of British children's humor comics. The format of "Miss T" also contributes to its sense of anarchy: many of her earlier four-panel strips run vertically down the page rather than horizontally or appear in oddly shaped sequences, such as long vertical panels that take up the whole page (#94). In the strip itself, panel borders are often sharply angled or entirely absent (as in fig. 3.1), and dialogue appears in jagged or misshapen speech balloons (e.g., Vic's singing). Miss T appears in color in a few of the annuals, surprisingly revealing herself as a blonde, but in fact works better in black and white. Collins's blunt lines and numerous embellishments (such as Vic's saliva, the line indicating the direction of his gaze, or the cuckoo

ASTONISHING ARTISTS 69

Figure 3.1. "Miss T" (*Misty* #62). Written and drawn by Joe Collins. Reproduced with permission of Misty™ Rebellion Publishing IP Ltd.; copyright © Rebellion Publishing IP Ltd., all rights reserved.

Figure 3.2. "Day of the Dragon" (*Misty* #16). Art by Homero, writer unknown. Reproduced with permission of Misty™ Rebellion Publishing IP Ltd.; copyright © Rebellion Publishing IP Ltd., all rights reserved.

signifying his "funny turn") create a mise-en-scène of mayhem appropriate for this "dee-lightful" "witch of the whimseys."

Jaime Rumeu i Perera (1930–2003), also known Homero or Romeo, was a key Spanish artist of this time, with a background in British romance comics. He worked through Creaciones Editoriales from the early 1950s and drew for many of the romance comics in the 1960s, including the strips "Susette" in *Cherie* (DC Thomson, 1960) and "Juliette" in *Romeo* (DC Thomson, 1957–74). During this time, he often signed his work "Romeo," later changing to "Homero" (after Homer) and using this pseudonym on his subsequent work for comics such as *Misty* and *Tammy*. He continued to work for the Spanish, British, and Swedish markets in the 1980s. He drew seven of the *Misty* serials ("Day of the Dragon," "The Cult of the Cat," "The Black Widow," "The Nine Lives of Nicola," "Nightmare Academy," "The Ghost of Golightly Towers," and "The Haunting of Hazel Brown") and five single stories. His style combines wide or chiseled faces with strong expressions against detailed and clean backgrounds (figs. 3.2, 5.1, 9.2a, 9.2c).

Brian Delaney drew regularly for a number of British girls' comics, although I have found virtually no published information on him. He has been recognized as the artist on the strips "The Professionals" and "Hart to Hart" (*Tops/TV Tops*, DC Thomson, 1981–84) and as a contributor to many other DC Thomson titles, including the strips "Tom Smith's Schooldays" and "Buddy's Super Personality Series" in *Buddy* (1981–83). He also provided the strips for most of Fleetway's *Grange Hill* annuals (1981 onward). He is named as the artist on the Scandinavian version of Alfred Andriola's *Kerry Drake* (main artist ca. 1984–90) and also on two issues of the Swedish comics anthology *Serie-Magasinet* (published 1948–2001) in the early 1990s. He was linked to Temple Rogers Artists Agents and may have been involved in a design group with the science fiction artist Chris Moore in the early 1970s (Gallagher 2000; Holland 2007, 2008). His name has also been associated with *Jackie* and *Romeo*, and he drew the *Misty* serials "Paint It Black," "The Four Faces of Eve," "Midnight Masquerader," "The Secret World of Sally Maxwell," and "The Loving Cup." Based on the dates of identified work, it seems possible that *Misty* features some of Delaney's earliest comics art, which is characterized by bold lines, high-contrast black-and-white fills, and uncluttered panels with empty backgrounds (see fig. 4.1).

John Armstrong loved drawing as a child and picked it up again during his time in the Far East in World War II, participating in an art course at the Lim Chin Tsong Palace in Rangoon in the years after the war. When he returned to England, he studied art at Middlesbrough's Constantine College (which is now part of Teeside University) and worked as a commercial artist for an advertising agency in Newcastle. He came to comics through work for *June and School Friend* in the 1960s, working freelance alongside doing book illustrations for educational titles for Pitman Publishers, and bringing with him Mario Capaldi, who got back in touch with John after their time at art school when he heard he was working in comics. Armstrong worked extensively for both DC Thomson and IPC, for whom he did his most famous girls' comics work: "Bella at the Bar" for *Tammy* (1974–84). In *Misty* he drew the serials "Moonchild," "End of the Line," and "The Silver Racer-Back," as well as a number of single stories. Armstrong's art uses extensive photo references (Bella was based on his niece, and he photographed skaters at his local ice rink as reference for many of his stories), and he is particularly good at human anatomy. His favorite *Misty* strips to draw were the sporting elements of serials "The Silver Racer-Back" and "Moonchild," and the single story "Dead Man's Eyes," which ends on a dramatic image of an oversized skull. Other single stories such as "Take Two" were less satisfying, as "I wasn't good at drawing things like sharks" (Lillyman 2009). His *Misty* pages are dramatic, with a lot of variation of panel size, and his characters frequently break panel borders ("Bella's feet and arms were always going into the next frame, for example, because I liked that"). As a consequence, Armstrong's work looks very free on the page and also has a sense of depth and realism from its use of foreshortening. For example, figure 3.3 shows a dramatic start to the third installment of "Moonchild," where the composition, perspective, and layout all emphasize Rosemary's suffering. Recognized as one of the greatest girls' comics artists of all time, Armstrong died on August 27, 2018, at the age of ninety-four.

Eduardo Feito worked on British comics from the mid-1960s, first contributing to *Boyfriend* (City Magazines, 1959–66). His art has been described as having a classic girls' comics style and has appeared in *Diana*, *Judy*, *Misty*, *Tammy*, and *Bunty* (his last British girls' comics work, in the 1990s). He drew the *Misty* serials "The School of the Lost . . . ," "A Leap through Time," "Hush, Hush, Sweet Rachel," and "Wolf Girl," and some single stories. His style is detailed, with a fine line and carefully shaded backgrounds (see, e.g., fig. 10.3).

John Richardson was born in Eston and, after trying his hand at being a farmhand and a professional wrestler, decided to pursue illustration. His first strip was "Phantom of the Fells" in *Bunty* #348–358 (September 12, 1964–November 21, 1964), followed by "The Mean Arena" in *2000AD* (beginning prog 178, September 1980). His work also appeared in *Tornado* and *2000AD* in the 1970s, and he continued to draw for *2000AD* into the 1980s and also for *Scream!* and *Eagle*, as well as a "Famous Five" strip for a Danish Enid Blyton fanzine. Toward the end of the decade, he drew cartoon strips for a number of motor and computing magazines, including "Tina Tailpipe" for *Super Bike*, "Pwlong" for a CB magazine, "Super CC" for *Custom Car*, and the beloved "Jetman" strip for *Crash*, based on the Spectrum computer game *Lunar Jetman* (1984). He claims his style was heavily influenced by Frank Bellamy's work on the old *Eagle*

ASTONISHING ARTISTS 73

Figure 3.3. "Moonchild" (*Misty* #3). Art by John Armstrong, written by Pat Mills. Reproduced with permission of Misty™ Rebellion Publishing IP Ltd.; copyright © Rebellion Publishing IP Ltd., all rights reserved.

comics (Paddon 1987), and one can certainly see similarities in his precise line and almost cinematic close-ups (see figs. 2.2, 8.3d, 8.4a, 11.4).

Isidre Monés Pons was born in Barcelona in 1947. His interest in art was enhanced by his discovery of the Pre-Raphaelites, the symbolists, and Persian miniatures, which he discovered in 1968, and some of his early sketches display these influences (Monés 2014).[9] He worked as a book illustrator and for advertising agencies and then joined Selecciones Ilustradas in the early 1970s. He drew his first comics and his most famous work for Warren, beginning in January 1973 with *Vampirella* and *Creepy*, and adding *Eerie* to his roster later in the year. He combined this with art on DC Thomson's *Commando* and *Bullet* in 1976, alongside more work for Warren in 1979, and continued to draw for DC Thomson on "Starhawk" in the 1980s (*Starblazer*, 1979; and *The Crunch*, 1979). Monés's experience in horror comics made him well suited for *Misty*'s tales, particularly those of high Gothic and grotesquerie, such as "Mirror . . . Mirror" (#37) and "Flight from Fear" (#92) (see figs. 8.2, 8.6, 10.1, 10.4). His work appears in *Misty* from #2 onward, although mostly in the first half of the comic's run, for which he provided twenty-two single stories that often feature monstrous creatures or horror archetypes. His only *Misty* serial, "House of Horror," which appropriately deals with zombie waxworks, features in the final few issues. He was a prolific children's book illustrator over the following decades, along with illustrating puzzles, games, and DVD covers, working with many different techniques. He is still a freelance artist, living in Barcelona and promoting his work at https://isidremonesart.blogspot.co.uk.

Monés remembers *Misty* fondly, saying:

> I always had a suspicion that there is a sector of British women between forty and forty-five years old traumatized by those comics that I drew. I overlapped them with my Warren work, and I did not disguise the terrifying aspect very much. I remember the cat ["Miss Cassidy's Cat . . . ," #50], . . . the girl trapped in the amber ["Perfect Specimen," #67], the haunted house ["House of Horror," #96–101], the monsters of the circus ["The Simple Job," #56], and the story of the medieval plague ["Flight from Fear," #92]. (Monés 2018)[10]

I spoke with him about many of his stories, and he prefers the ones that contain more detailed work, going beyond realism to conjure an evocative mood. Tavinjer (2015) describes Monés's art as having "passion that grows from deep roots in setting, in place, in atmosphere," and his work on *Misty* shines particularly in its depiction of creepy buildings and uncanny creatures. I was able to share with him some of his pages from "House of Horror" that he had not seen for nearly forty years, as the publishers did not return any original artwork. His response was "PHEW!!! It is horrifying! How can they make those comics for girls!"[11]

Jorge Badía Romero (also known as Jordi Badía Romero, and sometimes working under the pseudonyms Jobaro or Jorge B. Gálvez) began his comics career in the 1950s, drawing for romance and adventure titles in Spain. He moved into British comics in the 1960s and '70s, drawing romance titles for Fleetway and DC Thomson. He also drew for Warren's horror titles in the 1970s and was drawing for *Tarzan* in the 1980s. Roach characterizes Jorge as one of the most prolific artists in girls' comics, claiming that he worked and played to excess: drawing three or four pages each day and then indulging in drink and food, leading to a heart attack in his thirties. For *Misty* he drew the serial "Screaming Point" and eighteen single stories (see, e.g., fig. 9.1b). His brother Enric Badía Romero (born 1930) is also identified as the artist on three stories for *Misty*, though he claims he never drew for this comic (K. Richardson 2018). Enric is most famous for the newspaper strip "Modesty Blaise," which he drew from 1969 to 1978 and from 1986 to 2001, interspersed with his strip "Axa" in the *Sun*.[12] The brothers often teamed up (signing "Badía" for "Badía Bros") in the 1960s and 1970s and had previously worked on *Spellbound*, drawing the lead strip "Supercats." Many of the other Spanish artists involved with *Misty* (such as Romero, Freixas, Redondo, and Franch) had also worked on *Spellbound*.

María Barrera Castell was born in Barcelona in 1937, the only child in her family. She was just thirteen when she first began taking on the mostly male art world of Spain by showing her work to agencies. She drew for many of the 1950s Spanish romance comics (*Sissi*, *Jana*, *Pulgarcito*) and also worked as a book illustrator. She joined Creaciones Editoriales in the 1970s and produced work for *Mirabelle*, *Jinty*, *Misty*, *Tammy*, and the Dutch *Tina*. She drew a lot for *Mirabelle* in particular. She worked for Bruguera for a long time, frequently accepting British comics work because it was better paid, and she had a dream to one day live in the United Kingdom. She was one of the few female artists who worked on *Misty*, for which she drew the serial "The Body Snatchers" and fourteen notable single stories, including "Roots" (#1). She married another Spanish artist, Guillermo Gesalí, and continued to draw well into her seventies. Gesalí sometimes contributed pencils, and they would collaborate, but María always finished the work using a thin bamboo reed pen and ink (Gesalí 2017). She is a detailed artist who often uses character features such as hair to distinguish and emote, and her fine line work is well suited to the comics' black-and-white printing, as can be seen in figure 3.4 (see also figs. 9.1a, 10.2).[13] She is now eighty-one and still lives in Barcelona, although she draws very little today.

So little information is available on Juan Ariza (also sometimes called José Ariza Peláez) that we cannot even be certain of his name. Ariza drew some

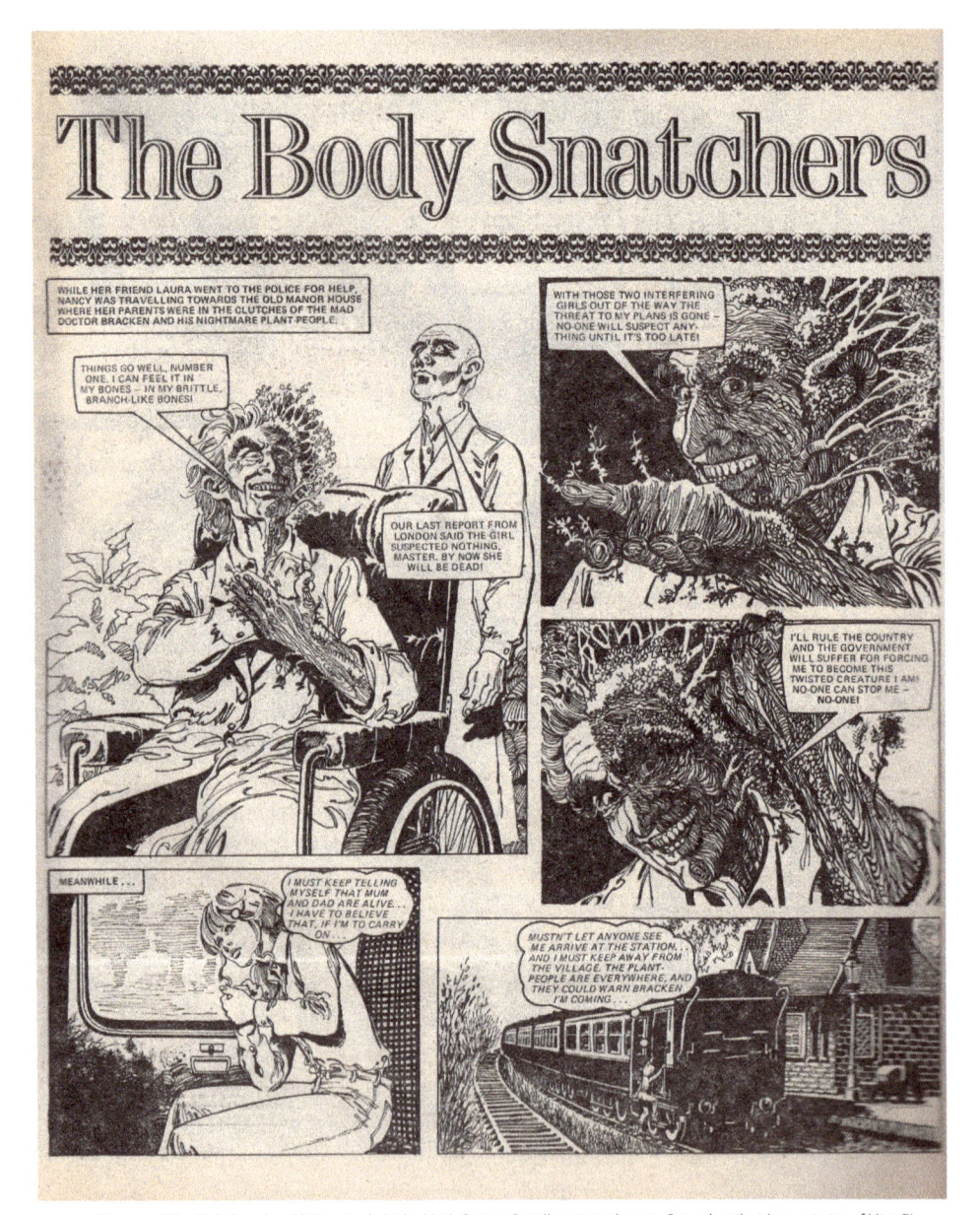

Figure 3.4. "The Body Snatchers" (*Misty* #101). Art by María Barrera Castell, writer unknown. Reproduced with permission of Misty™ Rebellion Publishing IP Ltd.; copyright © Rebellion Publishing IP Ltd., all rights reserved.

British romance comics in the 1960s, primarily for smaller publishers like Micron and Pearson. He worked extensively for Spanish publishers such as Bruguera and Esin in the 1970s, providing illustrations for children's books and adaptations such as the collection *Joyas literarias juveniles* ("Aventuras de Huck Finn" and "La Flecha Negra"). He likely came to *Misty* through Blas Gallego or Carlos Guirado. He drew twenty-three single stories for *Misty*, where his work particularly shines. It has a somewhat static quality that is perhaps reminiscent of fashion illustration, but the comic's black-and-white print emphasizes its delicate curling lines and fairy-style ethereality (see, e.g., figs. 6.1, 8.3a, 8.4b, 8.4d, 9.1d, 11.2).

Carlos Guirado did very little for the British market, although he has been identified as the artist on nineteen of the *Misty* single stories. As such it is likely he came to *Misty* through Blas Gallego, along with other artists such as Martin Puigaget, who drew the notorious *Misty* strip "The Pet Shop" (#24) (discussed in chap. 13). Gallego himself has been identified as the artist on eleven of the *Misty* single stories. Born in 1941, he had previously drawn British romance comics in the 1960s, starting with DC Thomson's *Star Love Stories* in 1968. He moved to London in 1973 and lived there for some years, working for comics such as *Melanie, Mirabelle, Misty*, and *Pink*. He would also draw for *House of Hammer* and women's magazines such as *Woman's Realm* and *Woman's Weekly*. After leaving London, he worked for many companies around the world, including the United States, and today lives in Barcelona. Gallego became close friends with Gil Page (the IPC managing editor who worked with Barrie Tomlinson on *Scream!*), and his artwork is dark and sensual. He specializes in erotic and fantasy art, particularly painted pages, posters, and covers.[14] He did not draw many of the *Misty* stories himself, and his memory of the work he produced is unclear, as he explains: "At that time all magazines took the artwork originals and we have not any drawing at all, or any copy. For this it is very, very difficult . . . impossible to remember" (Gallego 2016). His art displays a great deal of texture and movement, and his characters' body language conveys their mood as much as facial expression.

A number of other significant Spanish artists drew small amounts of work for *Misty*. For example, Jordi Franch Cubells (1936–80) drew the serial "The Salamander Girl" and the single story "Garden of Evil" (#53). Franch was an established artist for many girls' comics through both Selecciones Ilustradas and Bardon and was particularly prominent in *Jackie*. Jesús Redondo Román (known as Jesús Redondo and born 1934) is another artist of note, still living today, who drew the serials "Long Way from Home" and "Hangman's Alley" and two single stories. He also previously worked on *Diana, Jackie, Spellbound*, and *2000AD*.[15] Josép Gual Tutusaus (also known as Josép Gual or José Gual) was another Barcelona artist who also drew for *Eagle* and *2000AD* in the 1980s, as well as *Creepy* and *Eerie* for Warren, and a number of Spanish horror and crime series (*Le Vicomte, Hallucinations, Phantasms*), before commencing a lengthy run on "George and Lynne" (*Sun*) beginning 1982. He drew the *Misty* serial "Danger in the Depths" and sixteen other single tales (see, e.g., figs. 8.4c, 9.1c, 9.3). Carlos Freixas, one of the most prolific artists in girls' comics, also worked on *Misty*, contributing one story. Freixas was born in 1899 and came to Spanish comics in the 1930s from a background in illustration, having worked on the literary magazine *Lecturas* (1917–present), where he developed a precise, restrained style that would continue in his comics work.

José Cánovas Martinez (known as José Cánovas) was another artist who contributed to *Misty*. He was recognized in Spain as a highly political artist, working at the time of Franco, and was one of the creators and artists involved in the review magazine *Troya*, which focused on political satire and protest stories. His art is dark and surreal and often parodic. In Britain he also drew for the *Candy Floss* comic. He drew fifteen single stories for *Misty*, including "Mask of Fear" (#39; fig. 11.3). Cánovas is often confused with José Casanovas (born José María Casanovas Magri, 1934–2009), who worked on many British girls' comics stories, including "Ella on Easy Street" for *Tammy*, "Dora Dogsbody" for *Jinty*, "Have-a-Go Jo" for *Princess Tina and Penelope*, and "The Nine Lives of Nat the Cat" for *Sandie*, as well as extensive work on *2000AD*.[16] However, they are two distinct artists, and Casanovas did not contribute to *Misty*.

Alongside the Spanish talent were a number of established British artists. Ken Houghton died in the 1980s but during his career drew for comics such as *Battle Picture Weekly* ("Rat Pack") and *Tammy* ("Leap for Louise," "Castaways on Voodoo Island," "Lady with the Lamp") in the 1970s, and *Look and Learn* ("Laura Doone") in the 1980s. He also worked for DC Thomson, mentoring a young Sean Phillips, who did ghost penciling for him. Houghton drew eleven single stories for *Misty*, including "Moodstone" in the first issue and "Mirror Mirror on the Wall . . ." (#61; fig. 11.1). Houghton has a characteristic way of drawing splayed hands, and a very clear drawing style. This complements his page layouts, as he often throws many panels together dynamically (overlapping, without borders) with little white space to break up the page. Peter Wilkes also drew a number of strips for IPC's girls' comics in the 1970s and 1980s, including "My Heart Belongs to Buttons" (*Jinty*, 1979), "Tansy of Jubilee Street" (*Jinty, Jinty and Penny, Tammy and Jinty*, 1981–93), and "The Comp" (*Nikki*, 1985–89; *Bunty*, 1989–2001). He drew three single stories for *Misty* and continued to draw for *Tammy and Misty* after the merger. Wilkes draws clearly, often creating rippling waves of hair or shadows (see, e.g., figs. 9.4, 11.5). Prolific girls' comics artist Douglas Perry also contributed a story to *Misty* (and two reprinted pieces in the annuals), although the bulk of his other work was printed in *Tammy* and *Bunty* (for a very complete list of his other works, see Scott

2016a). Chris Lloyd (née Wiskin) joined IPC around 1965, firstly retouching artwork on *Love Story Picture Library* and going on to work on titles such as *Princess*, *Penny*, and *Look and Learn*. She was art editor on a number of IPC's pop music magazines and also provided artwork for many comics, particularly dummies of new publications and illustrations for various articles (including craft features for *Tammy* and *Misty*'s free gift "astro-cards"). She worked at IPC for around twelve years before taking voluntary redundancy to go freelance and raise a family.

Mike Brown was another key contributor to *Misty* with the comedy series "Wendy the Witch," which had previously been published in *Sandie* (1972–73) (see fig. 5.3). Brown came to IPC from Odhams Press, one of the companies that was incorporated into IPC and ceased publishing in 1969. He drew comedy strips such as "The Group" and "Wiz War" in *Pow!* (1967–68), which merged into *Pow and Wham!* (1968), and was then absorbed into *Smash!* (1966–71). Other work included "Brenda's Brownies" for *Sandie*, and the strip "Smart Alec" in *Krazy* (1976–78), then merged into *Whizzer and Chips* (1969–90). He also drew the strip "Super Dad" in this comic and ghosted and inked a number of Leo Baxendale strips. His work has a quintessential "British humor comics" style and is sometimes confused with that of Leo Baxendale.

British portraitist Shirley Bellwood is the final—but perhaps most visible—artist involved with *Misty*. Bellwood was a painter and illustrator as well as a comics artist. She was born in Pool in Wharfedale and studied at Leeds College of Art, subsequently living in London and then moving to Malvern in later life.[17] She began working on comics in the 1950s, with her first work believed to be on C. Arthur Pearson's *Glamour Library*, and she went on to draw for titles such as *Mirabelle*, *Romeo*, *Roxy*, and *Valentine* and, later, for girls' comics such as *Sally*, *Jinty*, and *Misty*. She also provided work for many publishers and magazines (see J. Freeman 2016), including the *People's Friend*, where she illustrated many short fiction stories and serials using the brush name Sandy Rose (Blair 2018). She came to *Misty* because she had worked with Jack Cunningham on some of the older romance comics and was suggested by staff editor Norman Worker as the perfect person to bring Misty to life (Cunningham 2017). Bellwood provided fifty-four delicate pen-and-ink drawings of Misty for the comic's inside cover, some of which were recolored to use as cover images, posters, games, greeting cards, and calendars in the weekly issues. She also produced ten full-color paintings that were used as posters and covers for the annuals (1980–86) and holiday specials (1978–80).[18] She based Misty's appearance on herself—even Misty's cat (on the cover of Annual 1981) is Shirley's own cat Habibi. Outside comics, Bellwood was a highly respected portrait painter who held major exhibitions with the Royal Portrait Society and regularly took commissions from peers and politicians. She died on February 1, 2016, in hospital in Worcester,

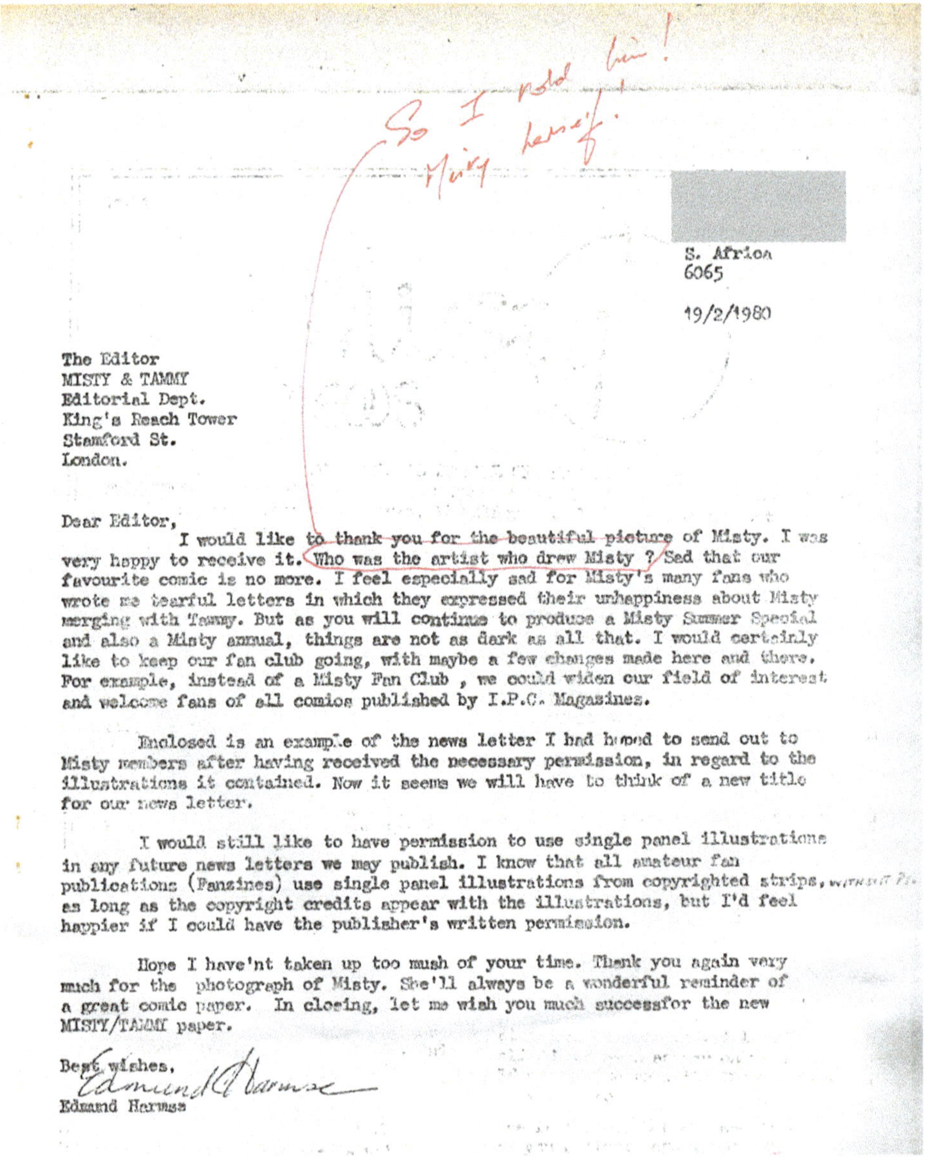

So I told him! Misty herself.

S. Africa
6065

19/2/1980

The Editor
MISTY & TAMMY
Editorial Dept.
King's Reach Tower
Stamford St.
London.

Dear Editor,
    I would like to thank you for the beautiful picture of Misty. I was very happy to receive it. Who was the artist who drew Misty ? Sad that our favourite comic is no more. I feel especially sad for Misty's many fans who wrote me tearful letters in which they expressed their unhappiness about Misty merging with Tammy. But as you will continue to produce a Misty Summer Special and also a Misty annual, things are not as dark as all that. I would certainly like to keep our fan club going, with maybe a few changes made here and there. For example, instead of a Misty Fan Club , we could widen our field of interest and welcome fans of all comics published by I.P.C. Magazines.

    Enclosed is an example of the news letter I had hoped to send out to Misty members after having received the necessary permission, in regard to the illustrations it contained. Now it seems we will have to think of a new title for our news letter.

    I would still like to have permission to use single panel illustrations in any future news letters we may publish. I know that all amateur fan publications (Fanzines) use single panel illustrations from copyrighted strips, as long as the copyright credits appear with the illustrations, but I'd feel happier if I could have the publisher's written permission.

    Hope I have'nt taken up too much of your time. Thank you again very much for the photograph of Misty. She'll always be a wonderful reminder of a great comic paper. In closing, let me wish you much success for the new MISTY/TAMMY paper.

Best wishes,
Edmund Harmse

Figure 3.5a. Forwarded fan letter from reader Edmund Harmse, annotated by editor Norman Worker to describe Shirley as "Misty herself."

ASTONISHING ARTISTS 81

Figure 3.5b. Shirley Bellwood. *Left to right*: Photo of Shirley Bellwood in her youth, ca. 1960s, courtesy of Elizabeth Gaunt. *Woman in Shawl* (self-portrait), reproduction of life-sized oil painting by Shirley Bellwood, courtesy of Elizabeth Gaunt. *Lace Collar* (self-portrait), reproduction of life-sized oil painting by Shirley Bellwood, courtesy of Elizabeth Gaunt.

at eighty-four. Her paintings really capture character, and this is what shines through in Misty's face. In particular, Bellwood's self-portraits show a similar determination, and she shares her character's jet-black hair, penetrating gaze, and delicate features (fig. 3.5b).

Bellwood's drawings of *Misty*'s host character in particular helped frame the comic as mystery and suspense rather than outright horror, complementing the high-quality art that graced its interior pages. Beautiful and ethereal, Misty was a tantalizing embodiment of the attractive side of Gothic, whose dual qualities of attraction and repulsion have also been noted by many critics (Botting 2001). Her seductive appearance and ghostly form gestured toward the contemporary New Age witch, suggesting magical power without transgressing the boundaries of the female body and feminine behavior. As Germanà (2013, 17) notes, the witch is a "simultaneous embodiment of female marginalisation and feminist subversion," whose abnormality and monstrosity are often characterized by either sexless sterility or savage sexuality. Germanà continues: "Female beauty is acceptable as long as she is the object of the controlling male gaze; when she strays from the literal and metaphorical enclosures designed for her body by patriarchal authority she becomes a threat to the very foundations of masculine power" (62). Although positioned as a strong and controlling figure within her world, Misty's seductive beauty and supplicative welcomes simultaneously enable her to stay within social norms, balancing against her power and enhancing her allure (see chap. 7 for further discussion).

As Pat Mills (2016a) explains: "Misty worked well. . . . She is this beautiful witch-like character, and I'm sure it would have had an appeal to a lot of readers and—being a little cynical about it—possibly the more middle-class kids, or middle-class mum would see it as 'safe,' whereas if they had seen the kind of covers I had in mind, they might have said, 'Oh, no, I don't want my Daisy reading this kind of nonsense!'"[19] This manipulation of the comic's visual image to produce a less confrontational publication aligns with *Misty*'s branding as a "mystery story paper." Alongside this, its vast range of artists provided high-quality work that conveyed a sense of drama and dynamism and complemented the comic's taut storytelling, as the next chapter continues to explore.

CHAPTER 4

VISCERAL VISUALS

With gripping stories supported by a wealth of artistic talent and a seductive, ethereal cover girl, *Misty* was a truly striking comic. This was backed up by the insanity of its interior page designs, some of which pushed the principles of comics layouts to the limit. In this chapter, I look more closely at the ways in which *Misty*'s editorial and artistic team developed and exploited the visual conventions of British comics to enhance its storytelling. My discussion here draws on quantitative analysis of a random sample of ten *Misty* issues to explore the idiosyncrasies of its style, research that was conducted by Paul Fisher Davies and supported by Bournemouth University's Centre for the Study of Journalism, Culture and Community. This quantitative analysis is complemented by qualitative readings of how these visual features work in practice to enhance a story. Finally, I reflect on these research findings using comics theory and Gothic theory, with particular focus on techniques of transgression and excess.

Experiments with layout in British comics go back to Frank Bellamy's work on *Eagle* in the 1960s (which contained dynamic and varied panel shapes and sizes) and are characteristic of many titles. DC Thomson's *Warlord* (1974–86) was a particularly important comic in this regard: it "tore up the rule book" by having longer stories, bigger images, and "punchier" layouts and artwork (Roach 2016). When 2000AD launched in 1977, it adopted a similar approach, which Pat Mills attributes to the vision of art editor Doug Church. Mills (2016a) gives Church credit for the "impact and energy" that characterized 2000AD's pages, explaining that Doug would critique scripts and suggest more dynamic images, often leading to rewrites. This visual legacy continued in the comic's run: David Roach joined 2000AD in 1988 and recalls artists being told to "make it punchier" and to have "one big panel per page" (Roach 2016). Bodging was often used to deliver this, and in particular on the work of some artists—Roach (2016) names Guirado and Busom, among others.

This type of visual dynamism can also be seen in *Misty*. Figures 1.1, 3.3, and 6.1 all show pages that use a large opening panel to launch a story, which was common in the comic. Mills (2016a) argues that the visuals of "The Cult of the

83

Cat" and "The Black Widow" (both written by Bill Harrington and illustrated by Homero) in particular owe something to Doug Church, saying: "There is clearly a *2000AD* influence there.... All that incredible Ancient Egypt.... They are trying to get that *2000AD* sense of spectacle." Mills goes on to suggest that *Misty* is "copycatting" here and that its stories often use size and spectacle unwittingly, bringing in exciting visuals without an overall sense of artistry.

While there is no doubt that the pages of *Misty* were confrontational and dramatic, I want to respond to this claim by exploring how the comic uses its visuals and arguing that in fact a Gothic aesthetic structures the page. While I had initially hoped to identify the characteristics of particular artists, the discovery that panel shapes, borders, and sizes were often bodged by the editorial staff led me to revise my research questions and instead analyze the *Misty* "house" style. My aims were to (1) explore the use of artistic layout in *Misty*; (2) investigate the sufficiency and usefulness of existing comics theorists' taxonomies of page layouts; and (3) consider the usefulness of Gothic theory in understanding aspects of page layout. These aims map onto the following objectives: (1) identify formal page features through inductive cataloging and use quantitative and qualitative analysis to draw conclusions about their significance; (2) apply established comics theories to the findings and reflect on their value; and (3) reinterpret and reflect on the findings through the lens of Gothic theory.

The methodology took the form of quantifiable analysis of a random sample of pages, tagging elements such as panel borders and tiering, and supplementary layout features such as arrows and depth. This was complemented by close qualitative readings of tagged examples that explored the use and impact of these features. Bournemouth University's Centre for the Study of Journalism, Culture and Community provided support for this small-scale research project, which also produced some of the data discussed in chapter 7. I am indebted here to my research assistant Paul Fisher Davies, who coded and tagged these common image features using Scrivener software.[1] To do this, a random sample of ten issues was generated, using a random-number generator to select a nonrepeating list of tens and units so as to avoid clumping. The total data sample collected thus comprised 320 pages, of which 70 were nonstory pages, 8 were "Miss T," and 1 was "Wendy the Witch." Discounting these pages of prose features and the comedy series as nonrepresentative left 241 pages of story, which made up the narrative sample. Impactful features of these pages were then manually identified and tagged, with the list of tags increasing as the study continued. These tags included panel features such as angled borders, round borders, open borders, jagged borders, and so forth, along with page layout features such as arrows, color, inset panels, and splash pages. The pages were also categorized in terms of their relationship to a standard "grid"

VISCERAL VISUALS   85

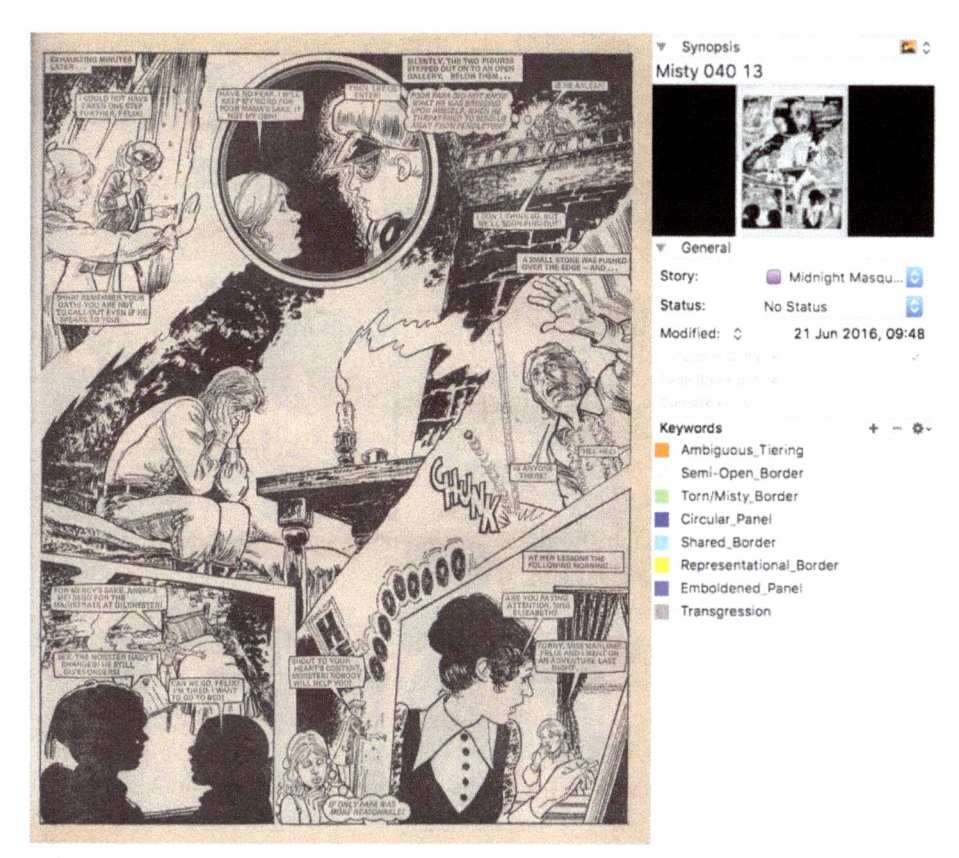

Figure 4.1. "Midnight Masquerader" (*Misty* #40). Art by Brian Delaney, writer unknown. Reproduced with permission of Misty™ Rebellion Publishing IP Ltd.; copyright © Rebellion Publishing IP Ltd., all rights reserved.

or number of tiers.² It should be noted that pages can include many features, and the following figures must be considered in light of this. So, for example, one might suspect that a number of particularly dynamic pages affected the figures given. However, my meta-analysis of the findings confirms that this is not the case, and the features tagged are spread across the entire sample. That is to say, there are no pages that received no tags; even those that appear simple and perpendicular still have at least one dynamic feature, such as an open panel border or staggered tier. For example, Homero's work on "Day of the Dragon" (fig. 3.2) is one of the more static layouts but contains many semiborderless panels and transgressed panel borders. Similarly, María Barrera Castell's work in figure 3.4 appears straightforward at a glance but in fact contains a split tier, a staggered panel arrangement, a semiopen border, and transgressed panel borders.

Figure 4.1 shows the tagging possible on an individual page. This extract from "Midnight Masquerader" contains a number of different panel border features, including semiopen edges, shared borders, a representational border (the candle smoke), and a torn or misty border (e.g., along the bottom edge of panel 1). The page also has a dynamic selection of panel shapes, including a circular panel that is emboldened (although its contents are not especially significant). As a result of the varied panel sizes and shapes, the tiering on this page is ambiguous; it is hard to fit it into a grid layout.

AIM 1: EXPLORE THE USE OF ARTISTIC LAYOUT IN *MISTY*

Panel borders are one of the primary features of the comics page and are the material by which layout is most easily and materially identified. A wide range of nonstandard borders were identified and tagged in *Misty*, as shown in table 4.1.

The data indicate that by far the most common panel border idiosyncrasy is the borderless panel (which is either entirely open or lacking one or more sides), which appears on the majority of the pages analyzed. This effect is generally achieved either by using blank space to create an implied border or by overlaying consecutive images so that they appear contiguous. Unpanelized sequences (which appear less often) are a similar category that overlaps with this, referring to instances where several distinct events or time periods are rendered within the same panel. For example, this might include the visual strategy known in comics as the De Luca effect, where a character is repeated in the same panel to indicate movement (Gravett 2008). Borderless (and semibordered) panels and unpanelized sequences appear in many of the figures included in this book. The analysis also found that while these types of open panels appear quite often, they are not used consistently in support of modalized images. To be clear: this means that a lack of border often has no significance to the narrative events and is generally simply decorative. The frequency with which this device appears might indicate that it is a historically or culturally situated method, or simply (as Cunningham suggests) that panel borders were often removed by editorial to give a sense of free movement.

The category of angled sides appears on nearly one-third of the pages studied and refers to "vertical" panel borders that are angled other than 90 degrees. Although these are sometimes used for action panels, again this is by no means consistent, and this type of border is often used simply to create visual dynamism on the page. A similar tendency is found in emboldened panels, which sometimes mark significant events but in the main are decorative. Circular panels, when used, often appear centrally, framing faces, but have no other significance. Curved borders are also predominantly decorative, other than in

Table 4.1. Panel border types in *Misty*.

Border Type	Pages
Open border/borderless	138 (57%)
Semiopen border	133 (55%)
Angled sides	78 (32%)
Circular panel	43 (18%)
Emboldened panel	39 (16%)
Shared border	23 (10%)
Overlapping border	21 (9%)
Torn or misty border	17 (7%)
Curved border	10 (4%)
Unpanelized sequence	10 (4%)
Representational border	9 (4%)
Jagged border	8 (3%)
Modalized border	5 (2%)
Rounded border edges	3 (1%)
Nested enclosure	1 (<1%)

one instance where they signify hypnotic music being played ("The Jukebox," #28), and the same can be said of rounded border edges, which are rare.

Modalized borders are defined as instances where the border has an explicit relationship with the narrative events (e.g., a cloud shape to indicate a dream or memory). A particular type of modalized border overlapping with this category is the representational border, which has a clear pictorial quality, for example, shaped like a cat, candle smoke, or a crystal ball. However, many of the foregoing categories are sometimes used as more subtle modalizing features. For example, jagged borders with sharp angles are normally used in comics to indicate a split, as in a telephone conversation or similar. In *Misty* they instead often indicate a startled character or a change of consciousness. A further modification of this type of line that may be unique to this comic is the torn or misty border, which encloses the panel with a meandering line reminiscent of smoke or mist. Both types are sometimes diegetically motivated or modalizing but are often simply decorative.

Some additional page features were also identified. These were largely found to be marginal: arrows to indicate reading direction appear just once (<1 percent); and inset panels appear on thirty-four pages (14 percent), although I should note that this is a slippery category, as often the circular panel border noted earlier shares this feature. Splash pages appear twelve times (5 percent), always as the first page of a story. They are often ambiguous and merge story logo and content: for example, "The Loving Cup" incorporates a large panel of the cup itself into the first page of every episode. These elaborate story logos are not limited to the serials: all the *Misty* stories have a visually marked title. Sometimes this is text only and conveyed in an oversized or elaborate font ("Date with Death," #76) or accompanied by an image from the story ("The Fetch," #2). But at other points these are elaborate bookplate-style panels that might contain a unique image (as in the cameo of Rachel in "Hush, Hush, Sweet Rachel") or intricate border ("The Body Snatchers," fig. 3.4). While the title fonts of the serials are consistent, the accompanying images can change (as in "Paint It Black"). So it seems that even *Misty*'s paratextual elements such as story logos are attention grabbing, experimental, and inconstant.

Perhaps the most significant of the page feature categories that were analyzed is transgression, where character limbs or other objects break an enclosing panel border or other spatial container, which occurs on ninety-three pages (39 percent). I have argued in other work (Round 2017) that these instances of aesthetic transgression reflect the comic's themes: uncanny and uncontained, focusing on rule breaking and its consequences. The more extensive analysis carried out for this project reveals that aesthetic transgression can have a modalizing function, as in panel 1 of figure 4.1, where Elizabeth's hand is perhaps reaching out to push open the door or simply to lean on a wall. However, such transgressions are also often just decorative (as in fig. 3.2, where Dave's and Gayle's hands break the panel borders).

These quantitative and qualitative analyses demonstrate that *Misty*'s visual devices tend toward the experimental and dynamic. However, they are most often used simply for ornamentation. This is particularly apparent in the treatment of panel borders and the use of emboldened lines or nonstandard shapes. When modalizing features appear, they tend toward the emotional and symbolic rather than the prosaic—for example, indicating heightened emotion (jagged border) or reinforcing the central motifs of the story (representational border).

AIM 2: INVESTIGATE THE SUFFICIENCY AND USEFULNESS OF EXISTING COMICS THEORISTS' TAXONOMIES OF PAGE LAYOUTS

The inductive nature of the tags that emerged during the research was complemented by the application of comics scholarship. Two key theoretical influences informed the approach to tagging the page layouts. The first is the notion of the "tier," which is an important organizational principle of the comics page

Table 4.2. Tiering in *Misty* page layouts.	
Number of Tiers	**Pages**
3 tiers	155 (64%)
2 tiers	38 (16%)
Ambiguous	27 (11%)
4 tiers	18 (7%)
1 tier (splash page)	13 (5%)

and is prominent in francophone discussion of *bandes dessinées* (as *bandes*, or "strips," are integral to the French name for the medium). The work of Benoît Peeters (1991), Thierry Groensteen (2009, 2012), and Renaud Chavanne (2010) supports the search for tiered patterns as a principle in the *Misty* layouts. However, this project found that while tiers do seem to be an organizing principle for most *Misty* pages, they are not always clean and at times can be highly ambiguous. Pages were tagged according to their number of identifiable tiers, with ambiguous tiering also noted (this category is nonexclusive). In general, sequences of panels follow the upper edge of the page, often with a ragged or staggered lower border, and a similar tier runs across the lower edge of the page with a ragged or staggered upper border. This creates a third tier across the middle of the page, formed by loose or damaged borders shared with the top and bottom tiers.

Although table 4.2 demonstrates that the tier system underpins the majority of pages, this seldom takes the form of a straightforward grid. Variations such as staggering (where the upper and lower edges of panels in sequence do not line up) and tilting (where the baseline that defines reading progression is at an angle rather than horizontal) are common. Staggered tiers appear on ninety-six pages (40 percent), and tilted tiers are found on eighty-nine pages (37 percent) (see figs. 3.3, 3.4). These appearances are not limited to pages tagged as "ambiguous," although staggering and tilting do often feature here.

The second theoretical model is taken from the work of Neil Cohn (2014), who argues that one feature of comics page layouts that guides the reader is "blockage," whereby the reading path is negotiated every time the reader abuts against a border "T" junction and must thus read downward rather than across. Using data from a study in which he asked participants to describe how they would read a page of blank panels (Cohn 2014), Cohn argues that experienced comics readers confronted with blockage will depart from the traditional "Z" reading path. However, the *Misty* pages analyzed call into question Cohn's methodology and the validity of his definition. "Blockage" seldom appears in *Misty*, where just three pages of the sample (1 percent) contain clear examples.

By contrast, staggered, ragged, or tilted tiers (where the upper and lower edges of sequential panels do not line up) appear much more frequently. But while these do create some sense of "blockage," the panel content requires the reader to continue along the "Z" reading path.

The foregoing quantitative analysis demonstrates that, based on this sample, none of the *Misty* pages feature clean, enclosed, perpendicular panel layouts, and regular gridding is generally absent. While the three-tier structure is frequent, these tiers are generally rough and improvised runs that emerge out of the page space (i.e., following the top and bottom page edges), rather than being created from straight, regular lines. This use of angularity and variability places *Misty* much closer to 2000AD than to other girls' comics such as *Mandy* and *Judy*, which both favor four-tier structures and tend more to perpendicular panelization (although variations in borders are still frequent in the small sample of these titles that was considered). *Misty* does not look like the American postwar comics or like its contemporaries.

Returning to the findings from a qualitative perspective, Thierry Groensteen's "system of comics" provides some backing for the dramatic and dynamic nature of the page layouts and even an explanation for their apparently arbitrary nature. Groensteen's formal investigation of comics argues that comics are made up of iconic solidarity: that is, comic book pages and images have multiple various relationships of interdependence. He identifies two main components to this: the spatio-topia (which deals with spaces and places on the page), and the concept of arthrology (which deals with the way one image is related to another, either linearly [restricted arthrology] or as a network [general arthrology]). In his investigation of the spatio-topia, Groensteen (2009, 48) describes the work of Guido Crepax as using "diffracted layouts, where the panel's frames do not have two parallel borders and are not square, [so] the page has been subjected to the empire of obliques, of points, and of apparently arbitrary cuts." He draws on the work of Bruno Lecigne to analyze these "destabilising grids," whose reading argues that they coincide with eroticism or violence. In Lecigne's parsing of Crepax's art: "The page seeks to circumscribe the limits of pleasure through formalization. It must enclose (signify) the inexpressible. . . . [As a] voyeur, the reader is equally constrained to interiorize with this constant laceration of space the processes of sadism itself" (Lecigne 1982, 23). Groensteen extends this analysis of "unstable layouts, baroque frames" (2009, 48) to the work of other artists such as Andreas. However, he argues further that although it is common to relate the frame's structuring function to its expressive function when its form is dynamic and attention grabbing, these choices always have an expressive value. He proceeds to analyze the diminishing (rectangular) panels of Bill Griffith's "The Plot Thickens" (1980); pointing out that here it is the panels' relative size (or area) that reinforces the ironic and paradoxical message of this comic, rather than their shape (or form). Essentially Groensteen is saying that square, regular panels do not lack expressive qualities. They can be affective when one considers the entirety of the page's spatio-topia and takes into account other features like panel area and site. He continues to suggest that this is true of all contemporary comics where page layout has been deliberately chosen rather than imposed.

This discussion helps illuminate the variable use of dynamic layouts in *Misty*. Lecigne's notion of a "laceration of space" (a phrase with Gothic and violent connotations) certainly has relevance to the form and site of *Misty*'s panels, apparent in their angular shapes and staggered positioning. Panel area also comes into play as the varied panel sizes and inclusion of splash pages also speak to *Misty*'s themes of transformation and transgression in the manner identified by Groensteen. Further, the discovery of an editorial policy that added these features explains their indiscriminate use on the page.

AIM 3: CONSIDER THE RELEVANCE OF GOTHIC THEORY TO OUR UNDERSTANDING OF ASPECTS OF PAGE LAYOUT

In previous work, I have compared the way in which *Misty* and *Spellbound* use a Gothic aesthetic by applying Farber's (1972) early definition of cinematic Gothic. Farber defines Gothic films as "sharing arresting distortions in mood and cinematic technique . . . often in the setting of lush, ominous decay . . . a very distinctive kind of baroque and self-conscious expressionism, relying on unusually over-ripe, even violent visual exaggerations and refractions" (1972, 95). He draws attention to key visual components that include black costumes and settings, "weird" lighting and unsettling camera angles, exaggerated shadows, and large, asymmetrical settings and composition (Wheatley 2006, 9). Writing more than forty-five years later, Spooner (2017, 49) offers the following definition of twenty-first-century Gothic style, which she acknowledges is varied but "can be recognized by a combination of features including intensive chiaroscuro; crowded space; intricate detailing; an emphasis on line; distorted proportions; a saturated color palette or combinations of black, white and red; ornate fonts; and deliberately retro or archaic styling." Spooner's definition crosses media, referring to a wide range of contemporary texts, products, and brands, such as the films of Guillermo del Toro and Tim Burton, Chris Riddell's illustrations, or *Emily the Strange* merchandise and products. Spooner later applies similar terms to an analysis of the castle in *Edward Scissorhands* (Tim Burton, 1990), describing vast rooms seemingly composed according to Horace Walpole's concept of "sharawaggi" or lack of symmetry. This architecture is apparently constructed without right angles: the few straight lines are broken and jagged; windowpanes are irregularly spaced; the curving lines of the staircase and windows are suggestive of organic forms. The overall effect is both stark and overelaborate, creating a distinctive sense of timelessness, in which the architecture evokes Gothic precedents but cannot be matched to any specific historical style. (Spooner 2017, 63)

Taking the two definitions in combination produces a list of Gothic visual features that include exaggerated shadows or chiaroscuro; distorted proportions; skewed angles; asymmetry; baroque or intricate ornamentation; and motifs of age or decay. Of this list, those that relate to the page's formal properties (Groensteen's spatio-topia) rather than panel content (such as shadows or motifs of age) are all present in the pages analyzed from *Misty*. The comic uses panel sizes that vary from splash pages to small proportions, creating an effect that is nonregular and resulting in distorted proportions. Acute and oblique angles appear on one-third of the pages examined, resulting in asymmetrical layouts that are further emphasized by varied border shapes and patterns (the different panel borders also contribute to the "emphasis on line" that Spooner notes). Particular features such as the torn or misty border or curved or circular edges also emphasize *sharawaggi*—creating an asymmetrical organic effect and avoiding rigid lines. Varied tiering also contributes to the asymmetry and is so dramatic that one-tenth of the pages cannot be clearly defined or classified. The page layout as a whole thus becomes intricate and baroque in its excess.

Therefore, many of the common features found in these pages contain Gothic overtones. In other work (Round 2019), I explore the presence of formal transgression in comics, arguing that comics narratology is inclined toward breaking its own rules and boundaries, thus challenging reader identity. Botting (1996) has written of Gothic's characteristic formal "transgression" and "excess," and Wolfreys also argues that "to transgress is to appeal to a Gothic sensibility" (2008, 98). Comics' particular methods of breaking boundaries, such as transgressing panel borders or removing these containers entirely, thus directly speak to the Gothic. Wolfreys (2008, 98) argues that Gothic form and content "[present] us with narratives . . . in imminent threat or crisis. . . . The narrative drive presents the threat to space and identity, ontology or being." In *Misty* the space of each storyworld is under constant threat by the breaking of panel boundaries, just as the story content interrogates identity, as I explore in the next chapter.

One might argue that the conflicting drives on the page are also characteristic of Gothic, as they create a set of paradoxes. For example, asymmetry and *sharawaggi* are defined as organic effects, and the round edges, circular panels, and open edges seen on the *Misty* pages also conjure this sense. By contrast, the panels that tend toward acute angles and the use of features such as jagged edges go against this, conveying dramatic and deliberate lacerations. A similar dialectic might be identified in the relationship between surface and depth. The elaborate borders and frames of the comics page create an appearance of baroque excess that draws attention to its surface, juxtaposing this against the depth that is apparent in the panels' content. If, as I have suggested, Gothic is an affective and structural paradox, such tensions and contradictions seem integral.

In *Misty* the page is consistently transgressive. Panel borders are varied and experimental in form: they are often angled, liminal, or indeterminate (ragged, misty) or broken in some way. This dynamic variation is constant: every page of the sample analyzed contains one or more examples. These exciting formats are most often used for a purely decorative purpose with no clear narrative meaning, although in some instances they are modalizing and have ties to the story content. However, it does not necessarily follow that they have no sense of artistry. Perhaps they are best read as reflecting the overall sense of *Misty* and Gothic and comics: as transgressive and excessive.

CHAPTER 5

SHOCKING STORIES

Misty's dramatic visuals and Gothic style reinforce its story content, which tends toward the dramatic, transgressive, and supernatural—tales of ghostly possessions, horrific transformations, alien abductions, mysterious cults, dramatic kidnappings, attempted murders, and malevolent traps. The next few chapters explore the ways in which this comic develops distinct story features that rearticulate horror and Gothic tropes from the surrounding media of the 1970s. To provide a foundation, this chapter first introduces the various types of *Misty* story. Here I explore the differences between its serial, series, and single stories, analyzing their use of Gothic tropes such as the Gothic heroine, the "comic Gothic" or "whimsical macabre," and the excess of the cautionary tale. I look closely at some representative examples of each format, setting the groundwork for more detailed analysis of various aspects (influences, story features/formulas, host characters) in the following chapters.

Like most of the girls' anthology comics, *Misty* contains a mix of serial stories, recurring characters, and complete (single) stories. The appearance of these different formats can be broken down as shown in table 5.1.

The *Misty* serials are ongoing sagas with continuity, appearing in an average of ten installments. They are held distinct from the series, which contain stand-alone episodes with no continuity except their recurring characters, and in *Misty*'s case are all comedies ("Miss T," "Wendy the Witch," and "Cilla the Chiller"). The *Misty* singles are one-shot stories with unique characters and no continuation. They are predominantly original, although the *Misty* annuals include twenty reprints from *Sandie*, *Jinty*, *June*, and *Tammy*.

MISTY'S SERIAL STORIES AND GOTHIC HEROINES

The *Misty* serials all follow the same rough outline. We are introduced to a female protagonist, who quickly develops a problem of some kind. This may be the manifestation of a supernatural power (visions, telekinesis, telepathy) or

Table 5.1. Breakdown of serial, series, and single comic strip stories.

Source	Format	Medium	Stories	Episodes
Original	Serial	Graphic	32	339
		Text	1	2
	Single	Graphic	302	302
		Text	84	84
	Series	Graphic	2	89
Reprint	Single	Graphic	21	21
	Series	Graphic	1	18
Total			443	855

the intrusion of a mysterious or magical object (a box of paints, a ring, a mirror, a car, a swimsuit). Alternatively the protagonist may find herself trapped in an unhappy situation (a new family, school, or world) or become aware of some deception (a secret, prisoner, or plot of some kind). The story line develops as she discovers new information relating to the item or her situation. These categories can overlap: for example, Gayle's mirror in "Day of the Dragon" shows that she is the reincarnation of Cheng Hsiao Feng, and Nicola's cat ring reveals her destiny as the Chosen One of Bast ("The Cult of the Cat")—blurring the lines between internal powers and external objects. Similarly, magical objects or external forces can also serve as the source of antagonism and create a situation from which the protagonist struggles to escape ("Journey into Fear," "Paint It Black," "The Silver Racer-Back"). Many trapped protagonists also become aware of a mystery or deception of some kind: for example, "Nightmare Academy" revolves around Sharon's attempts to discover the secret that Madame Nocturne is hiding, and Sarah remains at Pendleton Manor to investigate its secrets ("Midnight Masquerader").

However, one common feature of this plot is its focus on a protagonist who has to accept or overcome some aspect of herself, which underpins eleven of the thirty-three serials.[1] This is often a hidden part or special power and might be revealed by a mysterious or magical object. A good example is "The Cult of the Cat," which was the lead story in the first issue of *Misty* and one of just two of its serials to spark a sequel ("The Nine Lives of Nicola").[2] Written by Bill Harrington with art by Homero, it tells the story of Nicola Scott and her acceptance of her destiny as the Chosen One of Bast. The story cuts between Egypt and England, as a messenger, Charmian, is dispatched to awaken Nicola to her gifts so that she can take her role as a high priestess in the Temple of Bast. Charmian follows Nicola around, placing a cat ring on her finger while she sleeps. Nicola cannot remove it and then begins to develop catlike traits (fear of water, ability to climb and balance, light-reflective eyes) and has new knowledge and visions of Egypt. The tension comes from Nicola's fear at the "slow frightening cycle of change" she undergoes (#7) and her sightings of Charmian, and also from our uncertainty as to the cult's intentions, which are framed ominously and as a potential threat throughout. For example, Charmian insists, "You must learn to follow without question!" (#2), and members of the cult implore, "Give her [Nicola] the fortitude to accept her fate" (#3). Even in the final episode, we are still unsure whether the cult wishes Nicola harm, as Charmian removes Nicola's powers while she is climbing, causing her to fall. The resolution that Nicola is only required to send her "secret self" to Egypt, remaining physically with her family in the new knowledge that she is "a very special person," is entirely contained in the final two pages and arguably a bit of an anticlimax. This might have been one reason for the story's return as "The Nine Lives of Nicola" (#53–64), which offers an actual antagonist as the Temple of Bast is attacked by the Cobra King and Nicola must help save the cult.

Nicola can be read as a persecuted and pursued Gothic heroine in flight in both stories, per Orianne Smith's (2013, 129) comments on this figure:

> Each Gothic heroine is an exemplar of female sensibility born into a world that is blind, indifferent, or hostile to her special qualities. Each must pass through a liminal state in which her true identity is concealed, and all are relentlessly pursued by a Gothic villain intent on depriving them of their virtue, their inheritance, or both. Finally, in an act of Providence, each is rewarded with a happy ending in the final few pages.

The framing of the cult's intentions as dangerous and villainous encourages a reading of the story in this light, which is continued in its sequel, where Princess Ravala pursues Nicola. Commenting on the Radcliffean Gothic, Orianne Smith (2013, 144) notes further that "it is precisely the geographical and social displacement of the Gothic heroine that enables her to come into contact with, and to transform the lives of, as many people as possible," and so the dislocation between the Egyptian mythology and Nicola's life in modern England adds to this reading.

While the plot of "The Cult of the Cat" may be a little stretched, its delivery is tense, and the story is visually ambitious. Harrington's writing conveys Nicola's frustration effectively as she repeatedly demands, "Leave me alone. You and your . . . your cats and your snakes" (#10), to no effect. Homero's art creates the spectacle of ancient Egypt through pyramids, stone carvings, temples, priests and priestesses. The story's opening splash pages are particularly impressive, featuring gatherings of acolytes in mystic rituals, burning incense, scrying, and chanting. The main body of the story sustains this exoticism by constantly cutting between the two locations. This creates a hallucinogenic quality, as Egypt is evocatively drawn and the location jump is seldom signified by narration. The frequent transformations (from human to cat) add to this dreamlike quality and are beautifully rendered in repeated imagery using the De Luca effect (fig. 5.1). Along similar lines, shadows and reflections are manipulated to emphasize the illusion (#1, #3), and panel borders are often elaborate and representational, for example, shaped like cats (#3, #6).

The alternate scenario of a protagonist trapped or otherwise sucked into an unhappy or mysterious situation (such as a new family, school, or world) features nineteen times.[3] Lucy is sent to stay with her creepy uncle in "Screaming Point," Lizzie narrowly escapes Madame Blaze's "House of Horror," Elena is trapped in ancient Greece ("A Leap through Time"), and Jenny is prevented from leaving "The School of the Lost . . ." An indicative example is "The Sentinels" (#1–12), in which an old tower block provides Jan Richards with access to a terrifying world where the Nazis won World War II, which she struggles to escape. She encounters doubles of her family and friends, and after Jan's father becomes trapped in a Nazi prison, Alt-Jan must ultimately give up her own father to take his place. The story is surprisingly dramatic and graphic, with helicopter chases (#4), a splash page of Jan's brutally beaten father (#11), and a horrifying scene in which her pet dog Tiger is eaten alive by rats (#4) (fig. 5.2). Capaldi's art is dynamic and realistic throughout the tale, using light and shade to lead the eye through the layout, and bringing in an adventurous edge. The page layout of figure 5.2 literally foregrounds the swarming mass of rats (see panel 5) while simultaneously giving the reader a direct look at Jan's and Sally's fright. The composition uses inset and circular panels to build toward the mounting horror, making it the central subject of the panels and the page as a whole.

These "trapped" scenarios do not have to be supernatural: Toni's attempts to escape her father ("Whistle and I'll Come . . .") and Jackie's efforts to help her Gran ("The Cats of Carey Street") are also examples of heroines who are trying to resolve or escape from a threatening situation. Similarly, the magical items discussed earlier may not be beneficial and instead take on or enable the role of antagonist.[4] Sometimes the two themes are inextricably entwined: for example, in "Paint It Black," Maggie's box of paints allows her to create wonderful pictures, but this causes her father to imprison her out of greed and immerses her in the Thursby family mystery, and only when she has helped Amy can she be free.

These trapped protagonists depict the second type of Gothic heroine: confined and incarcerated. By focusing on a trapped heroine in peril, the serials draw on "The dreaded Female Gothic image of the imprisoned woman" (Davison 2004, 62). This represents women's historical fears about their autonomy

Figure 5.1. "The Cult of the Cat" (*Misty* #1). Art by Homero, written by Bill Harrington. Reproduced with permission of Misty™ Rebellion Publishing IP Ltd.; copyright © Rebellion Publishing IP Ltd., all rights reserved.

Figure 5.2. "The Sentinels" (*Misty* #4). Art by Mario Capaldi, written by Malcolm Shaw. Reproduced with permission of Misty™ Rebellion Publishing IP Ltd.; copyright © Rebellion Publishing IP Ltd., all rights reserved.

and status as property. As Davison (2004, 54) explains: "The married woman of the period was frequently commodified and became a femme couverte under established law—a woman whose autonomy and identity were denied as she was regarded as her husband's property. Under such circumstances, marriage signalled a figurative death for women." Anxieties about agency and identity underlie these stories (Davison 2004; Horner 2010; Tóth 2010).

Critics have therefore read the Gothic heroine narrative as the search for an "achieved, finished identity" (Brownstein, cited in Kaplan 1983, 83); a tale of "emotional growth" (Davison 2004, 50) in pursuit of wholeness and completion (Tóth 2010; O. Smith 2013). Voyages of self-discovery that end in happy homes characterize many of the *Misty* serial stories. In "Moonchild," Rosemary escapes her abusive family life and unwanted powers when her mother leaves and her grandmother dies, and she finds her new place living with her best friend Anne (#13). The Hudson family adopt Toni at the end of "Whistle and I'll Come . . ." (#56), Salah claims her temple at the end of "The Salamander Girl" (#9), and Sammy's family adopt her twin Jane at the close of "Don't Look Twice" (#66). But even if the protagonists are not given new places, their bildungsroman journey enables them to change and be happier with their old place. For example, in "The Cult of the Cat," Nicola initially struggles against her destiny, saying, "No, no, go away. Keep out of my head. I hate your gods and your cats" (#7), but she ultimately accepts her new identity as "a very special person, the chosen of Bast" (#12). As Tóth observes: "The gothic heroine must inevitably go through transformations of personality in order to formulate a separate and independent identity" (2010, 23).

In the *Misty* serials, "Heroinism thus becomes a process in self-awareness" (Wright 2017, 18), where pursued or imprisoned characters rise toward a happy ending and self-acceptance (even though this is sometimes tinged with ambivalence after great sacrifice; see chap. 10). In this, the serials contrast with the single stories, which in general provide a transgressing heroine with swift and direct punishment (although it is worth noting this is often a form of incarceration). The tension between the two types plays an important part in giving balance to the comic, and I explore these differences further in chapter 8.

The contrast also had a commercial imperative that has been discussed and critiqued by fans, creators, and critics. Pat Mills claims that "one of the reasons for the decline of *Misty* was they went for too many one-shot stories" (2016a), and Jenni Scott (posting as comixminx) also "attribute[s] the failure of the title to having run too many one-off stories" (Comics UK 2015). These claims are not entirely correct: my analysis of every tenth issue shows that at *Misty*'s start the serials dominated, with four or five serial installments and two to three single stories in each issue. This weighting flips around halfway through the run, where each issue contains two to three serials and four to five singles. It then evens out toward the end, with three serials and three singles in every issue. Mills (2016a) describes the move to include more single stories as "pure laziness" and "an easy way out" when compared with crafting a longer serial, even of the adaptive type that he pioneered with "Moonchild" and "Hush, Hush, Sweet Rachel." As he explains: "It would have been a natural thing, for example, to have other Stephen King stories and had a hotel, or a giant werewolf.... They didn't want to do that because it requires a commitment; you've got to sit down, you have to read a 400-page novel.... You've got to analyze it, and then you can say, 'Can I make this acceptable for eleven- to twelve-year-old girls?'"

Prigmore (2016a) responds to the criticisms by explaining that the editorial team

> used the self-contained stories to try out new writers and artists. There was a variety of styles to suit their particular skills: mystery, weepie, humor, and so on. Also, a few complete pages in hand meant gaps could be plugged if the post was late from Spain or people were ill, etc. We had thirty-two pages to fill every week, and it could be touch and go sometimes! . . . I know Pat Mills has said he thought there were too many one-offs in *Misty*, but I don't agree. What does a new reader get if they buy, say, issue five and it's full of serials? "The story so far" can only tell you so much. But with one or two complete stories there is satisfaction to be had. And some stories, like music, only need a short time. Any longer and they lose something. Personally, I think much of the greatest literature is found in the short story.

While the combination of single and serial stories likely had both commercial and artistic reasoning behind it, *Misty* also differed from the other girls' comics in another significant way: its lack of recurring characters. Serials ended after an average of ten episodes, and as Mills (2016a) points out, "There was no what you might call mystery equivalent to Judge Dredd, a character that would be in the comic all the time." However, "regulars" of this kind get a mixed reaction from the readership: marckie73 comments, "I never cared for them. With me it's more like: Oh, no. Not again a Bella or Molly Mills story . . ." By contrast, Phoenix feels the complete opposite, saying: "I always loved the regulars. They were like old friends coming back to meet me again" (Comics UK 2015).

Regardless of taste, Marionette (Comics UK 2015) argues that "regulars are what gives a comic its identity. The most successful comics have all had multiple regular character serials. It's always perplexed me why *Misty* had little beyond a cover girl." Tammyfan agrees, pointing out that "any old girls' comic can run serials—it's the regulars like The Four Marys or Bella Barlow that give the comic its particular identity and separate it from the pack." She continues: "Miss T was the only *Misty* character to endure because she was the only regular—besides Misty herself" (Comics UK 2015). While their popularity may be in dispute, the lack of regular characters is certainly one reason that *Misty*'s identity was quickly lost when it merged into *Tammy* (see chap. 14). However, I would suggest that the lack of regulars might also be the reason that Misty herself developed such a clear identity and received such a strong response from the comic's readership (see chap. 13).

MISTY'S SERIES CHARACTERS, COMIC GOTHIC, AND THE WHIMSICAL MACABRE

Misty's only "regulars" are the comedy series characters "Miss T," "Wendy the Witch" (reprinted from *Sandie*), and "Cilla the Chiller" (reprinted from *Princess Tina*). Of these, Miss T (created by Joe Collins for *Misty*) appears the most frequently. As noted, her stories most often see her as the victim of her own magic spell, for example, replacing her broomstick with an errant vacuum cleaner (#2) or turning herself into an apple pie (#7) or monster (#8). Puns are quite common: for example, after seeing "Draculump" star "Christopher Glee" in an advert for dental care, she sighs, "Life has no bite anymore" (#9), and she offers Vic the Vampire "stake and chips" in #62 (fig. 3.1). Ironic commentary also comes from her cat or in textual asides.

"Miss T" is complemented by occasional reprints of Mike Brown's series "Wendy the Witch," about a younger character whose spells often help her to avenge herself on bullies. Figure 5.3 shows a good example. In this episode, Wendy's spell goes awry, and she falls into ice water, regaining the cold she was trying to lose. The circular nature of the plot (where she ends up in the same state as the start), the backfiring of her magic, and the commentary element of the numerous little asides ("My teddy witch" in panel 3, and the indicators "Heave" and "Freezing" in panel 9) are all typical of British comics. In subsequent stories, Wendy has her revenge on bullies Enid and Nellie, who steal her sweets and chips and entangle her in a skipping rope, again with a typically British feel and plenty of puns: "Tee! Hee! Well she got her des[s]erts, alright!" (#55), and "She's had her chips now, eh, monster?" (#60). The supporting cast of characters (which include Enid, Nellie, Rosie, and Nosey Nelly) gives the strip a feel similar to *The Beano*'s "Bash Street Kids" (Leo Baxendale) or "Dennis the Menace" (devised by George Moonie, David Law, and Ian Chisholm) as Wendy gets "the slipper" from her mum (Annual 1979).

"Cilla the Chiller" (writer and artist unknown) appears only in the *Misty* annuals. Cilla is a schoolgirl ghost who haunts a stately home, playing tricks on its visitors and residents, in particular feuding with child guests such as Nellie

SHOCKING STORIES 103

Figure 5.3. "Wendy the Witch" (*Misty* #54). Art by Mike Brown, writer unknown. Reprinted from *Sandie*, April 8, 1972. Reproduced with permission of Misty™ Rebellion Publishing IP Ltd.; copyright © Rebellion Publishing IP Ltd., all rights reserved.

(Annual 1982). She tends toward practical jokes, although she also sometimes scares people away accidentally ("Eek! She's a spook and she spoke!" Annual 1981). Again, puns are common, and the art is in a typical British comics style, reminiscent of the work of Reg Partlett or Leo Baxendale.

While the dominant perception of Gothic is as serious or weighty fare that responds to social trauma and articulates fears and anxieties, some critics analyze its comedic aspects. Horner and Zlosnik (2005) point toward the incongruity of Gothic, arguing that it "opens up the possibility of a comic turn that deliberately exploits the fragile boundary between comedy and horror" (Zlosnik and Horner 2013, 122). Rather than setting up "serious" and "comic" Gothic texts in opposition, they argue that the two are best viewed as a continuum, with horrifying stories that contain flashes of hysteria at one end, and parodic interpretations with moments of shock at the other. They argue that comedy is present in all Gothic texts and that by demonstrating the horrors of an uncanny and unstable world Gothic also celebrates the possibilities that are released. For these critics, Gothic is "always teetering on the edge of self-parody," and its "tendency to the sinister grotesque is easily converted to the comic flamboyance of the grotesque as excess" (2013, 124–25). In a comic like *Misty*, where protagonists are so often punished by their own actions backfiring, Miss T's and Wendy's misadventures invite exactly the "conscious, self-reflexive engagement" with this theme that these critics identify (125).

Spooner (2017) also draws attention to pleasurable or celebratory images of Gothic in the media, arguing that they are on the increase since the millennium. Her work stresses that "Gothic is not co-extensive with horror and cannot be reduced simply to its affective qualities" (2017, 54)—in short, arguing that fear is not the sole definition of Gothic. She points toward critics such as Weinstock and Botting, who criticize today's camp and humorous Gothics, and argues instead that Gothic's sensationalist and aesthetic qualities have always been a source of pleasure. In particular, she explores the work of Tim Burton as representing a playful, postmodern Gothic that draws on aesthetics over affect, where "the images *are* the story" (66).

Spooner (2017, 99) identifies a type of Gothic that she names the "whimsical macabre," which "reconfigures the gruesome and grotesque as playful, quirky and even cute, and often draws on imagery associated with childhood." She expands on this definition to explain: "The whimsical macabre deliberately fuses the cute, fanciful and quirky with the gloomy, gruesome and morbid. It brings together images of, or associated with, childhood, often filtered through a retro or neo-Victorian lens, with Gothic and horror iconography, to create a gently comic effect.... [It] is defined principally through its playful, quirky manipulation of Gothic style and imagery."

The parodic adventures of Miss T, Wendy, and Cilla certainly fall within both of these definitions. While *Misty*, as a 1970s British comic, may look entirely dated today, there is juxtaposition between the style of its comedy strips and the rest of the artwork. The comedy series are self-consciously retro and childish, harking back to a previous generation of British comics (*The Beano* et al.), which was at its peak in the 1950s and addressed a younger audience. The visual contrast between the comedy series and the rest of *Misty*'s stories supports their definition as whimsical macabre, as does their playful tone. The misadventures of Cilla, Miss T, and Wendy are filtered through "images of childhood" and also fuse dark themes (death, backfiring spells, bullying, and isolation) with humor and playfulness.

MISTY'S SINGLE STORIES: CAUTIONARY TALES WITH A STING

Misty's single stories are, almost without exception, four-page cautionary tales with a shocking twist or horrifying "sting in the tail." Rayner (2012) is referring to these stories when she explains, "Within *Misty*'s pages, the slightest moral flaw led to suffering and/or death," and muses on the "horrific fates that were in store for all girls who broke the law." In this, *Misty* followed in the footsteps of the pre-Code American horror comics. This genre had significant impact on the comics industry in both Britain and America in the 1950s. Crime and horror comics took over newsstands in America from the late 1940s, and by the early 1950s, fifty to one hundred horror titles were being released each month, the majority published by Atlas (later to become Marvel) (Trombetta 2010). Negative public attention led to a Senate investigation and the ultimate censorship of the industry with the 1954 Comics Code,[5] concerns that were shared in Europe owing to the exportation of titles.

The most frightening and famous of these comics were produced by Entertaining Comics (EC), led by Bill Gaines and editor Al Feldstein. EC had only a small market share (less than 3 percent) and was competing with numerous imitators, but the company's legacy survives to this day. EC produced anthology comics with host characters (discussed further in chap. 7), often adapting ideas from classic horror and science fiction writers, and using narrative strategies such as direct address, dense and visceral language, a trick ending, and the addition of an extra layer of fiction. A particular EC trademark was the shock ending: in the words of editor in chief Bill Gaines, "If somebody did something really bad he usually got it. And of course the EC way was he got it the same way he gave it" (Diehl 1996). These often include O. Henry–style reversals that involve an ironic twist of fate or overturned expectations. For example, big-game hunters end up as heads on someone else's wall, or wives who connive to kill their husbands become the victims of their own plans. This karmic tone in particular continues in the *Misty* single stories, where every imaginable sin is met with poetic justice. A small selection might include the following:

Cathy cons an old lady out of a moodstone ring, which then sucks all the color out of her life ("Moodstone," #1); a gossip columnist is crushed to death by the books of names and notes she has kept on her acquaintances ("Sticks and Stones," #16); clothes-thief Ann is turned into a fashion dummy ("When the Lights Go Out!" #18); cruel siblings Vivien and Steve trap a mouse in a maze until it dies of exhaustion, but they are in turn locked in a maze by sentient apes ("The Pet Shop," #24); Sally awakens a real ghost while teasing her scared cousin ("The Last Laugh," #29); mugger Cath causes an old lady to be hit by a bus but is then run over herself ("Dead End," #34); Dana kills her twin sister Erica so that she can claim the money she has inherited, but is then accused of the murder Erica committed to get it ("Two of a Kind," #38); Sue takes a creepy mask to win a Halloween competition but then cannot remove it ("Mask of Fear," #39); Rita steals a jigsaw but ends up trapped in one ("The Final Piece," #44); penniless Lois enlists a witch's help to trade places with wealthy Cora but once the swap has been completed finds out that her new body is dying ("If Only," #47); Lisa steals a clock but discovers she will have to wind it forever ("Slave of Time," #55); greedy orphan Effie is literally killed with kindness by her adopted family ("Heart's Desire," #56); jealous Anna puts a gypsy curse on her sister, but it backfires ("Two Left Feet," #59); a fraudulent medium says she will exorcise a demon from Camilla, but it enters her instead ("The Mark," #60); Olivia summons the spirits of her teachers to cheat on a test, but they will not leave ("The Disembodied," #68); cheat Alison is given a magic pen but continues to cheat, so it breaks and covers her with irremovable ink ("A Stain on Her Character," #72); Sally destroys her dad's snail experiments, but the snails trap and immerse her ("House of Snails," #77); Kate scares her little sister with monster stories and is attacked by a monster herself ("Monster Movie," #87); vandals break some stained glass windows and end up trapped in the new ones ("Crystal Clear," #99); and jealous Roma drugs her cousin and cuts off her beautiful hair but is then consumed by ghostly hair growing out of the floor ("Crowning Glory," #101).

This formula dominates the single stories. While a handful offer uplifting tales of redemption or reward (e.g., "A Little Bit of Magic," #39; or "A Girl's Best Friend," #48), the vast majority are vicious morality tales where a wayward antagonist or protagonist is presented with a darkly apt punishment. There is something blackly humorous about this sort of poetic justice that chimes with Horner and Zlosnik's research into Gothic comedy discussed earlier, as the outcomes combine the uncanny and the melodramatic, sometimes producing farcical humor. In addition, Spooner's exploration of the whimsical macabre specifically refers to the cautionary tales of Heinrich Hoffmann and Edward Gorey, who, despite working more than a century apart, take the same "gleeful delight . . . in subjecting the bodies of their child subjects to inventive violence" (2017, 105). Cautionary tales also informed the British public information films of the 1970s, and the next chapter will look more closely at such influences.

The serials, series, and single stories in *Misty* intersect with Gothic in quite different ways. While the serials offer persecuted Gothic heroines who ultimately negotiate threats to their identity or escape imprisonment, the comedy series provide a version of the whimsical macabre that revolves around the childlike and farcical. The single stories take a still different angle, serving up vicious cautionary tales with outcomes that are both horrifying and hilarious in their excess. In the next chapter, I consider these ideas against the context in which *Misty* was produced, exploring the impact of its surrounding culture and media.

CHAPTER 6

HORROR AND GOTHIC IN THE 1970S

Flares and hippies, Tupperware and mustaches, orange and brown decor, and psychedelic rock music are some of the more common memories of Britain in the 1970s. While *Misty*'s nationality, "big visuals," and links with Pat Mills have meant that an association with *2000AD* has frequently dominated the limited critical attention paid to this comic to date, I want to go in a new direction and instead explore some of the cultural influences that shaped *Misty*, which was definitely a child of its time. This chapter first discusses the political context of 1970s Britain, which manifests in the presence of social commentary in *Misty*. I then consider the surrounding atmosphere of British cultural and literary horror, with a particular focus on the horror and mystery stories being offered to children and shown on television and in schools. I argue that *Misty*'s stories are strongly influenced by the atmosphere of cultural horror emerging in Britain in the 1970s, particularly by ideas of transgression and punishment expressed in horror cinema and public information films.

CULTURAL CONTEXT AND SOCIAL COMMENT

Leon Hunt (1998, 5) suggests that many narratives surround the 1970s and that they often combine a discourse of nostalgia with a narrow focus on a particular aspect: bad taste and fashion, political incorrectness, recession and power cuts, vulgarity or grottiness. These metonyms are used to construct the decade variously as a "golden age" or a "fall" (and sometimes both simultaneously). Many scholars and historians note a slide from optimism to "surliness and introversion" (Gibbs 1993, 38), although they do not agree on the tipping point. The postwar consensus crumbled during this decade, which began and ended in Britain under a Conservative government (1970–74 and 1979–97), interspersed with a marginal Labour government (1974–79). While there were important liberal victories (such as the Equal Pay Act 1970 and the Race Relations Act 1976), the early 1970s also saw a series of restrictive legislative acts such as the

Misuse of Drugs Act (1971), the Immigration Act (1971), the Criminal Damage Act (1971), the Prevention of Terrorism Act (1974), and the Industrial Relations Act (1974). These came about partly in response to the legal reforms of the "permissive" 1960s (L. Hunt 1998), but also contemporary political actions such as ongoing utilities strikes (leading to a three-day week for many workers, with dire financial consequences), and a series of IRA bombings (starting in Ireland in 1971 and moving to England from 1972 onward). Global nuclear war between the United States and the Soviet Union was also a threat, and the concept of mutually assured destruction became ingrained into the public consciousness. Nairn speaks of "cultural despair" (1977, 51), and Goodman (2014, 121) notes "a feeling of impending conflict and the threat of potential annihilation." Britain during this time also saw large-scale demolition and rehousing, swinging inflation (Wasson 2016), and uncomfortable ethnic relations or outright racism as second-generation migrants moved into suburbs. Brotherstone and Lawrence (2017, 11) claim that "the political climate was souring," and Marwick (1982, 249) argues that "perhaps violence, race tension and terrorism are the most important social phenomena of the 1970s."

Yet at the same time foreign travel was on the rise, boundaries were being pushed, and amazing evolutions were occurring in technology, music, and film. The US Voyager Program sent probes into new reaches of outer space (1977). Televisions had also become ubiquitous: in the mid-1950s, around one-third of British homes had a television set, but by 1973 this figure had risen to 93 percent (BBC 2014). Videocassette recorders also gained popularity: in Britain the competition between the VHS and Betamax formats peaked in 1976, but by the end of the decade, VHS had effectively won the war. Modern computing was born with the invention of the Intel processor in 1971, and home computers were released in 1977, becoming popular in the 1980s. Video games such as *Pong* (1972), *Tank* (1974), and *Space Invaders* (1978) were invented. Advances in LCD technology also introduced affordable digital watches and pocket calculators, and microwave ovens also increased in popularity toward the end of the decade as their price dropped. It must have felt like the future had arrived.

Johnny Mains (2017, 8) claims that "the seventies were a very twisted time," Wasson (2016, 316) describes them as "a terrible time," and Turney (2010, 264) draws attention to the conflicting drives that underpinned British society:

> The 1970s encapsulated social and cultural confusion, war and rebellion, economic decline (inflation was 27% in 1975) and environmentalism, and it fused the local with the global in unprecedented ways. The threat of potential social disarray exemplified by Watergate and the first resignation of a US president, the rise of trade unionism ("the winter of discontent," 1978–79) and impending strikes and accompanying shortages, the horrors of Cambodia

and an increasing concern about world energy resources (the 1973 oil crisis) challenged the status quo as never before.

Misty's stories, then, can be read as articulating specific British fears of this decade, including environmental concerns, animal rights, globalism and progress, and poverty and delinquency. Ecological threats are a key theme: for example, pollution is the true evil in stories such as "The Monster of Lavender Lagoon" (#77), where an evil factory owner is punished for contaminating the lake. In "Cathy and the Nature Spirits" (#83), Cathy is distressed when her father sells off some land, and she tries to warn the "nature spirits" that live there. When the first tree is cut down, she appears there injured, and he calls off the sale, resulting in her being returned to her bed unharmed. In "The Forest" (#77), Lorna is warned by a dream to care for the woodland the way that her father does. "Looking for Something Special" (#73) also draws attention to neglected nature and the sadness of a deserted seaside through its nameless lead character, who ultimately transforms into a pile of sand ("Unloved, unwanted now . . . / . . . just sand once again. / Think of us, beneath your feet. Tiny, separate grains. Liked so briefly and then deserted . . . / And yet we so nearly found it—love!"). Nature's living qualities are foregrounded as it is personified in our narrator.

Juan Ariza drew all the stories just mentioned, except "Lavender Lagoon" (art by María Barrera Castell). Ariza's delicate style and fragile, curling flourishes suit these ethereal tales and fairy characters. The art thus emphasizes the link between people and the land that underpins these stories' content (via the monster of the lagoon, Cathy's injury, Lorna's "touch of death," and the "sand-girl"). This is in itself a peculiarly Gothic theme, as the landscape acts as a metonym for the psyches of characters or lends itself to Marxist interpretation as a "projection[s] of historical conflicts of power and thought that have been pushed beneath the veneer of society" (Yang and Healey 2016, 8). Many critics have explored the use of Gothic landscapes to reflect and reveal the dark elements of culture and humanity (see, e.g., K. Ellis 1989, where she argues that Gothic landscapes are full of imprisoning spaces; my own work on revenant landscapes in *The Walking Dead* [Round 2014b, 2015]; or Yang and Healey's 2016 edited collection). Here the marginalized and disempowered positions of Cathy and the sand-girl are echoed by the neglect of their landscapes.

Layout and coloring also reinforce this message, as in figure 6.1. This opening page foregrounds the natural, as Cathy's repose in the forest dominates the space. The composition also works organically with the layout as she leans against the border of the first panel. The forest teems with life (nine different creatures are shown in this single panel), and Cathy's knowledge of it is also emphasized as she lists the plants she picks. All these details are juxtaposed against her parents and the domestic setting: a place of rules and work, as her

Figure 6.1. "Cathy and the Nature Spirits" (*Misty* #83). Art by Juan Ariza, writer unknown. Reproduced with permission of Misty™ Rebellion Publishing IP Ltd.; copyright © Rebellion Publishing IP Ltd., all rights reserved.

mother washes up and her father speaks of "terms" and "solicitors." They are unsmiling and more formally dressed (collars, waistcoat) and, along with the builder's vehicle, are the only sources of dark coloring on the page. This underscores their negative role in the tale.

This message is further emphasized by the narration and focalization of these tales, which all take the side of nature. The same strategy is used in the prose stories that deal with similar subjects and often contain a heavy dose of nostalgia or discourse of loss when discussing nature and village life, representing an ambivalence toward globalism and progress. For example, in the text story "Green Fizz" (Holiday Special 1979), Harriet discovers that her gran is a witch and that her corner shop has been providing the village with a drink that makes people contented and happy. Her gran explains: "But the supermarket has put a stop to all hopes of that.... It's taken my trade, dear," and because of this, "the milk of human kindness" is no longer able to get to everyone. Progress is seen as a threat and is used similarly in "Curse of the Roman Sword" (Holiday Special 1979), where a series of events (a proposed supermarket and new road) threaten Moira's village; and in the serial "The Cats of Carey Street," where Jackie's gran's house is due to be demolished (#30–40). "The Story of Little Wytching" (text, #72) also laments the changes in village life: "Years ago, the craft shop sold little hand-made peg doll witches on broomsticks, lovingly made by the local gypsies. Now they were all mass-produced in Hong Kong or Taiwan." Again, big corporations and globalization threaten happiness and tradition. Only one story in the entire *Misty* run represents progress as a force for good: "The Collector" (#68), where a haunted postbox that has been trapping people inside is torn down for town redevelopment, releasing them all. But even here the narrative stance again aligns the reader with the past by using second-person address ("You stand at the corner of a country lane, friendless and forgotten").

Environmental stories make up the bulk of the *Misty* tales that deal with nature. Thirty-six of the 443 stories (8 percent) revolve around plants, forests, and other natural themes (rainbows, weather, etc.). Of these, sixteen show nature as a threat, such as "Alien Seed" (#20), in which Libby's uncle grows a carnivorous plant; or the serial "The Body Snatchers" (#92–101). This story loosely follows the plot of the 1950s novel and film (remade in 1978), as Nancy's friends and teachers are replaced by plants. In the other twenty stories, nature is a helpful force: locusts save Jenny's plane ("The Swarm," #9), a rainbow brings sisters Karen and Lisa together ("At the End of the Rainbow," #64), and an elm tree protects Marla ("A Friend in Need," #66). The near-even split between good and bad nature reflects a Gothic ambivalence about the safety of our environment, although I should note that the number of positive depictions rises significantly if we include animal and pet helpers.

Misty also engages with animal rights—a movement that was sparked by an article in the *Sunday Times* by Brigid Brophy (1965) and then founded in the United Kingdom in the early 1970s by the Oxford Group. Today it is a global campaign; however, traces of its early rise in Britain can be seen in a number of *Misty* stories. As well as characterized or sympathetic animals (e.g., in the serial "Wolf Girl"), a number of tales carry an explicit message about associated issues such as hunting ("The Changeling," #9; "The Horn and the Hounds and the Hunted," #96; "The Last Hunt," #95), animal capture, cruelty, and testing ("The Purple Emperor," #12; "The Experiment," #100; "The Tadpole Terror," #83; "The Pet Shop," #24), and vegetarianism ("Food for Thought," #91) and veganism ("Ring of Confidence," #16–17).

These themes are neatly slotted into recurring *Misty* story tropes and narrative devices, such as magical items and prophetic dreams or twist endings and poetic justice (see chap. 8). For example, in "Ring of Confidence," Angela's ring will give her great wealth if she harms no living creature; however, as she quickly discovers, "Is there nothing we use that doesn't involve animals suffering in some way?" (#16). In "The Horn and the Hounds and the Hunted," Amanda's dream teaches her, "No—I will never hunt! Because now I know the fear of the fox . . . !" (#96), and Cora's nightmare reminds her to go back and save the tadpoles her sister has left on the windowsill because "they have just as much right to live as we do . . . !" ("The Tadpole Terror," #83). Human protagonists often become the victims of hunting, testing, or eating, along with parodies of, or objections to, the associated rhetoric. For example, Fleur dies trying to escape a testing laboratory disguised as her home in "The Experiment" (#100), while the commentary reads "Don't be silly—such tiny creatures can't think and feel in the way that we do" and juxtaposes her image with the rat in a cage alongside her. In "Food for Thought" (#91), Betty and Jill are enjoying their holiday, particularly the barbeque and seafood, when they are caught by alien fishermen. Their giant prawn-like captors complain, "Won't be able to do this much longer if those environmentalists back home have their way," and also comment on the meager amount of meat on humans as "too much effort." They ship the girls away on a journey that "seemed like an eternity to a terrified Betty and Jill," to be served as an exotic starter at a dinner party. As they are about to be devoured, another alien muses, "I think it is immoral to eat other creatures. . . . They may not be as intelligent as you and I. But they have feelings. They know pain and grief and terror." Its companion responds: "You do talk such nonsense sometimes. Animals don't have feelings," and the scene showing the girls being eaten ("AAAAARGH..!") is juxtaposed with their friends on earth enjoying a barbeque. The aliens' appearance and comments clearly parody carnist rhetoric, and the bleak ending underscores the irony. One of the most dramatic of these stories (and which sparked objections from *Misty* fans, as discussed in chap. 13) is the punishment of Vivien and Steve, who allow a mouse to die of exhaustion in their homemade maze and are then locked in a maze themselves by the giant ape owners of the shop they got it from ("The Pet Shop," #24). By including animals as pets as well as food and test subjects, *Misty* raises the issue at both a domestic and corporate level and makes it relevant to its child readership.

Social issues such as poverty and rehousing are also raised, and again progress is often demonized. For example, in "The Cats of Carey Street" (#30–40), Jackie's gran is being run out of the street she grew up on by Council town planners. The urban environment is often depicted as a tough and threatening place, especially for the lower classes: in "Whistle and I'll Come . . ." (#43–56), the persecuted heroine Toni muses, "I'd like to be in the country! I went there once when me real Dad was alive. Can't remember it too clearly, except that it was all green and lovely" (#46). Toni has an abusive alcoholic stepfather and becomes homeless and hungry, reduced to stealing bread despite her honesty, as she objects, "No, Albert! I can't just take one, that's stealing!" (#46). The story covers a variety of social issues including domestic abuse, alcoholism, organized crime, truancy, stealing, and homelessness, and also features a wider ethnic range of characters than any of the other tales, as Toni's friend Selina Sinclair is black.

Nonwhite characters rarely appear in *Misty*: even the "salamander girl" Salah is pale skinned, with blonde hair and golden eyes. When nonwhite characters do appear, they are generally stereotyped, such as Michael Lee, the inscrutable Asian antagonist in "Day of the Dragon" (#10–19), who has a "sinister smile." However, black protagonist Angie is a notable exception ("So You Want to Be a Star," #74), particularly as her ethnicity is not a factor in her story. The Sinclair family are described as "numerous, noisy and cheerful" (#51), and Toni muses, "No wonder Selina's so cheerful, living with a magic family like this." The lack of diversity is sadly common in British comics and children's books of the era, which often tend toward either invisibility or outright racism. Although nonwhite characters do appear in some comics, they are generally restricted to a supporting role, and their depiction is not always strong. For example, the South American characters Malincha and Chana play principal roles in the *Jinty* stories "Sceptre of the Toltecs" (1976–77) and "Alice in a Strange Land" (February 17, 1979–June 9, 1979), but as Scott (2014b, 2017b) points out, these stories contain numerous inaccuracies and some dubious depictions. A more positive example is the Indian girl Nirhani ("7 Steps to the Sisterhood," *Jinty* 1978), best friend of the lead character Shelley (Scott 2014a). However, nonwhite protagonists are occasionally allowed the lead role in British girls' comics. One of the earliest examples is the Japanese protagonist Yum-Yum, who appears in "Yum-Yum in Search of Her Sister" (*Diana* #26–36, August 17, 1963–October 26, 1963; later reprinted in

Mandy #694–704, May 3, 1980–July 12, 1980). Nadine, a black protagonist, stars in the fun-filled sports strip "Life's a Ball for Nadine" (Jinty and Penny 1981), and "Cotton Jenny" was a very popular serial in *Bunty* #1455–68 (November 30, 1985–March 1, 1986) (see Comics UK 2012) for further discussion and examples). As noted, racial tensions were widespread in 1970s Britain and are apparent in much of the entertainment media of the time. The dominance of white characters in *Misty* is therefore unremarkable, although disappointing.

Of the other social issues I have mentioned, a strand focused on stealing, mugging, vandalism, and bullying features most strongly in *Misty*. It is not tied to ethnicity and instead comments on the moral panic around youth culture that appears in many decades of British history, whether aimed at hippies in the 1960s or skinheads and punks in the 1970s. Stanley Cohen coined the term "moral panic" in the 1970s and emphasizes the role of the media and use of the visual in creating a moral panic, pointing out that "the public image of these folk devils was invariably tied up to a number of highly visual scenarios associated with their appearance" (such as the Mod/Rocker fights on Brighton beach) (Cohen [1972] 1987, 20). However, Marsh and Melville (2011) emphasize that moral panics are not a new concept, citing the craze of "garroting" (an especially violent form of mugging) in Victorian London reported in the pages of *Punch*, and suggesting that the reaction is common to delinquent aspects of any society's youth culture or working class (e.g., the more recent panic over "hoodies," where again the panic is associated with a strong visual marker). Tebbutt (2016) also argues that youths have often been made to act as a symbol for adult fears of the future, paying particular attention to areas such as legislation, social norms, gangs, sexual behavior, leisure activities, and identities. Delinquent "folk devils" can be found in many comics from previous decades, such as the story "Wynne against the Beatniks" in *Diana* (1965), in which a gang of scruffy beatniks (drawn with unruly hair and gaunt features) make Wynne's life miserable.

Misty's young delinquents are similarly marked, from their working-class speech to trashy clothing and bad attitude, such as the gang leader Norma in "Moonchild," who fights, bullies, smokes, and disrespects her mother: "See you, Mum. Don't nick any of me fags on your way out" (#11). Pat Mills writes Norma as an unrelentingly malicious character ("Rosemary deserves to be hurt for being so weird," #7; "She deserves to be punished for being so creepy," #10), and John Armstrong's artwork emphasizes her hardness through severe black hair in the style of Joan Jett. Whether Norma is lounging with her feet up in a record shop, knocking Anne unconscious in a hockey game, or creating havoc in the kitchen, she is a force of chaos and unrelenting malice. Of course, she is punished for this and ends up trapped in the blaze her cigarette has started.

Many of *Misty*'s single stories feature delinquent protagonists rather than the antagonists that characterize the serials. In "Room for One More" (#39), Julia and her gang of "hoodlums" threaten a shopkeeper that they will "do him over proper," and go on a rampage until she is run over fleeing the law. Burglar Kate pulls a knife on a householder, which "gives me a chance to scarper a bit sharpish!" ("Framed," #75), but her theft ultimately backfires on her. These wayward protagonists often end up far worse off than the serials' antagonists. Severe punishments and moral lessons are fitted neatly into established *Misty* story types; dishonest protagonists either steal from the wrong person or take a magical item that backfires drastically. Sometimes the lesson is even often spelled out in direct address: "You won't bully strange old women in the street, will you, girls? Who knows what kind of gardens they might have?" ("The Revenge of Granny Godner," #41).

Misty's stories reflect many of the emergent concerns of the 1970s, such as environmentalism, animal rights, social tension, and delinquency, which are incorporated into the comic's plots of enchanted items, wishes, and hidden powers or rearticulated in terms that a child audience can relate to. It is highly likely these stories were written by Malcolm Shaw, described as "very right on" by Wilf Prigmore (2017b), and whose socialist worker and communist politics are confirmed by his widow Brenda Ellis (2016). Many parallels can also be found in concurrent comics, such as the story "Fran of the Floods" (Alan Davidson and Phil Gascoine, *Jinty*, January 17, 1976–September 11, 1976), in which a flicker of the sun leads to climate change with apocalyptic results. However, the *Misty* stories also draw heavily on the surrounding atmosphere of horror, which was invading mainstream entertainment in the 1970s.[1] Film, television, books, comics, and games all embraced the genre, and not just in texts aimed at adults.

HORROR IN THE MEDIA

When we think of 1970s horror cinema, the tendency is often to privilege American films. Cinema had become more violent throughout the 1960s, in part thanks to the introduction of the Motion Picture Association of America (MPAA)'s rating system. After groundbreaking independent films such as Romero's *Night of the Living Dead* (1968), horror became extremely visible in the mainstream: Marriott and Newman (2006) claim that *The Exorcist* (1974) was the first horror to make it to the upper levels of *Vanity Fair*'s box-office champ charts, quickly followed by *Jaws* (1975). There was a move toward "pure" horror, without explanation or backstory—Jaws bites because that's what sharks do—that extended into films such as *The Texas Chainsaw Massacre* (1974) and *Halloween* (1978). The decade also saw a turn toward teenage concerns: whereas

Rosemary's Baby (1968) is about a middle-class white woman in Manhattan, and horror had previously focused largely on adult concerns and protagonists, the dominant focus moved toward teenagers as both victims and heroes, such as in *The Last House on the Left* (1972), *The Texas Chainsaw Massacre* (1974), *Black Christmas* (1974), *Carrie* (1976), *Halloween* (1978), and *When a Stranger Calls* (1979). While teenage horror had been seen in the 1950s (*I Was a Teenage Werewolf*, 1957), these stripped-down new horrors offered a simplicity and brutality that often combined with a heavy dose of ambiguity via an unhappy ending (introduced in the 1960s in films such as *The Birds*, 1963; *Dance of the Vampires*, 1967; and *Night of the Living Dead*, 1968).

The changes in the American movie industry and the types of films being released also led to pressure in Britain. A new AA certificate (aged fourteen upward) was created in 1970, and the age for the X rating was also raised from sixteen to eighteen. British cinema was therefore getting strong realism from America and sexually explicit art house films from Europe (*Last Tango in Paris*, *Emmanuelle*), leading to a strong sense of ambiguity and confrontation in its own films. Whereas British horror had been dominated by Hammer in the 1950s, other companies such as Amicus (founded in 1962) and Tigon (founded in 1966) emerged in the 1960s. Amicus was most famous for its portmanteau horror films, four or five short horror stories linked by an overarching plot, such as *Dr. Terror's House of Horrors* (1965), *Tales from the Crypt* (1972), and *Vault of Horror* (1973). Leon Hunt (1998, 147) argues that these "grim flarey tales" became especially prominent mid-decade and are characterized by a contemporary setting and hints of sexploitation (operating around a "repressive hypothesis") and become more resonant when considered against the crisis backdrop. Key British directors such as Norman J. Warren (*Prey*, 1977; *Terror*, 1978) and Pete Walker (*House of Whipcord*, 1974; *Schizo*, 1976), often working with writers such as Dave McGillivray (*Frightmare*, 1974; *Satan's Slaves*, 1976), produced shocking and subversive contemporary horrors with ambiguous endings. The message was "You're not safe"; unlike the 1960s, horror was not normative, and equilibrium was not always restored. The sexualized and graphic content meant that debates emerged about reregulation of values and content (stemming from a wider vein of worry about pop culture), running alongside a consumerist deregulation of the industry itself (the rumblings about "video nasties" would begin in the late 1970s).

Marriott and Newman (2006, 113) describe the horror film as being "at its zenith" in terms of output and diversity in the 1970s. The decade can be read as a classic and political age of horror where cultural value and box office appeal were used to negotiate a place for horror. In its wake, critics such as Robin Wood ([1983] 2003) brought serious scholarship to bear on the genre, arguing for horror as "the return of the repressed": a dramatization of the duality of the repressed self / the Other and example of the dream-film analogy. Wood claims that in the 1970s horror became "the most important of all American genres" (1979, 76), and subsequent research has similarly applied psychoanalytic approaches and connected these films with the politics of their cultural and historical context (civil rights, women's movement, antiwar demos, etc.). Scholars such as Clover (1992), Creed (1993), and Halberstam (1995) draw attention to the treatment of the feminine Other, and later work continues to investigate the identity politics of horror from perspectives such as class, gender, ethnicity, and sexuality (Roche 2014). While many critics looking at British horror prioritize the first half of the decade (Pirie, Hutchings, Sanjek), they too show a consensus toward interpreting these films with reference to their cultural backdrop.

As well as articulating cultural concerns, the mediality between cinema, television, film, radio, and literature also shaped the formats and themes that emerged. British horror and Gothic literature had been popular in previous decades (Dennis Wheatley, Ramsey Campbell) and gained further traction in the 1970s from best-selling writers such as James Herbert (*The Rats*, 1974) and Graham Masterton (*The Manitou*, 1976). American writers such as Ira Levin (*Rosemary's Baby*, 1967), William Peter Blatty (*The Exorcist*, 1971), and Stephen King (*Carrie*, 1974) also brought supernatural forces to the mainstream. Their success inspired a boom market of cheap pulp horror paperbacks, which imitated these literary novels' extreme scenarios and transgressive forces while adding a heavy dose of excess, titillation, and nihilism. Hendrix (2017, 9, 138) examines this trend, which started in the late 1960s and would run until the early 1990s, when the genre was rebranded as the more mainstream "thriller." He stresses the pulps' no-holds-barred approach, lurid painted covers (from artists such as Jeffrey Catherine Jones, Jim Thiesen, and Jill Bauman), and controversial subjects, such as "Jewish monster brides, sex witches from the fourth dimension, flesh-eating moths, homicidal mimes, or golems stalking Long Island." These are books that pull no punches and "[respect] no rules except one: always be interesting" (9).

Cinema was also looking to literature for stories, and many high-profile adaptations became box office hits, such as *Rosemary's Baby* (dir. Polanski, 1968), *The Exorcist* (dir. Friedkin, 1973), and *Carrie* (dir. De Palma, 1976). Cinematic formats also invaded television: the decade saw the rise of the "television movie" in the United States, whereas the United Kingdom moved toward anthologies and serial dramas. American horror comics had used the anthology format in the 1940s and 1950s, and it became a staple of both radio and television in the 1960s and 1970s. Early shows included *Lights Out* (NBC radio, 1934; NBC television, 1946), *The Twilight Zone* (CBS, 1959), *Thriller* (NBC, 1960), and *Mystery and Imagination* (ITV, 1966). In the 1970s, the format became strongly associated with horror through series such as *Night Gallery* (NBC, 1969–73), *Dead of Night* (BBC, 1972), and *Ghost Story* (BBC, 1971–78; 2005)—and would of course be used by *Misty*.

When asked about the influences that led him to create *Misty*, Pat Mills (2015) comments:

> I didn't have access to EC Comics, apart from a British compilation called COMIX, which included a few. That was certainly inspiring and I hugely admire the few examples I read. Superb! Most of my inspiration, though, comes from British sources. The *Pan Book of Horror* tales were around at the time. *Tales of the Unexpected* etc. And some weird dreams—if I'm lucky!
>
> Also, then and now, anything I pick up in the media.... Scary stuff! I find there's nothing to beat real life.

Certainly a number of high-profile real-life horror and mystery stories in Britain resonated throughout the decade. The Highgate Vampire case caused a media sensation around the desecration of graves at Highgate Cemetery (London) and sightings of a ghostly figure. The publicity spanned from 1969 to 1975, kept alive in the media by the rivalry between involved parties, a series of alleged sightings, a mass vampire hunt (March 1970), and subsequent acts of vandalism and desecration. Alongside this were more serious violent crimes that included child murder cases, such as the ten-year-old murderess Mary Bell (1968); the "Monster of Worcester," David McGeary, who killed three children and impaled their bodies on nearby garden railings (1973); and thirteen-year-old victim Carl Bridgwater (1978), who was shot when delivering newspapers. "Yorkshire Ripper" Peter Sutcliffe was active between 1975 and 1980, killing thirteen women (and attempting seven more) until he was finally arrested in 1981. All were notorious cases that shocked Britain and resonate to this day in living memory.[2]

The Pan Book of Horror Stories series that Mills cites as an influence are low-cost paperback collections of short stories, launched in 1959 and initially edited by Herbert van Thal.[3] The series ran to thirty collections and is notable for including classics such as George Langelaan's "The Fly" alongside Bram Stoker, Edgar Allan Poe, and Agatha Christie. The stories are often remarkably sadistic and gory (such as George Fielding Eliot's "Copper Bowl" or Seabury Quinn's "The House of Horror"), but there are also excruciating tales of psychological terror, such as Jack Finney's "Contents of the Dead Man's Pocket" (where our protagonist climbs out on a high ledge to retrieve an invaluable piece of paper) or William Sansom's "The Vertical Ladder" (where a climbing dare goes very wrong). These are claustrophobic, nerve-gnawing stories. They sit alongside uncanny events and archetypes such as séances, werewolves, ghosts, and mad scientists, and while certainly adult fare, many stories ring true with the *Misty* ethos. In Joan Aiken's "Jugged Hare," an unfaithful wife is punished, Oscar Cook's "His Beautiful Hands" sees a beautician takes revenge on the father who abandoned her, and in L. P. Hartley's "W.S.," a fictional character comes alive to kill his creator. The tales are frequently bleak or sometimes blackly humorous (as in "Dead Man's Pocket"), ending in mutilation, madness, or misery for protagonists. The strands of retribution and justice and the stories' unfinished or hopeless endings find an echo in *Misty*'s single stories and other entertainment of the time.

Jacobs (2000), Cooke (2003), and Wheatley (2006, 31) explore the development of Gothic horror on television, noting the sense of trepidation and anxiety that initially accompanied this and the conviction that Gothic was "an unsuitable genre for domestic transmission." Wheatley discusses the ways in which early examples reference diverse filmic traditions and often rely on the unseen and uncanny. Some 1970s examples continued this tone, such as *Tales of the Unexpected* (ITV, 1979–88), initially based on a selection of Roald Dahl's adult short stories before branching outward. The subject matter of the *Tales* is mostly adult: cheating spouses, wagers with high stakes, and everyday sadism or attempted cons that are punished dramatically through twists of fate. It is these twist endings that tie the *Tales* most closely to the fare of *Misty*. For example, in "The Landlady" (S01E05, 1979), Billy's landlady reveals a gruesome taxidermy collection of former tenants, which he seems about to join. In "Royal Jelly" (S02E01, 1980), a father feeds his daughter royal jelly to make her grow (but into what?), and the episode closes with her mother's horrified scream and a disturbing buzzing noise. "Georgy Porgy" (S02E09, 1980) enters the Oedipal nightmare of a clergyman who ends up in an asylum, believing he is being eaten alive. In "The Flypaper" (S03E01, 1980), Sylvia becomes one of a series of schoolgirl disappearances after being lured to a house by a motherly lady who pretends to save her from a sinister man. The final scene shows Sylvia terrified and trapped (intercut with images of flies stuck to flypaper) as the couple pull the blinds closed and grab at her clothing. The stories' themes tend toward the uncanny as "kitchen sink" realism, everyday characters, and low-cost British production values are combined with themes of mutation and transgression. The *Tales*' uncanny strangeness and uncertain perilous endings are in clear keeping with *Misty*'s plots, and although the television broadcast of *Tales* did not begin until midway through *Misty*'s run, the Dahl short stories were published beforehand in collections such as *Kiss Kiss* (1960) and mainstream magazines like the *New Yorker* in the 1950s and 1960s.

Alongside suspenseful fictional horror in literature and television, 1970s Britain also saw the rise of the public information film aimed at children. These were exactly the type of cautionary tale that *Misty*'s single stories patterned.

They included animated series such as *Charley Says* (Richard Taylor Productions, 1973) and a series of live-action short films that did not shy away from showing graphic violence or using the conventions of the horror genre. For example, *Lonely Water* (Central Office of Information, 1973) was aimed at preteen children and warned of the dangers of drowning. Narrated by Donald Pleasance in a slow and eerie cadence, it opens: "I am the spirit of dark and lonely water: ready to trap the unwary, the show-off, the fool," and, after showing a number of dangerous scenarios, all containing a mysterious hooded figure in the style of Death, ends with the echoing promise "I'll be back!" *Play Safe* (Central Office of Information, 1978), a collection of three short films about the dangers of electrocution, is most notorious for its first installment "Frisbee," in which young Jimmy is electrocuted after climbing a pylon to retrieve his Frisbee (the extended version includes a particularly graphic image of his legs on fire).[4] These films aren't afraid to show dead bodies, blood, or mutilation, such as the infamous *Apaches* (dir. Mackenzie, 1977), which warns of the dangers of playing on farmland, including being crushed by various machines, drowning in slurry, and drinking poison (complete with bloodcurdling screams of pain). The decade also saw a series of fireworks safety films warning of blindness and burns (described in graphic detail), and *Never Go with Strangers* (dir. Erulkar, 1971), which features ominous shadows looming over a terrorized child, jarring music, an animated red filter over the stranger's car, and a hideous transformation of his face using animation.

The "twist of fate" that characterizes all these films can also be found in *Misty*'s single stories. A vandal who damages an electricity pylon unwittingly causes the death of his own sister (*Play Safe*, 1978). A boy who throws a firework accidentally blinds his girlfriend (*Firework Girl*, 1975). Danny, our narrator in *Apaches*, reveals at the end of the film that the "party" he has been talking about is his own funeral. We can note similarities here with the sort of ironic tragedy that the *Misty* single stories often end on. For example, in "The Frankenstein Papers" (Annual 1984), Professor Sansom lights a fire that melts ice and frees the creature, but the fire gets out of control, and he dies in the blaze. Witch Old Meg is also burned to death by children playing with matches ("The Story of Little Wytching," #72). Rachel is hit by a car while trying to prevent her own death ("You Can't Cheat Tomorrow," #36). In "Ghost of Christmas Future" (#48), a group of passengers think they have escaped a bus crash but later discover they are all dead.

While some of the public information films were only shown in schools "under responsible adult supervision," many were broadcast on television during the children's programs. In the 1970s there were only three television channels and no breakfast or daytime shows: broadcasting ran from approximately midday to midnight, and the BBC in fact closed down at 2 p.m. before restarting at 3:30 p.m., as it was assumed everyone was either at school, at work, or too engrossed with housework. Despite this, the decade saw an increase in children's programming and produced a large number of fictional shows that can only be described as terrifying.

For example, *Ace of Wands* (Thames/ITV 1970–72) followed a stage magician with supernatural powers, whose investigations included characters transformed into dolls, an evil ventriloquist dummy with hypnotic powers, a deadly hallucinogenic gas, and a machine with the ability to paralyze. While the plots are very different, some of these motifs have similarities to the *Misty* stories "A Turn for the Worse" (#44) and "The Devil's Dummy" (#69). The anthology horror program *Shadows* (Thames/ITV, 1975–78) spanned from traditional stories of witches, ghosts, and myths to child abuse and dark urban fantasy. Again, we can see echoes in *Misty*: in "The Man Who Hated Children" (*Shadows* S03E05), our antagonist slowly transforms into a tree, a punishment meted out in "The Treatment" (#75) and "Voices in the Wind" (#42). *Children of the Stones* (HTV/ITV, 1977) exploited the horror trope of the small, creepy village with strange or vacant inhabitants, combined with *Invasion of the Body Snatchers* (1978), and parallels can be found in *Misty* in "Who Pays the Ice Cream Man?" (#52) and "The Body Snatchers" (#92–101). Children's Gothic television continued to have a strong presence in the United Kingdom in the 1980s, for example, in shows such as *Dramarama* (ITV 1983–89), *The Box of Delights* (BBC, 1984), and *Moondial* (BBC, 1988). Critics such as Butler (2008), Peirse, (2010), and Wheatley (2013, 679) have discussed the dark and sinister tone of these series, in which "children become immersed in supernatural worlds in which they must confront the past (and themselves)"—a description that equally applies to *Misty*, in particular to its serial stories.

Horror and Gothic for children were also invading the page. In 1974 Alan Frank published *Horror Movies*, aimed at the younger reader and lavishly illustrated with film stills and archive footage. *Monsters and Vampires* (Frank 1976) and *A Pictorial History of Horror Movies* (Gifford 1976) followed, also focusing on cinema and containing plenty of illustrations. *The Usborne Guide to the Supernatural World* was published in 1977, composed of three small paperbacks titled *Haunted Houses, Ghosts and Spectres*, *Vampires, Werewolves and Demons*, and *Mysterious Powers and Strange Forces*. These pocket-sized books were aimed at a younger audience and collect facts and myths from around the world. They are extensively illustrated in color, with original art and some particularly striking renderings of beasts and demons. Other children's books such as *The Hamlyn Book of Ghosts in Fact and Fiction* (1978) also bring together historical legend and "authenticated" stories alongside proven hoaxes and famous fictional examples. This book contains some disturbing photographs (a shattered skeleton, a shadowy figure) and illustrations, such as one of the Exmoor Black Dog (42, 151, 30). The collection as a whole is factual rather than sensationalist, but its angle is striking, arguing definitely for the existence of ghosts as a type of *"visual telepathy.... They are facts.* Pictures seen by the mind's eye.... A ghost is just a *footprint* on time" (155). The series continued with *Horror* (1979), *Mysteries* (1983), and *Monsters* (1984), which have a similar tone and whose painted covers (by Oliver Frey) bring a dramatic sense of gravitas to their subjects. The *Mysteries* book concludes with the question "Could Plato have been right, or is the legend of Atlantis a rather nice fairytale?" (153) and ends with a quotation from *Hamlet*: "There are more things in heaven and earth, Horatio / Than are dreamt of in your philosophy" (I.V.167–68). The supernatural is definitely not limited to fiction here.

British comics were also not exempt from the horror and supernatural craze, although things were perhaps more subtle owing to the legacy of the American horror comics. *Pocket Chiller Library* was a small-format horror- and crime-themed comic book series published by Top Sellers between 1971 and 1977 (137 issues), each telling a different stand-alone tale with titles like "Killer Doll" (#4) and "Gibbet of the Damned" (#87). These bleak stories often end badly for their wayward protagonists, such as "Beyond Death" (#105), in which the murderous Logan Gibbs is mummified and entombed, cursed to "[walk] the dark and terrible regions beyond death" for eternity. His screams to be released and pleas for any reply give way to a final page on which he is shown utterly alone, surrounded by menacing shapes of darkness, while the narration concludes that "the answer would be long in coming." Death is also the fate of Derek Stanton, who falls victim of his own scientific experiment and is turned into a bat-like creature ("The Bat," #119). Female protagonists are generally innocent girls thrown into a dangerous situation and fare slightly better: for example, stories such as "Everlasting Night" (#112) and "Mangled Mind" (#113) see their heroine escape, often with the help of a romantic interest, although supporting female characters die in their stead.

For younger comics readers, "munster" titles such as *Shiver and Shake* (IPC, 1973–74) and *Monster Fun* (IPC, 1975–76) provided comedy-horror strips aimed at preteen readers. These often reference established horror, such as "Frankie Stein," devised by Ken Reid and introduced in *Wham!* (1964), then resurfacing in IPC's *Shiver and Shake* (1973–74) and *Whoopee!* (1974–85, drawn by Bob Nixon) and also appearing in *Monster Fun* as editor. Similar examples might include "Gums," a shark with false teeth, who debuted in *Monster Fun* #35 (1976, written by Roy Davies, with art by Bob Nixon and later Alf Saporito). Comedy horror strips with child characters or school settings were also common, such as "Rent-a-Ghost Ltd." (*Buster*, 1969–79; *Wow!*, 1982–83; originally by Reg Parlett), "Hire a Horror" (*Cor*, 1970; Reg Parlett), "The Ghosts of St. Gilda's" (*June and Pixie*, early 1970s; creator unknown), "Wendy the Witch" (*Sandie*, 1972–73; Mike

Brown), "The Girls of Grimley's Grammar" (*Tammy*, 1973–74; Mike Brown), and "Cilla the Chiller" (*Princess Tina*, n.d.; creator unknown). This subgenre would continue into the 1980s with strips such as "Creepy Comix" (*Wow!*, 1982–83; *Whoopee!*, 1983–85; *Whizzer and Chips*, 1985–90; Reg Parlett), "Fright School" (*Buster*, 1985–88; Reg Parlett), and "Strange Hill" (*Whizzer and Chips*, n.d.; Tom Paterson). The original *Misty* comedy series "Miss T" clearly comes from this mold.

ECHOES AND ADAPTATIONS

Misty's story titles and content are constantly referring to the surrounding atmosphere of horror and Gothic. Many of the serial stories contain superficial namechecks, such as "Whistle and I'll Come . . . ," which recalls the BBC's *Whistle and I'll Come to You* (dir. Miller, 1968), an adaptation of an M. R. James ghost story (1904). The title of the *Misty* serial "Hush, Hush, Sweet Rachel" echoes the movie *Hush . . . Hush, Sweet Charlotte* (1964), a psychological thriller about infidelity and a falsely accused murderess, and the TV movie *Sweet, Sweet Rachel* (1971), a pilot for the subsequent series *Sixth Sense* (ABC, 1972) about a murderer who uses extrasensory perception. "The Four Faces of Eve" namechecks the 1957 movie *The Three Faces of Eve*, a dramatic treatment of dissociative identity disorder. The titles thus connote murder and psychic danger by referencing big-name texts with Gothic, horror, and mystery overtones.

The content of some of the serial stories is also directly adapted from the surrounding media. Pat Mills comments: "I said we should look at all the kinds of female adults' fiction that were around at the time, and do girls' comics versions of that" (Mills 2011)—a strategy that had already worked well in his boys' comic *Action* ("Hook Jaw" and "Death Game 1999" are based on *Jaws* and *Rollerball*). A number of the *Misty* serials adapt contemporary horror books and films in different ways. For example, "End of the Line" (Malcolm Shaw and John Richardson, #28–42) recalls the movie *Death Line* (1972), where people are kidnapped by the cannibalistic descendants of a group of Victorian tube tunnel workers trapped underground. "The Sentinels" (Malcolm Shaw and Mario Capaldi, #1–12) shares its alternate history setting of Nazi-occupied Britain with *It Happened Here*, a 1964 British film. It perhaps also takes its title and scenario from *The Sentinel* (Konvitz, 1974; movie adaptation dir. Winner, 1977), in which protagonist Alison discovers that her Brooklyn apartment building contains the gate to hell and that she has been chosen by God to be its guardian. Shaw's writing often uses preexisting texts as a jumping-off point, combining a new genre (such as science fiction) or plot events (Ann's hunt for her father) with the catalyst or backdrop of an existing text. By contrast, Mills's rewritings more directly rework the key story elements into more juvenile forms, removing the sex, death, and gore. "Moonchild" (Pat Mills and John Armstrong) is a direct adaptation of Stephen King's *Carrie* (1974), and "Hush, Hush, Sweet Rachel" (Pat Mills and Eduardo Feito) retells Frank De Felitta's *Audrey Rose* (1975, adapted into a film in 1977). But while both Carrie White and Audrey Rose/Ivy Templeton end up dead, their *Misty* equivalents Rosemary Black and Lisa Harvey escape the supernatural and find happy, secure homes.

The structure of "Hush, Hush, Sweet Rachel" follows a similar pattern to *Audrey Rose*, but told from the perspective of the child rather than adult characters and with consequent changes to the themes and tensions. *Audrey Rose* is mainly focalized through parents Janice and Bill Templeton and occasionally through other supporting characters. Their worries about apparent stalker Elliot Hoover and love and fears for their daughter Ivy form the basis of the plot, and the story begins when Janice first becomes aware of Hoover. It then follows the family through her acceptance of his unbelievable story, uncanny evidence of the reincarnation and a kidnapping court case, finally ending in tragedy when regressional hypnosis is attempted on Ivy. In the rewritten "Sweet Rachel," the plot follows a similar pattern: Lisa meets the mysterious Mrs. Prendergast and then experiences a series of episodes of childlike behavior and nightmares, until the reincarnation claims are introduced in the fourth installment, after which the story revolves around her struggle to accept them and prevent herself lapsing into Rachel's personality. Lisa's friends play a key role in helping and supporting her, particularly against antagonist Rosie, who tries to ruin Lisa's popularity at school by encouraging her childlike behavior. Ultimately Lisa's visions end when Mrs. Prendergast falls to her death.

In "Moonchild," Rosemary Black discovers her telekinetic powers after a dangerous practical joke is played on her at school, and the negative attention continues from bully Norma and her gang. Rather than prom night, the culmination of the tale is a party that they throw for Rosemary, at which they give her mean gifts, a disgusting cake, spray her with paint, and blindfold her, causing her to fall off a balcony. Rosemary's reappearance rising into the air is pure *Carrie*—drawn from the bullies' perspective and with the menacing threat "You've had your turn. Now . . . it's mine" (#12). As in *Carrie*, the house also catches fire (albeit due to Norma's smoking), but everyone escapes, and after the death of her grandmother and her mother's departure, Rosemary's powers vanish, and she goes to live with her friend Anne.

The sexual element is removed from both, as Rosemary's powers are unrelated to puberty, and there is no concern that Mrs. Prendergast's intentions toward Lisa are unsavory. The gore also vanishes—there is no shower scene or bucket of blood—but resonances remain, such as when Norma's gang decide to throw a birthday party for Rosemary and begin chanting, "Shame! Shame!"

(#9) rather than "Plug it up!" This retains the animalistic bullying and mob mentality that is so striking in *Carrie*. Finally, the tragedy is removed, and both stories sacrifice the outsider rather than the child to achieve this end, as Mrs. Prendergast and Rosemary's grandmother both die, enabling the young protagonists to move on.

Misty's persecuted heroines, moralistic tales, and ambiguous or unhappy endings are strongly resonant of the atmosphere of cultural horror emerging in Britain in the 1970s. Politics and society were fractured and uncertain, with racial and social tensions and emergent environmental movements warning of danger. Horror cinema brought together transgression and punishment to warn "You're not safe," and the dialogue around these films drew attention to the demands of moral guardianship. Public information films similarly demonstrated the consequences of careless behavior in a world of threats. Horror literature for both adults and children offered ambiguous outcomes and conveyed an uncertain and supernatural reality. The need for a guide or friend to help navigate or escape this dangerous space must have been strong and is a service that Misty herself provided for her readers, as I explore in the following chapter.

CHAPTER 7

OUR FRIEND OF THE MISTS

Misty, our eponymous host, guided readers through the 101 issues of her weekly comic and lived on into the 1980s in various annuals (1979–86) and reprints (explored further in chap. 14). She plays a unique role as a combination of fictional editor, host, and cover girl. This chapter first explains the background to host figures in comics, particularly noting their affinity with the horror genre. I then reveal how Misty herself originated, based on interviews with the comic's original creative team, and explore the ways in which her depiction uses Gothic tropes. Misty's appearances on the inside cover are cataloged and analyzed alongside the welcome message that she offered readers. My discussion here focuses on the use of Gothic themes and notes the dominance of naturalized and feminized symbols that offer a sense of time and history. I also demonstrate that the language used suggests a journey and employs an alliterative and poetic tone alongside Gothic images of the body and isolation.

HORROR AND HOSTS

Horror hosts are an established feature of the genre across media, looking back to radio programs such as *The Witch's Tale* (WOR, 1931–38), which was hosted by Old Nancy, "the Witch of Salem." She provided the inspiration for subsequent radio narrators such as Raymond in *Inner Sanctum Mystery* (Blue Network, 1941–52), and also the basis for EC Comics' host the "Old Witch."[1] Real-life figures would also host a number of later horror television shows such as *Alfred Hitchcock Presents* (CBS and NBC, 1955–65), *Boris Karloff's Thriller* (NBC, 1960–61, 1961–62), and *The Twilight Zone* (CBS, 1959–64), which was hosted and narrated by its creator, Rod Serling. The British television show *Tales of the Unexpected* (ITV, 1979–88) continued in a similar vein, as the author Roald Dahl introduced each episode with a teasing summary of its themes or his inspiration.

In comics the most famous examples are EC Comics' "Ghoulunatics": the Crypt-Keeper, Old Witch, and Vault-Keeper, who respectively hosted *Tales from the Crypt* (1950–55), *The Haunt of Fear* (1950–54), and *The Vault of Horror* (1950–55), although each would also appear in the others' titles. The Ghoulunatics' purpose was predominantly humorous. They served as a distancing frame around the stories, with their terrible puns and comedic comments creating a protective layer between the child reader and the horrible events. Jones (2015, 127) argues that the Ghoulunatics were functions rather than distinct characters, pointing out that "the distinctions between the [EC] hosts were minimal," and "physical samenesses, the likeness of function, voice and attitude shared by the three blurred their identities."

In the following decades, Warren Publishing introduced Uncle Creepy and Cousin Eerie, hosts of *Creepy* (1964–83) and *Eerie* (1966–83), and Vampirella, who hosted *Vampirella* (1969–83) between 1969 and 1970. DC Comics created brothers Cain and Abel as hosts of *House of Mystery* (1951–83, 1986–87, 2008–present) and *House of Secrets* (1956–78, 1996–99) anthologies, coming on board in 1968 and 1969 respectively. Marvel embraced the figure less but still devised characters such as Headstone P. Gravely and Roderick "Digger" Krupp for the anthology titles *Tower of Shadows* (1969–75) and *Chamber of Darkness* (1969–74). These key figures sit alongside a number of other minor hosts from each company, and other publishers such as Charlton Comics also had numerous host characters in their horror and suspense titles from the 1960s onward.

British anthology comics also had hosts, often linked explicitly to the more scary sections of the comic, which might be due to the characters' horror genre legacy. Hosts first emerged in British girls' comics in the 1960s, perhaps following the American comics, but also growing naturally out of the stories' structures. Before this time, many girls' comics stories began with a paragraph of background, such as "Debby West wanted to join Melwin's Circus with Spot, her performing dog" ("Call of the Circus," *School Friend*, March 5, 1960). Alternatively, the protagonist may introduce her story, for example, "I am Meg Baring, a stage magician" ("The Girl Magician Tells a Secret," *School Friend*, February 13, 1960) or "My name is Anne Howard and I'm a nurse at Trenent Cottage Hospital" ("No Love for Jenny," *Diana* #141, October 30, 1965). The development of a separate figure to perform this function therefore seems a logical step, and two distinct types of host (serial and series) can be identified in British girls' comics.

The series host is a character who bookends a nonsequential group of stories that are unrelated except in their theme (in much the same manner as the EC or DC hosts). The first and most famous series host to feature in British girls' comics is the Storyteller, who would appear in various titles between 1965 and

1982. He is introduced in the first issue of the merged *June and School Friend* on January 30, 1965, as the narrator of "The STRANGEST Stories Ever Told": "a new series of stories that will thrill and intrigue you." His first tale is "The Haunted Bank" (artist Mike Hubbard), in which penniless Eric is tempted to steal from his job but thinks better of it after some strange supernatural happenings and receives the money he needs by another means. The Storyteller introduces and wraps up the tale, which also uses unassigned narration throughout, and provides an epilogue in which he explains what happened to Eric afterward. Although the Storyteller does not interact with story events, the borders between his world and the storyworld are hazy, for example, as he ends "The Diary from the Past" (February 27, 1965) with the explanation "She could never bear to lay eyes on that picture again . . . so her father gave it to me!" He was popular, surviving multiple mergers and often gaining approval in the letters page (e.g., see *Tammy*, May 17, 1975).

Diana's Man in Black follows, first appearing in "Star of Doom" (*Diana* #197, November 26, 1966). He is a Dracula-esque character with black hair and Victorian attire, who addresses the reader directly, opening his first story with the following lines: "I am your storyteller, the Man in Black. Don't be frightened. Come a little closer and let me tell you of the strange mystery of a girl called Drusilla. Her life is controlled by the—STAR OF DOOM."

He provides this preface and an epilogue that complements the unassigned narration that runs throughout the story. The Man in Black wraps up by promising "another story that will send shivers up your spine" in next week's issue. Although he does not participate in his stories, his speech often incorporates the drawn title (as in "Star of Doom"), and like the Storyteller, his explanations sometimes weave him into the storyworld, such as in "The Two Faces of Perlita" (a *Dorian Gray*–style story), which he closes with the words "The Princess died within the hour. . . . The carving came into my possession—but I've no elixir, which is just as well" (*Diana* #232, July 22, 1967). He was often drawn by David Cuzik Matysiak, who drew a number of regular DC Thomson strips.

Other girls' comics also had series hosts, most often older male characters. These authoritative patriarchal characters frame their supernatural stories with morals, explanations, and sometimes questions. *Spellbound* (1976–78) was the home of Damian Darke, a tall, older man in old-fashioned attire (high collar, ruffled shirt front) with a raven atop his shoulder, who reads from a weighty book. Drawn by Brian Lewis, he appears weekly from the first issue, in "Spectre from the Flame," in which a ghostly judge saves protagonist Jane from an intruder. His epilogues either summarize the outcome ("Another Pair of Hands . . . ," #54) or raise questions: for example, "Well, what do you think? Was it just a tattered old rug, she had picked up while sleepwalking? Or was it INDEED the Cavalier's Cloak?" ("The Cavalier's Cloak," #37).

Other more diverse host figures also appear. "Gipsy Rosa Remembers" was published in *Diana* for a time (n.d.). *Judy* (1960–91) occasionally featured a character called She of the Shadows (who it seems appeared only in the annuals); a glamorous-looking veiled lady in long black dress and gold jewelry. *Judy*'s most famous host character is Bones, who presents "Tales from Skeleton Corner." This "nerve tingling new series" launches with "Flower Power" in *Judy* #1632 (April 20, 1991), in which Carly uses a homemade flower lotion on her face but is horrified when later her skin withers like dead flowers. Bones is more EC Comics than paternal storyteller, and he often matches his speech, jokes, and attire to the story's events, such as wearing a baseball cap with the logo "Say It with Flowers" in "Flower Power."

Gypsy Rose first appears in *Jinty and Lindy* in "The Ring of Death" (January 29, 1977), launching "Gypsy Rose's Stories of Magic and Mystery."[2] She breaks with the previous dominant type of host by being young and female, and also by participating in her own tales. In the majority of these, she acts as a "supernatural consultant," advising on hauntings and other troubling events. However, later tales begin to reduce her to a bookending role, and by 1980 her appearances are all reprints, not just of previous Gypsy Rose tales but also of old Strange Stories from *Tammy* and *June*, where the Storyteller's panels are simply replaced with ones featuring Rose. After *Jinty* merges with *Tammy* on November 28, 1981, the Storyteller and Gypsy Rose rotate as hosts of the Strange Story slot (with new material) until July 1982, when the slot is rebranded as a "Tammy Complete Story" with no narrator. The Storyteller appears once more, in "The Fireside Friend" (a "Tammy Complete Story," December 15, 1982), which he opens with a warm welcome and closes with questions, but after this he vanishes quietly.

As well as these liminal host figures, many girls' comics serials had their own dedicated storytellers. I call these characters serial hosts, as they are confined to a particular serial story. The first of these that I have found is Jackie Flynn, the narrator of "Bridget at War," who first appears in *Diana* #146 (December 4, 1965). Jackie bookends all ten episodes of this serial story, where he addresses the reader directly and sometimes interjects comments. He has an anecdotal style with a slightly acerbic edge and is also a somewhat ghostly presence compared to the depiction of the main events, as he is drawn in pencils only and (aside from the opening sequence) against an empty background.

Other later examples of the serial host in the 1970s and 1980s include "Madame Marlova Remembers," in which Madame instructs her pupils with inspirational stories of famous ballerinas (*Debbie*); Miss Hatherleigh, the caretaker of "Cremond Castle" (*Spellbound*, *Nikki*); Megan Dolwyn, who tells customers the histories of her dolls in "Dolwyn's Dolls" (*Bunty*); Tamsin Treco's grandmother in "A Tale from the Toy Museum" (*Bunty*); Beverley Jackson, who knows the story behind every button in "The Button Box" (*Tammy*); and Jade Jenkins

(*M&J*), whose Saturday bring-and-buy stall is made up of objects that all have stories to tell.[3] Briony Coote names this category of stories the "Collective Storyteller," as the tales often come from a collection of sorts, but I find the term "serial hosts" a better fit, since many do not have a physical collection of objects, and also because "collective" confuses the issue by implying they are multiple. These characters differ from the series host because they are confined to a particular storyworld, although they may then tell a number of unrelated embedded stories.

Both types of host problematize the boundaries between fiction and reality, and the series host in particular is a liminal figure, as the host's status within the diegesis or storyworld is uncertain. Jones (2015) argues that the function of the host character is to tell the reader how to read the story, drawing attention to the way in which the EC hosts reframed the frightening events as schlock comedy. In this light, the differences between the British host characters are interesting. Whereas they all address the reader directly with introductions and background at the start of the tale, their treatment of the story's end varies. They can raise questions, provide explanations, offer morals, or interfere with plot events. They may step in and out of the diegesis, address the reader directly, break the borders between the text and paratext (e.g., by introducing elaborately drawn story titles in their dialogue), and have speech that shifts back and forth between different representational forms (such as narrative boxes and speech balloons), gives way to unassigned narration, or appears in different layers of story (for a full discussion, see Round 2014a, chap. 7). In this sense, their role can be read as Gothic, as it echoes the textual strategies used in novels such as *Frankenstein*, which contains multiple narrative frames (Captain Walton's letter to his sister retells the story told to him by Victor Frankenstein; Frankenstein's story contains the creature's story; and the creature's story contains the story of the DeLaceys. These layers collapse when the characters meet in the Arctic). The transgressions of expected diegetic boundaries and the embedded nature of the told stories support a Gothic reading of the host character.

As recurring characters, the hosts of girls' comics also helped to shape the distinct identity of each publication. This was complemented by the comics' use of girls' names as titles, which were often then attached to a "cover girl" image, editorial message, or other feature. For example, *June* labeled its letters page "June's Postbag," accompanied by a drawing of a dark-haired girl. When the comic merged into *Tammy* in 1974, June took her place on the cover as Tammy's younger sister (Tammy is the older blonde girl, and June becomes a blonde with pigtails). They have a dramatized story in one issue circa 1978, but their appearances are otherwise limited to the paratext of the cover. The characters behind some of the other titles are less well defined, although still implied. *Jinty*'s earliest issues include the header "Jinty's Bits and Pieces" on the letters and puzzle page, and her existence is also suggested by features such as a crafts page that says, "Jinty Made It Herself . . . so can you!" (*Jinty* #14, August 10, 1974). However, there is no space that presents Jinty as a character who speaks to us. A year later, only "Jinty's Bits and Pieces" remains, and after the merger with *Lindy* (November 8, 1975), even this is removed. Before its merger into *Jinty*, *Lindy* also had a similar host, who greets us on the first letters page ("Lindy's Letter Box"), where she confesses, "I'm pretty nervous writing this, my very first letter to you all, but the Ed. said that as the paper's named after me, I'd better have the first say." A photograph of a young teenager accompanies this message, and it is the only contact we have with Lindy, although the editorial "Laurie's Life" (also accompanied by a photograph of "Laurie," an older teenager) frequently refers to Lindy, claiming that the two share an office and work on the comic together. The tactic is developed by DC Thomson's "Supercats," who appear in their own weekly strip and also present a separate double-page spread in each issue of *Spellbound*, where one of the team addresses readers directly and invites them to join the Supercats Club (the page has competitions, letters, a code-breaking message, and features such as exercises or recipes). The comics' identities are reinforced in peripheral spaces like this, and *Misty* uses a similar strategy.

MISTY'S ORIGINS AND FUNCTION

That IPC's new mystery comic for girls should have a host character was the suggestion of its subeditor Bill Harrington:

> Bill thought, because we used to have a storyteller in *Tammy*, and I think before that in *School Friend*—it's quite an old idea of having a storyteller—he thought it'd be quite nice if we got some sort of a guide, a figure who can direct what we're doing and tell the kids what's going to happen next. . . . I think his character was Nathan somebody. He seemed to be a fairly spooky-looking character. We put this down as one of the ideas. Gradually as we had a few ideas, we did take them to John Sanders and the directors, but Nathan was thought to be far too creepy and potentially a child molester; they didn't like the idea of him at all! (Prigmore 2016a)

The idea for Misty as this host appeared after the comic's name was decided, and so the character came about almost "by accident" (Cunningham 2017). Pat Mills (2016a) acknowledges that "the credit for the character of Misty comes from Wilf Prigmore," and she was ably visualized by Shirley Bellwood as an embodiment of feminine mystique and dark beauty. As well as conjuring an image of Gothic and mystery, rather than outright horror, Misty performed a number of functions within each issue. She is a mix of cover girl and host, and her official role is as the comic's fictional editor, like Tharg the Mighty One from 2000AD. In *Misty*'s original weekly run, she never bookends a story, although she often does so in the specials, the annuals, and in *Tammy and Misty* after the merger. These appearances are presumably to replace the opening panels of stories taken from older sources.[4] They are mostly taken from Shirley Bellwood's artwork: for example, the introductory panel to "Prince of Lightning" (Annual 1981) is a cropped image from the inside cover of *Misty* #38.

When Misty does introduce or close a tale, her function is consistently questioning, and thus quite different from the Ghoulunatics and the other girls' comics hosts. For example, in "The Sea Maid" (Holiday Special 1979), Misty opens the tale by narrating: "Anne Goodwin and her mother had been invited to spend a few weeks with friends who lived on the rocky Cornish coast." The friends tell Anne the myth of the Sea Maid, a Siren who tricks sailors into crashing their boats on the nearby Wreck Island. Anne hears voices one night and rescues two twin girls from the island, only then to be told by the girl's mother that she couldn't have heard them cry for help, as both are dumb. The final panel then has Misty wrap up the tale, asking, "Did Anne hear anything on that night? Anne is convinced that she did, just as she is sure that the stories of the Sea Maid 'luring sailors to their doom' are all wrong. Perhaps the voice was the Sea Maid's way of proving her innocence by saving two lives!"

Here Misty fulfills one of the functions of the EC hosts—offering explanations and reassurance—but with a feminist twist, as she digs deeper into the story to defend the reputation of the Sea Maid, rather than adding an ironic distance from the tale's events. In addition, her tone is quite different: she is neither humorous nor patronizing, and she addresses readers on their level, rather than as boys and girls (or "boils and ghouls" in EC-speak). Puns do exist in *Misty* (e.g., "mummy" [#19], "green fingers" [#2], and "scared of her shadow" [#58]), but they take place within the story, not as a form of external mockery as in EC's comics ("The two men refused to swallow Old Coley's story, and so . . . heh, heh, they got swallowed up instead" ["Terror in the Swamp," *Vault of Horror* #15]). While the Ghoulunatics' joking summaries and terrible puns provided closure, Misty's own contribution is less definite in both content and phrasing, raising questions and uncertainties ("perhaps"). In "Curse of the Roman Sword" (Holiday Special 1979), she also runs counter to the official "truth" and raises questions rather than providing answers, saying: "Most are sheer superstition, but the story of Moira Turner makes one think." In "Melody from the Past" (Holiday Special 1980), Misty's epilogue again only raises questions: "Did she hear a piano playing that stormy night—or was it merely 'dream' music?"

Jones points out that the Ghoulunatics also took on the role of editors and responded to readers, as well as introducing and ending the stories and sometime appearing in frontispieces, "inviting readers into the magazine" (134). This is the closest parallel to Misty's most dominant function, which is to welcome us to the issue every week. However, in contrast to the Ghoulunatics, IPC developed Misty into a person whom readers desperately wanted to know more about (see chap. 13), with an entire world and character being slowly unveiled. In Misty's introduction to the first issue (scripted by Wilf Prigmore and hand-lettered by Jack Cunningham), she teases, "Perhaps one day I'll tell you my story..." Prigmore admits that the team had no idea whatsoever what her story would be at this point, and the fragments of information that appeared in her responses on the letters pages and her introductions were made up on an ad hoc basis. "The first two or three issues, we really didn't know quite what she was. We'd really thought she was dead, but we'd be playing for time, thinking, 'What are we going to do with it?'" (Prigmore 2016a).

Misty represents the Gothic of her era.[5] Her ghostly appearance recalls the contemporary New Age witch, who Nick Freeman (2016, 746) claims was a "significant aspect of countercultural life in Britain" in the 1960s. He argues that witchcraft features heavily in early modern writing (folklore, children's literature, and fantasy) and, when present in later texts, is often modernized in some way ("in the service of ecology, feminism, spiritual renewal, and personal development")—noting that the "good witch" frequently appears in the Gothic film (2016, 745–46). Misty's long black hair, flowing robes, and star charm necklace all fit with this image, and she almost always appears in a wild, natural environment (such as the sea, a lake, forest, or mountain) or sometimes among ruins or rocks.

Roper (2012, 6) points out that "the wildness of mountains and deserted landscapes . . . became part of the iconography of witchcraft," and "journeys featured, too, in the stories of witches' flight." Misty's welcomes are notable for drawing extensively on images of the body and the journey, as we are constantly urged to "walk," "journey," "quest," "venture," "step," or "follow" Misty elsewhere—crossing, it is implied, into another world. Punter (2017, 94) also argues that the witch reminds us "of the undecidable. . . . [She] has rather to do with transient, becoming, halting, temporary, liminal states." *Misty*'s realm and her physical status are both left undefined, a transitional place where she is simultaneously both elsewhere, and "always with you."

Roper (2012, 3) argues that the witch is "symbolically and psychologically capacious" and can be morally ambiguous and strongly attractive despite her association with evil (in this instance, the dangers of Misty's realm, within which she exists as a reassuring presence). Misty's gentle and attractive qualities are a clear demonstration of the 1970s reclamation of the witch from the "universal metaphor" (Germanà 2013, 64) that it had become under patriarchal control. Rather than a wizened or threatening figure characterized by either androgynous sterility or ferocious sexuality, the New Age or pagan witch was strongly associated with nature, tranquillity, and spirituality. Whereas "the [traditional] witch's abnormality is arguably linked to her anti-maternal function" (65), Misty is consistently shown in natural and fertile surroundings. Although her welcomes in each issue do not quite position her as Earth Mother, she is consistently framed as a friend who guides with care and concern.

Because of this approach, a great deal of the comic's appeal was Misty herself; unlike the Man in Black, Damian Darke, the Storyteller, or even Gypsy Rose, Misty is a companion and role model for readers, and her presence goes beyond framing stories in a few panels. Not intimidating in any way, she was intended to be a "calm" and "reassuring" presence (Prigmore 2016a). In a sense, she is both present and absent in the comic, as although she doesn't appear in any of its main run of stories and was late to arrive on the cover, her words frame each issue and respond to selected letters, and her image appears more than once. This, along with her witch-like appearance, also helps to shape her as a ghostly and magical presence, in an undefined and liminal realm, which is further enhanced by the visuals and lexis of her weekly welcome.

MISTY'S GOTHIC IMAGERY AND LANGUAGE

Throughout the weekly issues, Shirley Bellwood's artwork, Misty's welcome (scripted by the editors), and her brief responses to letters are really our only contact with the character. The annuals and specials offer a little more access to Misty, as she bookends fifteen stories and even appears in four text stories (Annuals 1982, 1983, 1985, and 1986), as well as some additional features and even interviews (Holiday Special 1980, Annual 1982).

As noted, Bellwood produced a total of ten color paintings and fifty-four black-and-white drawings of Misty.[6] The drawings appear on the inside covers of the weekly issues and are delicate sketches that often feature extensive dot work. Rather than being reminiscent of comics' Benday dots (used for coloring and exploited in Roy Lichtenstein's pop art series), these instead give an ethereal air, and perhaps one could even say that comics style is being subverted here. The paintings appear on the covers of seven of the eight annuals (1980–86) and as posters in all three of the specials (also appearing on their covers in 1979 and 1980). A letter from Norman Worker dated October 10, 1984, refers to Bellwood's final painting of Misty, saying, "It is no exaggeration to say that it brought a lump to my throat. Your beautiful painting says goodbye—I believe it is the best of the many superb Mistys you have done—and there is sadness there, quite unmistakably" (Worker 1984). The painting uses darker hues than all of Bellwood's previous ones, and Misty's raised hand is perhaps waving goodbye to us. Misty also appears on the cover of fourteen weekly issues in color, as well as in two games, two calendars, and two sets of Christmas cards, all adapted from Bellwood's black-and-white inside-cover drawings.[7] Like the other *Misty* covers, which blow up single panels from stories, these would have been cropped and colored in house, and some of the images are also reused (with more dramatic neon coloring) as the covers for the eight *Best of Misty Monthly* comics that were released in 1986 (fig. 7.1).

Although the inside covers seem different, there are in fact only fifty-four different base images, and only twenty of these are unique (i.e., appear only once).[8] The rest are duplicates that have been reworked in some way (cropped, tilted, mirrored, or even combined), each between one and five times. The reuse begins early: #6 is the first issue to reuse a previous image by cropping a section from #2. As the comic continues, the repetition is sometimes quite blatant: for example, #14 crops and mirror-flips the previous week's image (#13) with an additional bat. In other instances, the manipulation can be quite complicated: for example, #88 takes Misty's face from #18 and the moon and sea background from #57 (fig. 7.2). The last unique piece of art appears in #81, and the final new piece of art appears in #83 (and is then reused in #94). The majority of reused images come from the first twenty issues, although certain later images are also popular picks for reuse: #36 (where Misty appears beside a moonlit pool and is framed by weeping willows; see fig. 7.3) is used four times in all.

Table 7.1 shows the breakdown of reused images. In addition to the ninety-nine issues represented, there is one issue where Miss T delivers the inside-cover greeting (#91), and one issue where this welcome is absent (#48). In fact, December 1978 seems to have been a particularly problematic month, as no greeting text appears in four consecutive issues (#45, #46, #47, and #48), and no new inside-cover images appear during this time. As noted, #48 omits Misty entirely and launches straight into "Hush, Hush, Sweet Rachel."

Although the altered versions may emphasize different connotations (e.g., cropping out wider nature scenes in favor of focusing on Misty herself), looking closely at the corpus of fifty-four original images seems more likely to avoid false conclusions based on repetition. As part of the research project supported by the CsJCC and conducted by Paul Fisher Davies, different nodes were tagged in each image, relating to Misty's pose, her shown features, and the background details. An example is shown in figure 7.3, accompanied by table 7.2, which lists in order of frequency the twenty most common nodes. The columns refer to the number of individual tags, the number of pages on which they feature, and aggregate totals of both. Where appropriate, nodes combine totals from more detailed subcategories: for example, "foliage" covers tags such as branches, leaves, grass, and flowers.

OUR FRIEND OF THE MISTS 137

Figure 7.1a. Inside cover of *Misty* #53. Reproduced with permission of Misty™ Rebellion Publishing IP Ltd.; copyright © Rebellion Publishing IP Ltd., all rights reserved.

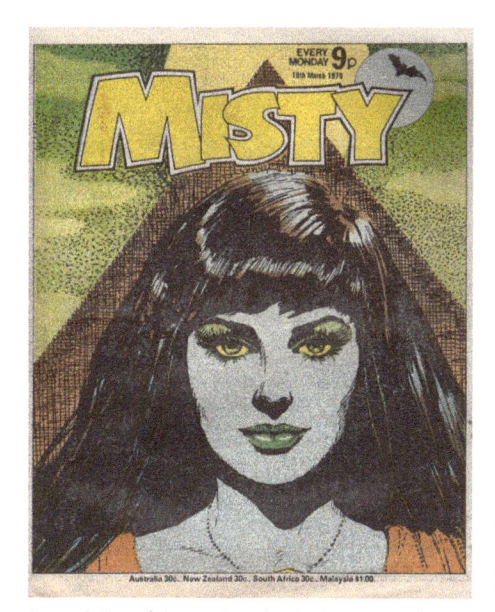

Figure 7.1b. Cover of *Misty* #57. Reproduced with permission of Misty™ Rebellion Publishing IP Ltd.; copyright © Rebellion Publishing IP Ltd., all rights reserved.

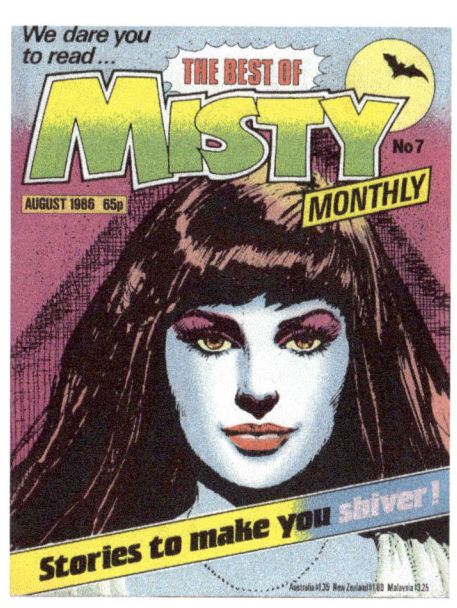

Figure 7.1c. Cover of *The Best of Misty Monthly* #7. Reproduced with permission of Misty™ Rebellion Publishing IP Ltd.; copyright © Rebellion Publishing IP Ltd., all rights reserved.

138 OUR FRIEND OF THE MISTS

Figure 7.2a. Inside cover of *Misty* #18. Reproduced with permission of Misty™ Rebellion Publishing IP Ltd.; copyright © Rebellion Publishing IP Ltd., all rights reserved.

Figure 7.2b. Inside cover of *Misty* #57. Reproduced with permission of Misty™ Rebellion Publishing IP Ltd.; copyright © Rebellion Publishing IP Ltd., all rights reserved.

Figure 7.2c. Inside cover of *Misty* #88. Reproduced with permission of Misty™ Rebellion Publishing IP Ltd.; copyright © Rebellion Publishing IP Ltd., all rights reserved.

Table 7.1. Reuse of inside cover base images.

Times Used	Issue #	Number of Base Images	Total Images Produced
Used once	1; 3; 4; 5; 8; 17; 19; 21; 23; 29; 32; 34; 35; 37; 41; 50; 62; 68; 77; 81	20	20
Used twice	2 + 6; 7 + 10; 12 + 85; 16 + 44; 20 + 64; 22 + 60; 24 + 38; 25 + 43; 26 + 95; 28 + 51; 30 + 98; 31 + 47; 33 + 39; 40 + 66; 42 + 70; 49 + 63; 53 + 101; 54 + 71; 56 + 80; 57 + 84; 58 + 75; 61 + 92; 65 + 89; 69 + 100; 76 + 82; 78 + 86; 83 + 94; 87 + 93	28	56
Used three times	9 + 52 + 73; 15 + 46 + 79	2	6
Used four times	13 + 14 + 27 + 67; 18 + 45 + 88 + 96; 36 + 55 + 74 + 90	3	12
Used five times	11 + 59 + 72 + 97 + 99	1	5
Total		54	99

To look first at Misty herself, we can see that her pose and appearance are frequently obscured in some way: her full body appears less than half the time (in just twenty of fifty-four images), and she may appear translucent or hide some part of her face (in profile, tilted, sideways, or shadowed). Sometimes she avoids eye contact entirely. Her appearance is extremely feminized: hair wisps appear on nearly all the pages (and are abundant within these, as sixty-one separate nodes were coded across forty-three pages); her neckline features nearly half the time, and her star necklace almost as often. Although her full body appears just twenty times, and her feet are never shown, her hands feature significantly more (a theme that is backed up by the analysis of her language and its themes of touching and feeling, as I will explore).

Moving on to her surroundings, Gothic symbols unsurprisingly dominate here, with bats being the most frequent (although they are not numerous or flocking and generally appear either singly or in pairs). Other background features are similarly eerie but also strongly naturalized and feminized, such as the moon (whose shape is sometimes duplicated or used to frame text) and stars (like the bats, stars are most often found in isolation, rather than covering the night sky). Other natural features shown are mist lines, clouds, and foliage. Water is a recurring theme, whether pools, waterfalls, or droplets, and is sometimes complemented further by features such as shells, starfish, rushes, and water lilies.

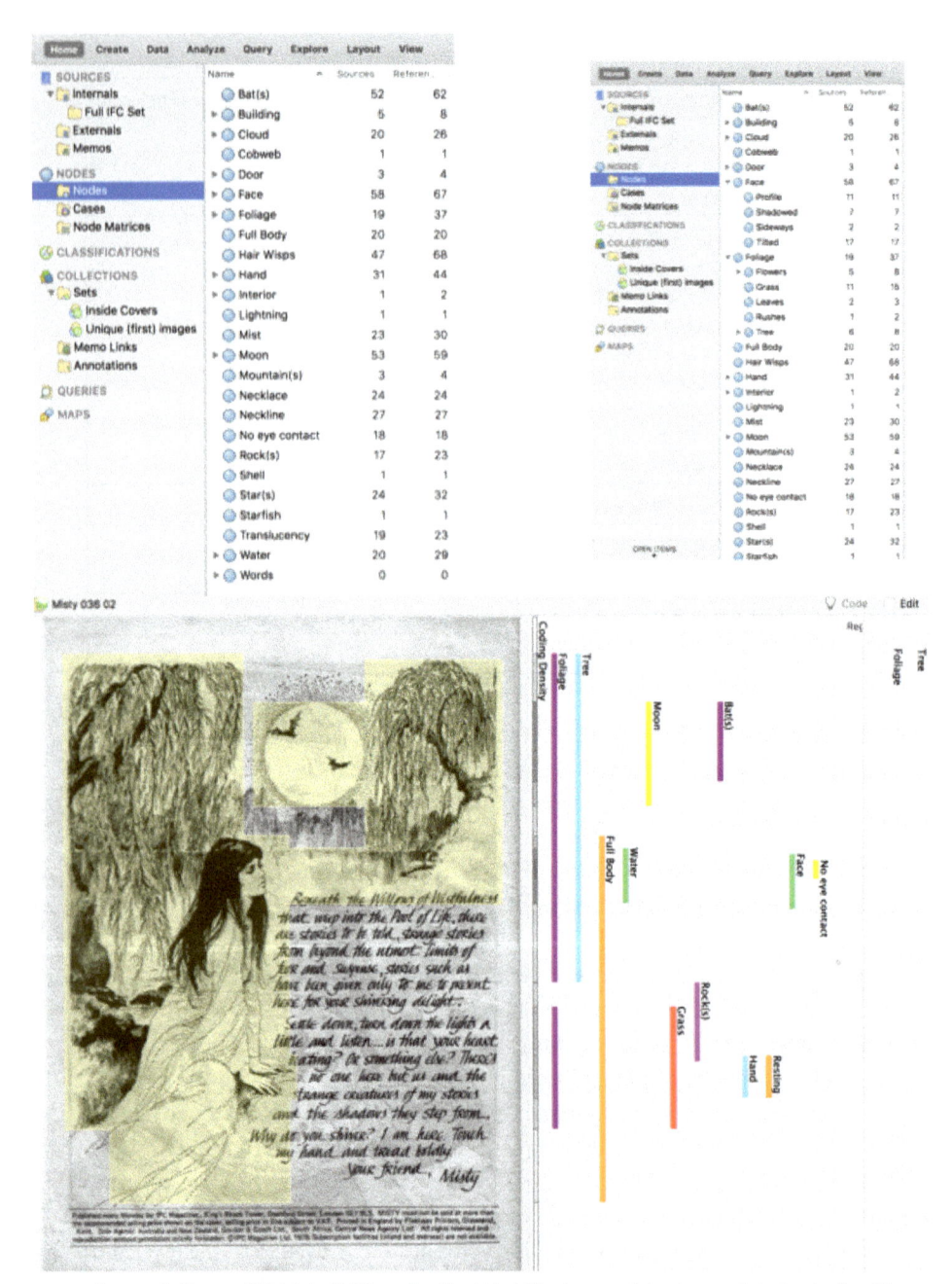

Figure 7.3. Inside cover of *Misty* #36 with NVivo coding. *Top right*: additional screengrab showing unpacked categories (face, foliage). Courtesy of Paul Fisher Davies. Reproduced with permission of Misty™ Rebellion Publishing IP Ltd.; copyright © Rebellion Publishing IP Ltd., all rights reserved.

Table 7.2. The twenty most common visual nodes tagged on inside covers.

Nodes	Number of Pages Tagged	Number of Tags	Aggregate Number of Tags	Aggregate Number of Pages Tagged
Bat(s)	48	58	58	48
Moon	48	49	53	49
Hair wisps	43	61	61	43
Face	28	28	63	54
Neckline	25	25	25	25
Star(s)	24	32	32	24
Necklace	24	24	24	24
Hand	23	30	44	31
Mist	20	27	27	20
Full body	20	20	20	20
Water	19	26	28	19
Translucency	19	23	23	19
No eye contact	18	18	18	18
Rock(s)	17	23	23	17
Face\Tilted	16	16	16	16
Cloud	14	17	25	19
Hand\Resting	12	14	14	12
Foliage\Grass	11	15	15	11
Face\Profile	11	11	11	11
Cloud\Cumulus	7	8	8	7

While the natural strongly dominates, a sense of time and history is also emphasized through ancient features such as rocks (see table 7.2) and mountains (four instances across three pages). Also present are ruins (two pages), cobwebs (one page), and ancient sites such as Stonehenge (two pages). Buildings and human constructions appear rarely (five pages in total) and when present are often in decay or juxtaposed against the natural world. The only interior features present are also self-consciously Gothic: doors (three pages) and keyholes (once), heavy curtains (once), and staircases (once). In this way, visual tropes of Gothic, the natural, the ancient, and the obscured dominate the inside covers throughout.

As well as our glimpses of Misty, the poetic greeting she offers also sets the tone for the issue, which is noted by reader Elizabeth Tring (#84), who says: "The letter you put at the beginning is good because it sets you in the right scary atmosphere to read your stories." The language and appearance of these welcome letters can also be analyzed fruitfully. Initially written by editor Wilf Prigmore and then taken over by Malcolm Shaw and Bill Harrington (Prigmore 2016a), the lexis has a mystical tone and often challenges the reader or urges her to take action in some way. Cunningham's calligraphy complements this by giving a genteel and personal air. Issue #36 (fig. 7.3) contains an exemplary address, as follows:

> Beneath the Willows of Wistfulness that weep into the Pool of Life, there are stories to be told, strange stories from beyond the utmost limits of fear and suspense, stories such as have been given only to me to present here for your shivering delight.
>
> Settle down, turn down the lights a little and listen . . . is that your heart beating? Or something else? There's no one here but us and the strange creatures of my stories and the shadows they step from. Why do you shiver? I am here. Touch my hand and tread boldly.
>
> Your friend, Misty

The alliteration of key words such as "suspense," "strange," "shivering," and "shadows" sets the thematic tone for the contents and helps frame the issue as something to be explored and overcome. The greeting also contains a strong sense of place (the "Willows of Wistfulness" and the "Pool of Life") and instantly immerses readers in these new and mysterious locations, asking them to "settle down" and "listen" (which in this instance sits a little oddly against "turn down the lights," blurring a sense of place between self and Other). There is a strong sense of embodiment ("heart," "hand"), and Misty herself is a reassuring, guiding presence ("I am here"). She addresses readers on their level ("Your friend, Misty") and can even be read as supplicative (as she "present[s]" stories for the reader's "delight"). The reader is being questioned ("Is that your heart beating?" "Why do you shiver?") and challenged ("Touch my hand and tread boldly").

Extending this analysis to the corpus as a whole is illuminating.[9] Readers are constantly being urged to do something, and the comic is presented as an elsewhere location for them to explore. "Can" and "dare" feature prominently, and "you" dominates in the phrasing: "you [too] can" appears eight times, and "we can" is used four times and "I can" just twice. Thus the welcomes make ongoing linguistic attempts to link Misty with the reader and to present her as a guide or companion. On two occasions, she greets us as "my sisters of the mist" (#29, #39) and once as her "children" (#84). Analyzing "dare" and "will" across the entire corpus reveals a link with Gothic metaphors such as the journey. As well as being dared to read the comic's contents, the reader is challenged to "be my companion" (#66, Summer Special 1978), to "brave the midnight way" (#69), and to "tread boldly" (#36, #51), "softly" (#42), "warily" (#54, #57), or "fearlessly" (#79). The comic is defined as an otherworldly location as we are invited to "journey" with Misty (#88, #98), to "quest" (#14), or to "venture" (#11, #12, #16, #20, #49, #66, #69, Holiday Special 1979, #90) along "misty ways" (#37, #93), "unknown paths," or "untrodden ways" (#40). These metaphors function in addition to simple invitations to "come with me" (#25, #35, #43, #51) or "follow me" (#42, #56, #79, #97). Verbs such as "step" (#34, #36, #40, #49, #50, #53, #63, #70, #77, #80, #83, #85, #89, Holiday Special 1980) and "walk" (#58, #80, #84) also feature prominently and are used to give a sense of Otherness of place: for example, "Step into another world with me" (#70). "Step into the unknown with . . ." is also a common cover strapline (used on the covers of issues #15, #19, #22, #29, #32, #72, #73, #87).

The Otherness of place is further enhanced through Misty's references to a number of distinct locations within her realm. These are the Cavern of Dreams (#7, #19, #24, #29, #30, #91), the Pool of Life (#3, #5, #16, #36, #62, #82), the Mountains of Mystery (#28), the Willows of Wistfulness (#36), the Gate of the Year (#49), the Wilderness of Willows (#55, #90), the Sea of Solitude (#84), the Stones of Sanctuary (#42), the Doorway to the Dawn (#21), the Sands of Time (#23), and the Land of Beyond-and-Beware (#89). The use of capitalization demarcates these places from more general references such as the "shadow way" or the "land of nightmare." Their lexis is strongly alliterative, and many are somewhat clichéd. When these phrases are used in the greetings, they are also often accompanied by an image that reinforces their meaning, which suggests that the editor devised them based on the image selected for the inside cover that week. For example, all the references to willows show Misty alongside some willows, the Gate of the Year shows her gazing through a broken stone window frame or gateposts, and the Doorway to the Dawn is depicted as an arch of rock. A blurring of her world and ours also takes place around these locations, as real places may be drawn and renamed, such as Stonehenge ("The Stones of Sanctuary," #42) or the Durdle Door coastal rocks in Dorset (inspiring the "Doorway to the Dawn," #21; and the "sands of solitude," #38). These doublings of place seem very Gothic and stress the metaphorical nature of Misty's realm.

Gothic references to the body also appear as we are invited numerous times to "touch" Misty, most often her hand (#31, #36, #56, #68, Holiday Special 1979, #93), or to "take" her hand (#21, #63, #69, #88, #89, Holiday Special 1980). "Touch" appears five additional times and is most often related to "you" (#95) or "the followers of Misty" (#65), along with other sensory experiences such as "ice-cold touch" (#82) or "fingers of ice that touch your spine so you can catch your breath" (#52). Eyes feature six times: we are invited to look into Misty's eyes three times, but equally to adopt her position ourselves, for example, "take a look at things through my eyes—the eyes of Misty" (#6). The repetition of "eyes" in this sentence reinforces the symbol, and the reader is invited to occupy the position of both self and Other, another instance of doubling.

In nearly all the greetings, the reader is constantly being urged or challenged to take action of some type, even if it is simply to "behold" or "marvel" or, more prosaically, "write," "read," "listen," or "place an order." Only five greetings place the reader in an object grammatical position, and even these still directly involve the reader. For example: "Out of the mists I come to take you by the hand into the world of shadows" (#60), or "once again I wait to guide you through the midnight lands of shadows and suspense" (#64).[10]

In general, the lexical choices made are revealing, and table 7.3 below displays the fifty most common words used in the inside-cover greetings. Unsurprisingly, the most common word is "misty," which appears more than twice as often as the second-most used word, which is "mist" (!). We might expect the word "misty" to dominate, since she signs her name every week, and of course discounting these ninety-five instances reduces the total significantly.[11] The appearance of "friend" is also interesting; however, Misty only signs herself "Your friend [and guide] [of the mists]" on fifty-seven occasions, and so this word's dominance is not solely due to her characteristic sign-off. However, taking these facts into account means that "world" then becomes a highly dominant feature of her greeting, thus stressing the sense of place that has already been discussed. The greetings also emphasize time (week, coming/waiting), and the other choices are also notable for indicating dualities often found in the Gothic, such as the tension between coming and waiting and an emphasis on the seen/unseen (look/shadows, mysteries).

Nonetheless, on some occasions, the mask slips (as it were), and jarring references to material aspects of the comic (such as the free game or Christmas cards) or specific stories appear (see, e.g., #29, #30, #32, #44). Analyzing the phrasing closely in this manner suggests that #76 may be the work of a different voice, as the long sentence of additive clauses without punctuation seems cumbersome, and the usual poetry is lost. Perhaps this is the point at which Shaw retired as editor and Norman Worker took over:

> I move in many mystic circles seeking always the spine-tingling shudders of true nightmare and believe I have found an extraordinary blend of suspense and fright in a new serial beginning very soon about a very unusual horse which I urge you not to miss.
> Till our next misty meeting,
> Misty
> (#76)

Although many of the word choices used here are common to the greeting lexis (e.g., "spine-tingling" and "shudder"), there are words that are only used here: strikingly these include "believe" and "urge." We could perhaps suggest that the reader's belief or faith is never called into question otherwise. A similar disruption occurs in issues #29 and #30, which (along with #91, discussed hereafter) are the only instances of the word "issue" and in which the contraction "I've" also appears:

> Greetings my sisters of the mists,
> While every issue of Misty is shiverful of mystery and menace that nobody else can bring you, and this issue certainly has its share of strange shapes in the shadows and heart-stopping surprises, just a word about next week's offering.
> That will be a very special issue of Misty in which TWO serials begin and I've devised a game in which every one of you will at last be able to join me in the Cavern of Dreams. Think of that!
> You simply can't afford to miss it,
> Misty
> (#29)

In contrast to the other greetings, these two instances engage the reader in more fiscal terms, such as "urge you not to miss" and "you simply can't afford." The closing exclamation point also seems more in keeping with contemporary language than Misty's usual idiom, and contractions in general are rare in her speech. "I'll" appears only four times in the entire run, and a more poetic, timeless tone is achieved by using full modal verbs such as "I shall," "I/you will," "I/you must," and so on.

The other departure from Misty's seductive and ethereal welcomes occurs in #91, where Miss T instead greets us:

> As it's trick or treat time Misty thought it'd be quite a trick for me to give you all a treat and join my friends in the great Hallowe'en party in her Cavern of Dreams while she's out polishing up the monsters and grabbing the ghouls for this week's weirdly wonderful, tremendously terrifying and shudderingly spine-tingling Hallowe'en issue of Misty.
> Your witch of the whimseys,
> Miss T

Again contractions are used ("it'd," "she's"), and colloquial slang ("grabbing," "weirdly"), and "issue" appears again. Miss T's alliteration is more direct than Misty's (pairing words together, rather than periodically returning to the same alliterative letter), and the effect is lessened. Joe Collins's art on this page also emphasizes the chaotic and overblown, as a gaggle of overlaid monsters accompany Miss T.

The words that dominate the greetings ("mist," "world," "shadows," "mystery"), and the recurring images of other worlds and the body are a clear fit with Gothic themes. My opening definition of Gothic noted its tendencies toward the hidden, unseen, and unknown, represented here by the visual and verbal references to "shadows" and "mist." Gothic's ability to both disturb and appeal is also conveyed in these pages, along with its transgressive and seductive qualities, as Misty invites us to cross over to another place with her, promising us frights and delights in equal measure.

Searching for terms related to the Gothic concepts of haunting, excess, and the unseen also produces interesting results and is particularly relevant to this study, as my own formalist approach to comics is based on these three key Gothic tropes (Round 2014a). In this model, I approach the comics page layout using the concepts of haunting (or temporal or spatial disruption), excess (or artificiality), and the crypt (or the Other or unseen). Considering the findings with this framework in mind is illuminating. Misty's invitations to follow her or otherwise move elsewhere can be seen as a disruption of place, and the greeting from #36 cited earlier in particular blurs the lines between the reader's space and Misty's own (combining the request to "turn down the lights" with her location at the Pool of Life).

Her lexis emphasizes time and place, and alongside the dominant use of "world," the journey motif suggests that she is constantly leaving/returning from some "domain" that is other than where the reader is. This is strongly linked to temporality, where terms such as "coming," "waiting," and "week" dominate, and "time," "night," and "now" also appear frequently (see table 7.3). Looking at common word stems around the theme of time is interesting: "hour" collocates to "witching," "misty," or "midnight" most often, instilling a sense of mystery and dread; but "waiting" refers to Misty herself more than twice as often as it does to "monsters" or other terrors, which counterbalances this. "Once" collocates to "again" or "more" in every instance except one ("never shiver more than once," #63). As such it gives a sense of cyclical temporality: we do these things "once again" and "once more"—reinforcing the eternal, otherworldly state. I have discussed in other work how a view of time as potentially static or cyclical characterizes the page layouts and contents of many comics narratives (see, e.g., Round 2013; 2014a, chaps. 3 and 7), and chapters 11 and 12 of this book also explore the construction of timelessness in *Misty*'s story content.

Connotations of excess are also apparent in the usage of words such as "all" and "every," which emphasize some emblematic terms. A common usage of "all" links a number of Gothic phrases, including "all the children of the mists gathered together" (#26), "all the creeping creatures of the shadows" (#81), "all the dwellers of darkness and those who move in mystery" (#25), "all the fear and fright" (#81), "all the mists of time" (#12), and "all the secrets of time and all the tales of unknown things" (#34). The named entities conjure suitably Gothic tones, and, tellingly, "all the other creatures of the night" (#37) and "all the other denizens of the shadows" (#82) are also named—bringing in the Gothic Other and also the impression of a vast horde of additional creatures. There are also frequent references to unnamed terrors, when, for example, "all" collocates to "all that is breathtaking and spine-tingling" (#17), "all that has come creeping here" (#35), "all that is eerie, weird and frightful" (#34), "all that lurks in the long shadows" (#75), and "all that move in the moonlight stillness" (#41). "Most" collocates to "secret" (or "dark and secret") every time it is used (#50, #69, #94), and "utmost" links to "breathtaking and spinetingling" (#17) and "utmost limits of fear and suspense" (#36) on the two occasions it appears. "Every" is more prosaic in focusing mainly on the material level of production and the readers themselves, for example, "every [single] one of you" (#29, #30), "every week" (#6, #35, #74), "every letter" (#1, #3, #4), "every issue" (#29). However, "every" does also bring in some Gothic elements, such as "every dark corner" (#79) or "every corner where the darkness lies" (#88), "every faceless fear" (#20), "every footstep" (#85), "every whisper and shadow" (#98), and "every thrill's a chill" (#1). In these instances, notions of excess are used to emphasize Gothic themes, and particularly to draw attention to great masses of beings ("all the other . . .") and unnamed or hidden things ("all that lurks," "darkness," "faceless," "shadow").

These usages also emphasize the unseen, which is the key feature of the crypt. "Look" is a common word, and readers are asked to "look [up]on" "shadows" (#68, #75), "terrors" (#69, #72), "[the] mysteries [and marvels]" (#9, #12, #40, #58), "horrors and monsters and mysteries" (#95), "nameless monsters" (#89), "that which is OTHER" (#25), "the THINGS" (#87), "the creatures of the night" (#21), and "the shuddermakers" (#31). All these instances are threatening (only slightly counterbalanced by the inclusion of "marvels"), and the only positive examples are "the wonders of the other side of midnight" (#93) and "into the mystic waters" (#82). In addition, all this looking is done by the reader, rather than Misty herself, and only the moon otherwise "looks down" (#32). Seeing is thus a device to engage the reader that is often combined with fear and the unknown as it collocates to the unnamed in my earlier analysis. This is further emphasized by two instances where the reader is advised to "look behind you" (#17) or "look over your shoulder" (#86).

The unseen and hiddenness are also apparent in Misty's appearance. As noted, the delicate lines and dots of the inside-cover drawings often depict her as transparent, and she is frequently shadowed (e.g., in profile or with half her face obscured) or appearing in mist. Her appearance never includes feet,

Table 7.3. The fifty most common word stems used on the inside cover greeting.

Rank	Word	Count	Weighted Percentage	Including
1	misty	146	4.31%	misty
2	mists	70	2.07%	mist, mists
3	friend	68	2.01%	friend, friendly, friends
4	world	50	1.48%	world, worlds
5	shadows	44	1.30%	shadow, shadowed, shadows
6	week	44	1.30%	week, weekly, weeks
7	comes	39	1.15%	come, comes
8	mysteries	34	1.00%	mysteries, mysterious, mystery
9	waiting	33	0.97%	wait, waited, waiting
10	look	31	0.91%	look, looked, looking, looks
11	story	31	0.91%	stories, story
12	midnight	30	0.89%	midnight, midnights
13	fears	29	0.86%	fear, fearful, fearfulness, fears
14	time	28	0.83%	time, times
15	moon	26	0.77%	moon
16	tales	24	0.71%	tales
17	places	23	0.68%	place, places
18	creatures	22	0.65%	creatures
19	things	21	0.62%	things
20	dare	20	0.59%	dare, dared, daring
21	secret	20	0.59%	secret, secrets
22	way	20	0.59%	way, ways
23	every	20	0.59%	every
24	take	20	0.59%	take
25	night	19	0.56%	night
26	hand	19	0.56%	hand, hands
27	gather	19	0.56%	gather, gathered, gathering, gatherings
28	may	17	0.50%	may
29	strange	17	0.50%	strange
30	follow	17	0.50%	follow, followers, following
31	terror	17	0.50%	terror, terrors
32	bats	16	0.47%	bat, bats

33	part	16	0.47%	part, parted, parting, parts
34	guide	15	0.44%	guide
35	meeting	15	0.44%	meet, meeting
36	now	15	0.44%	now
37	one	15	0.44%	one, ones
38	letter	15	0.44%	letter, letters
39	must	14	0.41%	must
40	page	14	0.41%	page, pages
41	step	14	0.41%	step
42	beyond	13	0.38%	beyond
43	next	13	0.38%	next
44	read	13	0.38%	read, reading
45	shiver	12	0.35%	shiver, shiverful, shivering, shivers
46	still	12	0.35%	still, stillness
47	make	11	0.32%	make, makes, making
48	dreams	11	0.32%	dreamed, dreams
49	lurk	11	0.32%	lurk, lurking, lurks
50	even	11	0.32%	even

and instead she vanishes toward the bottom of the page, with solid pen strokes breaking down into dotted lines that merge with her dress. In fact, the *Misty Annual 1982* printed an "Interview with Misty" in which one of the questions asks, "Have you got legs? We never see them?" Misty replies that "the mist does not need legs and travels quicker without them," but when she wishes to "materialise," she has them if she wishes—but still "tend[s] to drift." The lexis here links her firmly with the intangibility of mist and the natural world.

It thus seems logical to read Misty as a kind of spirit guide and her realm as one that shadows ours. She suggests in the letters page that she is constantly with us and refuses to assign any definite location to her realm, replying to one reader:

> Do you know the story of the man who wandered the world for a lifetime looking for Happiness and came home only to find it was in his own back garden all the time? Well, my Misty World is a bit like that, Malgosia. I often see you, my readers, but if you see me it will be in dreams or perhaps in the briefest glimpse on a misty day—Misty. (#44)

So, unlike the cover girls in other girls' comics or EC's horror hosts, the character of Misty is more than a function and has a thematic purpose that supports her comic's mystery content. She plays an essential role in developing the world of the comic, rather than simply lending her name and image or subverting scares with a joke. Her welcomes to each issue are topically and visually focused on mystery, nature, history, and the body. Gothic motifs of bats, moons, ruins, and mist are used to set this tone but always appear in low numbers: we are more likely to see single bats and a few trailing branches, rather than swarms of creatures or dense, impenetrable forests. The aesthetic tends toward isolation and remoteness but sits in tension with a Gothic excess that often shapes Misty's language. The obscured and unseen are also themes that dominate both visually and verbally, alongside a sense of history and temporality.

Rather than simply noting the frequent appearance of Gothic motifs in Misty's image and language, I have analyzed data on their overall frequency, combinations, and juxtapositions to argue for their symbolic meaning. My findings suggest that the blending of references to nature, isolation, Otherness, and the body is closely related to the trajectories of Gothic. In the next chapter, I look more closely at the main story content of the comic, using a similar process of inductive coding to explore how the tales themselves use and develop Gothic tropes.

CHAPTER 8

A TAXONOMY OF TERROR

"Pacts with the devil, schoolgirl sacrifice, the ghosts of hanged girls, sinister cults, evil scientists experimenting on the innocent and terrifying parallel worlds where the Nazis won the Second World War" (Rayner 2012).[1] There is no doubt that *Misty* pushed the boundaries of readers' expectations, but what other conclusions can we draw about its stories' narrative structure and themes? In this chapter, I conduct qualitative and quantitative research into the entire corpus of *Misty* stories. I discuss Pat Mills's girls' comics formulas and explore how far *Misty* follows them. I then identify the most common themes and story types based on inductive analysis of the story summaries.

Horror and trauma were not new subjects in girls' comics. The trend goes far back, and contemporaries such as *Tammy* were notorious for their "slave" stories, in which indignities and tragedies were heaped on a protagonist week by week. The classic example is "Slaves of War Orphan Farm" (Gerry Finley-Day and Desmond Walduck, *Tammy* #1–24, 1971), in which protagonist Kate is tortured by vindictive foster carer Ma Thatcher. As well as imprisonment and slave labor, Kate is terrorized by guard dogs, beaten unconscious, and escapes numerous murder attempts. Other examples include "Stefa's Heart of Stone" (Alison Christie and Phil Townsend, *Jinty*, August–December 1976), in which Stefa's best friend dies, her mother is hospitalized, her dad loses his job, and she suffers chronic indigestion. A number of these stories end in tragedy, such as "Nothing Ever Goes Right" (Maureen Hartley and Paddy Brennan, *Judy* #1102–18, 1981), whose heroine Heather consistently tries to help people despite suffering accidents, scarring, exclusion and bullying, chronic illness, hospitalization, and a series of unhappy homes with foster families and relatives. Her mother leaves the family and is then killed in a car accident, her father's new shop burns to the ground, and then he nearly drowns before dying in hospital. Ultimately Heather dies and is buried in an unmarked grave, but although nobody knows of her fate, she is remembered by all the people she has helped. The story is dramatic, laid out in angular panels that zigzag across the page (see Lorrsadmin 2014 for examples), so although the grid structure is preserved, it feels less blocky and static than some other girls' comics stories (see, e.g., my discussion of *Spellbound* in Round 2017). It is also bleak, with scant payoff at the end, and this bleakness is intensified because Heather is a likable character who continues to try to do the right thing despite the cost. However, *Misty* took the tragic story to new depths with its dramatic denouements and brutal payoffs.

UNHAPPY ENDINGS AND UNFORTUNATE PROTAGONISTS

Rayner (2012) says that *Misty*'s stories "eschewed happy endings with a bitter relish. The heroines, or usually antiheroines, who populated its strips and text stories had only to betray the tiniest fault or foible and that was it—they would die horribly, or be disfigured, or be transported to an unholy realm of evil. Redemption came rarely to these unfortunate schoolgirls."

This is my recollection of *Misty* too—but is it accurate? Do the stories usually end badly? Are there more antiheroines than heroines? Is redemption unlikely? To answer these questions, I analyzed the content of *Misty*, across all the comics, annuals, and specials, including all stories (both graphic and text) but leaving out the comedy series "Wendy the Witch," "Miss T," and "Cilla the Chiller" discussed in chapter 5. The following analysis combines quantitative data with qualitative analysis of some indicative examples.[2] It uses either the individual episode (total 748) or the complete story (total 440) as the unit of coding, depending on the question being asked. By triangulating my research in this way, I hope to give an objective sense of the weighting given to different themes, and to identify patterns and common tropes.[3]

First: the protagonists. Using the complete story as the unit of coding, there are 309 (70 percent) good protagonists and 131 (30 percent) antiheroines. This is extremely significant in light of Rayner's comments. But although there are fewer bad protagonists than we might remember, they are generally memorable. Their character is clearly marked in the first pages of a story, either through their own dialogue or by an omniscient narration. For example, Nancy Pierce's first words in "The Girl Who Walked on Water" (#35) are "Shut up, you old windbag!"; and in "The Fetch" (#2), we are told early on that "Anita Clark wasn't worried that her snobbish ways won her no friends." The majority of good protagonists are similarly marked by their behavior, and it is further notable that *all* the serials have a good protagonist. Toni Ballard in "Whistle and I'll Come . . ." (#43–56) is a good example. She is the only one in her family who cares for their dog Albert, and in the story's opening scene, when she is beaten by her stepfather for accidentally waking him up, she cries out, "I-I'm sorry! I o-only wanted Albert's lead" (#43). The story revolves around her efforts to escape her stepfather and find a happy home for herself, and protagonists like Sandy Morton ("Winner Loses All!" #78–94), Elena Hare ("A Leap through Time," #30–36), and Jackie Dow ("The Cats of Carey Street," #30–40) are also gentle, victimized heroines, more sinned against than sinners. This means that if we take the episode as the unit of coding (thus focusing on the weekly experience of reading the comic), then the number of good protagonists rises to 617 (82 percent).

Moving to consider the tales themselves, 158 (36 percent) have a negative ending, 91 (21 percent) have an ambivalent outcome, and 191 (43 percent) contain a positive resolution. But although the ratio of bad endings is not as high as Rayner and I remember, combining the categories reveals that the majority of the stories (57 percent) do finish in a negative or ambivalent manner, with the protagonist in a dangerous situation or an explicit note of fear or doubt. For example, Nancy Pierce ends up trapped at sea after stealing shoes that allow her to walk on water (#35), and "The Ring of Confidence" (#16–17) promises Angela's impending death as she realizes she is unable to live without harming anything. By contrast, a positive ending is defined as one where the protagonist achieves her goal or gains liberty; for example, Jenny finds "true friends for evermore" and escapes "The School of the Lost . . . ," which burns to the ground (#22). However, this positive sense can be undermined by the sacrifices characters have made or a bittersweet tone, producing an ambivalent outcome. For example, Sandy's father sacrifices his life for his daughter in "Winner Loses All!" (#94), and Rosemary Black in "Moonchild" gets a happy new home but at "a terrible price" (#13). Narration may also be used to create uncertainty: for example, "Journey into Fear" concludes "Or would it?" (#27), and "The Black Widow" ends on a questioning "The End?" (#33).

Ambivalence is certainly relevant to my definition of the Gothic, which draws attention to its dual or contradictory qualities. Andy Smith (2013, 415) points out that labeling Goth subculture is "fraught with ambivalence and ambiguity." Masschelein (2013) argues that ambivalence has informed the literary and critical conceptualization of key Gothic concepts such as the uncanny. In particular she points to Todorov's (1975) exploration of the fantastic, whose "hesitation" echoes the "intellectual uncertainty" and "ambivalence" of Freud's uncanny, where the familiar is made strange. However, ambivalence remains relatively underexplored and undefined, although an unpublished master's thesis by Enki (2008, iii) claims it as an inherent characteristic of Gothic and defines it more fully as "the realm of uncertainty that is represented by neither/nor conditions as opposed to the realm of certainty represented by modern either/or conditions." Ambivalent endings are those that carry mixed feelings or are left unexplained or unresolved—neither a happy outcome nor a sad one.

However, what is striking in *Misty* is that negative or ambivalent outcomes are not confined to the actions of a bad protagonist. Cross-referencing the

Table 8.1. Story endings and protagonists.				
Stories	Ending			
Protagonist	Negative	Ambivalent	Positive	Total
Bad	98 (75%)	7 (5%)	26 (20%)	131
Good	60 (19%)	84 (27%)	165 (53%)	309
Total	158 (36%)	91 (21%)	191 (43%)	440

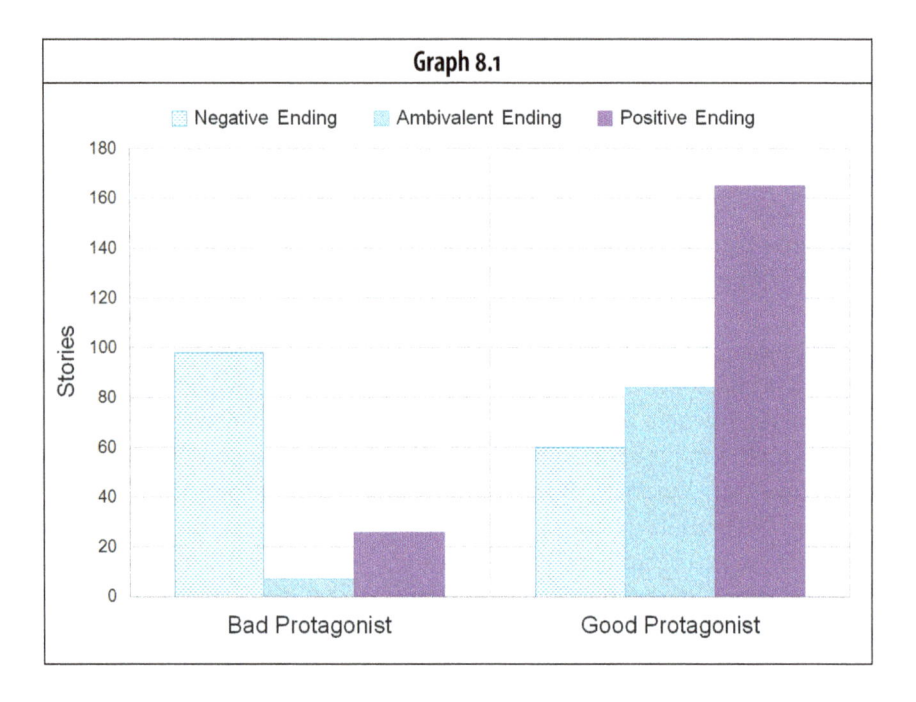

Graph 8.1

story endings against the protagonist type reveals that nearly half of the good protagonists nonetheless meet a nasty end, as shown in table and graph 8.1.

As the table and graph show, 46 percent of the good protagonists meet a bad or ambivalent end. While bad protagonists are admittedly more likely (80 percent) to meet these fates, it is significant that nearly half of the good girls are nonetheless punished. We can therefore argue that *Misty* does not convey a message of mere chance, or even of moral justice, but rather that "bad things will happen to bad people—but they also often happen to good people."

At the other end of the scale, and in further support of these findings, even the stories that end positively are not simple, uplifting tales and generally arrive at a happy end only after extensive danger and peril. Taking the story as the unit of coding, just eleven (3 percent) of the tales follow a simple happy trajectory and have an Uplifting Moral (MO), being a story of good deeds or a lucky encounter. These are all single stories, so the figure reduces to just 1 percent if we take the episode as the unit of coding, suggesting that this type of narrative was rare in the weekly experience of reading the comic. Along similar lines, it should be noted that, until the final episode, the protagonists of the positive-ending serials (twenty-two stories, which account for 12 percent of the positive endings) often find themselves in increasingly uncanny or unhappy circumstances, as befits the Gothic heroine who suffers numerous trials and obstacles on her way to fulfillment (Tóth 2010). These weekly cliffhangers contribute further to the sense of peril that characterized *Misty*, and if they are themselves counted as ambivalent "endings" (using the episode as the unit of coding), then 74 percent of the installments end negatively or ambivalently.[4]

Imperiled and persecuted, the Gothic heroine is a figure who "screams for us all."[5] Whether pursued or imprisoned, she is constantly under threat, and it has been argued that the genre creates victimization by using female fears of annihilation as a plot convention (Meyers 2001). However, while scholars continue to debate the Gothic heroine's positive qualities (see chap. 10), Moers ([1976] 1978) reads her as a subversive figure, and later critics such as Anne Williams (1995, cited in Corson 2010) concur, arguing that her suffering leads to triumph over patriarchal power. Only through continued struggle and revolt can the heroine achieve fulfillment, and Tóth (2010, 29) concludes that "those who refuse to subordinate themselves, eventually gain their reward."

But how easily is this reward achieved—or how rare is redemption? If we take the episode as the unit of coding, 226 installments (30 percent) of the *Misty* tales feature a character who is redeemed or rewarded in some way because of her own actions. Kate gives her archaeologist grandfather a vision of the city he is searching for before he dies ("Curse of the Condor," #19), Judith's investigation helps Miss Thistlewick complete her penance for a deadly boat trip ("The Haunting of Form 2B," Annual 1980), and Anita Clark changes her snobbish ways after a nightmare in which she is buried alive ("The Fetch," #2). While not all these examples involve the tale's protagonist, and "The Haunting of Form 2B" is a *Jinty* reprint, they do indicate that redemption actually has a fairly strong presence in the *Misty* tales.

So if redemption actually happens quite a lot, and the unhappy endings are not as dominant as claimed, why is *Misty* so well remembered for this feature? One explanation might be the stories' extreme nature. Looking more closely at the content emphasizes how harsh the outcomes often are: generally out of all proportion to faults such as rudeness, selfishness, or vanity. Girls are trapped permanently in magical items such as crystal balls, snow globes, music boxes, or weather houses ("The Collector," #88; "Old Collie's Collection," #82; "A Turn for the Worse," #44; "Uncle's Nasty Hobby . . . ," #63). They might be aged prematurely ("Fairy Gold," #37; "One Hour in Time," #66), ousted from their bodies ("If Only . . . ," #51; "Who Killed Teacher?" #70), or transformed into something monstrous such as a caterpillar ("Finder's Creepers," #62) or a shop dummy ("When the Lights Go Out!" #18). They can also die in a number of horrible ways, often to return as ghosts: by drowning in a swamp ("A Room of Her Own," #69), being eaten by wolves ("A Spell of Trouble," #24), or burned to death ("Black Agnes," #59; "Mrs. Grundy's Guest House," #86).

While the majority of these victims are bad protagonists, a large proportion of the good protagonists are punished, as noted, and often for quite minor mistakes, such as Caroline, who avoids a dentist appointment and is turned into a vampire ("Sweet Tooth," #78). In addition, in a handful of tales (five, or 1 percent), the bad outcome is completely and entirely undeserved—provoking the response "It's not fair!" In "Old Ethna's House" (Holiday Special 1979), Joy and her friend are tricked by Ethna, who asks them for help but then turns them to stone with her Medusa eyes. Gloria inherits an evil cauldron that creates monsters in "Pot Luck" (#57), and Mary Connaught is imprisoned by her charge in "The Governess" (#79). In "The Dryad Girl" (#100), Shala gives up her immortality after falling in love with a boy she sees, but is repulsive in human form (fig. 8.3a). In "A Dog's Life" (fig. 8.1), Mrs. Abbot is reunited with her long-lost grandniece Jane, who shows her how selfish and mean her pet dog Ling is—but before Mrs. Abbot can change her will in Jane's favor, Ling causes an accident that kills Jane (although her death is unseen). Here the image of Jane falling dominates the page, and Ling is a demonic background character with glowing slits of eyes. The story's end point further emphasizes the dog's agency, as Ling breaks the fourth wall to gaze smugly at the reader, a strategy that is also used on the previous two pages. So although bad or ambivalent endings do make up more than half of *Misty*'s stories, the mark they made on readers' memories is not necessarily due to the quantity. Rather, the extreme nature of the punishments and the lack of provocation may be responsible for this impact. Rayner acknowledges this moral ambivalence in a later article (2014), saying, "The beauty—or horror—of *Misty* was that you didn't even have to be an evil person for a terrible fate to take you—you only had to have one tiny little moral hiccup, if that, to be damned for all eternity," but my research emphasizes that even this "moral hiccup" is not always required.

CATEGORIES AND FORMULAS

Various critics and creators have attempted to classify the different types of girls' comics stories. Coote (n.d.) provides an inductive list of "unofficial headings" for serials, but these categories are numerous and varied, and taken solely from comics that she has access to, excluding some titles entirely. Her labels range

A TAXONOMY OF TERROR 157

Figure 8.1. "It's a Dog's Life" (*Misty* #9). Art by Jacques Goudon, written by Wilf Prigmore. Reproduced with permission of Misty™ Rebellion Publishing IP Ltd.; copyright © Rebellion Publishing IP Ltd., all rights reserved.

quite widely from the very specific ("Busy Parent Syndrome") to the very wide ("Bullying," "Friendship Problems") and may refer equally to story formats ("Daily Diary"), characters ("Doppelganger"), plot tropes ("Magic Object"), or other means of classifying. There is also substantial crossover; for example, it is unclear what the difference is between categories such as "Hampered Girl," "Saboteur," and "Nasty Troublemaker" (all of which involve a heroine being held back in some malevolent way).

Other critics and creators have suggested wider categories that can be applied to the serials. Pat Mills (2011, 2014a, 2016a) states that the girls' comics were written to a distinct set of formulas,[6] as follows:

Slave story (SL): about hardship and bullying, focuses on a victimized individual or group that is systematically exploited and abused.
Cinderella story (CI): a down-on-her-luck heroine in unfortunate circumstances.
Friend story (FR): the heroine's desire for a friend is paramount.
Mystery story (MY): can be as simple as "What's inside the box?"

All these categories resonate with Gothic themes. The Slave story is based on persecution and control, as a malevolent villain or powerful institution is responsible for the denigration and mistreatment of our heroine. This type of story titillates by transgressing the reader's expectations. It drives toward excess by heaping new indignities and punishments on the protagonist each week and seeking to outdo itself with each new installment. Slave stories were popular in many girls' comics, with the most famous example being "Slaves of War Orphan Farm" (Gerry Finley-Day and Desmond Walduck, *Tammy* #1–24, 1971), as noted. Mistyfan (2014b) points out that the setting can be based on an activity (swimming, ballet), an institution (workhouse, school), or something more unusual such as a dystopian world or totalitarian society. The protagonist can take on various roles, such as the slave who refuses to be broken or the secret helper working undercover. Mistyfan (2014b) also notes that this type can often be combined with a Mystery strand. *Misty* stories such as "House of Horror" (#96–101) and "The School of the Lost…" (#13–22) combine the Mystery and Slave formulas as disadvantaged protagonists are tortured in various ways by their peers or teachers. Some of the single stories also followed the Slave formula: for example, in "Garden of Evil" (#53), Tansy is captured by a wicked queen and made to work in her garden of poisons, until the queen dies and her kind sister takes over.

The Slave story shares some qualities (such as an oppressed Gothic heroine) with the Cinderella story, which focuses on an unlucky or unfortunate protagonist. The key differences seem to be the isolation and passivity of the protagonist, as she is often without help and consistently tries to do good rather than rebel or fight back, placing her in danger of being crushed by her ordeals. As a passive character whose development is enabled only by the interventions of the villain (Tóth 2010), Cinderella can certainly be read as a Gothic heroine. Cinderella stories became a trend after Alan Davidson and Miguel Quesada's "Little Miss Nothing" (*Tammy and Sally* #18–31, 1971), in which poor Annabel Hayes is forced to work on her family's market stall, and her attempts to kick-start her dressmaker ambitions by selling her own goods are constantly destroyed by her family. Perhaps the most heartrending example in *Misty* is "Whistle and I'll Come . . ." (Mario Capaldi, writer unknown, #43–56), which heaps misery on protagonist Toni. Pursued by her violent stepfather after the death of her dog and her mother, she is also harassed by various teachers, tramps, criminals, and thugs before finally finding a happy home. The Cinderella formula appears in *Misty*'s shorter stories too, but it is often combined with a twist ending or comeuppance for the villain that alters its impact. For example, in "Sprig of Heather" (#81), Polly sells lucky heather, but her mean stepfather takes all her money until she meets some fairies ("the Manikin") who agree to help her, and when she wakes she finds he has been press-ganged (other similar examples include "Seal Song," #10). A less clear-cut example might be "Cry Baby!" (#68), in which adopted Catherine is constantly teased by her older sister Sarah, which makes her cry—but when her tears drop in a wishing well and she gets one wish, the next day Sarah is transformed into a crying baby. While Catherine's passivity and victimization fit the Cinderella formula, in *Misty* a "Just Desserts"–style ending dominates these types of single stories and is often revealed in a final dramatic panel (see also "The Gravedigger's Daughter," #78; "The Haunting of Hazel Brown," #41–42; and "Was It Just . . . a Game?" #14). I discuss this type of ending later in this chapter.

Although it does not always end well, the Friend story is perhaps the most positive in *Misty*. Like the Cinderella story, it focuses on the Gothic theme of isolation through a lonely protagonist whose search for companionship drives the story. "Wolf Girl" (#65–80) is a pure Friend story, as all Lona wants is to fit in somewhere, either with the wolf pack or in human society. In many of the shorter *Misty* stories, the friend is nonhuman, taking the form of an animal ("Friends," #101; "Silverwing," #15; "Fangs for the Memory," #38), a tree or spirit ("A Friend in Need," #66; "The Dryad Girl," #100; "Cathy and the Nature Spirits," #83), or a ghost ("Catch Me If You Can . . . ," #69). "The Ghost of Golightly Towers" (#81–94) is another good example of the Friend story, as Amanda is bullied in her children's home until she finds companionship in Sir Giles and ultimately they help each other.

Finally, we come to the Mystery story, whose ambivalent, inexplicable, and uncanny qualities are intrinsically Gothic, and of which Mills (2011)

Table 8.2. Pat Mills's formulas as used in *Misty*.

Mills's Formulas	Stories	Episodes
None	182	182
Mystery	145	176
Friend + Mystery	41	164
Friend	41	56
Cinderella + Mystery	6	46
Cinderella + Friend	4	40
Mystery + Slave	3	34
Friend + Mystery + Slave	2	22
Cinderella + Friend + Mystery	1	13
Cinderella	11	11
Slave	4	4
Total	440	748

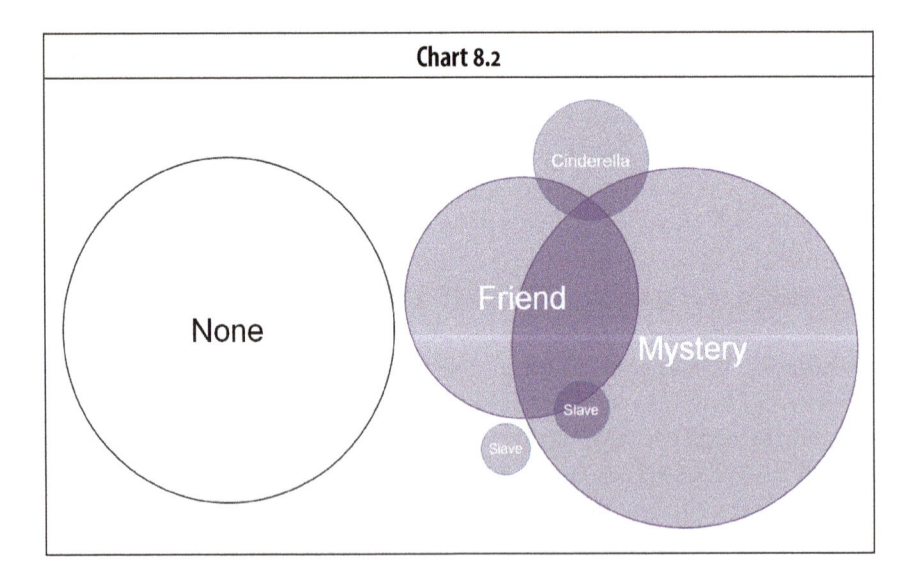

Chart 8.2

memorably says, "The explanation can be complete crap, and it usually *was*, and it doesn't matter!" In *Misty* this can indeed be as simple as "What's in the box?" ("Black Sunday," Summer Special 1978) but in other instances stretches to many installments: "Nightmare Academy" (#65–76), "The School of the Lost …" (#13–22), "The Silver Racer-Back" (#83–91), and many more are strong examples. Mills (2017b) adds that "school mysteries were particularly important. And/or weird schools." Critics such as Truffin (2008) draw attention to the

Gothic qualities of school settings in American fiction as places of power and control, and M. Smith and Moruzi (2018, 6) argue that in contemporary young adult fiction the traditional school story is often adapted and transformed by the Gothic, enabling female protagonists who are "unique, disruptive, and potentially transformative." In the *Misty* school mysteries, tension arises from a mysterious event or inexplicable problem that the protagonist is in a unique position to unravel. Knowledge is doled out slowly: for example, in "Nightmare Academy" Sharon witnesses a series of uncanny events that cause her suspicions of Miss Nocturne to slowly grow over the first six episodes with absolutely no resolutions or explanations offered until she witnesses Miss Nocturne change into a bat (#70). The remaining six episodes then offer a series of reveals (Miss Nocturne is icy cold, she has no reflection, shows her fangs) before wrapping up with a dramatic finale in which Sharon saves the school and Miss Nocturne is (accidentally) killed. What is startling is the lack of information given in the first half of the serial, and a similar pattern is followed in "The School of the Lost...," where we are never quite sure what the threat to Jenny actually is until the penultimate episode, which reveals that she is to be a sacrifice to the devil at the school's gala day.

Stories can, of course, combine more than one formula and often do: Mills (2017b) points out that "'Little Miss Nothing' [written by Alan Davidson with art by Miguel Quesada, *Tammy*, 1971] was also a Cinderella story, but the heroine's desire for a friend was paramount. That is the key motivation in this age group of girls and that should include *Misty*, albeit in a mystery context." "Moonchild" (#1–13) is also "partly a Friend story," as the bullies try to undermine Rosemary's relationship with Anne. Other serials such as "The Four Faces of Eve," "The Loving Cup," and "The Secret World of Sally Maxwell" also combine the Mystery and Friend formulas, featuring isolated protagonists whose search for a friend is jeopardized by the mystery. Even "Paint It Black" contains elements of the Friend story, as Maggie realizes she needs to help the ghost of Maria Thursby and find out what happened to her. A variation takes place in "Winner Loses All!," which primarily combines the Mystery and Cinderella formulas as poor Sandy struggles to help her alcoholic father and resolve her deal with the devil against a series of obstacles. However, Sandy's isolation means that the story also contains elements of the Friend story, as her companionship with her horse Satan forms a major part of the narrative and is contrasted to the bullying she receives from Jocasta.

Table and chart 8.2. show the categories of formulas used in the *Misty* stories. Using the episode as the unit of coding (total 748 installments), the Mystery formula is by far the most prominent, appearing in 455 episodes (61 percent), followed by the Friend formula (295 episodes, or 39 percent). The two are also the most popular combination: 22 percent of the stories combine the Mystery and Friend formulas, which is far ahead of the next most popular category of the pure Friend stories, which make up 7 percent of the total. The rest of *Misty*'s tales fall into the Cinderella and Slave categories (in that order), in various combinations, but in the majority of cases these are again combined with the Mystery or Friend formulas. It is interesting to note that the Slave story features the least of all and is barely present in its pure form (less than 1 percent). It is more common when combined with the Mystery (5 percent) or Mystery and Friend (3 percent) formulas. So although Mills's formulas do obviously inform some of *Misty*'s stories, they don't dominate in the same way as in other comics. For example, the *Tammy* Slave stories mentioned earlier systematically heap indignities on the protagonist each week: see, for example, "Waifs of the Wigmaker," "The Camp on Candy Island," "Serfs of the Swamp," "Slaves of the Hot Stove," and "The Four Friends at Spartan School" (Tammyfan 2013). However, this type of suffering is not the primary focus of the *Misty* Slave stories. For example, in "The School of the Lost . . . ," the bullying that Jenny experiences and the drugging of the other schoolgirls are secondary to the intrigue, which raises new questions each week: Why is Jenny's photo on the chapel altar? Why is she not allowed to leave? Why are the villagers scared of her?

In addition, many of the *Misty* stories (182, or 24 percent) do not fall into any of Mills's formulas. For example, in "Avalado's Portrait" (#11), Maria and her younger brother outwit a blackmailing artist who has painted a magic picture of her. It is difficult to fit this reactive adventure into any of the categories. It is also notable that these nonconforming stories are all single stories, the shocking cautionary tale for which *Misty* is so well remembered. This perhaps suggests that this story type is more completely its own, while the serials fit more closely with the story patterns from other girls' comics. *Misty* departs from Pat Mills's rules in other ways, too: Mills (2014a) stresses the need to have the protagonist's name in the story title, which is something *Misty* rarely does, just twenty-seven times in its overall total of 443 stories (6 percent).

COMMON PLOT TROPES

My alternative approach to analyzing *Misty*'s stories has been developed from analysis of the plot summaries to create inductive categories. Rather than applying a preexisting typology (such as Mills's formulas), I instead noted similarities between the stories as they emerged, thus producing a gradually expanding list of plot tropes. I am not suggesting that the creators wrote with these ideas in mind, but simply demonstrating that the 440 noncomedy stories in *Misty* exhibit a number of common features, as follows. Please note that the first three categories can take either positive (+) or negative (−) form:

External Magic (M+/M−): The protagonist or an affiliate finds or receives a magical item, a charm or curse, or enters a magical or haunted place. This can be positive (M+) or negative (M−). M+ examples include "Paint It Black" (#1–18), in which Maggie's box of paints helps her seek justice for Maria; or "Crystal Clear" (#99), where Katey traps some vandals by using a crystal ball. M− examples might include "Date with Death" (#76), in which Bea and her friend disappear into a calendar they have stolen; or "In The Labyrinths of Her Mind . . ." (#56), in which mean Judy is terrorized by a tape recorder that hisses creepy rhymes at her.

Internal Power (P+/P−): The protagonist discovers that she has some sort of special ability or power, such as prophetic dreams, telekinesis, haunting, or suspicions of reincarnation. This discovery might be empowering and useful (P+) or harrowing and debilitating (P−). For example, in "Room for Dreams" (#7), Ann's prophetic dreams make the family lots of money and rid them of her violent uncle, whereas in "Darkness at Noon" (#80) Julia has horrific visions of the destruction of Pompeii that nobody believes.

Wish or Promise (W+/W−): The protagonist or an affiliate makes a deal or promise in exchange for certain benefits or receives wishes (these may then go awry). In "A Girl's Best Friend" (#48), Carla's sight is restored thanks to her guide dog Belle (W+), whereas in "If Only . . ." (#51) Lois swaps lives with rich Kora only to discover she is dying (W−).

Science Fiction (SC): The mystery is explained by some sort of rational frame, perhaps involving science or technology, or simply as a dream. The frame does not have to be plausible or even possible, but it is offered as a logical explanation for seemingly impossible events (Todorov's "supernatural explained"). For example, a character is revealed to be a waxwork ("The Bitter Tale of Sweet Lucy," #35), clockwork ("The Clock Maker's Daughter," #40), or robot ("The Family," #6; "The Experiment," #100); aliens intervene in the narrative ("Titch's Tale," #26; "The Visitors," #28; "Food for Thought," #91; and more); or another explanatory frame such as a giant chessboard or board game is used ("Master Stroke," #23; "Madhouse!" #90). Scientific experimentation also appears, as in "The Silver Racer-Back" (#83–91) or the fog that causes Sally's telepathy ("The Secret World of Sally Maxwell," #48–60).

It's a Trap (T): A malevolent antagonist lures the protagonist into danger, which she may or may not escape. For example, Old Rosie feeds girls to her roses ("How Does Your Garden Grow?" #74), Mad Mary traps Karen and her dreams in a crystal ball ("The Collector," #88), and teacher Mary Connaught is locked in a cellar by her malevolent charge ("The Governess," #79). Traps are directed at the deserving and undeserving equally: Old Ethna pretends to need help but then turns her rescuers to stone ("Old Ethna's House," Holiday Special 1979), but villainous protagonists also receive their share ("Yet Another Teacher for Molly," #46; or "Hard Harry's Last Game," #36, which both feature criminals who receive a form of justice). Characters sometimes escape their fate (Ginny avoids a poisonous scratch in "The Monkey's Claw," #4), but most often they do not.

Actions Backfire (B): A deliberate act by someone in the story (whether protagonist, affiliate, antagonist, or secondary character) has unhappy and unexpected consequences. For example, rude Laura pushes over an old lady and is cursed ("One Hour in Time," #66); Sally swats a bee and is turned into one ("Queen's Weather," #18); and delinquent Glenda becomes trapped in a tree ("The Treatment," #75).[7]

Redemption (R): A benevolent person helps the protagonist, or the protagonist provides someone else with help; a wrong is righted. Polly is helped by the Manikin ("Sprig of Heather," #81); "The Cats of Carey Street" help Jackie and her gran (#30–40); and a team of rabbits help Emily stand up for herself ("Run, Rabbit, Run!" #64).

If we take the episode as the unit of coding, these tropes appear in the quantities shown in table and graph 8.3.

The most common feature is Actions Backfire, which occurs in 230 (31 percent) of the episodes—but this is by a very slight margin, as Redemption appears in 226 (30 percent) of stories. The magical items, powers, and wishes that appear are consistently more likely than not to be negative in nature, with the largest margin falling within wishes, which very rarely turn out well. Deliberate traps are a relatively common feature (167, or 22 percent of episodes), and a rational frame also appears perhaps more than we might expect given *Misty's* supernatural appearance (137, or 18 percent of the episodes).

The various categories create a large number of different combinations, of which I reproduce the top ten in table and graph 8.4. Perhaps unsurprisingly, the most common combination is M− B (a negative type of external magic, combined with the backfiring of actions of the protagonist). For example, in "You Can't Cheat Tomorrow" (#36), Rachel is given a crystal ball by a gypsy and warned not to try to see her own fortune, but she does so anyway, leading to her death. This says something about personal responsibility: as in the 1970s public information films, the message seems to be that bad things can happen, but there is still accountability. Dangerous objects require harmful or careless

Table 8.3. Common plot tropes in *Misty* stories (by episode).

Episodes	Format		
Plot Type	Serial (341 episodes)	Single (407 episodes)	Total
B Actions Backfire	42	188	230
R Redemption	130	96	226
M− Negative External Magic	51	126	177
T It's a Trap	102	65	167
SC Science Fiction	78	59	137
M+ Positive External Magic	73	47	120
P− Negative Internal Power	81	35	116
P+ Positive Internal Power	59	37	96
W− Negative Wishes	27	17	44
W+ Positive Wishes	0	4	4

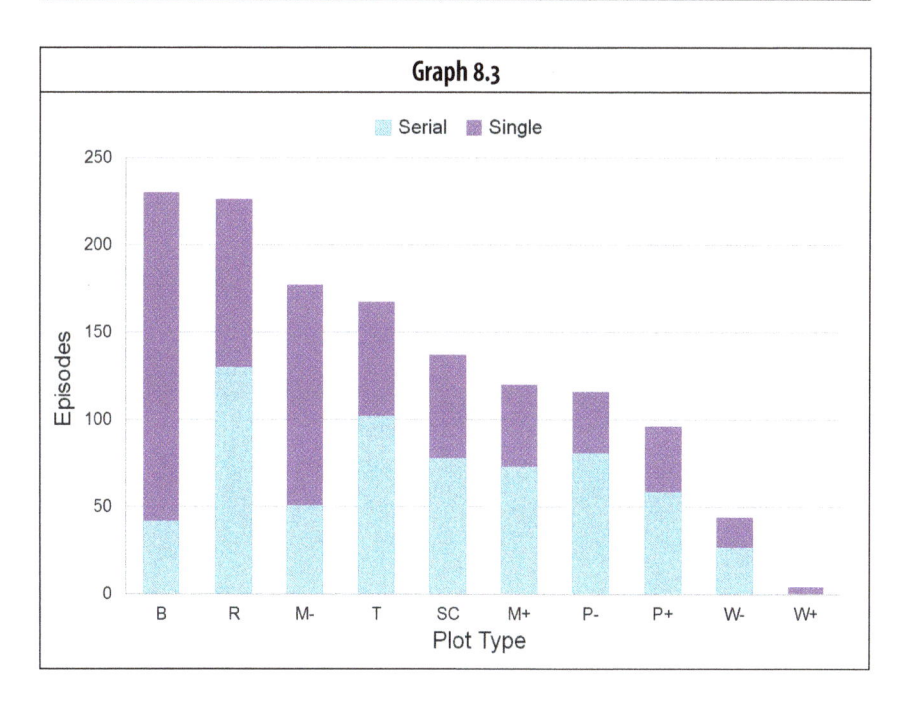

Graph 8.3

actions to have impact; the combination of M− T (negative magic combined with a deliberate trap) appears much less often, as shown.

However, the second most featured combination is M+ R (a positive magical force combined with a helper or other sort of redemption), counterbalancing the foregoing warning, as it offers almost the opposite message. For example,

Table 8.4. Combinations of plot tropes in Misty stories (by episode).

Episodes	Format		
Plot Type	**Serial**	**Single**	**Total**
M— B Negative External Magic, Actions Backfire	4 (1%)	74 (18%)	78 (10%)
M+ R Positive External Magic, Redemption	46 (13%)	26 (6%)	72 (10%)
T It's a Trap	41 (12%)	19 (5%)	60 (8%)
P— SC Negative Internal Power, Science Fiction	34 (10%)	2 (0%)	36 (5%)
P+ R Positive Internal Power, Redemption	24 (7%)	10 (2%)	34 (5%)
P— R Negative Internal Power, Redemption	26 (8%)	4 (1%)	30 (4%)
M—T Negative External Magic, It's a Trap	20 (6%)	9 (2%)	29 (4%)
P— Negative Internal Power	11 (3%)	18 (4%)	29 (4%)
M+ Positive External Magic	18 (5%)	9 (2%)	27 (4%)
B Actions Backfire	0 (0%)	27 (7%)	27 (4%)

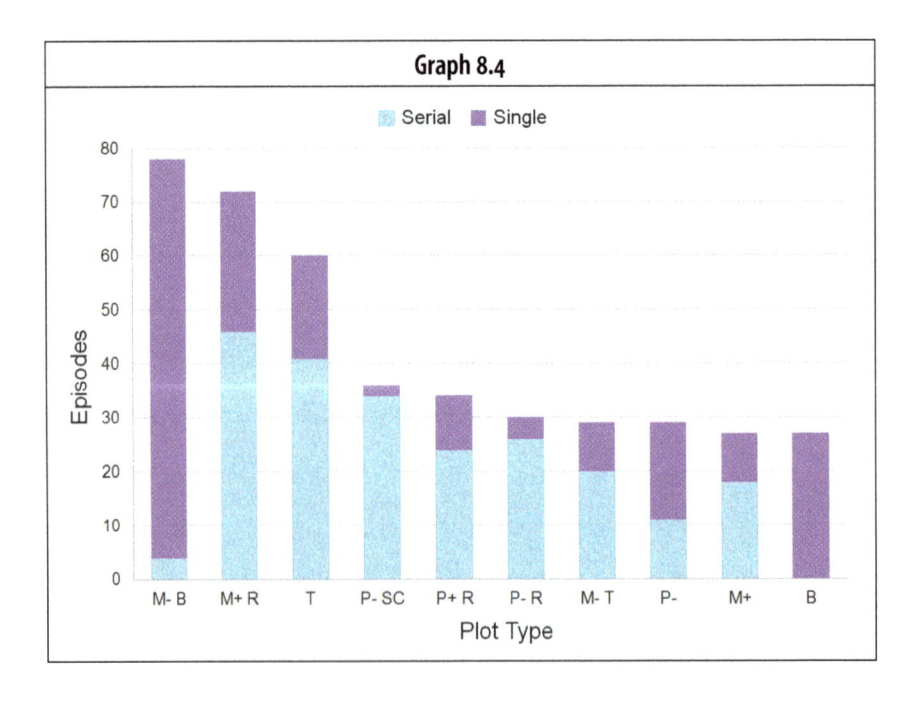

Graph 8.4

while on holiday, Jenny's brother Peter kills a locust against her wishes, but on their flight home a swarm of the insects saves their plane ("The Swarm," #9). In "A Friend in Need" (#66), Marla is watched over by an old elm tree that ultimately saves her life. In "Living Doll" (#72), Barbie follows a mysterious doll and saves a little girl from drowning. It therefore seems that magic is not inherently bad or dangerous, and its intrusion into protagonists' lives can have positive benefits.

With this in mind, it is also interesting to note that the following two most frequent combinations steer away from supernatural objects and magical forces, although they might still contain mythical or fantasy characters or horror archetypes (see chap. 11 for further discussion). Protagonists are simply lured into traps: for example, Sheila is captured by an evil mermaid ("Mermaid," #88), Jilly escapes zombies ("Night of the Dead," #94), and Harry joins the ghosts of children in quicksand ("Hard Harry's Last Game," #36). The next most common category introduces supernatural powers, but with a rational frame that explains them away; for example, Tina's vision of a star that is heating earth's atmosphere is just a dream ("Rogue Star," #63). This combination is predominantly weighted toward serial episodes such as "The Four Faces of Eve" (#20–31), "The Secret World of Sally Maxwell" (#48–60), and "Don't Look Twice" (#57–66). These stories all rationalize their protagonists' uncanny visions and special powers: Eve is made up of the bodies of four different girls and has dreams of their memories, Sally's visions have been brought on by a gas she inhaled, and Sammy has been sharing the experiences of an unknown twin sister.

A final point to note from these data sets is that they show a clear distinction between *Misty*'s single stories (where negative magic and unintentional consequences dominate) and the serial episodes (which contain the bulk of the positive magic and redemption and are also more likely to contain a trap). The ratio of difference between the singles and the serials is significant throughout the table (often 2:1 or more), showing that they use and combine their tropes in quite different ways.

STRUCTURE AND MEDIUM

As well as these various types of plot catalyst, the *Misty* stories also use a number of dramatic devices, particularly in their endings. Two that are of note are as follows:

> Shock Twist (TW): A final twist or inversion in the tale that reverses our expectations: for example, the seeming antagonist is actually a friend, or the monster is not who it seems. In "The Sad Eyes of Sorrow" (#49), Frankenstein's creature is appearing in a freak show and is assumed to be wearing a mask, but the end reveals that the monstrous face is his real one and his human face is a mask he wears. In "Witch Hunt" (#99), Frida and her infant sister Anna are captured by witch hunters, but the ending reveals that baby Anna is the real witch.

Just Desserts (EC): An EC Comics–style payoff where the villain "gets it how they gave it" via dramatic or gruesome poetic justice. Shoplifters are turned into dummies ("When the Lights Go Out!" #18); dishonest gardeners are sucked into plants ("Voices in the Wind," #42); Nan steals magic shoes but then cannot walk on dry land without sinking ("The Girl Who Walked on Water," #35); and Perri falsely enters an essay competition for disabled children and ends up in a wheelchair ("The Prize!" Holiday Special 1979).

We can observe some crossover here with the earlier categories: for example, many of the Just Desserts endings are brought about when Actions Backfire; and a Shock Twist often accompanies the Science Fiction frame. However, these two features are notable for their dominance. The Shock Twist ending is present in eighty-seven (20 percent) of the stories, and Just Desserts are meted out in 123 tales (28 percent). They share twenty-nine (7 percent) of the tales (all single stories), and so the overall combined total is 181 (41 percent), which seems significant when we consider their nature. How surprising is a shock twist, a quirk of fate, or an ironic punishment if it happens nearly half the time?

This paradox is perhaps representative of the dual impetus that characterizes Gothic (subversive/conservative, horrifying/attractive, etc.). While critics such as Cavallero (2002, 123) have argued that Gothic texts embody Roland Barthes's (1973) notion of *jouissance*, discomfiting and unsettling the reader, Gothic theorists have not, perhaps, paid as much attention to the other side of Barthes's argument: the text of *plaisir* that offers a readable and familiar pleasure. Barthes's essay in fact has a Gothic bent: he describes the experience of reading de Sade as a process of "cutting," creating "two edges," one obedient and conformist, the other mobile and blank, and proposes that the pleasure of reading lies in the seam between these two sides: a place of compromise and loss (6–7). Barthes argues that this is true of culture and manifests in language, and the pleasure of reading is therefore taken not from narrative suspense but from these points of abrasion and conflict. They produce the text of *plaisir*/pleasure (comfortable, euphoric, aligned with culture and its norms) and the text of *jouissance*/bliss (discomfiting, unsettling, bringing us to a crisis of culture and language). While Barthes goes on to discuss the relationship between the two categories ("Is pleasure only a minor bliss? Is bliss nothing but extreme pleasure?" [20]), it is in the combination of the two that his philosophy meets the Gothic. He describes the text as a fetish object and notes its duality (both inside and outside language), bringing corporeal and sensual meaning to the experience of reading, and couching much of his argument in Gothic lexis ("I am interested in language because it wounds or seduces me" [38]). The scholarship on Gothic comedy that I have already discussed, the conservative impetus that can be read in many Gothic texts, and the familiar patterns of "shock twist" or

A TAXONOMY OF TERROR   169

Figure 8.2. "Flight from Fear" (*Misty* #92). Art by Isidre Monés, writer unknown. Reproduced with permission of Misty™ Rebellion Publishing IP Ltd.; copyright © Rebellion Publishing IP Ltd., all rights reserved.

"poetic justice" highlight that within the Gothic we also encounter an experience of *plaisir*, supporting the view of Gothic as an affective and structural paradox.

In other work (2014a), I claim there are three key Gothic aspects of comics narratology: the use made of the space of the page (haunting); the active role of the reader (crypt); and the multiple points of view and perspectives combined on a page (excess). I have already discussed the dynamic page layouts used in *Misty*, but the comic uses a particular narrative strategy that combines the latter two aspects (active reader, multiple perspectives). This strategy is to mislead the reader by using the medium (ME), such as by giving us a limited point of view or excluding us from certain visual information. For example, dreams are presented as reality in "The Dummy" (#4) and "Fancy Another Jelly Baby?" (#71). We are unable to distinguish a trick spider from a real one in "Red Knee—White Terror!" (#1). This happens in twenty-five of the single stories (6 percent), which use the comics medium to misdirect us or align our point of view with that of the protagonist as we share her dreams or visions. For example, in "Flight from Fear" (#92), Lucy abandons her maid Peg when she flees the plague in London. In this story, an extended dream sequence is presented as reality: a panel in which Lucy reclines in her coach, thinking, "I'm too tired to move!" is followed by the caption "But moments later . . ." before her coach is taken on a wild ride into a graveyard, where she is nearly thrown into a plague pit (fig. 8.2). The panel in which the pit looms before her dominates the page with its size, perspective (as Lucy screams toward us), and color (contrasting white and black shading). Although the following panel, in which she wakes from the dream, is placed centrally, it is one of the smallest on the page, and its black background and shape hide rather than flag its significance. By contrast, the graveyard scenes in her dream are dramatic nightmares of dereliction enhanced by the acute angles and abundance of details (see, e.g., panels 1–2): broken gates and overgrown foliage surround horrifying revenants dressed in rags and covered with plague boils. Here layout and style combine to misdirect the reader and problematize the distinction between fiction and reality.

In addition, on a number of pages, the final reveal is kept from us until the final panel (fig. 8.3; fig. 8.6 is also a good example). In all these instances, characters remain with their backs to us or are otherwise obscured before a dramatic or grotesque final image, which is given extra emphasis by the panel area, form, and site (Groensteen 2009). These pages are all drawn by different artists, and so the use of layout and panel size is arguably house style, as discussed in chapter 3. Along similar lines, final panels may also be used to reveal something to the reader that is hidden from the protagonist, as, for example, in figure 8.4. This provides a different form of shock ending that hinges on reader activity (as we must recognize the threat in the panel) and uncertainty (as the outcome for the character is undecided).

A TAXONOMY OF TERROR 171

Figure 8.3a. Horrifying final pages: "The Dryad Girl" (*Misty* #100, art by Juan Ariza). Reproduced with permission of Misty™ Rebellion Publishing IP Ltd.; copyright © Rebellion Publishing IP Ltd., all rights reserved.

Figure 8.3b. Horrifying final pages: "Dead Man's Eyes" (*Misty* #79, art by John Armstrong). Reproduced with permission of Misty™ Rebellion Publishing IP Ltd.; copyright © Rebellion Publishing IP Ltd., all rights reserved.

A TAXONOMY OF TERROR   173

Figure 8.3c. Horrifying final pages: "The Eyes of the Gorgon" (*Misty* #21, art by Rafael Busom). Reproduced with permission of Misty™ Rebellion Publishing IP Ltd.; copyright © Rebellion Publishing IP Ltd., all rights reserved.

Figure 8.3d. Horrifying final pages: "The Pig People" (*Misty* #95, art by John Richardson). Reproduced with permission of Misty™ Rebellion Publishing IP Ltd.; copyright © Rebellion Publishing IP Ltd., all rights reserved.

Figure 8.4a. Reader activity in final panels: "The Haunting" (*Misty* #7, art by John Richardson). Reproduced with permission of Misty™ Rebellion Publishing IP Ltd.; copyright © Rebellion Publishing IP Ltd., all rights reserved.

Figure 8.4b. Reader activity in final panels: "Shadow of a Doubt" (*Misty* #58, art by Juan Ariza). Reproduced with permission of Misty™ Rebellion Publishing IP Ltd.; copyright © Rebellion Publishing IP Ltd., all rights reserved.

A TAXONOMY OF TERROR   177

Figure 8.4c. Reader activity in final panels: "Danger in the Depths" (*Misty* #85, art by Josép Gual). Reproduced with permission of Misty™ Rebellion Publishing IP Ltd.; copyright © Rebellion Publishing IP Ltd., all rights reserved.

Figure 8.4d. Reader activity in final panels: "Catch Me If You Can" (*Misty* #69, art by Juan Ariza). Reproduced with permission of Misty™ Rebellion Publishing IP Ltd.; copyright © Rebellion Publishing IP Ltd., all rights reserved.

Before concluding, it seems worth pausing to analyze how all these different categories work together in a single story, "Mirror . . . Mirror," which is included at the end of this chapter in its entirety (fig. 8.6). By chance—or maybe fate—*Misty* #37 was one of the issues randomly selected for coding, and so my analysis also draws on the visual tags discussed in chapter 4, which are shown in figure 8.5.

At the most basic grid level, the first page has two tiers, which increase to three and four tiers across the next two pages, before dropping back to three tiers on the final page. This layout becomes ambiguous on the third page, which also contains the most tiers—this is where the magical activity reaches its peak. Panel borders and boundaries are varied and dynamic throughout: circular panels are used more than once at the start, and open and borderless panels appear on every page, further complemented by panels with shared borders and semiopen edges. Angles are used to create a sense of disorientation and danger: three of the four pages have a tilted base, giving a slanted angle on the puzzling events, and angled vertical edges appear in addition to this on the final page, conveying further shock through contrast with the previous three.

The story is a combined Mystery and Cinderella, and at its start we are firmly aligned with Linda. The medium contributes to this effect, as the circular panel "zooms in" on her hurt feelings. By bringing us physically close to her, it encourages our identification, and its circular form gives the panel extra emphasis by making it stand out from the other shapes on the page. The situation is one that most children can empathize with—being laughed about behind your back—and also plays on the insecurity that many teenagers feel about their looks. This is further emphasized on the second page in a similar panel, where we learn that she does not get on with her stepmother, and the (albeit innocent) question she asks only makes Linda feel worse about herself. Despite Linda's curt responses and cynical thoughts, at this stage in the story, she is our Cinderella, and we feel sorry for her.

When the magical item enters the story, it is described in distinctly fairy-tale terms ("Gaze into it for a full minute first thing in the morning and last thing at night") and, of course, comes with a warning ("Don't let any harm befall it, I warn you . . ."). The pace picks up in these panels (the bottom row of page 2), as they are tall and narrow. They also lack borders, creating white space in the middle of the page that prevents it from appearing too crowded despite the heavy dialogue.

The following page introduces the transformation: Linda's face appears multiple times in an unpanelized sequence, using the De Luca effect. An image of her posing in a bikini emphasizes her changed figure and provides a counterpoint to the opening image of page 3, where a frumpy Linda stares into her mirror. In contrast to the other three pages, this one is composed entirely of

180 A TAXONOMY OF TERROR

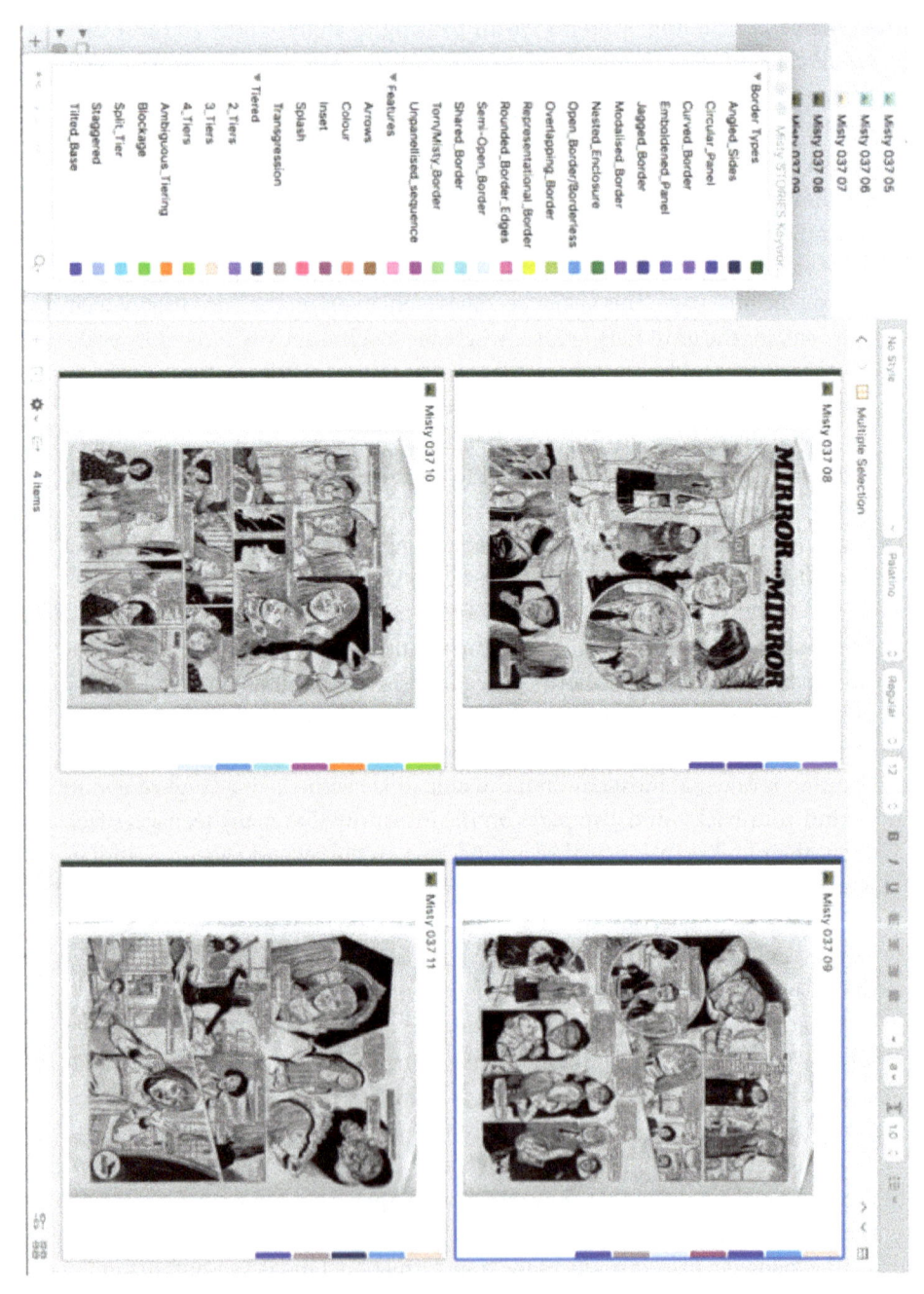

Figure 8.5. Tagged pages from "Mirror . . . Mirror" (*Misty* #37) using Scrivener. The colors shown on the right of each story page relate to the full list shown on the left-hand side. Courtesy of Paul Fisher Davies. Reproduced with permission of Misty™ Rebellion Publishing IP Ltd.; copyright © Rebellion Publishing IP Ltd., all rights reserved.

straight square lines: the regiment of time passing. Again we see people talking behind Linda's back, but in this instance we are not given the closeness to her that we had at the start of the narrative. The moment when the mirror is broken in fact puts us close to her mother's hurt face as she slams the door behind her after Linda calls her jealous and ugly.

On the last page, the story's full impact comes from its dramatic unhappy ending. This is hidden from us until the final grotesque panel: Linda keeps her back to us in the middle row of the page. The scene is given added power, since Linda's mother has fainted in the background and is lying in the hallway, and Linda's dialogue ("Oh no! Oh no-oo-oooh!") emphasizes her despair. The composition of the final panel also adds impact, as it confronts us directly with Linda's misshapen face as she gazes toward us while viewing her reflection in the bathroom mirror. The angles return on this page, along with the sense of space in its top row as Linda shrugs off the accident but worries about it in her dreams. This then gives way to sharply angular panels that increase the dramatic tension. The closing narration has a knowing tone ("But Linda might not want to use the mirror today. . . . She may never use a mirror again"), emphasized by the final pun ("face yourself"). It aligns the reader again with Linda, bringing us into the story with direct address ("After all, would you want to face yourself every morning, like this . . .") and abandoning us here.

The story closes with a typical *Misty* negative ending that sounds quite permanent ("never . . . again") and combines a magical item with the backfiring of the protagonist's actions. The identification we have felt with Linda (as focalizing character, protagonist, and victim of the same bullying and insecurities that many teenage girls experience) only sharpens the impact. Linda has been vain and mean, and it is because of this that the magic mirror has been broken. In addition, she has been punished by poetic justice: because she became vain about her beauty, her beauty is what has been destroyed. On the last page, the final image of Linda's shattered face (bottom right) pairs with the first panel (top left), which shows her reflection in the shattered glass of the mirror. This doubling increases the feeling of poetic justice and inevitability.

"Mirror . . . Mirror" and the other *Misty* stories mobilize shocking and magical plot tropes alongside Gothic themes of isolation, persecution, power, and excess. These stories' outcomes are often extreme and confrontational, and although the fare of *Misty* is not as consistently negative as readers might remember, it is perhaps more disturbing owing to this variety and inconsistency with moral "rules." Protagonists are more often good than bad, but this does not guarantee them a happy ending—many of the tales punish rather than reward. Although girls who are selfish or dishonest are very likely to get their comeuppance, redemption is possible, and accidental or undeserved bad endings for good characters also feature prominently. This creates a strong moral message but adds a sense of ambivalence, as character behavior does not always equate with outcome.

In some respects, the *Misty* stories do follow aspects of what Pat Mills calls the "formula." More than half the stories are based on one or more of his categories, such as a Cinderella or other persecuted Gothic heroine who is our focalizing character, and whose search (for answers, escape, a friend, or home) drives the plot forward. However, Mills's formulas apply much more to *Misty*'s serials than to the single stories, and the Mystery formula dominates completely; the other formulas appear most often in combination with it.

The majority of the *Misty* stories revolve around an encounter with a mysterious object, event, person, or ability. Protagonists may receive enchanted or magical items or powers or be the victim of a trick or a trap, but these external factors are seldom effective alone. Characters' own actions are most often the catalyst for their downfall—and *Misty*'s stories do, more often than not, end in downfall or on an ambivalent note. Faustian bargains are made, and wishes are indeed granted, but often with horrifying consequences that are narrowly avoided—or not. The story endings in particular draw on the unexpected, providing shock twists or brutally poetic justice, and the space of the page and the active role of the reader are often used to enhance the emotional affect. Gothic duality is created through the presence of both *plaisir* and *jouissance*, enhanced by other aspects of the publication I have already discussed, such as the comedy series and Misty's reassuring presence. In the next chapter, I continue to explore the combination of such diverse or opposed strategies for creating fear.

A TAXONOMY OF TERROR   183

Figure 8.6. (pages 183–86) "Mirror . . . Mirror" (*Misty* #37). Art by Isidre Monés, writer unknown. Reproduced with permission of Misty™ Rebellion Publishing IP Ltd.; copyright © Rebellion Publishing IP Ltd., all rights reserved.

AYE, IT'S EASY FOR ME, RIGHT ENOUGH! 'COS I'VE GOT THE SECRET, LASS. THE SECRET OF REAL BEAUTY. HEE,HEE... MAYBE ONE DAY I'LL SHARE THE MAGIC WITH YOU.
WHAT A BATTY OLD DEAR! WHAT CAN SHE KNOW ABOUT IT? AND IF SHE HAS GOT A SECRET, WHY DOESN'T SHE USE IT ON HERSELF?
AT HOME, THINGS WERE STRAINED AS USUAL. LINDA JUST COULDN'T GET ON WITH HER STEPMOTHER...
WHAT'S ON THE AGENDA TONIGHT, LINDA— GOING ANYWHERE SPECIAL?
DON'T BE FUNNY! WHERE COULD I BE GOING? WHO'D WANT TO TAKE ME?
THAT OLD CRONE WAS WRONG! IF I WAS BEAUTIFUL I'D HAVE NO PROBLEMS AT ALL! I COULD GO ANYWHERE... DO ANYTHING!
NEXT DAY, ON THE WAY HOME FROM SCHOOL, SHE MET THE OLD WOMAN AGAIN...
HOLD ON, DEARIE, I'VE BEEN WAITING FOR YOU.
WHAT ON EARTH FOR?
I'VE DECIDED TO SHARE MY SECRET WITH YOU... MY MAGIC WILL GIVE YOU THE BEAUTY YOU'VE ALWAYS DESIRED. WE'LL SEE IF IT GIVES YOU THE HAPPINESS YOU EXPECT IT TO!
THIS IS NO ORDINARY MIRROR, DEARIE. GAZE INTO IT FOR A FULL MINUTE FIRST THING IN THE MORNING AND LAST THING AT NIGHT, AND THE MAGIC WILL DO THE REST. YOU WILL NOTICE THE CHANGES AT ONCE.
SHE'S TOTALLY FLIPPED! A MAGIC MIRROR, HAH!
I'LL TAKE IT ANYWAY. IT'S GOT A FANCY FRAME AND I NEED A MIRROR FOR MY ROOM. BUT IMAGINE JUST GIVING IT AWAY!
BUT TAKE GOOD CARE OF IT, GIRL. DON'T LET ANY HARM BEFALL IT, I WARN YOU...

A TAXONOMY OF TERROR 185

THAT SILLY, UGLY FOOL! SHE BROKE MY MIRROR! I COULD KILL HER FOR THAT!
BUT WHAT CAN IT MATTER? I'LL FIND THAT OLD CRONE, SHE CAN MAKE ME ANOTHER ONE. AND EVEN IF SHE CAN'T, I KNOW I'M BEAUTIFUL ENOUGH ALREADY.
BUT AS SHE SLEPT, THE OLD WOMAN'S FINAL WORDS CAME BACK TO LINDA . . .
TAKE GOOD CARE OF IT, GIRL. . . NO HARM BEFALL IT. . . I WARN YOU. . .
AND NEXT MORNING. . .
Y-YAWN. . . OH, WHAT A NUISANCE. I'LL HAVE TO USE THE BATH-ROOM MIRROR TO GET READY THIS MORNING. . .
BUT LINDA MIGHT NOT WANT TO USE THE MIRROR TODAY. . . SHE MAY NEVER USE A MIRROR AGAIN. . .
AAAARGH!
WH-WHAT'S WRONG? WHAT ARE YOU SCREAMING AT? TELL ME?
AFTER ALL, WOULD YOU WANT TO FACE YOURSELF EVERY MORNING, LIKE THIS. . .
OH NO! OH NO-OO-OOOH!
THE END

CHAPTER 9

TERROR, HORROR, AND FEMALE GOTHIC

There is little doubt that *Misty* is so well remembered because of its ability to cause fear; Collings (2012) refers to "a legion of females who had experienced the terror and insomnia that was *Misty*," describing it as "literally terrifying" and "a potential 'life ruiner.'" Rayner (2012) says: "*Misty* was hardcore and scared the hell out of me." Gibson (2015, 133) cites a reader named Elsa, who describes it as "my introduction to horror/occult/general weird shit writing." The existence of this book testifies to the impact that a single horrifying image from *Misty* had on me. But, as discussed, *Misty* was not intended to be a horror comic. So what use does it make of fear? This chapter explores the construction of terror and horror and then moves to consider these terms from a gendered perspective, reviewing the critical development of Female Gothic to arrive at a working definition. I carry this definition forward into the next chapters and use it to cultivate my notion of Gothic for Girls.

TERROR AND HORROR

Despite its claims to be a "mystery" comic, the covers of *Misty* predominantly use images of terror (the speculative unseen) or horror (the recoil from a shocking image). They can be broken down as follows. Of 101 issues, forty-one (40 percent) show a fearful reaction (wide eyes, screaming, running); thirty-six (36 percent) show a hideous image (a skeleton, monster, or animal); fourteen (14 percent) show an image of Misty herself; and ten (10 percent) contain some other nonthreatening or abstract image (horses, fairies, etc.). I would argue that the covers that show fear with no source (as in fig. 9.1) demonstrate terror, since they focus on the sensory reaction and contain obscuration. By contrast, covers with a dangerous or unnatural creature (as in fig. 9.2) create horror. Where a cover contains both a horrifying image (such as a giant locust) and a terrified reaction to it (such as a girl screaming), I have classified the cover according to the one that is the most dominant based on its size, color, and position. My

188　TERROR, HORROR, AND FEMALE GOTHIC

Figure 9.1a. Terror-based covers: *Misty* #4 (art by María Barrera Castell, "Roots"). Reproduced with permission of Misty™ Rebellion Publishing IP Ltd.; copyright © Rebellion Publishing IP Ltd., all rights reserved.

TERROR, HORROR, AND FEMALE GOTHIC 189

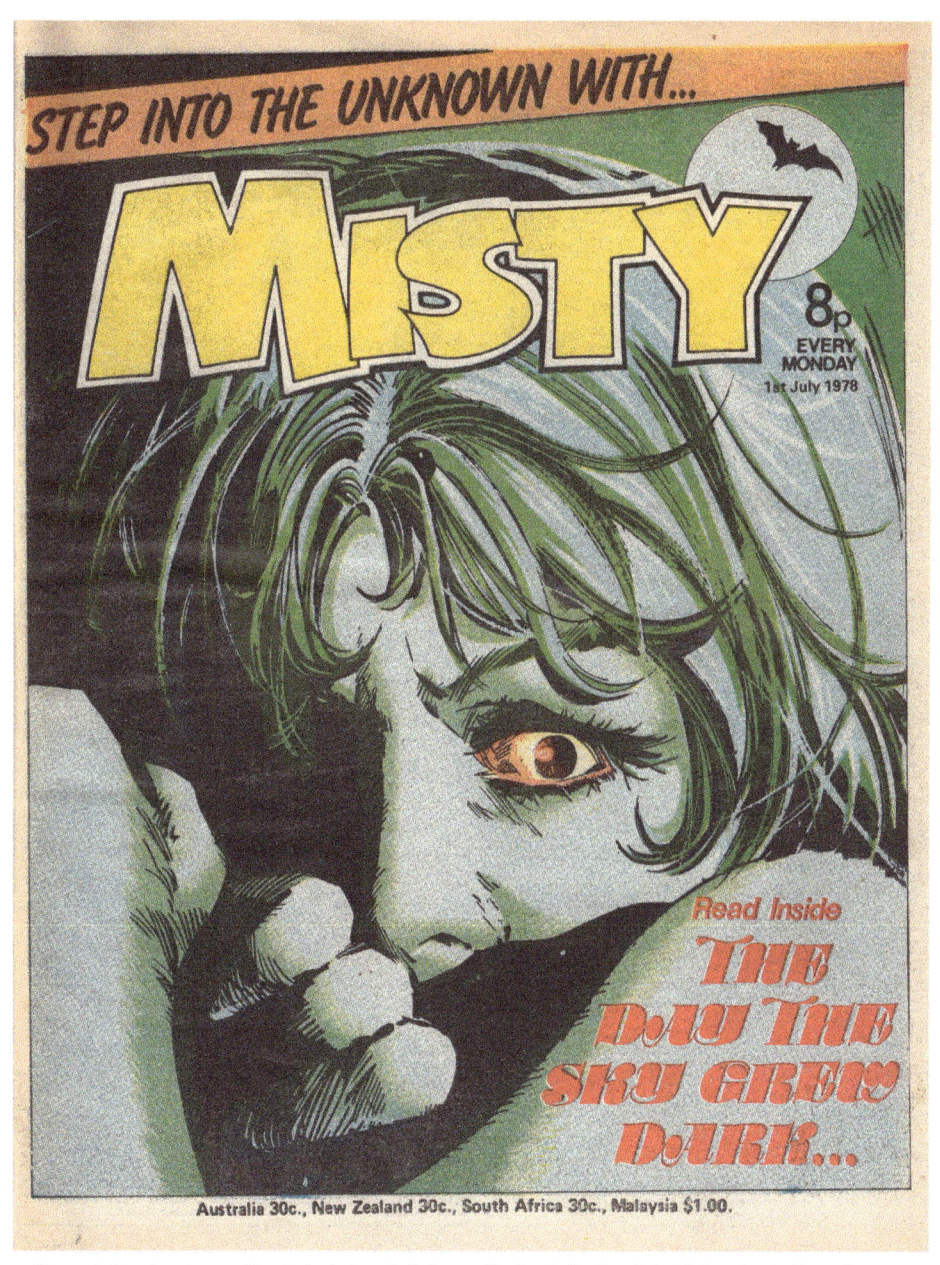

Figure 9.1b. Terror-based covers: *Misty* #22 (art by Jorge Badía Romero, "The Day the Sky Grew Dark..."). Reproduced with permission of Misty™ Rebellion Publishing IP Ltd.; copyright © Rebellion Publishing IP Ltd., all rights reserved.

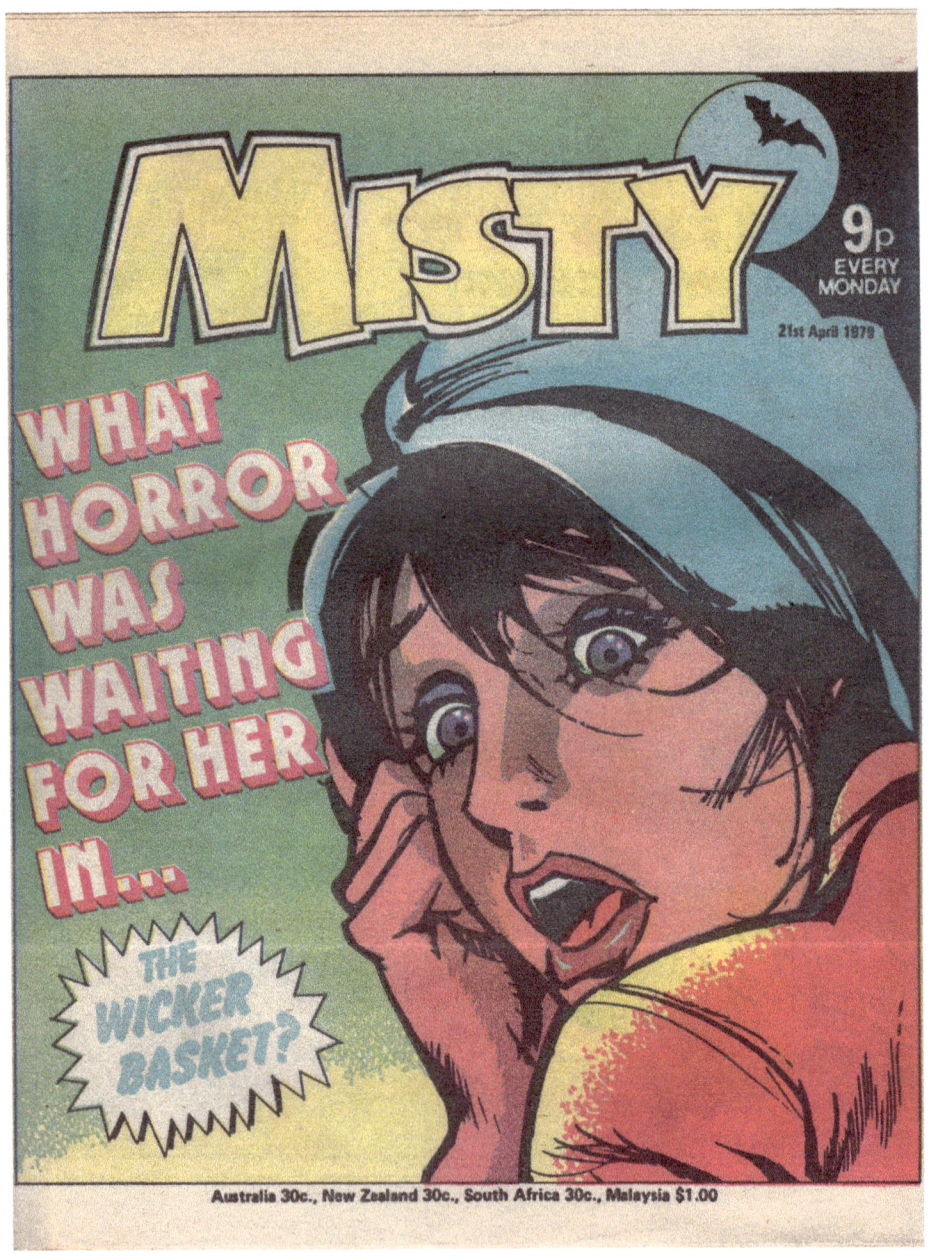

Figure 9.1c. Terror-based covers: *Misty* #63 (art by Josép Gual, "The Wicker Basket"). Reproduced with permission of Misty™ Rebellion Publishing IP Ltd.; copyright © Rebellion Publishing IP Ltd., all rights reserved.

TERROR, HORROR, AND FEMALE GOTHIC   191

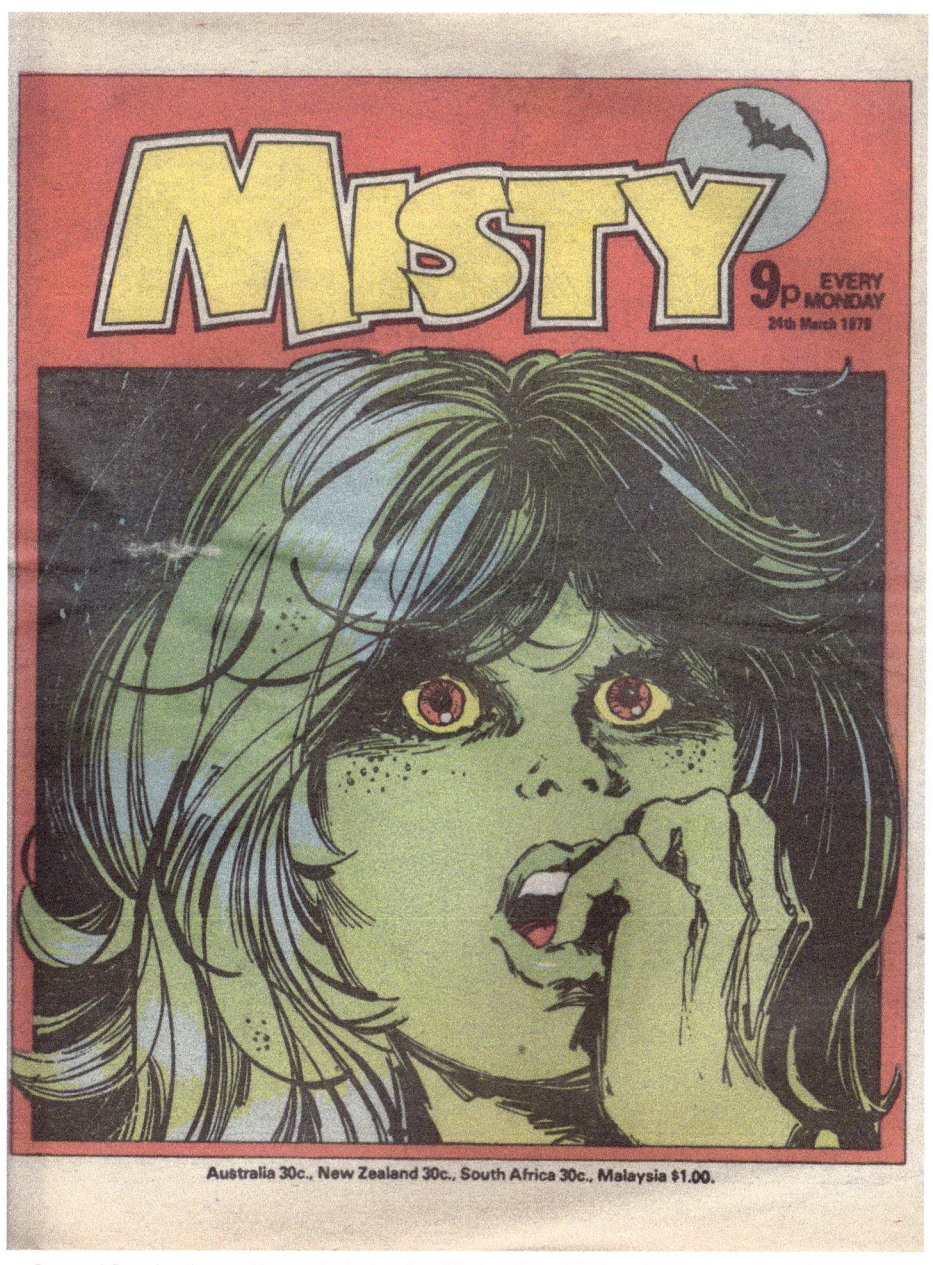

Figure 9.1d. Terror-based covers: *Misty* #59 (art by Juan Ariza, "Shadow of a Doubt"). Reproduced with permission of Misty™ Rebellion Publishing IP Ltd.; copyright © Rebellion Publishing IP Ltd., all rights reserved.

Figure 9.2a. Horror-based covers: *Misty* #18 (art by Homero, "Skullduggery"). Reproduced with permission of Misty™ Rebellion Publishing IP Ltd.; copyright © Rebellion Publishing IP Ltd., all rights reserved.

TERROR, HORROR, AND FEMALE GOTHIC 193

Figure 9.2b. Horror-based covers: *Misty* #72 (artist unknown, "The Story of Little Wytching"). Reproduced with permission of Misty™ Rebellion Publishing IP Ltd.; copyright © Rebellion Publishing IP Ltd., all rights reserved.

Figure 9.2c. Horror-based covers: *Misty* #61 (art by Homero, "The Cult of the Cat"). Reproduced with permission of Misty™ Rebellion Publishing IP Ltd.; copyright © Rebellion Publishing IP Ltd., all rights reserved.

TERROR, HORROR, AND FEMALE GOTHIC 195

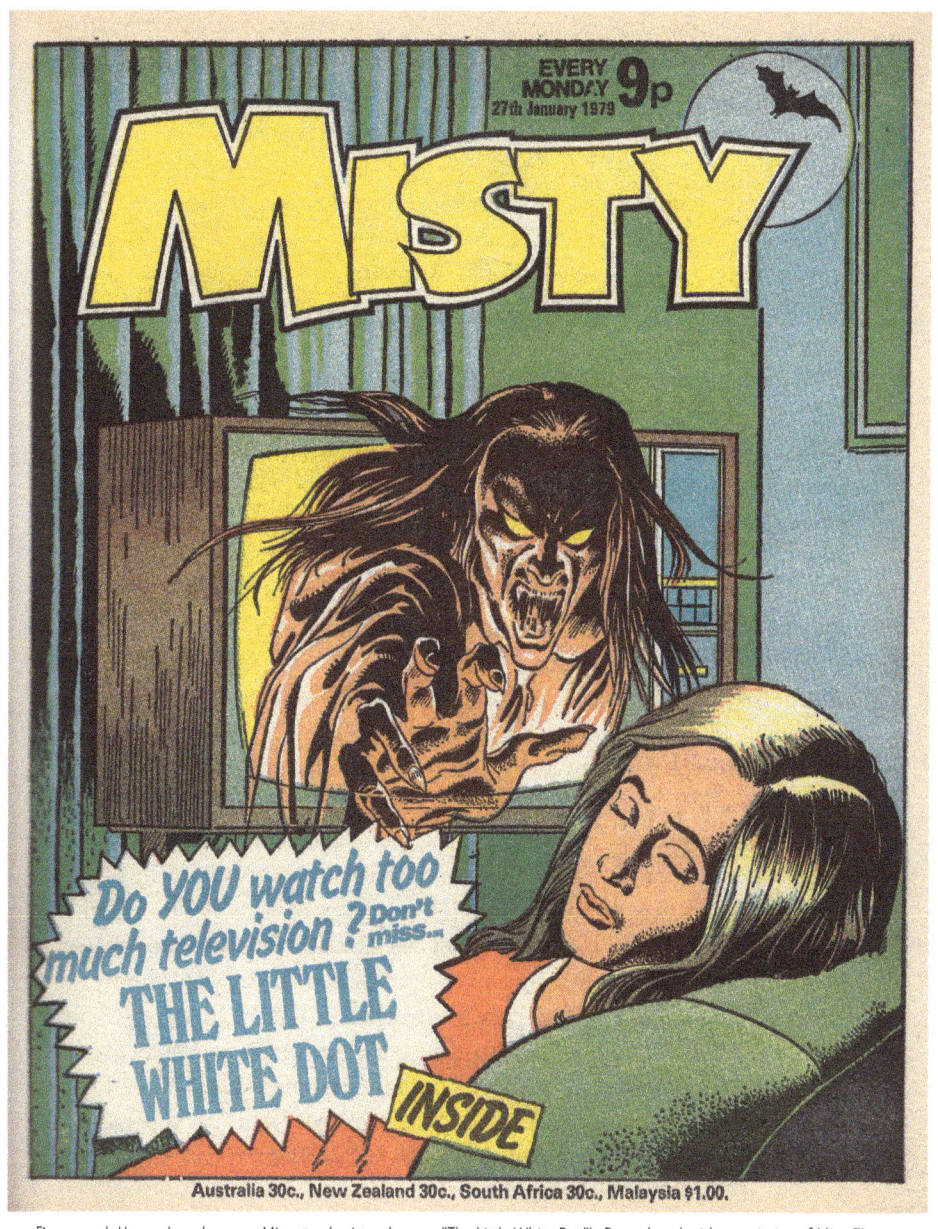

Figure 9.2d. Horror-based covers: *Misty* #51 (artist unknown, "The Little White Dot"). Reproduced with permission of Misty™ Rebellion Publishing IP Ltd.; copyright © Rebellion Publishing IP Ltd., all rights reserved.

findings show that the vast majority of *Misty* covers exploit either horror or terror, in roughly equal measure, rather than suggesting mystery and intrigue or soothing us with Misty's own image.

By contrast, the *Misty* story titles primarily create mystery and suspense rather than outright fear. As well as the allusions to existing texts noted in chapter 6, titles generally tend toward the suggestive rather than the explicit, for example, by referencing a mysterious item without explanation, as in "The Jukebox" (#28), "The Dummy" (#4), "The Swarm" (#9, Annual 1979), "The Silver Racer-Back" (#83–91), and others. Similarly, many titles are puns or knowing references to the story's content, such as "Examination Nerves" (#47), "The Writing on the Wall" (#76), or "Prize Possession" (#19). When the titles do use a Gothic lexis, they most commonly refer to a monster of some kind (such as a witch, vampire, gorgon, or fiend, which total nineteen instances in 443 stories, or just 4 percent) or a ghost or haunting (eighteen instances, or 4 percent). These are followed by evocative references to night or dark (also including the words "black" and "shadow"), which appear sixteen times (4 percent), and some quite visceral words around death ("dead," "kill," "blood," "bone," "grave," "tomb"), which total fifteen appearances (3 percent). The lexis of fear ("terror," "horror," "dread") is the next most common, featuring thirteen times (3 percent), followed by fatalistic words such as "fate," "doom," and "last" (nine appearances, or 2 percent) and magical words such as "curse," "voodoo," and "spell" (eight appearances, or 2 percent). The remaining word groups include "strange" (five instances), "revenge" (four), "cold" (three), "evil" (three), "sad" (three), "secret" (three), "spooky" (two), "scream" (two), and "broken" (one), which each account for less than 1 percent of the tales.

I have examined the appearance of both terror and horror in *Misty*'s content in previous work (see Round 2017, which compares *Misty* with DC Thomson's *Spellbound*), but the results bear repeating here. Using a discrete random sample of ten issues of *Misty* (containing sixty-four individual story episodes), I first discovered that all (100 percent) use some instance of fear. However, just fourteen of the stories (22 percent) rely on a monstrous image or effect to horrify (such as skeletons, gorgons, spiders, sea demons, a fire, rats, snakes, beetles, melting waxworks, and zombies). The remaining fifty stories (78 percent) do not show anything horrifying: although dramatic events and characters such as traffic accidents and witches feature, there is no grotesquerie or gore. Instead they raise tension through their narrative stance and by suggesting an impending doom.

A typical example of the horror-Gothic in *Misty* might be "Queen's Weather" (#18) (fig. 9.3), where Sally swats a bee and is attacked by a swarm that traps her in its hive. The page layout highlights her fear in the central panel, and Josép Gual's art also emphasizes the horror, depicting the bees as monstrous and alien. The final image juxtaposes her smooth, untextured skin against the giant

TERROR, HORROR, AND FEMALE GOTHIC 197

Figure 9.3. "Queen's Weather" (*Misty* #18). Art by Josép Gual, writer unknown. Reproduced with permission of Misty™ Rebellion Publishing IP Ltd.; copyright © Rebellion Publishing IP Ltd., all rights reserved.

Figure 9.4. "Hold Tight, Please!" (*Misty* #29). Art by Peter Wilkes, writer unknown. Reproduced with permission of Misty™ Rebellion Publishing IP Ltd.; copyright © Rebellion Publishing IP Ltd., all rights reserved.

bees' detailed, hairy bodies. A similar strategy is used in "Red Knee—White Terror!" (#1; see fig. 2.2), where a detailed image of the spider is foregrounded alongside physical sensations as it attacks Andrea ("It-it . . . w-wants . . . to . . . g-go . . . on m-my . . . hair!!!").

Conversely, the terror-Gothic informs stories such as "Hold Tight, Please!" (#29) (fig. 9.4), where June and Gail catch a mysterious, ghostly bus home from the disco. The story ends happily (they escape and make it home, where they discover that the bus they were supposed to take was involved in a fatal collision), but before this it creates a creeping terror that is emphasized through their wide eyes, isolation, and the obscuration of any information ("I can't see a thing out there"). Peter Wilkes's art uses heavily shadowed images, contributing to the feel of increasing nervousness and awakened senses.

For readers who remember *Misty* best for its horrifying images or shock story endings of grotesque transformation (as in fig. 8.3), these results are revealing. In general the horror remains largely unshown, and instead the tales terrify through the unseen and suggested. Townshend's (2016) claim that terror is sublime while horror is sensation chimes with Heiland's discussion of the creation of fear in Gothic novels, which is achieved "through their engagement with the aesthetic of the sublime or some variant of it" (Heiland 2004, 5). This is an encounter with something so powerful that we are awed and the borders of meaning and identity begin to crumble. *Misty*'s magical items, powerful witches, mysterious curses, and character transformations are all examples of encounters with the sublime, as protagonists are confronted with grand forces that destroy their sense of meaning and even their own identity as they are trapped, changed, or otherwise subsumed by greater powers. The struggles with identity that characterize the serials further support this interpretation.

FEMALE GOTHIC

The distinction between horror and terror has sometimes been conceptualized in male and female terms, for example, describing the writing of Ann Radcliffe as terror, and that of Matthew Lewis as horror. Gendered approaches to Gothic are fraught with difficulty, and "Female Gothic" in particular is a problematic term that has proved most valuable for the debates it has provoked, which I will explore here.

Some of the complications of the Female Gothic can be seen in the body of scholarship that has developed around the Gothic heroine. Such work has traditionally focused on the Radcliffean Gothic, with critics such as Moers ([1976] 1978) exploring the Gothic heroine as a critique of male oppressors: a blameless victim suffering under tyranny. But while scholars such as Horner and Zlosnik (2017, 186) claim that Radcliffe's fiction "features imperiled but resourceful young female protagonists," other scholars find these heroines more passive than resourceful and have argued that Female Gothic and Gothic feminism thus naturalize woman-as-victim (Meyers 2001, 10–11). They point out that these pursued and imprisoned women demonstrate a lack of agency (Horner 2010) and that their development is only enabled by the trials they undergo and the interventions of the villain (Tóth 2010). Horner (2010) argues that this "powerful legacy" continues until the twentieth century, when Gothic heroines (e.g., in the work of Fay Weldon or Angela Carter) become unruly and abject. However, scholars such as Clery (1995) challenge these readings of the Gothic heroine. Clery points out that the character defies patriarchal authority without support, and other critics (Corson 2010; Braude 1998; Hoeveler 1998) also note that the contemporary Gothic heroine embodies "a more progressive notion of female empowerment" (Corson 2010, 17) and "forms a more equal alliance with the hero" (Braude 1998, 103).

Contradictions and paradoxes like these abound in the debates around Female Gothic. Coined by Ellen Moers in *Literary Women* ([1976] 1978), "Female Gothic" originally referred simply to "the work that women have done in the literary mode that since the eighteenth century, we have called the Gothic" (90). Moers was the first to consider the Female Gothic as a distinct practice or set of literary conventions, located in the work of female writers. Her work followed more than a decade of consciousness-raising through feminist activism and was produced in a context where social attitudes toward women had changed greatly. By the mid-1970s, women had achieved many of the freedoms that they asked for, and gender inequalities and female issues were acknowledged to have value and weight, although the legacy of past inequalities still loomed large. The decade thus combined empowerment and optimism with a continued hangover of entrapment and limitation, and it is worth noting that *Misty* was also devised at this time.

Moers's pioneering analysis of the Female Gothic surveys different types of "heroinism" in the writing of high-profile female authors, analyzing their biographies alongside their works and identifying coded representations of domestic entrapment and female sexuality. From this analysis, Moers defines two types of Female Gothic: "traveling heroinism" (as in the work of Ann Radcliffe) and the "birth myth" (as in the work of Mary Shelley). Moers draws attention to the active agency of these Gothic writers and their heroines and points out that it was the (male) writers who came after Radcliffe who rewrote the Gothic heroine as "quintessentially a defenceless victim, a weakling, a whimpering, trembling, cowering little piece of propriety whose sufferings are the source of her erotic fascination" (137). Her reclamation of the legacy of female writers is continued in Gilbert and Gubar's seminal *The Madwoman in the Attic* (1979), which uses psychoanalytic theory to explore anxieties about space and authorship in nineteenth-century women's writing and takes the Gothic doubling of Jane Eyre and Bertha Rochester as its central metaphor for the predicament of the woman author. The authors argue that the "woman writer feels herself to be literally or figuratively crippled by the debilitating alternatives her culture offers her" (57), and the images of confinement, monstrous bodies, and uncontrolled growth (of hair or size) that characterize such writing represent how "a 'thinking woman' might inevitably feel . . . imprisoned within her own alien and loathsome body" (89). Modleski's ([1982] 1990) subsequent analysis of "mass produced fantasies for women" also applies psychoanalysis to the Gothic novel, arguing for a cathartic function that allows female readers to work through profound psychic conflicts, especially ambivalence and paranoia, and to explore them in relation to the systematic oppression of women in society.

Andrew Smith (2004, 80) summarizes that "for Ellen Moers the Female Gothic was characterized by concerns about motherhood and associated images of birth trauma. Later criticism focused attention on how specific structural features, including images of absent mothers and 'lost' daughters, were related to the form's anti-patriarchal politics." Many critics have pointed out that these 1970s models are more reflective of the ideologies of second-wave feminism than an objective description of the narratives of women writers. Fitzgerald (2004) draws attention to the way in which Female Gothic hitched itself to the "rising star" of feminism and thus became institutionalized as one of the means of uncovering lost traditions of women's work and literature. Ledoux (2017) also interrogates this period, noting the disproportionate critical weighting that is given to Radcliffe's writing. Ledoux points out that Female Gothic is frequently used as shorthand for a narrative of female victimization (often within the confines of domesticity and marriage), despite overwhelming evidence that engagement with these stories is much more complicated. She argues that categorizing works in this way creates more problems than it solves, and the development of a women's Gothic tradition was much more nuanced, slow, and organic than early critics and later feminists describe.

These early scholars define Female Gothic as originating in Romance and being concerned with ownership and property as the grounds for rights and personhood. Fitzgerald also draws attention to the ways in which this rhetoric ("maps," "territories," "breaking ground," "space," and "landmarks") dominates feminist criticism of the 1970s and 1980s. Female Gothic is effectively defined as a tale voiced by a woman, articulating female experience, and based on a typical plot. Miles (1994, 131) defines this as being about a heroine in flight, who is caught between pastoral and threat, running either from a sinister patriarch or toward an absent mother. He adds that in the 1980s this interpretation was reformulated to refer to the collective unconscious and its repressions, not the individual psyche of the author.

Whereas the 1970s critics read Female Gothic as interrogating motherhood and femininity, in the 1980s poststructuralist critics approached Female Gothic through a series of critical lenses, such as the feminist, romantic, transgressive, and revolutionary. Fleenor's edited collection (1983) explores debates around the conservative and radical qualities of Female Gothic in four main areas: mystique (its popular appeal), madness (the female experience in patriarchal society), monsters (isolation and sexuality), and maternity (the body as literary metaphor). These essays investigate the theme of female identity, rather than the gender of the writer, and are often conflicting. Taken together, they reflect the many facets of Female Gothic as it has been articulated by feminist criticism, and point toward the problems of literal representation, the insufficiencies and polarities of language, and the need for a literary and critical pluralism that recognizes the manner in which Female Gothic is shaped by a male reality and surrounded by a patriarchal society. Transcendence is not possible in this conception of Female Gothic, which instead articulates the struggle to survive in a patriarchal world and thus portrays a "common schizophrenia" shared by Gothic and the female experience, which has been formed by various dichotomies (patriarchal, feminist, Manichean, etc.) (Fleenor 1983, 28). Many of the chapters explore the roles offered to women, recognizing these "partial lives" not as "open possibilities" but as "traps" (K. Stein 1983, 129).

Sedgwick (1986, ix) also recognizes a divide in Gothic writing between the "male paranoid plot" and the "maternal or monstrous plot," focusing on key ideas of interment and possession such as "live burial." In her parsing, this can take many incarnations (literal, figurative, and structural): for example, conventual imprisonment as a plot event, the findings of phenomenological or psychoanalytic readings, or the salience of "within," such as when we find embedded stories within stories. Sedgwick devotes a whole chapter to the notion of "live burial" as underpinning language itself, where meaning is hidden within the signified. My own (2014a) examination of the comics medium as an encrypted space follows similar lines.

Kate Ferguson Ellis (1989) returns to the image of the castle to offer a social critique of the development of Female Gothic, rather than the Marxist or psychoanalytic approaches offered by other scholars. She argues that the changing social role of women in the eighteenth century required a new ideology of the female archetype, moving from weak and easily tempted to innocent and passionless. This redefinition narrowed the options for women to a point of passivity, against which the sensation novel appears as a reaction and protest. The heroine's terror is an enactment of these limitations—she cannot be allowed the knowledge of rape or violence—just as her flight enacts a political objection to the imprisonments offered to her by marriage. Ellis describes Female Gothic as an "insider" narrative, with the "outsider" Male Gothic running as a parallel discourse that explores the innocence of wandering (male) heroes in the face of shame (external) and guilt (internal).

Female Gothic is next revisited in a special issue of the journal *Women's Writing* (1994). By this point, critics had thirty years of scholarship to draw on, and so this collection has a retrospective and evaluative feel. The essays summarize Female Gothic's historical development and offer culturally situated analyses. They draw attention to a number of gendered features in Gothic, exploring the use of the sublime (Milbank, Botting), consumerism and luxury (Clery), and possession and doubling (Punter).

Anne Williams's *Art of Darkness* (1995) is the next landmark text to address gender in Gothic. It defines Gothic as a poetic tradition, like Romance, with both a male and a female genre. Instead of arguing for Gothic as an inherently female mode (that expresses "the ambivalently attractive, 'female,' unconscious 'other' of eighteenth-century male-centred conscious 'Reason'" [19]), Williams explores the complications and contradictions within such approaches. Her work argues that Male Gothic and Female Gothic refer to two distinct modes of writing, in general (although not always) practiced by writers of that gender. The two types contain clear differences in plot, narrative technique, and their treatment of the supernatural. Female Gothic provides a female-centered narrative (often with a limited point of view) and a happy ending that explains away the supernatural, bringing the heroine to completion (often via marriage). By contrast, the Male Gothic offers the dramatic irony of multiple focalizers or an awareness of the limitations of the point of view offered, accepts the supernatural as real, and ends tragically. Heroines in Male Gothic texts might survive, but they are not reborn or raised up; their stories often have an uncertain form of narrative closure and specialize in horror over terror, focusing on female suffering and positioning the audience as voyeurs (102–4). So whereas the "most crucial aspect of the Female Gothic plot [is] its constructive and empowering function for its female readers" (138), "the most oppressive anti-feminism is encoded in Male Gothic, organized around a 'female' 'other' both victimized and demonized" (136). Williams offers a close reading of Bluebeard's castle as an example of Male Gothic, reading its landscape as a complex metaphor for cultural power and gender arrangement—literally built on the bloody bodies of dead wives, like the patriarchy. She argues that "the Male Gothic heroine is, like Bluebeard's wife, caught in the ideology of a culture that reifies her 'female nature' as curious, inconstant, disobedient, weak, and that places her in a situation where those qualities will lead her into danger" (105). Williams's parsing and naming of her Male and Female Gothics is based on their perceived ideological stance, which is speculatively linked to the gender of the author. Although I dispute the gendering of these categories, particularly as it relates to authorship, the dichotomy between the two types of Gothic story that Williams identifies certainly appears in *Misty*. In general the serials accord with Williams's definition of Female Gothic, as heroines are cast into scenarios they do not understand, yet ultimately rise toward their happy ending, where the supernatural events of the narrative are explained or accepted. By contrast, *Misty*'s single stories match some aspects of Williams's definition of Male Gothic, as the reader must watch the protagonist's fall and tragic end.

This revisionist third wave of Gothic criticism tries to redress the essentialism and generality within Female Gothic and to explore its contradictions in a poststructuralist world. Howard (1994) argues that in fact there is no Female Gothic, simply the acts of women writers who appropriate Gothic discourse in very different ways. Other critics offer new terminology or try to counterbalance the evangelical stance of Female Gothic, as it can suggest a dichotomy between "bad" male Gothic texts and "good" empowering female texts (Baldick and Mighall 2012, 285). Hoeveler (1998) claims that many Female Gothic tales in fact enact a negative and demeaning form of femininity that she names "victim feminism": "female power through pretended and staged weakness." Suzanne Becker (1999) argues instead for the term "feminine Gothic" and stresses that this reflects the gender of the speaking subject, not the author. Creed's *The Monstrous-Feminine* (1993) responds to Freud's catchall figure of woman-as-castrated and instead suggests that the female terrifies as potential castrator, listing seven types of monsters that draw on feminine tropes.

These critics interrogate Female Gothic and draw attention to its essentialist and overgeneral qualities. They expose its inequalities, place the focus back on the text rather than the author, and attempt to redress the unequal amount of critical attention paid to particular authors (such as Radcliffe) and formats (by privileging the novel over the short story [Wallace 2004]). In their introduction to a special issue of *Gothic Studies* (2004) revisiting Female Gothic, Smith and Wallace (2004) argue that Female Gothic has developed away from psychoanalytic readings of historical novels as direct metaphors for family relations within patriarchal society. Instead it now includes contemporary authors across multiple media and literary forms and is plural and visible. They therefore argue that Female Gothic is a facet of Gothic's ability to problematize and interrogate norms rather than a gendered explanation for Gothic symbols. Many of the critics in this volume reconsider established tropes: domestic markers (Wright 2004; Wisker), property and a critique of luxury (Wright 2004), ghosts and live burial (Wallace; Horner and Zlosnik), and desire (A. Smith 2004; Palmer). Other essays explore new angles and approaches: DeLamotte considers the intersection of Female Gothic and African American Gothic, arguing that both tell the story of the repressed mother, and Wallace considers the short story format as a marginalized example. Subsequent collections from Wallace and Smith (2009) and Horner and Zlosnik (2017) have continued to pursue similar ideas. In *The Female Gothic: New Directions* (2009), the essays continue the discussion of ghostliness (Wallace), the sublime (Miles, Milbank), the body (Lippe), and the grotesque (Milbank), alongside new directions exploring subjects such as incest, race, and nationhood.

So what is Female Gothic? And how can we arrive at a definition that isn't absurdly tautological or essentialist? (*"Female Gothic is about feminine themes which are those that are about females."*) Like Ledoux and Howard, I personally find the term more problematic than useful: lacking nuance and ignoring the very different interpretations and gratifications that women may seek through their writing and reading. While Female Gothic initially aimed to recognize the marginalized female reader and writer, Buckley (2018) and Spooner (2017) both note that only a particular (Radcliffean) type of Female Gothic has been reclaimed, primarily through elevation by association with Romance. The tastes of younger readers (Priest 2011) remain devalued, and my exploration of Gothic for Girls seeks to address this.

However, because I am exploring a type of Gothic written explicitly for female children (the constructed readers apparent in *Misty*), it seems impossible to ignore the common qualities that established critics have found when taking a gendered approach to Gothic. My critical approach is textual and thus has little regard for the gender of the author. Nonetheless, having explored the development and debates surrounding Female Gothic, this critical review offers the following suggestions:

- Female Gothic explores the problems of female experience, which are multiple, varied, and nonessential. It thus takes different forms at different times and in different cultures. It might address concepts such as motherhood, body fear, possession, or domesticity but is not limited to such ideas. This does not necessarily require direct voicing from a female focalizer, protagonist, or narrator or address to a constructed female reader, although one or more of these may be present.
- Female Gothic performs rebellion and transgression (which may or may not be successful and can be destructive), for example, against imprisonment, patriarchal rule, cultural limitations and expectations, or something else. This can be read as subversive.
- Female Gothic has a simultaneous moral stance, often against dissolution (e.g., in the form of luxury). This is mobilized or juxtaposed against the enactment of desire and can be read as conservative.
- Female Gothic may contain domestic motifs or feminine psychoanalytic symbols (e.g., mirrors, doubles, boxes, purses, houses, churches, or ships).
- Female Gothic can be created by authors of any gender.

To avoid tautology, I have found it necessary to offer some suggestions of the symbols and concerns that Female Gothic might employ, while also recognizing that these are culturally, temporally, and geographically specific and thus subject to change. Here I take my cue from critics such as Andrew Smith (2004, 80), who argues that images of the double, models of desire, and specific constructions of gender all have a special place in Female Gothic. Moers also draws attention to the appearance of Freudian dream symbols in Female Gothic, and so, while the claim is not absolute, I suggest that gendered symbols might appear in these texts.

By suggesting ways in which Female Gothic can be perceived as both subversive and conservative, I have sought to reconcile this dichotomy, as these two qualities often appear together in Gothic writing. Baldick and Mighall (2012, 285) draw attention to the tendency in Gothic scholarship to smooth over this duality in favor of framing Gothic literature as "excitingly subversive" or "scandalously reactionary." However, we can acknowledge the copresence of rules and their breaking without continuing to an absolute definition of the text as either subversive or conservative, recognizing that it contains the potential for both and that the emphasis will be different in different works and for different readers. This view is also supported by Williams's conceptions of Female and Male Gothic, where either empowerment or punishment may result. Chatterjee also takes a wider view, arguing that Gothic is all about boundaries and the transgressions of, and anxieties about, them. I thus view the tension between traditionalism and transgression as a key Gothic quality, which can be used to address gendered issues.

I have avoided ascribing the use of particular narrative strategies (such as the grotesque, the sublime, or the abject) to Female Gothic, as the scholarship surveyed contains numerous contradictions here. For example, Miles (2009) argues that Female Gothic is about the sublime and Male Gothic is about the gaze. This divide lends itself well to the terror/horror categories previously explored; however, it is undercut by Milbank's essay in the same collection (2009), which argues that the grotesque is associated with the Female and the sublime with the Male. I have also tried to avoid overgeneral statements about what story endings "must" do, or regarding their treatment of the supernatural. While Williams's Male Gothic and Female Gothic certainly refer to two distinct types of Gothic story (both of which appear in *Misty*), based on her summaries, they both enact aspects of the female experience, and her broad claims about happy/tragic tones seem overly simplistic. In addition, the model of Female Gothic she describes seems overreliant on Radcliffe, with the Male Gothic then arising as its counterpoint, rather than being so named because of particular qualities or its appeal to a constructed reader of this gender.

However, I do accept the need to recognize the existence of Male Gothic for Female Gothic to exist. Although not the focus of my discussion, this raises the question: what might the Male Gothic be in response to my categories? I would suggest that it instead explores the possibilities of male experience, perhaps addressing concepts such as strength, competition, dysfunction, or weakness, while not being limited to such ideas or the presence of a male focalizer/protagonist/narrator. In its conservative aspect, it would perform and explore ideas of power and assertion (which may or may not be successful and can be destructive), for example, against internalization, rebellion, maternal control, or cultural limitations and expectations. Conversely, its subversive aspect would take an immoral stance, displayed as transgressive or destructive behavior (e.g., against duty, inheritance, or expectations) and mobilized or juxtaposed against responsibilities. Motifs of wildness or masculine psychoanalytic symbols (such as weapons, staffs, or tools) might appear.

By this rationale, *Frankenstein* is primarily a Male Gothic story—exploring naked ambition and power and sidelining female characters and concerns. This is perhaps a surprising stance given the number of readings of *Frankenstein* as an interrogation of birth or motherhood (Rubenstein 1976; Moers [1976] 1978; Bewell 1988; Winnett 1990). But if we leave aside the gender and biography of its author, we can find little in *Frankenstein* that speaks to female experience, and such readings have been overtaken by an equal body of criticism focusing on its interrogation of masculine themes (Davis 1992; London 1993; Daffron 1999; McGavran 2000). Victor's creation is not a birth horror of the type Mary Shelley experienced: there is no bodily danger or pain, and his emotional separation from his creature in fact goes against the notion of *Frankenstein* as being about maternal issues or obstetrics; the book is more easily read as a interrogation of paternal responsibility and male ambition. In support of this reading, Kate Ferguson Ellis (1989, 177) points out that the novel, like the work of Lewis, Godwin, and Maturin, "shift[s] the focus of the myth of the fall so that the site upon which the contest is played out is not the body of a woman but the mind of a man." This argument also finds a precedent in Botting's (1994) interpretation of *Dracula*, which compares Stoker's and Radcliffe's treatments of domestic virtue and property and thus describes *Dracula* as "a male romance" (187).

Having considered Gothic's gendered qualities and demonstrated that *Misty* contains both terror-Gothic and horror-Gothic, I now look more closely at the ways it combines this. The following chapters explore how *Misty* uses some of the most common themes, tropes, and motifs associated with Female Gothic. Some of these are taken from the work of the critics discussed, and others have arisen from my survey of the *Misty* stories, which revealed a number of recurring themes and symbols. My aim is to examine how *Misty* rearticulates Gothic tropes in a manner suitable for a young female audience, with a view to ultimately establishing the conventions of a Gothic for Girls.

CHAPTER 10

DEEP CUTS

Gothic Concepts and Identities

Gothic is so vast that deciding how to approach its presence in *Misty* has been no easy task. How can one break down over 250 years of literature into easily approachable themes or symbols—and what must be excluded? Is the castle more important than the attic; do madwomen deserve attention over monsters?

Drawing on the critical reviews from my introduction and chapter 9, and the taxonomy of common story types and symbols discussed in chapter 8, the next two chapters explore how *Misty* uses some common Gothic themes and symbols. This chapter focuses on underlying ideas and literary concepts: in particular the abject, the grotesque, and the uncanny. I discuss the ways in which these concepts are informed by transgression and transformation, and conclude by exploring the identity discourses offered in *Misty*. I consider how these ideas are rearticulated for a young female audience and reflect on the roles assigned to male characters. I argue that the *Misty* single stories often draw on Female Gothic themes (incarceration, transformation) to create the abject, whereas the serials express uncertainties about family figures and patriarchal authority. Chapter 11 then complements this discussion by examining the symbols, settings, and archetypes that appear in *Misty* and investigating their relevance to gender and the Gothic.

By doing this, I hope to explore the complicated relationship between depth and surface that characterizes Gothic. This relationship can perhaps also be understood as a tension between affect and aesthetic, between theme and trope, or between sensation and superficiality. Dedicating a chapter to underlying ideas and then moving on to consider their narrative manifestations will allow me to explore how Gothic themes and trajectories play out at the level of story, rather than simply identifying the presence of common tropes and symbols. Sedgwick (1986) argues that surface, not depth, provides the defining features of Gothic narrative, but motifs and symbols are insufficient to define Gothic and can lead to analytical dead ends. Spooner (2017, 53, 10) points out that much scholarship is still "mired in the Gothic shopping list." She argues that it is more productive to search for the uses made of Gothic than to attempt to categorize its appearances, and her analysis thus makes claims for the political significance of aesthetic performances of Gothic. It draws on the contexts of camp and dandyism to argue that postmillennial Gothic represents the "ascendance of a visual Gothic," where the "images are the story" (2017, 185, 66). The following two chapters build on this critical stance, in combination with thematic analysis. By examining Gothic's affective themes and aesthetic symbols and reflecting on the relationship between the two, I hope to offer a holistic consideration of the *Misty* stories that will inform my construction of Gothic for Girls.

FEMALE GOTHIC AND THE ABJECT

My definition of the Female Gothic first notes its focus on the problems of female experience. Critics have identified aspects such as the Gothic flight (Miles 1994), the trappings of property (Wright 2004; Punter 1998; Fitzgerald 2004), physical transformation and anxieties about the body (Wollstonecraft 1792; Fitzgerald 2004), and isolation and live burial (Irigaray 1987; Hoeveler 1998). These are brought together in the "feminine carceral," where the female body either is imprisoned or is itself experienced as a prison (Davison 2009).

My discussion of *Misty* in chapter 8 places a large proportion of tales (167) under the heading "It's a Trap." These can be read as reflecting the Gothic flight as heroines try to escape a particular fate. The identity fears that Gothic heroines articulate (whether pursued or imprisoned) are historically tied to property and wealth: Tóth (2010, 31) notes that the female body and property are intertwined and associated with each other in eighteenth-century literature, and Corson (2010, 21) also argues that in Ann Radcliffe's works, wealth and power are defined as a "tool for oppressing rather than empowering women." As such, we can add *Misty*'s magical-item tales to this discussion (297), as they problematize notions of property through the unexplained or unexpected qualities of these objects, which often become dangerous or gain their own agency. The tales of transformation (see, e.g., figs. 8.3, 8.6) also have obvious relevance to the abject breakdown of borders, as do the stories in which the protagonist meets an unhappy ending (158), as this often manifests as imprisonment of some kind.

Freud discusses being buried alive (as both a trap to escape and a tragic fate) as the most uncanny thing of all (Wallace 2009, n10). The idea is explored further by critics such as Horner and Zlosnik (2004), Ellis (2012), and Wallace (2009), who defines "live burial" as a powerful way of representing the traditional female experience of marriage, and Sedgwick (1986), who explores the ways in which the term underpins the Gothic potential of language itself.

In its literal sense, interment (and, indeed, marriage) seldom appears within *Misty* ("Marble Jaws," #70, is a notable exception), although imprisonment in a grave or coffin appears as a threat or dream in four of the tales ("The Fetch," #2; "Girl in the Graveyard," Annual 1980; "Screaming Point," #96; and "Flight from Fear," #92, shown in fig. 8.2). However, many of the unhappy endings leave a protagonist trapped in some way, or with some aspect of her identity erased or threatened. For example, in "The Final Piece" (#44), Rita discovers her own image in a jigsaw puzzle she has stolen, and when she puts in the final piece, she becomes trapped in place of its previous owner: figuratively buried alive (fig. 10.1).

This story combines a number of elements of the Female Gothic. The jigsaw is a dangerous magical item, and Rita's theft of it is a transgressive act. She attempts a flight from the cottage but is thwarted in a manner that emphasizes her buried status, since she is unable to leave owing to what she perceives as blinding daylight (as she might see if she was underground). She herself is uncannily doubled in the jigsaw image, problematizing her body and ownership of it. Her fate is one of live burial and isolation (she cannot leave until another comes to replace her), and she is incarcerated in a domestic and archaic setting—the remote cottage owned by the old lady she has replaced. Panel borders shaped like doorframes with pointed apexes emphasize this theme. The story's conclusion shows Rita wrapping up the jigsaw to entice a new victim to replace her in turn—giving us an uncanny scene of repetition that completes the cycle. Isidre Monés's art is heavily crosshatched, adding to the sense of claustrophobia, and the page layout also underscores this feeling: Rita is shrouded in shadow and enclosed in a series of dark, solid panel frames, only breaking them when she attempts to venture outside. By contrast, the woman she has freed escapes the panel borders and seems almost to address the reader directly with her gaze and pointing finger (panel 3). The reader shares Rita's perspective in panels 2 and 3, and thus also the sense of interment.

The story articulates feminine fears of incarceration and loss of autonomy and identity, for example, as women have historically been reduced to chattels through marriage. It may not be too much to read this movement as abject, Julia Kristeva's term for the confrontation with that which "disrupts rules, systems, boundaries," where "I am at the border of my condition as a living being" (1982, 3). The abject is the experience of identity disruption: a breakdown between subject and object. Rita's experience merges her identity with that of an object (the jigsaw) and removes her agency. The focalization and visual perspective used extend this experience to the reader, transgressing the borders of identity still further.

Another good example of abjection through disrupted identity can be found in the serial "Hush, Hush, Sweet Rachel" (#42–52). Protagonist Lisa experiences

GOTHIC CONCEPTS AND IDENTITIES 211

Figure 10.1. "The Final Piece" (*Misty* #44). Art by Isidre Monés, writer unknown. Reproduced with permission of Misty™ Rebellion Publishing IP Ltd.; copyright © Rebellion Publishing IP Ltd., all rights reserved.

a series of terrifying lapses where she loses all control over her body and actions, becoming little more than a conduit for Rachel's spirit. During these episodes, she speaks in Rachel's voice and completely forgets her own identity ("Lisa? Who's Lisa . . . ?" #43). The loss of control intensifies when her enemy Rosie realizes she can trigger Lisa's fugue state by calling her Rachel, and Lisa's helplessness increases further when she and her friends repeatedly try to speak to her mother about their worries, to no avail. More direct abject imagery is also attached to Rosie, whose grotesque bulk is combined with disgusting eating habits, as she eats food slops for a bet (#49) and leaves rotting sandwiches in her desk (#47). But throughout the story, the abject primarily threatens Lisa, as her identity is repeatedly attacked and shaken. The story's visuals emphasize this theme further, as the cover of *Misty* #42 shows Lisa with half of her face obscured, and at various points in the story she is juxtaposed against ghostly images of Rachel. In one case their images merge as Lisa looks into a mirror and her face vanishes entirely, replaced by Rachel (#48).

Serrato (2017, 53) points out that young adult fiction often uses Gothic themes to express the "problems of identity coherence and the abjectness of the self" that accompany puberty. In interrogating identity, *Misty*'s abject engages directly with this idea. While *Misty* does not often confront us with the abject in many of the disturbing and defiling forms that Kristeva suggests (such as bodily fluids, waste, and gore), its items and characters disrupt rules and cross boundaries, blurring the lines between subject and object and performing transgressive actions.

THE GROTESQUE

Grotesque imagery has been discussed (and often decried) by critics from Vitruvius (ca. 27 BC) to Ruskin (1851–53). Ruskin names the grotesque an essential quality of Gothic, also following Gothic's wider elegiac tendency by denigrating the "new" "grotesque renaissance" and comparing it unfavorably with earlier forms (1853). Other seminal critics such as Kayser ([1957] 1981) offer historical surveys that trace the development of the grotesque in art and literature, suggesting that it employs the fusion of different realms. Russo (1994) also notes the grotesque's liminal nature (between visible and invisible, ordinary and extraordinary) and associations with the feminine and abject.

Spiegel (1972) draws attention to the wideness and incompatibility of critics' definitions of the grotesque, which range from tragicomedy to juxtaposition to the Southern Gothic to a character type. Some (such as Novak 1979) write whole articles on the subject without once offering a textual consideration or summary of what the grotesque might be. Later scholars such as Gleeson-White

(2001) also highlight this absence, pointing out that often the grotesque is simply equated with Gothic and strange. Like Ruskin's discourse of loss, this again frames Gothic as something paradoxical, elusive, and difficult to define.[1]

Ruskin identifies two distinct strands of the grotesque: the "sportive" (playful) and the terrible or fearful (1853, xxiii), and the distinction is picked up by many later critics such as Russo (1994). Mikhail Bakhtin's use of the grotesque in his discussion of Rabelais and the carnivalesque is probably the most famous discussion of the first type. Bakhtin (1984, 26) explores the grotesque body as a form of play and protest created from the material body. It is composed of apertures and convexities, or points of entry or exit, and thus reveals its essence "as a principle of growth which exceeds its own limits only in copulation, pregnancy, childbirth, the throes of death, eating, drinking, or defecation." By contrast, critics such as Kayser ([1957] 1981) explore the uncanny and horrible forms that the grotesque can take, where it relates more strongly to the psyche as a cultural projection of an inner state.

Russo (1994, 29) points out that etymological investigations of the grotesque (from grotto to womb to maternal) and Bakhtin's production of a "general grotesque" both sustain a static and universalistic notion of the feminine that is psychologically and politically regressive. Russo instead investigates the grotesque through the lens of feminism, exploring its presence in "high" culture and modernity rather than the "low" forms of the carnivalesque. Her analysis approaches the grotesque as uncanny and strange, noting its paradoxes, such as the production of femininity based on simultaneous lack (cavern) and excess (unruly).

While Bakhtin has been criticized for stretching the concept of the grotesque to cover any female body, its relevance to the changes of the maternal body is clear, and Hélène Cixous famously defines the female as "the body without beginning and without end" (cited in Russo 1994, 67). The relationship between the sublime and grotesque (like the sublime and abject) is often invoked in this regard: Russo (1994) suggests that the grotesque might be considered an ironic fall from the sublime, and Milbank (2009) argues that the grotesque is associated with the female, while the sublime is linked to the male. She establishes the grotesque as a marker of creation and of "a desire to burst physical and social barriers and aesthetic categories, and to enact transgression" (86). Russo (1986, 221) similarly notes its relevance to the female body as a "site of desirous excess," and Gleeson-White (2001) also concurs that the grotesque expresses and affirms growth, promise, and transformation.

With this in mind, it is worth considering the handful of stories in *Misty* that deal with uncontrolled growth (six episodes, or 0.7 percent), particularly of hair ("Crowning Glory," #101; "The Queen's Hair," #43). As hair is a marker of femininity, this incarnation of the grotesque is explicitly female. In "Crowning

Glory" jealous Rona drugs her cousin Catherine and cuts off her hair—but after Catherine dies in an accident, Rona is unintentionally trapped in a crypt and consumed by golden hair that grows up from the floor. The tropes of female envy, hair, uncontrolled growth, and live burial mark this story as grotesque, abject, and uncanny. Artist Mario Capaldi intensifies the reading experience on the final page by assigning us a series of unnatural high perspectives and drawing a struggling Rona against a black background, consumed by swathes of hair that surge toward her with intent.

Kayser ([1957] 1981, 185) suggests that "suddenness and surprise are essential elements of the grotesque," and in *Misty* the "final reveal" is used effectively to achieve the grotesque in a number of stories, as already explored (chap. 8). For example, in "Mirror . . . Mirror" (#37, fig. 8.6), Linda's shattered face is hidden from us until the story's final panel, which is emphasized through area (taking up nearly a quarter of the page), form (the angled top edge of the panel leads the reader's eye to her face), and site (its privileged position on the page). "Spitting Image" (#79) ends with a similar reveal of the now-hideous Princess Rebecca, and in "One Hour in Time" (#66), Miss Pilgrim drops the tray she is carrying when she sees that her charge Laura has become horrifyingly aged and withered. In "Dead Man's Eyes" (#79, fig. 8.3b), Glenda is cursed with a gift of prophecy, and the last third of the page is taken up with her skull-like face against a black background. Melodrama also features in many of these reveals, via the protagonists' verbalized horror or the reaction of an onlooker, such as Linda's cry ("Oh No! Oh No-oo-oooh!" #37), Jill's scream ("Aaaaaaaaaahhh!") in "Roots" (#1; see fig. 10.2), Linda's mother fainting on the bathroom floor (#37), Miss Pilgrim's shock (#66), or the reflected image of Glenda's screaming friends (#79).

Other examples of grotesque or horrifying art include the half-man, half-plant Dr. Bracken (fig. 3.4), the skeletal Dr. Stark in "Mrs. Barlow's Lodger" (#19), and "The Thing from the Deep" (Annual 1985). The grotesque is used effectively in "The Uglies" (#62), in which vain Mandy finds herself in an "Ugly Pageant." Nearly half of the tale's final page is a dramatically angled panel showing a horde of "Uglies" clawing and climbing over themselves to get at her. Their grotesque takes the form of exaggerated features (lips, ears, noses), animal features (pig snouts, simian build), and human deficiencies (spots, baldness, snaggleteeth). In this tale expectations are inverted, not once but twice: the Uglies explain to Mandy that beauty is only skin deep before revealing themselves to be "even uglier" on the inside, and even after learning her lesson, she is not allowed to leave ("And Mandy screamed again, long and lingering, but no-one heard, no-one at all!").

However, and despite these notable hideous antagonists, *Misty*'s monsters are in fact more likely to be made by a personality flaw (laziness, rudeness, dishonesty, selfishness, etc.) than by any physical lack. Very few stories (just eight of the 855 episodes, or less than 1 percent) use the grotesque as a punishment, and unlucky heroines are more commonly confronted with the possibility of being trapped in a scenario or place with nightmarish qualities. While transformation is a frequent part of this, their new forms are not necessarily ugly. For example, Shirley trespasses into Old Collie's antiques shop and finds herself trapped in one of his snow globes ("Old Collie's Collection," #82), Caroline is transformed into a music box doll ("A Turn for the Worse," #44), and Colette's classmates turn into vampires ("A Breath of Life," #3). Alongside this sparing use of the grotesque, *Misty* also does not rely on its art to horrify, instead creating an atmosphere of suspense and mystery through its dramatic page layouts and themes such as the uncanny.

THE UNCANNY

The uncanny is often associated with Female Gothic. Modleski ([1982] 1990) names her chapter on Gothic "The Female Uncanny" (although she does not discuss the term), and Wallace revisits this idea in two separate essays (2004, 2009), where she argues for symbols such as the double and the act of being buried alive as quintessentially uncanny. Freud's *das unheimlich* is the horror of the familiar made strange and has been extended to stand for the repressed or marginalized elements of a culture (Masschelein 2013). Freud describes it as "that class of the terrifying which leads back to something long known to us, once very familiar" (1919, 1–2). He explores the etymology of the word in a number of languages, homing in on the German *das unheimlich*, which is an ambivalent word: it negates one meaning of *heimlich* (familiar, homely) but at the same time concurs with the word's second meaning (secret, hidden). *Das unheimlich* also sustains the presence of its antonym *heimlich* by encoding this word within itself (similar to "postmodernism"). It is thus an encrypting word, an example of live burial, and resonates with Female Gothic texts such as "Bluebeard" (Charles Perrault, 1697). Freud continues to explore uncanny symbols such as the double, offering a psychoanalytic interpretation of possible contributing factors. He notes that fiction offers many more means of creating uncanny effects than in real life, but the genre and setting of the tale affect this. For example, he argues that uncanny events are "very common in fairy stories" but are not recognized as such because feelings of fear are ruled out in this genre (16, 19).

Misty explicitly describes itself as uncanny on some occasions (e.g., promising "uncanny tales" and "uncanny new serials" in the welcomes to #8 and #30), and many stories revolve around a familiar object or setting that is made strange. A great example of uncanny story content is the one-shot "Roots" (#1),

Misty's very first "Nightmare" tale. Protagonist Jill goes to stay in Evergreen with her granddad for the summer but soon notices uncanny things in the familiar old village. Her eighty-one-year-old granddad carries her "heavy" cases "as though they were light as a feather"; Miss Carter, despite being at least one hundred, goes "whizzing up that hill" on her bicycle; and nobody seems to have died for over fifty years. When Jill wakes in the night and sees a figure standing outside in the rain, she initially explains her vision away as a scarecrow (an uncanny image in itself, as it parodies the human form), but the next night there are more, and she recognizes them as her neighbors. She confronts her grandfather, who explains that everyone in the town has literally put down roots (fig. 10.2).[2] This final reveal makes excellent use of the comics medium, taking place after a page turn, with shadows and composition both emphasizing Jill's shocked reaction, as well as the broken panel border and use of perspective to highlight her grandfather's "growing" leg. In fact, it was considered so shocking that Mills (2016b) has explained that he was forced to add a final "reassuring" panel (embedded in the corner of this one) in which Jill's shock and reaction are mitigated. This is somewhat clumsily positioned, although an attempt has been made to link it with the original composition by following the line of the grandfather's body.

The protagonists' uncertainties about the world around them are a particularly good fit for both Gothic and young adult literature. As Serrato (2017, 54) points out, this "entry into a realm of more complicated, less stable philosophical and moral discourses reflects the greater critical thinking and rethinking in which adolescents engage as they grow up." Suspicions of being surrounded by people who are not what they seem, and the subsequent discovery of a more complicated, threatening space, underlie a number of other *Misty* stories. In "Shadow of a Doubt" (#58), Mary suspects her friends and neighbors after hearing them plotting, and "Seal of Secrecy" (#20) and "Seal Rock" (#67) both feature girls who discover their own mysterious origins after being lied to by their fathers. This theme is particularly resonant, as in Gothic literature the family often serves as a metonym for the wider social structures of patriarchal society. Tóth (2010, 31) argues that "family has negative implications in the gothic novel," and many early Gothic texts problematize family relationships. For example, Walpole's and Radcliffe's male villains "represent various facets of patriarchal authority that work to marginalize female subjectivity" (Munford 2013, 225). *Misty*'s false fathers are an additional example of this, but its themes of mistrust and doubt are often extended further and made more explicit, for example, through the realization that whole worlds are contrived. In "The Experiment" (#100), Fleur realizes that her father is a robot and their house is made of plastic, and she dies when she tries to escape. Framing stories sometimes reveal the presumed storyworld as something fake (with male controllers): a chess game

GOTHIC CONCEPTS AND IDENTITIES 217

Figure 10.2. "Roots" (*Misty* #1). Art by María Barrera Castell, written by Pat Mills. Reproduced with permission of Misty™ Rebellion Publishing IP Ltd.; copyright © Rebellion Publishing IP Ltd., all rights reserved.

in "Master-Stroke" (#23) or a board game in "Madhouse!" (#90). Characters even discover that their own identity is false, such as Judy in "The Family" (#6), who searches for her father's "monster" but ultimately discovers that she is the creature (fig. 10.4).

This patriarchal and institutional mistrust appears particularly in the serials. In "Screaming Point" (#95–101), Lucy is sent to live with her Uncle Seth, who is not what he seems, and she ultimately discovers he is trying to reanimate the dead. In "The Body Snatchers" (#92–101), Nancy returns to her school after an illness to find that things are "a little bit odd. . . . A lot of the teachers seem kind of cold." The story operates in an atmosphere of suspicion and uncertainty, as Nancy constantly questions everything around her, and her speech frequently lapses into ellipses, for example: "What was that? I thought I heard . . . a noise . . ." "Oh . . . M-my . . . Wh-what is that thing?" (#96). María Barrera Castell's detailed and textured artwork enhances this uncertainty; for example, her rendering of Dr. Bracken (fig. 3.4) is particularly uncanny, as his half-human and half-plant face both sustains and destabilizes his humanity.

The many magical items that appear in *Misty*'s stories are also uncanny: for example, Maggie's box of paints, which seems ordinary but produces unexpected images ("Paint It Black," #1–18). In "Journey into Fear" (#14–27), Kev's car causes sinister events (Jan cuts herself on it although there are no sharp edges) and creates discord: "The happy Frazer household wasn't *its usual self* in the weeks that followed" (#14; italics mine). As the car's influence strengthens, Kev also becomes completely unfamiliar, acting like a 1930s gangster, and Jan notes: "He-he's changed!" When Jan and Kev try to find out more about the car's history, they are told "an uncanny story" by its previous owner, whose son also fell under its spell (#14). The language used to personify the car and the family is anthropomorphic but also strangely blank—it is "an evil black creature" (#14) and a nameless thing, simply "wicked! Evil!" (#21). Other everyday items with uncanny and eerie powers include a camera ("Smile," #100), garden gnomes ("Stone Cold Revenge," #14), a typewriter ("Prize Possession," #19), a tape recorder ("In the Labyrinths of Her Mind . . . ," #56), a pen ("A Stain on Her Character," #72), and mirrors ("Mirror . . . Mirror," #37; "Reflections," #53; "Age-Old Youth," #53)—many emphasizing writing or recording.

These uncanny items generally provide the catalyst for the story's events. Their power over the protagonist recalls traditional Gothic texts, where fascination with an object or idea can engulf the self (*Frankenstein*, *The Picture of Dorian Gray*). This might take the form of an unhealthy obsession with fashion, opulence, or ambition, which can drag protagonists down into dissolution or trap them in the permanency of an image or object (Wright 2004). Wright reads this as a moral critique of luxury and consumerism, arguing that it is commonly found in Female Gothic and particularly in the texts that contributed to the rise of Gothic in the late eighteenth century—ironically coinciding with its appeal to middle-class consumers. Punter (1994) also points out that problems of possession (including objects and property) are intrinsic to the Female Gothic. The forbidden object and its association with temptation, desire, and death are further explored by Mulvey-Roberts (2009), who argues that the curious protagonist colludes in her own fate and is a metonym for the reader (e.g., in "Pandora's Box" or "Bluebeard"). The protagonist's desire "to unmask the secret of otherness" (98) leads only to abjection: "perhaps the realisation of the ultimate 'knowledge' from which no curious seeker ever returns" (109). *Misty*'s dangerous items and transgressing heroines fit well with this Gothic conception of fragile identity and the dangers of luxury and self-indulgence.

PUBERTY AS A GOTHIC JOURNEY

Misty's use of the supernatural often twists these Gothic themes into metaphors for the experiences of a teenage audience. The abject threats to identity that underlie its stories frequently employ live burial, bodily transformation, and the feminine carceral. Grotesque bodies and uncontrolled growth also feature and are emphasized through dynamic visuals. Uncanny settings or objects create an atmosphere of doubt and uncertainty that often results in terror. As well as conveying explicit girlhood worries (friendship, bullying, etc.), these concerns about identity, control, and falsity are reconfigured into metaphors for negotiating puberty and femininity.

Kate Ferguson Ellis (1989, 219, 46) points out that power is the "central issue" of Gothic novels, in which "the terror of the Gothic heroine is . . . that, of being, in an unspecified yet absolute way, completely surrounded by superior male power." She argues that these novels are searching for a female subject and a resolution to the problem of evil inside the home as an "always already condition" (220). In this parsing, "The self is always a haunted self, a contested terrain that must be sought out, pursued into places where few would dare follow" (177). Gothic stories enact the struggle against patriarchal power that manifests both externally and internally, and the *Misty* tales articulate this.

For example, Lona in "Wolf Girl" (#65–80) has been raised by wolves and struggles to deal with her reintegration into society and her foster family. She finds herself howling at the moon when she feels alone and sad, and when she loses her temper and growls as she attacks some bullies, she despairs at being so "scared of all these new feelings and emotions boiling up inside me" (#66). Her animal "instinct" and behavior are overt metaphors for teenage angst, for example, as she muses, "I love my parents so much, but sometimes I feel I'm growing further apart from them each day" (#66). Her foster parents can't relate to her problems and tell her, "It's just teenage blues. Most kids go through a time of feeling unsettled. It passes!" (#67).

Fleenor (1983, 10) suggests that "the Gothic world is one of nightmare, and that nightmare is created by the individual in conflict with the values of her society and her prescribed role." This intensifies when Lona runs away and joins the wolf pack she has released from the zoo, as she then finds that "I-I don't fit in with them . . . and I'm out of place at home with my parents. I'm just a misfit!" (#74). The freedom Lona expects is not forthcoming in the wild, and she feels completely isolated: "The wolves have gone—the humans are scared of me. I-I'm completely alone!" (#77). The issue's final two panels represent Lona's conflict and her opposing lives as she first kneels upright in the rain and then collapses forward, her inverted pose and dark hair forming a vertically mirrored image (fig. 10.3).

The story is structured around Lona's repeated struggles against the lack of control she has over her own behavior and her feelings of not fitting in anywhere, even in the wolf pack. Lona flits between human and wolf society, constantly feeling outcast and in flight. This is emphasized further by her name, which phonically suggests "loner." Her behavior almost seems at its most human in the wild (making new clothes, adopting a baby, using fire) and

220　GOTHIC CONCEPTS AND IDENTITIES

Figure 10.3. "Wolf Girl" (*Misty* #77 and #80). Art by Eduardo Feito, writer unknown. Reproduced with permission of Misty™ Rebellion Publishing IP Ltd.; copyright © Rebellion Publishing IP Ltd., all rights reserved.

more animalistic in civilization (growling, howling, attacking). However, she ultimately breaks the cycle and returns the wolves to their cage at the wildlife park and herself to human society. But despite this positive ending, Lona's final thoughts are decidedly ambivalent and foreground the trapped position of women in society. As she locks the wolves in, she muses, "They think I've betrayed them, bringing them back here! But it's better to be a well-cared-for prisoner than a hunted victim without a leader" (#80). She then turns her attention to Anna, the human baby she has found, reminding them both of the "relatives" and "parents" who she hopes will be glad they have returned. The final image of Lona striding down the high street carrying baby Anna is accompanied by her thought "I must learn to take my place again . . . where I really belong!" while the wolves howl in the background (fig. 10.3). The central placement of this jagged speech balloon sustains and anthropomorphizes the wolves and juxtaposes their anguish with Lona's justification for her return. The image of her holding the baby and her references to family strongly connote motherhood, while her language (which is couched in terms of duty and uses words like "prisoner") indicates that the feminine carceral awaits.

A number of the serial endings are ambivalent in this way. In "The Secret World of Sally Maxwell," Sally claims to accept her telepathic powers, but her thoughts remain uncertain: "Its curse is all mine! I only wanted to lead a normal life . . . but things will never be normal." She continues, "I've come to terms with it. . . . I think that's as normal as I can ever hope to be . . . but it'll do!" (#60). Jan escapes the other world in "The Sentinels," but the doubles of her friends and family do not, and the story ends on her musing, "I hope they're all right Tiger. . . . Oh, I hope they're all right" (#12). Rosemary Black's final words to the reader in "Moonchild" are "I'm just an ordinary girl now . . . something I always wanted to be . . . but at what a price . . . what a terrible price . . . !" (#13). The visual strand is often used to reinforce this ambivalence: Rosemary stares straight at the reader in this panel, addressing her words directly to us and breaking the fourth wall. Similarly, in the penultimate panel of "Hush, Hush, Sweet Rachel," Lisa breaks the fourth wall to address us directly and explain, "It was Mrs. Prendergast who brought back all the memories of my previous life. . . . Now she's gone. . . . Poor Rachel can be at peace and I can be free." However, and although this ending is classed as positive, the final silent panel shows Rachel staring out at us from a black oval of shadow, echoing the serial's story logo (#52). It is not a happy image and perhaps conveys that she has been silenced and expelled, undermining the positivity of Lisa's words.

As explored in chapter 5, the *Misty* serials often have protagonists trying to accept some aspect of their self, which is the source of uncanny events. Reynolds et al. (2001, 6) cite Appleyard, who argues that teenage horror is often a metaphor for experiences of change and separation that are characteristic of adolescence, in particular the growing sense of "a split between the 'me nobody knows' and a changing personality" (1991, 109), and Rosemary Jackson (1981), who identifies the presence of a self split between benign/familiar and hostile/other as a manifestation of alienation in fantasy fiction. Gleeson-White (2001, 112) draws attention to "the felt 'freakishness' of the adolescent, particularly female, experience," and this sentiment is one that the *Misty* serials often try to reconcile. In "The Four Faces of Eve," Eve agonizes, "I'm a freak, a monster!" (#29), and later asks herself, "What sort of life can I expect . . . alone and just a creation of that monster Marshall's?" (#31). But when she finally tells her story to the circus folk, they not only believe her but also show her the way out of her situation, as Carol advises: "Three girls died. . . . You owe it to them to live a full happy life, don't you see?" (#31). This revelation is positioned in the center of the story's final page, in a circular panel whose form and site give it emphasis, and the page design slightly resembles a keyhole, perhaps indicating that Eve has finally unlocked the answer and escaped her dark past. Carol's father hides Eve from the police, taking her in and telling her, "I've got two daughters now," and the story ends on an unequivocally positive note.

While transformation and sometimes the grotesque are used as agents of threat or punishment in the single stories, the serials explore these ideas from the opposite angle. As Gleeson-White (2001, 112) argues: "A new account of the grotesque reveals that female adolescence might, rather, embody the possibility of endless metamorphosis." This can be a frightening thing: for example, in "The Cult of the Cat," Nicola is scared by the changes she perceives in her body, examining it one morning and finding that "everything's changing—my nails, my eyes . . ." (#6). Tinkler's study of girls' story papers between 1920 and 1950 observes that while appearance and beauty were appropriate topics of discussion, the development and maturity of the girl's body "[were] either ignored, diminished, or treated as abnormal" (1995, 161), despite large numbers of letters received on the subject (Hemming 1960). The physical and emotional changes experienced by the *Misty* heroines perhaps serve as metaphors for these worries, as the stories emphasize the characters' positive journeys of acceptance and growth. Learning to embrace and accept the change within oneself is a key part of the serials, as in "A Leap through Time," where Elena returns to her old life happier in herself after her adventures. She also discovers that her gymnastic abilities are within herself, as they continue after her crystal pendant is smashed (#36). This sort of struggle to either accept or expel some aspect of the self characterizes many of the serials, and identity is thus negotiated through their telling.

However, these identity negotiations are set within an atmosphere of paranoia and doubt that creates the uncanny, as discussed. As Sammy exclaims to her mother in "Don't Look Twice," "Wouldn't it be absolutely awful, Mum? To

GOTHIC CONCEPTS AND IDENTITIES   223

Figure 10.4. "The Family" (*Misty* #6). Art by Isidre Monés, written by Malcolm Shaw. Reproduced with permission of Misty™ Rebellion Publishing IP Ltd.; copyright © Rebellion Publishing IP Ltd., all rights reserved.

wake up and not know who you really are!" (#62). Her parents have not told her the truth about her adoption, and many of the other tales also foreground a fear of falsity, particularly patriarchal mistrust, which can have devastating consequences. In the final page of "The Family" (fig. 10.4), Judy's broken body dominates the page, and her face is turned away: her agency and identity have been completely removed in an example of abjection. As the narration warns, "Perhaps she shouldn't have hunted quite so hard for her father's . . . monster?" and while the ellipses and question mark create ambivalence, blame is nonetheless apportioned onto the female, who is "No child at all?"

Mills (2016a) warns against the use of bad fathers in comics (based on unsuccessful stories such as "My Father, My Enemy," *Tammy* #1–17), saying that "a girl reading those stories does not want to think ill of her dad. Right? So it could be a step-dad, it could be a cruel uncle, it could be whatever you like, but it cannot be DAD, because that's getting a little bit too close to home." *Misty*'s stories generally follow this rule, and the doubt cast on fathers in stories such as "The Family" and "The Experiment" is thus controversial. Other authority figures or family members are also revealed to be false and untrustworthy, as in "School of the Lost . . .," "Nightmare Academy," "The Body Snatchers," and "Screaming Point." Broken homes, divorced parents, and new partners also feature as villains, such as Jan's stepmother Sylvia in "Spider Woman" (Annual 1984) or "creepy Neville Chandler," who is dating Ann's mum in "End of the Line" (#28–42). "End of the Line" also plays out the theme of parental absence and falsity, as Ann sees her supposedly dead father trapped underground.

The presence of male characters in *Misty* deserves further exploration. Many stories feature paternal figures such as fathers, grandfathers, and uncles, and both male and female background characters appear throughout. However, named or active male peers (such as friends or brothers) are rare, appearing in just twenty-five of *Misty*'s stories (6 percent), and Kerry's brother Tony in "The Silver Racer-Back" is a notable exception. As a consequence, throughout the comic we get little sense of male support or of positive male relationships. In this, *Misty* follows the earlier schoolgirl papers of the type researched by Tinkler (1995, 130), who notes that these magazines managed compulsory heterosexuality by marginalizing and excluding male characters. Romantic relationships (whether explicit or implied) in particular are almost entirely absent in *Misty*, and Dave in "Day of the Dragon" is the closest instance of an ersatz boyfriend or partner. His relationship with Gayle seems quite romantic: they go to dinner together, argue and "make up" (#13), and often hold each other in a romantic way (see, e.g., panel 6 in fig. 3.2); however, this is mitigated by being named as Gayle's cousin, and there is no explicit romance. The only other romantic references are in "Midnight Masquerader," which suggests that Sarah may marry Mr. Pendleton (#46), and in "The Dryad Girl" (#100) who is rejected by Brian. There are a few additional instances of implied infatuation, such as "Somewhere" (Annual 1981), where Jinny spends all night talking with the ghost of a young highwayman, "Wolfsbane" (#70), in which Sara and Paul go to a disco together, and Stacey's invite to Ned in "The Jukebox" (#28), but these are left unsaid. There are also a handful of (mostly text) stories where characters discover a past love affair and help resolve it for the ghosts involved but are not directly involved themselves ("Down in the Cellar," Annual 1982; "I Must Catch the Last Train . . . ," #87).

When present, male characters feature most often as antagonists. They are often representatives of institutional authority, such as the scientists and doctors in "The Secret World of Sally Maxwell" and "The Four Faces of Eve." Alternatively they reference this sort of patriarchal power through social status, such as the cruel landowner in "Sure-Footed . . . to Eternity" (#3), the murderous Squire in "The Last Hunt" (#95), or Sir Mortimer in "Violets in the Moonlight" (#62), who unwittingly rejects his own daughter. But although male villains appear more often than female antagonists, they make up less than one-fifth of the *Misty* stories. Both male and female threats are far outweighed by tales featuring antiheroines who cause their own destruction, or stories that have no clear antagonist. Characters such as Felix in "Midnight Masquerader" complicate the issue still further, as Elizabeth believes Felix to be a friend, while Sarah is less sure, and at the close of the story "he" is revealed as Mrs. Pendleton in disguise. This very brief discussion shows that *Misty* concerns itself first and foremost with female characters and their problems, and the majority of male characters are patriarchal and parental, serving either as backdrop or as a threat.

Misty's stories draw extensively on Female Gothic themes. The single stories often use incarceration or transformation to create abject punishments for characters who transgress. Trickery and doubt are also employed, generating worlds of paranoia where the sting in the tale comes from a sudden realization that things are not what they seem. The serials also offer an uncanny atmosphere of mystery that might be created by the falsity of those around the protagonist, or through the protagonist's own compulsion to act in a way that is beyond her control. They thus provide a space for uncertainties about family figures and patriarchal authority to be explored and function as bildungsroman tales of self-growth. While most of the serial story endings are positive, one-third of them convey a strong sense of ambivalence, and the options available to the protagonists often comment on the limitations placed on women through domestic settings or familial relationships.

CHAPTER 11

SURFACE REFLECTIONS

Gothic Symbols, Settings, and Archetypes

Growing up is a perilous period, a negotiation of identity and a journey of individuation that constantly threatens to collapse into uncertainty and abjection. In this chapter, I explore the way that uncanny and abject themes are developed and expressed in *Misty* through Gothic motifs, settings, and archetypes. I identify the subject positions that the comic constructs for readers, paying particular attention to the use of the double, the Other, and symbols such as mirrors and masks. I then consider the settings of the *Misty* stories, arguing that many use the past to create an uncanny feeling of dislocation. The chapter concludes by examining the treatment of Gothic archetypes (particularly witches, vampires, and ghosts), demonstrating that these figures appear less often than might be expected, and are frequently handled subversively or sympathetically.

DOUBLES, OTHERS, MIRRORS, AND MASKS

The double or doppelgänger is a common Gothic motif. It may stem from the Manichean morality (of good versus evil) that characterizes traditional Gothic and provides a dualistic worldview. Doubling underlies the structure of the earliest Gothic texts (Walpole, Radcliffe, Shelley), and later Gothic stories develop the double as a motif to break down the barrier between self and Other. For example, in *Frankenstein*, Victor names his creature "my own vampire, my own spirit" (78), and later writers such as Anne Rice rework the vampire into our own image (Auerbach 1995). Sage (1988) argues that the double is linked to Protestant religious doctrine and represents the internal conscience or secret self. This duality can be read as a response to the human subject in crisis (Townshend) that rises in nineteenth-century literature and then moves into psychoanalysis. Freud's identification of the unconscious and psychological duplicity informs Jung's and Lacan's self and shadow self (subject and mirrored ego), as well as the Scottish psychiatrist R. D. Laing's publication of *The Divided Self* in 1960. Laing's study is an important countercultural text of the period, as it draws on philosophy to challenge medical orthodoxy, arguing for an understanding of psychosis as the lived experience (rather than hallucinatory symptom) of the tension between private and public personae.

Otto Rank's study *Der Doppelgänger* (first published in 1914) claims the double as a literary concept as much as it is anthropological and psychological. Like many Gothic symbols, the double is a contradictory idea: it replicates and preserves the self but also consumes and replaces it as a signifier of death. In "The Uncanny" (1919), Freud explores the double as the ultimate uncanny symbol: it represents the oscillation between narcissism and death, familiar and strange, self and Other. In particular he notes that the double manifests at two different psychic moments: the narcissism of childhood and the development of the conscience, as both enable separation and self-observation. Examples such as Stevenson's *Dr. Jekyll and Mr. Hyde* (1886), Wilde's *The Picture of Dorian Gray* (1890), and contemporary works such as Chuck Palahniuk's *Fight Club* (1996) make the dichotomy overt and use it as a plot basis, but Gothic consistently explores visual, metaphorical, and structural doubling.

Misty contains a number of examples of the double as hidden Other and uses it to demonstrate the performative nature of identity. "Prisoner in the Attic" (#61) literalizes the double as inner self, as elderly Connie Michaels is confronted by a mysterious girl while clearing some junk from her attic (the attic as metaphor for the psyche is established in books such as *Jane Eyre*). The girl reminds Connie of her own youthful idealism (sports achievements, suffragette protest, wartime nursing, and a political role in London—which ultimately corrupts her) and then reveals, "I am you and you are me—I am what you were before you forgot your ideals!" This panel breaks the fourth wall, allowing young Connie to address the reader directly, and is juxtaposed vertically with a panel that shows the elder, corrupted Connie berating a younger man. Young Connie then reveals, "You died when you came up here . . . and that was a week ago now!" and the final scene literalizes the death that the double brings as it shows her funeral. This use of a ghostly double also accords with the transgressive aspects of Female Gothic. Germanà (2013) argues that "in the late twentieth century the ghost crucially signifies the overcoming of structuralist dualism" (17–18), disrupting time and highlighting "the narrative black holes the reader is (subconsciously) exposed to" (141–42). Here the borders between a good and bad person collapse, dualism and temporality break down, and the story warns its constructed readers that they may not be able to control their destiny.

Doubles are also antagonists and threats. In "Mirror Mirror on the Wall . . ." (#61), Sally's reflection comes alive and tries to grab her so that they can change places (fig. 11.1). The page layout throughout the story is a mass of sharp angles and transgression—limbs extend over panel borders, characters are hurled into the air with curling motion lines leading the eye, and the gridding is entirely angular. The sound effect "CRASH" and Sally's shattered reflection share the same fragmented style, and the positioning also allows this image to double in function and disrupt time, existing both as dramatic event and as Sally's memory of it. Sally's final words also sustain the presence of her double in her present and invite the reader to share her fear that "she's still there and waiting!" in every mirror that they pass.

In "Shadow of a Doubt" (#58), Mary hears whispers coming from the barn at night and recognizes them as belonging to her friends, neighbors, and even family, who are "talking about k-killing . . . and some kind of revolution." She locks herself in her room but, in a dramatic panel of light and dark, is confronted by her shadow (fig. 8.4b). It speaks and reveals that it is they who have been plotting: "We are shadows . . . thousands of us . . . millions . . . and soon we shall rise up!" The plot literalizes the shadow self of repression, and the page layouts emphasize the point through their gridding: angular panel borders dominate three of the story's four pages, with only the third page (where Mary temporarily thinks she has a handle on the problem) returning briefly to stable 90-degree angles (fig. 11.2). The story's final angular panel is the most distorted of all, as befits its threatening ending (fig. 8.4b).

As well as her shadowy antagonists, Mary herself is doubled in a number of panels (e.g., as she listens at the barn door in fig. 11.2), but it is the appearance of her shadow that uses duplication most dramatically as her silhouette confronts her in a striking face-off. Throughout the story, Ariza's art allows Mary's wide eyes and flicked-up curls to dominate the panels she is in and lead the reader's eye through the first three pages. Moreover, in multiple panels, Mary gazes directly at us, further doubling identity as the reader mirrors her horrified stare and confusion.

In all these examples, the double brings explicit death (Connie's funeral, Sally's dog Toby, the threats Mary overhears), and many other supporting examples carry the same message. Some protagonists, such as Naomi in "The Guardian Lynxes" (#11) and Gayle in "Day of the Dragon" (#10–19), have historical doubles whose fate is tied to theirs. Again the double combines narcissism (Naomi and her father's desire to excavate the magnificent tomb; Gayle's longing for the "beautiful" mirror) with the threat of death (from the guardian lynxes; Chen and Chiang's romantic tragedy; and Michael Lee's use of the "Elixir of Life"). Classic Gothic dualities are also rewritten: in "The Shop at Crooked Corner" (#14), owners Josh and Abel are the same man, "doomed to live two different lives" in a Jekyll and Hyde–style scenario. "Hush, Hush, Sweet Rachel"

GOTHIC SYMBOLS, SETTINGS, AND ARCHETYPES   229

Figure 11.1. "Mirror Mirror on the Wall . . ." (*Misty* #61). Art by Ken Houghton, writer unknown. Reproduced with permission of Misty™ Rebellion Publishing IP Ltd.; copyright © Rebellion Publishing IP Ltd., all rights reserved.

230 GOTHIC SYMBOLS, SETTINGS, AND ARCHETYPES

Figure 11.2. "Shadow of a Doubt . . ." (*Misty* #58). Art by Juan Ariza, writer unknown. Reproduced with permission of Misty™ Rebellion Publishing IP Ltd.; copyright © Rebellion Publishing IP Ltd., all rights reserved.

uses reincarnation to explore the loss of control that the double brings. Entire worlds are also doubled, as in "The Sentinels," where an alternate reality "makes my world with all its faults look good" (#9), and whose duplicated characters are often marked by damaged bodies. Jan's mother notices that the double of her daughter does not have a cut on her hand after being bitten by her dog Tiger; and Alt-Jan responds in kind: "You're not my mother! You've no scar on your neck!" (#2).

The double demonstrates the "Other within," and perhaps even the position of the feminine in society, but Others appear repeatedly and overtly throughout *Misty*. The motif is even flagged explicitly on occasion: Misty's welcome in #25 invites us to "come with me and look upon that which is OTHER." Othering in *Misty* is a danger and a threat, but also attractive and exciting. Nicola is initially scared to discover her calling ("The Cult of the Cat"), and Lucy is terrified of her legacy and ancestors in "The Loving Cup," but both are able to use their inherited power and banish the evil that threatens them.

Misty's Others are often exotic, for example, bringing in ancient Egypt and the Orient, or fantastic characters such as in "The Salamander Girl" (#5–9). This story is initially set in Spain and then moves to Africa. It others its protagonist Salah from the beginning, introducing her on the cover in mysterious terms: "Who was she? What was her secret?" (#5). Throughout the story, characters such as Luis and Carmen either exploit Salah or are jealous of her and denigrate her verbally, calling her "freak," "savage," "witch," and "gypsy." In a remarkable reversal, Salah is blonde and fair skinned (and thus an identifiable heroine and focalizer for Western readers), but also positioned as the exotic minority in a world of Spaniards and dark-haired "Arabs," described as "like flame itself, all red and gold" (#6). Her Otherness is further emphasized as she refers to herself in the third person, saying, "Salah will not forget" (#5), and speaks in broken language throughout. Although Salah is our protagonist, we are kept external to her, and her decisions (e.g., to leave Luis and Carmen in #9) are never explained, just like her powers. The tale's ongoing narration gives a strong sense of simply watching her, rather than being allowed full access to her thoughts and feelings as with other *Misty* protagonists.

Spooner (2013) argues that masks, veils, and disguises in Gothic texts are not just props or plot devices but also represent a generic concern with surfaces. They can enable transgression by being carnivalesque or performative, or they can allow for self-transformation. Masks both reveal and conceal and in this way evoke doubleness: "Their horror frequently lies in its collapse; in the loss of control of the mask or the disguise, so that it estranges the bearer from his/her 'original' identity" (422). In "Mask of Fear" (#39), Sue borrows a mask from her uncle's creepy collection and wins first prize at the Halloween party she attends—but when she tries to remove the mask, she only finds another underneath, "and another . . . and another . . . and another . . ." Her mirror plays a central role in this unveiling, as this is where we see the mask repeated uncannily, and a jagged panel also marks the moment of reveal (fig. 11.3). Sue's own face is completely hidden throughout this page, removing all trace of her identity. The compositions of panels 2, 3, and 7 further emphasize this motif, as her back is turned to us, allowing the reflected mask to leer at the reader alongside Sue in the final panel. She is reduced to simply crying out, "Oh, no! No! No!"—losing control over her identity and her words and unable to return to her previous self.

In "The Sad Eyes of Sorrow" (#49), a human mask hides the creature's "real" identity, and Julie doesn't recognize "which was the mask, and which was the real me." Although the creature wears his "real" face for the act, it is nonetheless false: "All I can do is play the monster. . . . I deal in sadness and fear instead of laughter and happiness." Here the line between mask and face collapses (and thus between object and subject) as both are revealed to be a performance. His "sad eyes" are repeated as a dramatically colored motif in Julie's dream, rendered in psychedelic hues of orange, yellow, and green.

Classic Gothic dualities underlie many of the *Misty* tales, which use the double motif to comment on the performative nature of identity or emphasize its fragility. The medium is also exploited to double the gazes of characters and draw the reader into their experiences. The double frequently brings death and destruction, and it is often combined with symbols such as mirrors and masks. The significance of the mirror as a feminized symbol sits alongside the use of the mask. While masks are not a gendered symbol, critics such as Doane (1982, 1991) have explored the function of the mask and masquerade as enabling female access to the gaze, and (following debates in the work of Rivière, Lacan, and Irigaray) as a metaphor for the performance of female sexuality. In *Misty* masks are worn for parties and fairgrounds, gendered spaces of recreation and entertainment. Similarly, while doubled worlds such as in "The Sentinels" are masculine spaces of war and resistance, they are accessed through the domestic space (Jan's new home, a residential tower block). Othered spaces such as the world of "The Salamander Girl" also sustain familial structures, as Salah is exploited by Luis and his "spiteful daughter" Carmen. Doubles are thereby used to problematize and undermine identity, specifically in domestic situations. The reincarnated and historically doubled characters noted earlier support this motif further, though they can also be read as metonyms for the invasion of the present by the past, as I now discuss.

GOTHIC SYMBOLS, SETTINGS, AND ARCHETYPES   233

Figure 11.3. "Mask of Fear" (*Misty* #39). Art by José Cánovas, writer unknown. Reproduced with permission of Misty™ Rebellion Publishing IP Ltd.; copyright © Rebellion Publishing IP Ltd., all rights reserved.

HISTORICISM AND THE GOTHIC CUSP

The past is key to many definitions of Gothic. Davenport-Hines stresses "the strength of backward-looking thoughts" (1998, C3), and Kilgour (1995, 4) calls Gothic "a Frankenstein's monster, assembled out of the bits and pieces of the past." However, Baldick and Mighall draw attention to Gothic's anachronistic treatment of past and present, citing previous critics (McIntyre 1921) who note that "modern" heroes and heroines feature incongruously in novels with "historical" settings. They argue that this chronological discrepancy provides the central dramatic interest in these narratives, as contemporary characters (with whom the reader can identify) clash with archaic villains and threats. Miles names this position the "Gothic cusp" (1995, 87), situated between the modern and medieval world.

In *Misty* the Gothic cusp is used to create an uncanny alterity that comments on the contemporary moment. In particular it shapes the treatment of nostalgia, alongside the articulation of contemporary political issues such as environmentalism, animal rights, and delinquency. Although most tales in *Misty* take place in a recognizable urban environment (a village, town, or school), the setting is seldom clearly marked as 1970s Britain. While "town" connotes London in stories such as "Day of the Dragon" (a tube station sign is visible in the opening background), place names are rarely given, and characters' clothing is wildly varied (likely due to the international artists). Pleated skirts, school blazers, anoraks, jeans, shirt dresses, flowered smocks, patterned pinafores, checked trousers, knee-high boots, plain shirts, V-neck pullovers, round-necked dresses, and more feature. There are traces of 1970s style: Armstrong's "Moonchild" characters appear in miniskirts and flares; Redondo's girls wear denim dungarees and knitted tank tops/sweater vests in "Hangman's Alley"; and Feito draws Lona in a quilted gilet in "Wolf Girl" and Elena in striped, cuffed short-shorts in "A Leap through Time." But characters can really wear anything, supporting a reading of these "nameless places" as alterities—our world, but *dis-located*. This is further enhanced by their magical realist qualities, as places where enchantment does happen. The storyworlds thus carry a sense of displacement, often created precisely by the intrusion of the past into the present (the discovery of a magical item in a mundane shop, at a museum, or an archaeological dig). The past is also juxtaposed explicitly against the present day in serials such as "The Cult of the Cat," "A Leap through Time," and "Day of the Dragon."

However, O'Shea (2015a) points out that *Misty* commissioned "a significant number of stories which took place in the more distant past, usually . . . at some point after the turn of the Nineteenth Century, though up until the first decades of the Twentieth." Reviewing the comic's content reveals seventy-four stories set in a past time, of which nine are serials. This equates to 17 percent of the comic's stories, or 20 percent if the serials are weighted accordingly (175 installments out of a total of 855).[1] These tales are entirely or partially situated in a historical period or in an alterity with marked historical features (such as princesses, lords, slaves, or peasants). Many are tied to particular dates or events such as the Jack the Ripper murders in 1888 (#54), the Great Plague of London, 1665–66 (#59, #92), or the 79 AD destruction of Pompeii (#80). Their protagonists are generally maids or orphans or beggars: the downtrodden and victimized heroes common to *Misty* and other girls' comics. For example, Miranda (#12) is a beggar girl accused of witchcraft and sentenced to be burned at the stake; however, when a downpour commences, she is freed with the promise that she will be burned when it stops—but sixty years later it is still raining.

O'Shea (2015a) also notes that many of these historical tales echo classic Gothic literature. These include "The Weird Sisters" (Annual 1981), whose discussion of female insanity and its treatment in Victorian England evokes Collins's *The Woman in White* (1859); and "Strange Heritage" (Annual 1981), which resembles Brontë's *Wuthering Heights* (1847) in its Yorkshire setting and theme of doomed love. There are also a number of rewritten or reprinted Gothic tales—including an excerpt from Lewis's scandalous novel *The Monk* (1796)—and "diverse examples of literature by writers like Wordsworth and Poe, alongside tales of ancient Greece, Arthurian legends, and suchlike." To these I would add Wilde's *Dorian Gray* (reimagined as "Spitting Image," #79), not to mention the "True Ghost Stories" and other historical content. The story of the Borgias is fictionalized into "The Loving Cup" (#70–82) and also told in a feature in the *Misty* Annual 1980. Supernatural anecdotes about writers such as Mark Twain and Robert Louis Stevenson also appear (Annual 1982), along with the stories of people such as Vlad Dracul and Countess Báthory (Annual 1980), Rosemary Brown, Mary Shelley, and Jeanne Dixon ("Three Women," text, Summer Special 1978). In fact, *Misty*'s readers are positively encouraged toward transgressive literature and films: Annual 1983 contains a feature on Edgar Allan Poe, which recommends his tales to "the true Misty reader. . . . With their ingredients of premature burial, hideous execution, hypnotic trances, medieval plague and creatures breaking out of their tombs. They are all a 'must' for the Misty fan who has not encountered them." Other annuals contain features on the various incarnations of Dracula (Annual 1980) and horror stars such as Christopher Lee (Annual 1983). While these adaptations and citations might seem an odd fit for young readers, they demonstrate that *Misty* was aware of its relationship with classic Gothic and horror. They also look to the past to provide credibility by positioning *Misty* within an ongoing Gothic legacy.

The past is a key component in many scholars' textual definitions of Gothic. Hogle (2002) suggests a "Gothic matrix" composed of four categories: an

236 GOTHIC SYMBOLS, SETTINGS, AND ARCHETYPES

Figure 11.4. "The Choice of Silence" (*Misty* #62). Art by John Richardson, writer unknown. Reproduced with permission of Misty™ Rebellion Publishing IP Ltd.; copyright © Rebellion Publishing IP Ltd., all rights reserved.

antiquated space, a hidden secret, a physical or psychological haunting, and an oscillation between reality and the supernatural. This schema aptly describes nearly all the *Misty* stories, and I have trouble finding any that do not fit within it. Although most *Misty* tales have a contemporary setting, the intrusion of a curse, legacy, or spirit often provides the catalyst for events. For example, in "The Choice of Silence" (#62, fig. 11.4), deaf Amy visits the Egyptology exhibition at the museum (antiquated space) and is secretly addressed by a mummy (hidden secret) who asks for his freedom in exchange for her hearing. The color and layout emphasize the hidden nature of his words, which initially appear in ghostly yellow lettering, "FREE ME," and haunt her dreams that night (psychological haunting). She returns to set him free but changes her mind and destroys him (oscillating between reality and the supernatural as the evidence is destroyed and her miraculous hearing vanishes). A similar pattern takes place in other stories, such as "Pot Luck" (#57), where Gloria finds a secret hidden cauldron in Old Hazel's antiquated home but is then haunted by warnings about its evil nature, and although she locks it away, a supernatural creature apparently emerges. The monster is only partially shown, in the final images without narrative comment, and so arguably this demonstrates an oscillation by casting doubt on the outcome.

Hogle's matrix exposes the way in which fear in *Misty* comes from common Gothic elements. Punter also argues that Gothic contains "an emphasis on portraying the terrifying, a common insistence on archaic settings, a prominent use of the supernatural, the presence of highly stereotyped characters, and the attempt to deploy and perfect techniques of literary suspense" (1980, 1). Almost every *Misty* tale contains a secret or a haunting, and its unraveling treads a line between reality and the supernatural (as Hogle claims), to ultimately be revealed as one or the other. Punter's definition is equally valid, as *Misty*'s characters are not highly nuanced, and literary suspense is apparent in the vast number of twist endings or inverted binaries of good and evil (see chap. 8). What is interesting about both these models is that in *Misty* the "archaic setting" is the only criterion that is not always present, and instead the contemporary setting is often given Gothic qualities.

GOTHIC ARCHETYPES

Gothic's folkloric roots have given rise to some of the most famous icons of any literary genre: zombies, vampires, and werewolves cavort alongside skeletons, Frankenstein's creature, demons, witches, warlocks, and even the devil himself. While these archetypes are not the standard fare of *Misty*, they nonetheless appear on occasion.

I surveyed the entire run of *Misty* to see how often Gothic archetypes are used. The data showed that 171 of the 443 stories (39 percent) contain one or more archetypes (see table and graph 11.1).[2] However, I felt that the question I was asking was more about the comic's overall content from one issue to the next, and so table and graph 11.2 show the frequency of archetypes using the individual episode as the unit of coding (within 855 episodes).[3] Instances where archetypes are ultimately debunked (such as a skeleton puppet or an assumed ghost) are included, as my focus is on how frequently such archetypes are used, even if the use is parodic or misleading. The frequency of archetypes drops significantly if we discount satirical usage and the three comedy series. There remain some limitations to my method, as again the coding has been done by a single individual, and (for example) tales where "the dead" are mentioned in more general terms are not included. Nonetheless, this analysis gives a sense of the weighting given to named Gothic archetypes in *Misty*'s overall story content—and reveals that they appear less often than we might expect.

Rayner's (2012) *Guardian* article on *Misty* refers to "all the ghosts, zombies and eerie beings that haunted its pages." However, the first point to note is that Gothic archetypes like these feature in just 39 percent of the stories and similarly appear in less than half (350 episodes, or 41 percent) of the issue content when calculated by installment. My small-scale analysis of *Spellbound* found an even more extreme lack: just 14 percent of its comic strip content features Gothic archetypes (for a full discussion, see Round 2017). Conversely, five of the seven main comic strip stories in a single randomly selected issue of *Scream!* rely on established archetypes (71 percent). In the comic strip stories of the first five issues of EC Comics' *The Haunt of Fear*, archetypes appear ten times (50 percent). This distinguishes the girls' mystery comics from other horror comics. It also aligns them with a more traditional view of Gothic and in particular the first phase of the Gothic novel in the late eighteenth/early nineteenth century. In these early texts, monsters were "virtually unknown," in contrast to postmillennial culture, which holds monsters as "virtually synonymous with Gothic in popular identification" (Spooner 2017, 121).

By far the most common archetype is the witch; however, I should note that the comedy series "Miss T" and "Wendy the Witch" account for the majority of its appearances, and if we discount them, then the witch falls to third place. The following discussion therefore focuses on ghosts, vampires, and witches as the most frequent monsters used in *Misty*. It seems significant that these three archetypes all have a gendered aspect. Critical discussion of Female Gothic has frequently focused on its spectral qualities (Wallace 2009); the vampire problematizes gender boundaries through the penetrative bite; and the witch traditionally stands for female transgressions.

GOTHIC SYMBOLS, SETTINGS, AND ARCHETYPES   239

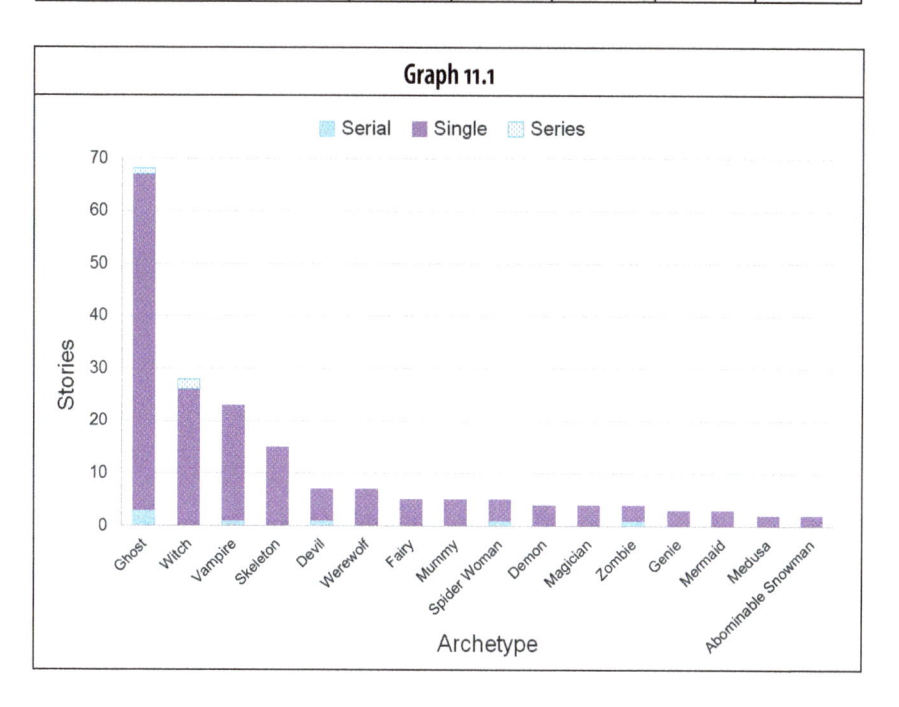

Table 11.1. Archetypes in *Misty* coded by story.

Stories	Original			Reprint		
Archetype	Serial	Single	Series	Single	Series	Total
Ghost	3	60	1	4	0	68
Witch	0	26	1	0	1	28
Vampire	1	22	0	0	0	23
Skeleton	0	14	0	1	0	15
Devil	1	6	0	0	0	7
Werewolf	0	7	0	0	0	7
Fairy	0	5	0	0	0	5
Mummy	0	5	0	0	0	5
Spider Woman	1	4	0	0	0	5
Demon	0	4	0	0	0	4
Magician	0	4	0	0	0	4
Zombie	1	3	0	0	0	4
Genie	0	3	0	0	0	3
Mermaid	0	3	0	0	0	3
Medusa	0	2	0	0	0	2
Abominable Snowman	0	2	0	0	0	2

Graph 11.1

Table 11.2. Archetypes in *Misty* coded by episode.

Episodes	Original			Reprint		
Archetype	Serial	Single	Series	Single	Series	Total
Witch	0	26	84	0	18	128
Ghost	33	60	5	4	0	102
Vampire	12	22	0	0	0	34
Devil	17	6	0	0	0	23
Spider Woman	14	4	0	0	0	18
Skeleton	0	14	0	1	0	15
Zombie	6	3	0	0	0	9
Werewolf	0	7	0	0	0	7
Fairy	0	5	0	0	0	5
Mummy	0	5	0	0	0	5
Demon	0	4	0	0	0	4
Magician	0	4	0	0	0	4
Genie	0	3	0	0	0	3
Mermaid	0	3	0	0	0	3
Medusa	0	2	0	0	0	2
Abominable Snowman	0	2	0	0	0	2

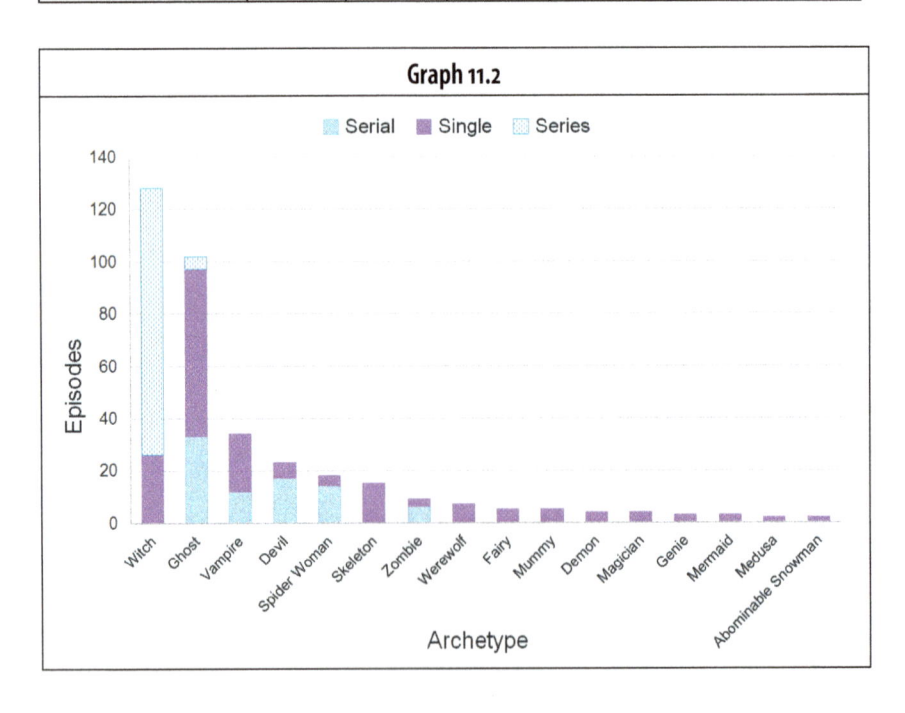

Graph 11.2

Wallace (2009) describes woman as a haunting and ghostly presence in Gothic, and Horner (2010, 323) points out that "many women authors used the idea of ghostliness to express this sense of inner conflict and lack of agency." Hoeveler and Irigaray also draw attention to the solipsism and isolation that characterizes Female Gothic. For Wallace too (parsing Mary Beard's concept of "the haunting idea" [1946, 77]), the dominant notion of Female Gothic is "woman as 'dead' or 'buried (alive)' within male power structures that render her 'ghostly'" (2009, 26). This is literalized in sixteen of the *Misty* stories where the protagonist either becomes a ghost or finds out that she is one already, like Connie Michaels in "Prisoner in the Attic" (#61). For example, in "Dark Secrets . . . Dark Night" (#13), Katrine is attacked by a vampire but has the last laugh as she reveals, "This train is haunted. By a ghost called Katrine!" and then "vanishe[s] into the night she loved." This type of ghosting is frequently tied to uncanny places: protagonists will feel drawn to a haunted house or garden, only to discover they are the ghost that haunts it ("The Garden," Holiday Special 1980; "The Dream House," #63). Ghosts in *Misty* are often benign: their most frequent usage is as a friend or helper, or a helpless entity needing aid, which features in twenty-nine stories. These include "The Ghost of Golightly Towers" (#81–94) and "Aunt Mary's Blessing" (#21), and friendly ghosts can also be animal helpers, as in "Whistle and I'll Come . . ." and "The Thing in Chains" (Annual 1982). Finally, ghost antagonists haunt a wayward heroine in twenty-two of the stories, such as "Black Agnes" (#59), where the murdering protagonist is pursued by her victims. These figures take the story as the unit of coding and can also be expressed as follows: Ghostly Protagonist (25 percent), Ghostly Friend/Helper (42 percent), and Ghostly Antagonist (33 percent). This analysis demonstrates that the ghost archetype is not simply an antagonist and is often aligned with the role or interests of the female protagonist.

Vampires are a common Gothic archetype and in particular have often been adapted for teenage girls, for example, in Stephenie Meyer's *Twilight* saga (2005–8) and Charlaine Harris's *Sookie Stackhouse/Southern Vampire Mysteries* series (2001–13).[4] In *Misty* vampires generally serve as outright antagonists but are often either ineffective or undermined in some way (e.g., via a twist ending or other debunking). Of the twenty-three vampire stories, more than half end positively (fourteen, or 61 percent), and many also subvert the myth. In "To See a Vampire" (#64, text), the dramatic opening description of a vampire movie is undermined by Karen's interruption "You great twit, you've let your choc-ice drip all over my sleeve!" and Eric later accidentally kills one with the same choc-ice stick. In another text story ("Don't Look Back . . . in Anger!" #23), a vampire "haunting" a derelict mansion is fake—just a trick of the developers to keep kids away. Laird Cameron in "Ratcatcher" (#27) is another good example of a visually stereotypical vampire (black clothes, long cloak, and black hair in a widow's peak with arched eyebrows and goatee beard), whose terrifying appearance is again undermined as he transforms into a bat and deals with the mice infestation at Doris's family home ("The mice were delicious . . . delicious!"). Inversion and twist endings also subvert the myth, and often protagonists under threat are revealed to be the real vampire—or something worse ("Forest of Fear," #89; "Dark Secrets . . . Dark Night," #13). One more notable feature is the number of times that Dracula is invoked by name (six, or 26 percent), and the visual markers associated with vampires are generally conventional (fangs, cloaks). The stories seldom depart from these stereotypes: the psychic vampire (Laycock 2009) in "Art of Death" (#89) and the vampiric ventriloquist's dummy in "The Devil's Dummy" (#69) are two significant exceptions. This suggests that *Misty* is keen to invoke the full weight of the archetype, if only to then undermine it through escape or subversion.

Finally, the witch appears explicitly in twenty-eight of the stories printed in *Misty*.[5] The moral ambiguity of the witch and its symbolic flexibility are discussed in chapter 7, where they are identified as a sign of recurrence and liminality (Punter 2017). Punter notes the witch's "periodic returns and recessions" (78), and it is important to note that the 1970s were a period of revival, as the archetype became politicized (for further discussion, see Round 2017). Key feminist texts such as Robin Morgan's *Sisterhood Is Powerful* (1970) and Mary Daly's *Gyn/Ecology* (1978) defined the witch as "female, untamed, angry, joyous and immortal" (Morgan 1970, 540) and celebrated a "hag-identified vision" (Daly 1978, 216). Radical feminists adopted the lexis of witchcraft, playfully referring to consciousness-raising groups as "covens" and using slogans that challenged the patriarchal view of the witch, claiming that "wicked witches were created by evil men" (Palmer 2004). The witch thus became a powerful container for "radical feminist connotations of female empowerment, marriage resistance and women's community" (Palmer 2004, 122), and the archetype's treatment in *Misty* mostly accords with this innovative and positive reinterpretation.

As noted, "Miss T" and "Wendy the Witch" account for the majority of the individual episodes in which witches appear. Alternatively they represent two (7 percent) of the total witch stories, which can be defined as comedies of errors. Witches are treated in four different ways in the other stories. The most common (eight tales, or 29 percent) is as an innocent victim or helpful force, as, for example, in "The Queen's Hair" (#43), where Queen Elvira imprisons the witch who helps her. Five of the tales (18 percent) have witches meting out justified (if extreme!) revenge, as in "Miss Cassidy's Cat . . ." (#50), where Jilly is shrunk to the size of a mouse after chasing her neighbor's cat. In seven of the tales (25 percent), witches are malevolent antagonists, such as One-Eyed Agatha, who destroys the village in "Night of the Dead" (#94). Finally, six stories (21 percent) feature protagonists who use or discover their own witch powers, such as "A

Picture of Horror" (#59), where Zoe traps her bullies in the pages of a horror comic (these tales also overlap with the categories of revenge [#14, #59] and innocent victim [#21]). This very brief list demonstrates that, in three-quarters of *Misty*'s stories, either witching is given some justification, or the witches themselves are unfairly victimized. In addition, although the visual stereotype of an aged crone dominates in the stories where the witch turns out to be good, across the other tales witches range from babies to old ladies.

Other Gothic archetypes receive limited attention in *Misty*. The undead in particular are marginalized: zombies rarely appear and are only explicitly mentioned in "House of Horror" (#96–101), where Madame Blaze's waxworks are revealed as zombies. The self-beating drum (#100) that controls them evokes the zombie's voodoo origins, although their uncontrolled rampage and grasping hands (#101) have more in common with George A. Romero's version. Zombie antagonists also feature in "Night of the Dead" (#94), where they are clearly a Romerian vision: rotting flesh, rising from graves, and seeking to tear apart Jilly, who is to be the "sacrifice for the dead." But even here their speech and single-minded mission (to avenge a witch who was burned by the townsfolk) recall the Haitian tradition rather than the dominant cinematic version.

The werewolf features in just seven *Misty* stories (this number does not include the serial "Wolf Girl," in which Lona is raised by actual wolves). Of these, werewolves are generally stereotypical antagonists (five tales, or 71 percent), as in "The Curse of the Wolf" (#60), "The Curse of Castle Krumlaut" (Annual 1983), "Forest of Fear" (#89), "Twin Catastrophes" (#67), and "Wolfsbane" (#70), where colleagues, friends, or family turn out to be infected. "Poor Jenny" (#17) is more interesting, however: Jenny fears she is a werewolf but dismisses this fear because the moon is out—but then the twist reveals that she is actually a wolf who turns into a girl at this time. The story plays with and inverts identity assumptions and emphasizes Jenny's confusion and the uncanny through recurring dream imagery of eyes and animal features. Her final transformation is a repeated image of her running and leaping forward in an unpanelized sequence, using the De Luca effect across the full width of the page. The plot inversion lifts the tale to a new level of pathos as we are left with the mute and silhouetted image of "Jenny" behind the bars of her cage (fig. 11.5).

The final instance of werewolfism in *Misty* is almost postmodern in its execution: in "The Simple Job" (#56), Terri's murderous uncle is killed by the Frankenstein's creature, Dracula, and Wolfman characters from their carnival's ghost train. (Ghost train characters also appear in "Last Train," Annual 1983, although there is no Wolfman.) In these instances, the fiction and tradition of the archetype are both acknowledged and reacted to—whether by inverting the tale ("Poor Jenny") or by incorporating an acknowledgment of its iconic appearance and existence ("The Simple Job").

244   GOTHIC SYMBOLS, SETTINGS, AND ARCHETYPES

Figure 11.5. "Poor Jenny" (*Misty* #17). Art by Peter Wilkes, writer unknown. Reproduced with permission of Misty™ Rebellion Publishing IP Ltd.; copyright © Rebellion Publishing IP Ltd., all rights reserved.

Overall, Gothic archetypes form a relatively small portion of *Misty*'s content. Rather than generic monsters or clichéd horrors, human flaws instead provide the driving force behind the fear. While some readers loved the archetypes (discussions about how to kill vampires feature multiple times on the letters page, as well as praise for Miss Nocturne), others were less keen (see chap. 13). The data analyzed in chapter 8 suggest that *Misty*'s stories are more likely to explore protagonists' actions and their consequences than to focus on archetypal antagonists, which this discussion further supports.

This analysis of Gothic symbols and archetypes has touched on many other Gothic themes that for reasons of space I have had to ignore. Old curses and past legacies are, of course, linked to many magical items, another example of the Gothic cusp. As Uncle Henry says of his mask, "Only I know its terrible secret" (#39), and past horrors come to life in many *Misty* tales, such as "A Stain on Her Character" (#72), where the school's founder punishes Alison for cheating. Masks and doubles in the tales I have examined frequently serve as agents of transformation, and this device appears as a punishment for both antagonists (as in "Mrs. Rossiter's Cats," #5; or "Cry Baby," #68) and protagonists alike ("The Treatment," #75). The relevance of uncontrollable and changing bodies to a teenage audience does not need to be stressed. Serrato (2017, 51) describes adolescence as a "distressingly transitional life stage," and Reynolds et al. (2001, 6) argue that "the image of monsters, aliens or other kinds of supernaturally powerful beings who take over the body of an ordinary person . . . provides the perfect metaphor for this stage in a young person's development." Change (as inherent to the female body and fertility) is also noted as a central concern of Female Gothic by critics from Moers ([1976] 1978) and Gilbert and Gubar (1979) to Gleeson-White (2001) and Hoeveler (2017).

Misty uses Gothic motifs of doubles, Others, and masks to explore the limits of female identity and particularly to represent issues of control and change. These motifs are frequently tied to feminine symbols (such as mirrors) and domestic settings. Historical doubles also allow the intrusion of the past into the present, which informs all the stories except those set in an explicitly historical period. In this way, all of *Misty*'s stories draw on some form of the Gothic cusp, where the past and present collide. But in contrast to this, the comic uses established Gothic archetypes much less frequently than we might expect, and its treatment of these monsters is often subversive or sympathetic.

CHAPTER 12

GOTHIC FOR GIRLS

So far, the discussion has demonstrated that *Misty* articulates many of the tropes and themes of the Female Gothic. Transgression and transformation are used to explore identity formation and fears of the body, addressing issues of control and change. Doubles express the Otherness of the female role, often reinforced by familial settings or domestic markers. The past intrudes on the present as characters and circumstance clash, creating an uncanny sense of dislocation. Truth is uncertain, expressing fears about family figures and patriarchal authority, and story endings are often unhappy or ambivalent, conveying entrapment and live burial. Stereotypes and archetypes appear less frequently than one might expect, and are often handled subversively and sympathetically.

Mapping these ideas onto my working model of the Female Gothic (chap. 9) confirms that *Misty* explores a number of the problems of female experience. In particular these relate to the physical and emotional changes of adolescence and fears of difference or isolation. The stories are produced by both male and female creators but are predominantly focalized through a female protagonist and set in a female world. Male characters rarely appear as helpers or friends and, when present, are most often either antagonists or patriarchal authorities. The stories offer subversion and transgression by exploring domestic entrapment and identity loss and undermining existing Gothic archetypes. They simultaneously express a conservative stance on the value of self-control and self-acceptance that is reinforced by the dangerous objects and desires and extreme punishments that feature. These themes are often conveyed through domestic and feminine motifs such as mirrors, doubles, families, and masks. The taxonomy of story types I proposed in chapter 8 also aligns with this definition of the Female Gothic by demonstrating that characters' own actions are often the catalyst for their downfall or redemption, and revealing the emphasis that the tales place on ambivalence.

This chapter builds on this analysis to explore how the treatment of these themes creates a Gothic for Girls. I argue that, despite the clear presence of Gothic material in texts for a young female audience, this subgenre is underexplored and marginalized. In this contention I follow Priest (2011), Spooner (2017), and Buckley (2018), who draw attention to the ways in which Gothic scholarship has historically devalued female tastes. They argue for the recognition of popular Gothic texts or subgenres aimed at disregarded groups such as young female audiences and consumers, claiming that taking such texts seriously "is also about taking seriously these marginalized audiences and allowing their tastes to help shape the Gothic canon" (Spooner 2017, 9). To do so, I survey existing work on childhood and Gothic, before moving to discuss the fairy tale and cautionary tale as subgenres of children's literature. I demonstrate that *Misty* combines Female Gothic tropes with explicit and implicit markers taken from fairy tales and cautionary tales. This creates an intertextual space that offers many possible subject positions to the constructed reader and produces an uncanny feeling of familiarity even as the tales push the boundaries of acceptability. The chapter concludes by relating *Misty* to some contemporary examples of dark fairy tales and arriving at a definition of Gothic for Girls.

GOTHIC AND CHILDHOOD

Critical interest in Gothic and children can roughly be divided into two types: analyses of the presence of children in Gothic writing and analyses of the presence of Gothic in writing for children (which later critics often use to interrogate the pedagogical aims of children's literature). Of the first type, Armitt (2017) surveys appearances of "the Gothic girl child" in fiction between 1845 and 2009 and concludes that the depiction of these characters remains surprisingly unchanged. She argues that "repeatedly, the Gothic girl child must undergo trauma on her journey towards womanhood" (72) and draws attention to the ways in which this journey is problematized. Gothic girl children may be prevented from maturing, held at the point of "becoming" (Poe), or otherwise infantilized and disempowered (Brontë, Gaskell). Nineteenth-century texts focus on relationships of power and express a preoccupation with seeing and shame (Oliphant, Henry James), whereas twentieth-century Gothic writing is more direct and moves the focus to the body via issues such as menstruation, attraction, and maturation (du Maurier, Carter, King). Metaphors of skewed mirrors, toys, dolls, and blood recur across these texts, and maternal or feminine bonds are depicted as fraught with danger, betrayal, or loss, producing a sense of isolation.

Georgieva (2013) also explores the depiction of the Gothic child, considering common character traits and features such as the journey toward realization and newly acquired knowledge (168). In particular she notes that models of abandonment and adoption are integrated into Gothic writing across the eighteenth and nineteenth centuries as part of the regularization of society through foundlings and orphans, waifs and strays, wards and protégés. She thus describes the Gothic child as both a character and a figure of style. Both critics note that the liminal and transient status of childhood informs this depiction: Armitt points to "the Victorian belief that pre-pubescent girls were particularly close to the spirit world and possessed clairvoyant powers" (2017, 63), and Georgieva describes the child as "a soul in transition" (168). Later scholars such as Carrington and Bruhm also consider the "evil child" as a manifestation of anxieties about child rearing (Carrington 2011), or as standing for other types of conflict, such as the clash between different theories of childhood as innate versus constructed (Bruhm 2006).

The alternate strand of scholarship on Gothic and children analyzes Gothic themes and structures in writing for children and young adults. While fear and juveniles might seem an unlikely pair, Jackson et al. (2008, 2) argue that children "have always had a predilection for what we now categorize as the Gothic: for ghosts and goblins, hauntings and horrors, fear and the pretence of fear." Subsections of this critical field include the concurrent historical development of Gothic and children's literature; affinities between the two genres (which both tend toward moral lessons and explorations of identity); the potential of Gothic to inform understanding of pedagogy and literary practice; and the psychological usefulness of horror and its treatment in children's texts.

Townshend (2008) explores the historical relationship between Gothic and children's literature, arguing that the two genres are intertwined. He explains that because nurses and carers habitually told folktales and fables to their young charges to scare obedience, concerns about the suitability of such tales began to appear, fed by class-based fears. This led to the creation of a children's literature with evangelical and moral purpose. Hymns and verse such as Isaac Watts's *Divine Songs* (1714) were deemed good for children, and publishers such as John Newbery created a literary market aimed directly at the young (*A Little Pretty Pocket Book*, 1744). Authors like Maria Edgewood and Mary Martha Sherwood provided moralistic and evangelical works, and writers such as Hannah More reclaimed the chapbook format from its associations with horror and sensation stories (*Cheap Repository Tracts*, 1795–98). Thus the emergence of a children's literature can be viewed as a reaction both to the older folktales and fairy tales and to newer Gothic romances and sensation novels.

However, despite this trajectory, Townshend (2008, 26) draws attention to an ongoing Gothic presence in children's literature, even of the pedagogical and worthy type. He notes the "hell and brimfire" in Watts's early work and the presence of "excruciating scenes of horror and terror" in evangelical writing for children more generally, such as the use of an executed body (rotting in a gibbet) in *The History of the Fairchild Family* (Sherwood 1818). This dramatic content was then preserved in part owing to contextual shifts in thinking about childhood. Scholars moved from arguing for the removal of all ghosts and fanciful elements from children's stories (Locke [1693] 1989) toward concerns that overprotecting infants from these things would instead render them overly fearful in later life (Rousseau [1762] 1979). Townshend argues that, as a consequence, sublime and fantastic literature began to be seen again as appropriate for children just as Gothic writing was being denounced as aesthetically inferior and unsuitable for adults. This brief history demonstrates the "literary polysystem" (Shavit 1986, ix) within which children's literature exists (and has always existed) in two concurrent (and often combined) forms: the acceptable/literary and the unacceptable/popular. Dividing children's books into "good" and "bad," often according to their educative potential, remains problematic, and later scholars explore the difficulties of defining and negotiating the pedagogical function of children's literature, drawing on the words of authors and readers to demonstrate that the line between instructing and indoctrinating is often hazy (Gooderham 2003, 166; Thomson 2004, 145; Buckley 2018, 71).

Some critics focus on the way in which Gothic children's literature problematizes education or can be used to inform our understanding of pedagogy and literary practice. Wellington (2008) reflects on a Gothic literature course she taught, applying the notion of "embedded pedagogy" to argue that the texts themselves contain lessons that influenced how she delivered them and how students responded. She demonstrates that, through Gothic themes such as shifting subjectivity, ambivalence, fear, and transgression, she and the students transcended their roles to appear as both victims and upholders of the "Gothic edifice" of higher education. Truffin (2008) uses a different methodology to explore the same areas, analyzing the depiction of the schoolhouse and its dynamics in the work of some contemporary American writers. She argues that their books use Gothic tropes and themes to articulate a suspicion of the academy and its guardians. School becomes "the loci of the Gothic experience" (26), where power relations structure all interactions (53) and the teaching role is one of abuse and cruelty (159). Truffin identifies this as "Schoolhouse Gothic": a set of representations voicing a "structure of feeling" (R. Williams 1977) about academia as dangerous and cruel. Her conclusions are situated with respect to critics such as Veeder (1998) and Winnicott (1982), as she argues that Gothic can act as a substitute for carnival or mediate the internal/external by liberating repressions (Truffin 2008, 158).

Many critics have traditionally argued for the psychological usefulness of Gothic children's literature in a similar manner. Boodman (2002, 185, cited in Cross 2008) identifies the uses young readers make of horror, claiming: "Books that deal with kids' deepest and often unspoken fears—of separation, abandonment, loneliness and death—can be therapeutic, far more so than tales that are relentlessly optimistic." Coats (2008, 91) argues that Gothic children's literature gives "concrete expression to abstract psychological processes, keeping dark fascinations and haunting fears where children can see them, and mingling the horror with healthy doses of humour and hope." Ernest Becker (1973, 19) claims that key tropes of the child's psyche include "terror of the world, the horror of one's own wishes, the fear of vengeance by the parents, the disappearance of things, one's lack of control over anything, really." For all these scholars, Gothic children's literature expresses the traumas of growing up and fears about the world.

Many other critics also recognize the usefulness of Gothic motifs to dramatize children's literature and young adult fiction and aid psychological growth. Cross (2008) claims that Roald Dahl's grotesque and overblown villains are Gothic. Coats (2008) demonstrates the applicability of Gothic to the depiction of female development, citing Neil Gaiman's *Coraline* (2002) and *Mirrormask* (dir. McKean, 2005). McGillis (2008, 232) also explores the "gothicising of puberty" in texts such as M. T. Anderson's *Thirsty* (1997) and *Ginger Snaps* (dir. Fawcett, 2000). It is worth noting that both stories end on a note of hopeless sadness with no escape from monstrosity for their protagonists. Pepetone (2012) explores the religious dimensions of "Kinder-Goth" by bringing a selection of classical children's literature texts to bear on J. K. Rowling's *Harry Potter* series. He draws attention to key features and recurring symbols such as mirrors, doubles, and masks, used to depict a divided self. Childhood locations such as schools are claimed as uncanny (A. Jackson 2008; Truffin 2008) and used to represent the psyches of uncertain protagonists (Crandall 2008). Issues of identity are explored through narratives of haunting and possession (A. Jackson 2008). Anna Smith (2008) argues that teenagers identify with the outsider status of liminal Gothic creatures and notes a trend for nonstandard archetypes (such as sympathetic vampires) in recent teen Gothic. Gothic's ambiguity is also claimed as having a ludic quality that benefits children, particularly when combined with humor (Cross 2008). McGillis (2008, 226) suggests: "Unwise choices may explain why the Gothic is a genre suited to stories about children and adolescents."

Psychoanalytic readings such as these argue for a pedagogical function of children's literature that aids the reader's development. The approach is particularly suited to subgenres such as the fairy tale or cautionary tale. The fairy tale is often claimed to do unconscious psychic work for children (Bettelheim 1975; Coats 2008) by offering a space in which fears can be projected onto villains and monsters, and assuring young readers of happy endings when trials have been overcome. Many fairy tales have a cautionary bent, such as Perrault's "Red Riding Hood" (1697), which warns of the dangers of trusting strangers. Meaning and memory are often reinforced by symbols and archetypes: for example, Red Riding Hood includes the forest as a wild and fertile place, the color red as symbolizing danger or puberty, and the act of rebirth in the versions where Red is saved. Like Gothic, fairy tale is rich with symbolism (where one object stands for another) and allegorical meaning (a hidden interpretation of an abstract idea, often political or moral).

These narrative strategies allow fairy tales and fables to convey both explicit and implicit lessons. For example, Aesop's fables (ca. 600 BC) contain explicit moral messages as postscripts, such as "appearances often are deceiving" ("The Wolf in Sheep's Clothing") and "slow and steady wins the race" ("The Hare and the Tortoise"). Later fabulists such as Charles Perrault also conclude their tales with a didactic warning, such as "Red Riding Hood" ("Children, especially attractive, well-bred young ladies, should never talk to strangers") or "Bluebeard" ("Curiosity, in spite of its appeal, often leads to deep regret"). While the Brothers Grimm added many Christian and puritan overtones to later versions of their folktale collections (see Loo 2014; Zipes 2014), the original versions also held an "organic" moral value that the Grimms tried to preserve without making it overt or didactic. They viewed their collection as an "educational primer of ethics, values, and customs" (Zipes 2014, xxx) from which young (and old) readers could gain wisdom and knowledge. All these storytellers use sins such as vanity ("Snow White"), greed ("Hansel and Gretel"), curiosity ("Bluebeard"), and pride ("The Swineherd," "King Thrushbeard") as plot catalysts. Such temptations are to be resisted, and personal faults must be overcome, or the consequences will be severe.

Critics such as Teverson draw attention to the strong strand of punishment and "protracted suffering" that characterizes many fairy tales and informs the related children's genre of the cautionary tale. Tatar ([1987] 1993, 25) defines cautionary tales as short prose narratives that "aim to mold behavior by illustrating in elaborate detail the dire consequences of deviant conduct." Notable examples include *Der Struwwelpeter* (Hoffmann [1844] 1848), in which children receive terrible punishments for transgressions: Augustus refuses to eat his soup and wastes away, Harriet plays with matches and is burned to death, and "Suck-a-Thumb" Conrad has both his thumbs cut off by the giant scissors of the "great tall tailor." The collected stories of *Max and Moritz* (Busch 1865) take a similar tone and warn of hooliganism as the duo terrorize their neighborhood but end up ground to bits and eaten by ducks. Cautionary tales employ fairy-tale-style villains or punishments to deliver a direct moral lesson of this type. In both genres, the horror is mitigated by excess and a lack of realism; characters are often reduced to stereotypes, and punishments are so grotesque as to be absurd.

The majority of scholarship on Children's Gothic to date has focused on identifying explicit moral lessons and constructing implicit psychological value from these tales (see, e.g., Jackson et al. 2008; Pepetone 2012; A. Jackson 2017). However, later critics such as Buckley (2018) have argued that such psychoanalytic readings are singular and essentialist, closing down the text by claiming to provide the "truth" about what it offers. Buckley's revisionist work argues that two main approaches dominate the treatment of the child in children's literature today. Scholars either identify an essentialist and universal child who is served by their psychoanalytic interpretation (Bettelheim 1975) or provide a deconstructionist or constructionist reading that demonstrates the child as a discursive construct of the book and thus representative of its social context (Ariès 1973; Lesnik-Oberstein 1994). Buckley points to the flaws in both methods, which argue for active reader engagement while simultaneously claiming that moral lessons are passively instilled, or reject the notion of a "real" reader while nonetheless identifying needs that are served. Instead Buckley explores reader agency within the pedagogical tensions of children's literature, using the critical frame of the nomad (Braidotti 2011) and looking at a selection of twenty-first-century Children's Gothic texts. For her the reader is not a "real" child but a conceptual persona constructed within and by the text through multiple intertextual intersections (Buckley 2018, 138). Gothic's "plural form" (Howard 1994) and its internal contradictions make it a particularly appropriate intertextual junction that can offer multiple possible subject positions to the constructed child reader.

With this in mind, we might reconsider the Gothic qualities that can be found in particular subgenres of children's literature such as fairy tales and cautionary tales. Rather than pursuing psychological and symbolic meaning from the Gothic tropes already analyzed, we should explore the positions of identification that the texts construct for their readers, and the intertextual sites that they draw on to do so. For example, *Misty* contains many reworkings of established fairy-tale tropes and symbols. Two tales are of particular note. The first, "Danse Macabre" (#52), depicts the story of Nadia, who lies and cheats to get the lead role in a ballet but collapses after the ballet shoes she has stolen force her to dance unendingly alongside a skeletal and ghostly chorus. This draws on Hans Christian Andersen's "The Red Shoes" (1845), in which Karen transgresses by first choosing and then continuing to wear her red shoes after they have been forbidden by her guardian. An angel curses her to dance without rest until, exhausted, she pleads with an executioner to chop off her feet. But she remains haunted by the shoes until she is finally able to fully repent, die, and go to heaven. Both stories share an overt moral lesson and key moments ("No more! Please! My feet are bruised and bleeding!"), and the *Misty* reworking draws explicitly on the fairy tale by having Nadia disobey so as to obtain the shoes. But it also reframes the story by combining it with the ballet setting (common in girls' comics) and the competition between Nadia and Lois for the lead role. The girls are demarcated by idiolects that flag their characters: while saintly Lois muses to herself, "I'd so love to be the star of the show," Nadia is antagonistic, thinking, "I've gotta make sure that little drip Lois doesn't get the part." Visuals emphasize the loss of control that the shoes bring Nadia, for example, using the De Luca effect in an unpanelized sequence of overlaid images as she finds herself unable to stop dancing. The comic thus constructs a number of different interpretative routes for its readers, depending on their familiarity with girls' comics, fairy tales, or both.

"The Forest of Fear?" (#89) similarly rewrites elements from various versions of "Red Riding Hood,"[1] and the story's subversive effect depends on these intertextual references. Protagonist Heidi loves Smirch Forest despite its creepy reputation, which is reinforced by opening images of wolves, bats, and bears. Passing through the forest to visit her grandmother, Heidi encounters a stranger who she suspects is a werewolf, and races ahead to save her grandmother. The stranger is already there, but she is able to order him off, as she is revealed to be a vampire in the final panel. Fairy-tale tropes are scattered throughout the story (Heidi's Papa is a woodman; she is asked to take food to her grandmother), and the tale's impact relies on reversing the implied knowledge. Again, it draws on the comics medium to do so, as Heidi is juxtaposed against apparent threats throughout (from menacing animals to the stranger in his witchfinder's hat and cape), and the final reveal is solely visual. The narration only refers to "the thing Heidi had become," against an image of her yellow eyes flooded with tears, with bright red lips and white fangs, as she cries, "I hoped you'd never need to know my secret, Grandmother . . . !" As Heidi outwits the stranger, this tale returns to earlier versions of the Red Riding Hood mythos, such as "The Story of Grandmother," which contains a *bzou* (werewolf) who is tricked by the peasant girl. Yet it simultaneously undercuts this trope as our heroine is revealed to be the monster of the piece, thus also recalling and juxtaposing the Gothic literary tradition of sympathetic monsters.

Other *Misty* tales also draw on established fairy-tale symbology, such as "The Fourth Swan" (#61) and "A Little Bit of Magic" (#39), both of which see persecuted characters change into swans and evade their tormentors. The motif of transformation and the symbolic qualities of the white swan echo stories such as Hans Christian Andersen's "The Wild Swans" (1838) or the Grimms' "The Six Swans" (1857) while reframing transformation as an escape, not a punishment. These *Misty* stories can be read as forerunners of a twenty-first-century Children's Gothic that constructs active child readers who can use their intertextual knowledge to access the multiple subject positions that the narrative offers them.

Contemporary Children's Gothic shares many qualities with older subgenres such as fairy tale that have an "affinity" to Gothic (Coats 2008, 78). However, it often uses intertextual references or a self-reflexive style to summon these older sources and negotiate the paradoxes of pedagogical aims. It thus provides a vehicle for moral lessons and warnings about the dangerous journey to adulthood while also questioning and problematizing simplistic visions of growth and maturation. It explores the divided self and issues of identity, interrogating notions of power and control, often through established Gothic motifs such as haunting and possession. It may use an isolated space or an uncanny setting or offer identification with monstrosity or the grotesque. It uses ambivalent endings and playfulness, constructing an active and knowing reader who can interpret these juxtapositions, and offering a variety of diverse subject positions. It thus creates distance from explicit horror, for example, through comedy or parody or stylization.

CHILDREN'S GOTHIC, FEMALE GOTHIC, FAIRY TALES, AND *MISTY*

Many of the features of Children's Gothic I have identified have already been noted as present in *Misty*. However, I would argue that Children's and Female Gothic are modified in this comic and brought together using fairy-tale tropes and narrative strategies. In this section, I analyze how *Misty* employs fairy-tale abstraction, magical realism, and conflicting gender roles to mediate between Children's and Female Gothic and produce a Gothic for Girls.

Fairy tale takes place in an abstract or undefined space and time that is distinctly Other ("Once upon a time" and maybe even "In a galaxy far, far away"). This timeless quality is created and enhanced by the use of archetypal symbols and characters in place of personal and realistic detail. Lüthi (1986, 11) argues that "in every sense, it [fairy tale] lacks the dimension of depth. Its characters are figures without substance, without inner life, without an environment; they lack any relation to past and future, to time altogether." Similarly, places are seldom identified or named. For example, Little Red-Cap's grandmother lives "out in the wood, half a league from the village," and the girl and her godmother live "in a small house at the end of the village" in the Grimms' "The Spindle, the Shuttle, and the Needle" (1843). Other tales (such as "Snow White") give no sense of place at all, and locations are situated only with respect to each other: the forest, the village, and the castle are often all that is needed.

Many of the *Misty* tales use this fairy-tale tone of detachment in their treatment of space. As noted in chapter 11, the past often intrudes into the present, creating a sense of dislocation and disconnection between characters and their circumstances. Combining the Gothic cusp with an absence of clear visual or temporal markers gives the *Misty* stories a timeless and abstract feel, creating the uncanny as the pseudo-familiar is made strange and set adrift. This is further enhanced by the textual treatment of place, which is seldom precise. In the majority of *Misty* stories, the location simply goes unnamed and undescribed, and action instead takes place in the home, school, or shop. When a place is named, it is often fictional, for example, Little Wytching ("The Story of Little Wytching," #72), Fiskfield ("The Jukebox," #28), the city of Ataris ("A Spell of Trouble," #24), or Chateau d'Arc ("Twin Catastrophes," #67). When real place names are used, they are not well known and generally connote either British-ness or exoticism, such as Nether Green (Sheffield) or Fenbridge (Cambridge), the settings of "Mrs. Barlow's Lodger" (#19) and "Journey into Fear" (#14–27). The city of Cori-Cancha in Peru ("Curse of the Condor," #19) is a real Inca temple, but its translation as "City of the Condor" is less accurate. Relative space is often used in a fairy-tale manner to situate the story: for example, Mrs. Barlow and her daughter live "in the small cottage opposite Nether Green church" ("Mrs. Barlow's Lodger," #19), and we are told only that the story of "Miranda" (#12) "took place in this very village."

Misty's characters perform against this abstract and uncanny backdrop. As Lüthi suggests, they can be read as characters without substance, inner life, or environment. Many are simply a transgression waiting to happen. In the single stories, the situation dominates; as in the stripped-down horror films of the 1970s, so the stories do not attempt psychological realism or explanation. Nan is just "a problem child" ("The Girl Who Walked on Water," #35), and the story gives no history or explanation for her behavior. Anna is vain ("Reflections," #53), Rita is a liar ("Web of Lies," #14), Della is spoiled ("Watch Your Step!" #25), Effie is greedy ("Heart's Desire," #56), Cath is a bully ("Dead End!" #34), Gail is lazy ("Full Circle," #58), and Sandra is selfish ("What Did You Say?" #85). There are a few exceptions: "Cave of Dread" (#2) opens with Steffie's childhood phobia of furry things (although no reason is given), which becomes the catalyst for the plot. But in the main, the *Misty* characters have no substance or inner life. Their stories begin and end with their sin and its punishment, giving no sense of a relationship to past or future.

We might expect the protagonists of the serials to offer more in the way of personality, particularly as their stories often deal with the threat and circumstance of change. However, even here characters are often reduced to little more than a set of fears or desires, and the struggle that the narrative portrays is that of stasis against movement. Rosemary simply wants friendship and acceptance ("Moonchild"), Elena battles against her timidity ("A Leap through Time"), and characters such as Jan ("The Sentinels") or Jenny ("The School of the Lost . . .") have few defining features. Their function in their stories is merely to explore the mystery. Toni in "Whistle and I'll Come . . ." is probably the most strongly defined character, but this is largely because she has Alfred to soliloquize to, allowing her to express some sense of history and longing, such as her memories of the countryside (#46).

Characters and locations in *Misty* are thus often left unnamed or only vaguely delineated, allowing them to act as a metonym for all such people or places, and perhaps to carry additional symbolic meaning. So "the village" stands for the neighborhood, sometimes nostalgically, and "town" is London or another big city, often negatively associated with progress or commenting on the hazards of the urban environment. Places such as Africa, Egypt, China, and Peru are exotic and Othered: potential sources of dangerous magical items and exciting self-discoveries. Similarly, vain, jealous, or selfish characters act as archetypal warnings for the reader, and the "Cinderella" characters stand for all girls who have felt themselves to be trapped and powerless.

The lack of detail has a distancing effect that is characteristic of Children's Gothic. Cross points toward the combination of comedy and Gothic in many children's works, arguing that it creates detachment, which is essential for the child's enjoyment. Other critics such as Cummins (2008) draw attention to the use of parodic and exaggerated characterization. With this in mind, we can read *Misty*'s characters as singular abstractions: little more than a parody of a particular sin or desire. This fairy-tale treatment creates a distance from the fear, even as other aspects of the medium or narrative may work to draw the reader in.

While *Misty*'s worlds and characters carry an uncanny sense of dislocation, the stories also contain elements of magical realism, which combines the mundane with the marvelous. Armitt (2012, 512) describes magical realism as "a disruptive, foreign, fantastic narrative style that fractures the flow of an otherwise seamlessly realist text." The term originates from art history, taking in magic realism (an artistic movement that foregrounds the fantastic or uncanny nature of everyday objects) and the subsequent literary movement of the same name (also known as marvelous realism), which takes the opposite angle. Magical realist literature expresses "the seemingly opposed perspectives of a pragmatic, practical and tangible approach to reality and an acceptance of magic and superstition" (Bowers 2004, 3). It juxtaposes the everyday with the supernatural for maximum effect, "erupting from a fissure in the ordinary, out of which the extraordinary flows" (Armitt 2012, 512). Armitt continues that when magical realism and Gothic combine, the supernatural takes center stage (rather than being "simply 'there'"), manifesting secrets that are given sinister resonance.

Although we can delineate clear differences between the depiction of everyday life in fairy tale and magical realism, an acceptance of enchantment is a defining trait of both literary genres. Todorov (1975) defines this mode of writing as the "marvelous": a world where enchantment and the supernatural exist. This is a characteristic of both fairy tale and magical realism. It is also apparent in *Misty*, with one important caveat: the existence of magic consistently comes as a surprise to the protagonists of its stories. This is not a fairy-tale world where enchantment is commonplace: a *Misty* protagonist confronted with her fairy godmother would be skeptical. This trope is acknowledged in some of the stories, often by using the comics medium to play with the reader (as discussed in chap. 8). For example, in "The Dummy" (#4), Rhoda catches sight of Beattie in her fairy costume and gasps, "What the . . . ?" before continuing, "F-for a moment I thought you were real!" The trick is extended to the reader with intertextual knowledge, as the drawn quality of the medium presents Beattie as possibly supernatural, before revealing that she is just an actress in costume.

We could also consider here the use of a rational frame (also discussed in chap. 8), which appears more in *Misty* than might be expected from a Gothic comic (137, or 18 percent, of the story episodes). These frames include dreams, aliens, time travel, tricks and cons that fake the supernatural, psychological conditions, machinery (clockwork or robotic characters), and other scientific experiments (on birds, snails). The first three need little explanation, although aliens in particular are often handled like the horror archetypes and expectation is reversed; for example, a tiny spaceship appears in "Last Encounters" (#32). The frames are also often combined: Jan's dream is revealed as the nightmare of an alien who is equally horrified by her appearance ("A Scream in the Night!" #47), and "Just Another Day" (#98) reveals the world as a dream of an alien character. Characters disguise themselves as monsters to terrify trespassers ("Don't Look Back . . . in Anger!" #23) or scare away rightful owners from their inheritance ("Prince of Lightning," Annual 1981). Sometimes psychology is used as justification, including hallucinations ("Last Encounters," #32), electric shocks ("The Little White Dot," #51), and telekinesis ("Ghost Hunters," Annual 1984). Science fiction also features; for example, Lucy is taken in by a kindly family after running away but melts when she sits too close to the fire and is revealed as a waxwork with a soul ("The Bitter Tale of Sweet Lucy," #35), and characters' discoveries that they or others are robots ("The Family," #6; "The Experiment," #100) have already been discussed in chapter 10. The intelligent snails that Sally's father has bred consume her after she tries to vandalize his experiments ("House of Snails," #77) in a story that is unremittingly bleak, as he sadly reflects, "They're all I've got left now Sally's gone. Doubt if I'll start up my experiments again, though."

Girls in *Misty* exist in a juxtaposed world. Their lives and priorities are of the mundane and everyday ("kitchen sink" realism, chores, and teenage worries) but simultaneously set adrift in fairy-tale abstraction (nameless places, empty characters, and stereotypes). These worlds are further disrupted by the presence of magic, which is a subversive and confrontational force. Its reality is not in doubt, but its presence is always an intrusion. However, my analysis of common tropes in chapter 8 shows that magical items and powers are most often combined with character actions, whether these are bad choices with unexpected and unhappy consequences, or positive acts with redemptive qualities. It therefore seems that *Misty* offers both conservative and subversive fare by combining moral rules with varied outcomes and often ending on a note of ambiguity.

Some stories demonstrate female restrictions and limitations (imprisonment, isolation, the feminine carceral), while other protagonists' struggles against these forces celebrate female strength and agency. In this they echo fairy tales. These have often been attacked for their problematic treatment of women, such as Perrault's heroines, who are passive ("Sleeping Beauty"), self-sacrificing ("Cinderella"), or wayward women chastised ("Red Riding Hood," "Bluebeard"). Gilbert and Gubar (1979, 36) also note that "Snow White" offers just two types of woman: the passive angel and the active witch. But by contrast, other fairy-tale protagonists are active, complex, and often ambiguous characters (as in the works of Marie-Catherine d'Aulnoy, Marie-Jeanne L'Héritier, and Catherine Bernard). The works of writers such as Hans Christian Andersen are easy to read as misogynist, as female characters are punished for their desires (red shoes, a prince) or rewarded for self-sacrifice (as in "The Snow Queen" and "The Little Match Girl"). However, Andersen's characters can also be interpreted as strong female agents enacting their own destiny, and scholars have also suggested autobiographical readings that place Andersen himself in the female character role, struggling between two classes and suffering in love (Teverson 2013). Zipes ([1986] 1993, 16) also discusses feminist adaptations in which "the women rely on their wits [or magic, symbolizing latent potential] which enable them to overcome oppressive conditions." While fairy-tale roles for women are not without problems, they are not as passive as appearances might suggest, and they negotiate power in a number of ways, offering diverse intertextual subject positions of the type that Buckley (2018) identifies and going beyond innocent virgin / wicked hag.

In her landmark book *The Beauty Myth* (1990), Wolf exposes the constructed and manipulated nature of these roles as part of a wider exploration of the complex social relationships between power, control, and femininity. Wolf argues that the qualities assigned to beauty are in fact designed to prescribe and control women's behavior, not appearance. So female competition, youth, and virginity are all made part of the beauty myth, devaluing age, knowledge, and power and asserting instead that women's identity is premised on attractiveness. Wolf continues to argue that definitions of childhood, female biology, and "women's work" are also ideals and stereotypes designed to control women (by requiring maternal supervision, positioning subjects as hysterics and hypochondriacs, and revolving around repetitive, time-consuming tasks). She points toward the ways in which women's bodies become sites of dispute and conflict, as the people inside them try to comply with ever-changing ideals of perfection that are intended to be aspirational and impossible to achieve. Like the girls' magazines discussed at the start of this book, fairy tales tread an ambiguous and paradoxical line that must articulate and address readers' interests and desires but avoid directly challenging patriarchy.

Orenstein also explores the contradictory nature of female roles in fairy tales. She notes that many lesser-known fairy tales celebrate ingenious girls, although she points out that none are free of problems (sexualization, violence, incest, etc.). These tales sit in contrast to the mainstream visions of fairy-tale femininity that are actively promoted and targeted at girls. Orenstein explores the appeal of the Disney Princesses, arguing that there are a number of reasons that girls engage with these characters and their brand (alongside other strongly gendered toys and clothes). One explanation she offers draws on established research into the appeal of gendered toys to suggest that very young children (under fives) don't understand that their own gender identity is fixed and cannot be altered by superficial changes. Products that clearly mark femininity are thus extremely appealing to this age group, who struggle with the concept of permanence in general.

Orenstein's book follows Wolf's research in exploring the cultural meanings of girlhood, as well as attempting to work through Orenstein's own ambivalent feelings about the contemporary Disney Princess obsession. She draws attention to the singular role of the Princess—there can be only one in each story, just one girl who is exalted above all others. She notes that this sense of isolation and competition continues in the Disney marketing, as although the Princesses sometimes appear together on merchandise, they do not share a storyworld and so never acknowledge each other on these products; each gazes off in a different direction. Orenstein argues that the Princess also stands as a figure of perfection, representing the increasing pressure on young girls to be perfect in a myriad of ways. Drawing on data from a large-scale survey of schoolchildren (2006), she explains that "instead of feeling greater latitude and choice in how to be female—which is what one would hope—they now feel they must not only 'have it all' but *be* it all: Cinderella *and* Supergirl. Aggressive *and* agreeable. Smart *and* stunning" (Orenstein 2011, 17). Contemporary expectations of girlhood thus straddle a contradiction, as girls must aim to fulfill all the new expectations as well as the old.

We can draw points from this analysis that reveal where Children's Gothic meets Female Gothic. For example, the fear of bodily transformation that underlies Female Gothic can perhaps be read not just as a metaphor for pregnancy but also as a continuation of the gender-based fears of young children, renewed in adolescence with the bodily changes that puberty brings. Isolation is both a defining trait of Female Gothic and apparent in the roles that are offered to girls in fairy tales. Fairy-tale worlds are undefined alterities that contain a sense of disconnection and distance, contributing to the solipsism that can be found in Female Gothic. Identity is interrogated and explored by the literatures of both childhood and Gothic, and Otherness and freakishness are problems that are enacted in both genres. *Misty*'s bodily transformations, solitary protagonists, empty worlds, and enactment of identity discourse and associated fears all cohere with these shared qualities, which lead me toward my definition of Gothic for Girls. But are these tropes common to other dark fairy tales for young female readers?

DARK FAIRY TALES FOR GIRLS

Fairy tales aimed at girls seem to take two forms: the saccharine or the shadowed. While adaptors from the Grimms to Disney have removed unsavory aspects and prettied up both characters and stories, a number of popular texts aimed at or given to young girls consistently combine dark themes with fairy-tale motifs. From *Alice's Adventures in Wonderland* to *Twilight*, these stories revolve around female protagonists awakening to strange worlds, and their struggles to negotiate or escape these.

Carroll's *Alice* (1865) is often remembered nostalgically as a whimsical childhood book, and the bright colors and happy anarchy of the Disney adaptation (1951) reinforce this impression. However, Alice experiences Wonderland as a confusing and frustrating place in which she is isolated. She often feels sad, alone, and trapped ("She walked sadly down the middle, wondering how she was ever to get out again" [12]), lost even in her own pool of tears. Her size constantly changes, and she questions her own identity throughout the text, for example, asking, "Who in the world am I?" (17–18) and "I know who I *was* when I got up this morning, but I think I must have been changed several times since then" (41). The key themes of Gothic for Girls are all present, and *Alice through the Looking Glass* (1872) develops many of these further through symbols such as mirrors and journeys.

Critics such as Rudd (2008) and Buckley (2014) argue that it is entirely possible to trace a Gothic strand in children's writing from the Victorian period to the present day. Buckley lists authors such as Frances Hodgson Burnett (*The Secret Garden*, 1911), John Masefield (*The Midnight Folk*, 1927), Philippa Pearce (*Tom's Midnight Garden*, 1958), Susan Cooper (*The Dark Is Rising* series, 1965–77), Alan Garner (*The Weirdstone of Brisingamen* trilogy, 1960–2012), Roald Dahl (*The Witches*, 1983), Robert Swindells (*Room 13*, 1989), Gillian Cross (*Wolf*, 1990), and Christopher Pike (*Spooksville* series, 1995–98), alongside publishers' series such as Point Horror (launched 1991) and Goosebumps (launched 1992). To this list I could easily add writers such as Penelope Lively (*The Ghost* of *Thomas Kempe*, 1973) and Gene Kemp (*Mr. Magus Is Waiting for You*, 1986),[2] and books for younger readers such as Ann Jungman's *Vlad the Drac* series (1982–94) or older ones such as Annette Curtis Klause's *The Silver Kiss* (1990). As Buckley (2014, 259) notes, these writers "have either invoked Gothic tropes, explored the potential of dark fantasy and uncanny time-slip narratives, published ghost stories or developed gruesome horror for children and adolescents." Many of their books tend toward magical realism and often deal with issues of isolation, estrangement, and incarceration. While not all are explicitly for girls, the domestic settings used by Hodgson Burnett and Pearce imply this, and the Point Horror series in particular was directly aimed at adolescent girls. Crawford (2014) notes that Stine, Pike, and Hoh also wrote young adult vampire fiction aimed at a female audience at the height of their popularity in the 1990s.[3] Reynolds et al. (2001, 17) discuss the Point Horror authors, alongside other writers such as David Almond, Philip Gross, Lesley Howarth, and Robert Westell, arguing that they provide "a form of frightening fiction which may be able to combat the miasma of hysteria and paranoia that can simultaneously paralyse and terrorize young people in contemporary society."

Later stories such as Neil Gaiman's *Coraline* (2002) also explore cultural adolescent fears by presenting an isolated protagonist trapped in a fantasy world. While the movie adaptation (2009) added a male companion, in Gaiman's novel Coraline is entirely alone, helped only by her cat. She enters an uncanny fantasy world populated by doubles from her own, including the villainous Other Mother—a literal Other and doppelgänger. Like *Alice* the story again conveys a loss of identity as Coraline is growing out of her childhood, feeling "bored with her toys" (13) and disconnected from her parents. Fears of transformation also underlie the narrative: her Other Father devolves into a grub-like creature, and the Other Mother's powers are to "transform, and twist, and change" (133). However, Buckley (2018) points out that an intertextual reading of *Coraline* is more productive than the psychological, as Gaiman characteristically litters his story with overt symbols of the uncanny and references to older sources.

Dark fairy-tale atmospheres continue to be picked up and rearticulated in other contemporary narratives for both boys and girls. Lemony Snicket's children's books focus on the Baudelaire family and their attempts to escape from Count Olaf. The plots have been read as allegories for the change from childhood to adulthood (Sadenwasser 2014; Austin 2013), and critics also note the ambivalence of the stories' endings and their problematization of Manichean morality (Olson 2011). Snicket's knowing and parodic tone complicates these readings and suggests escape for the informed reader. Tim Burton's works also find popularity with a teen and preteen audience (and, of course, incorporate *Alice in Wonderland*). An iconography of chaotic whimsy and stop-motion animation characterizes texts such as *Frankenweenie* (2012), *Corpse Bride* (2005), and *The Nightmare before Christmas* (1993). Although these films are not explicitly gendered, Spooner (2017) notes Burton's popularity with female audiences (and I would extend this claim to Gaiman's appeal as well). Many of their works deal with isolated and lonely protagonists and contain tropes of transformation, identity exploration, and Otherness within an intertextual frame.

When young adult fiction addresses itself explicitly to female readers, it again gives us a protagonist who is isolated or special in some other way and whose struggle to understand and negotiate her new identity underlines the text. Joss Whedon's television adaptation of *Buffy the Vampire Slayer* (1997–2003) is a key text here, with Buffy's struggles to accept her destiny becoming a strong focal point of the series. Book series such as Harris's *The Southern Vampire Mysteries* (2001–13) also revolve around "super powered" heroines like Sookie Stackhouse, whose telepathic powers set her apart from family and friends and whose continued discoveries about her identity underpin later plot developments. In both the novels and the HBO adaptation *True Blood* (2008–14), Sookie battles to retain her agency in a world of vampire friends and foes. While Bella Swan in Meyer's *Twilight* (2005–8) initially appears as a counterpoint to this, as an ordinary girl with no particular powers or abilities, Edward's love for her makes her special, and Crawford (2014, 162) suggests that Bella's gift is, quite simply, "pure will, in the service of pure appetite: no matter how much pain it causes her (or anyone else), she simply wants and wants and wants until, finally, she is given everything that she could desire, just for being herself." He also notes the text's use of intertextuality in its pursuit of wish-fulfillment fantasies, arguing that the first three books can be read respectively as optimistic reworkings of *Pride and Prejudice*, *Romeo and Juliet*, and *Wuthering Heights*, "except this time everyone ultimately gets what they want, and they are all allowed to live happily ever after" (171). Other popular television series such as *Once Upon a Time* (2007–present) follow similar questing protagonists immersed in intertextual worlds, such as Emma Swan, whose destiny as "the Saviour" is to help the fairy-tale inhabitants of Storybrooke reach their happy ending. Revisionist works such as *Wicked* (1995; 2003) and *Maleficent* (2014) also offer strong heroines and intertextual themes.

A large number of contemporary Gothic-themed stories thus construct a young female reader and use intertextuality to give her agency, of which I have given a very brief snapshot. While I am not suggesting that all Gothic narratives for this audience follow this pattern, many of the most popular have similarities. Protagonists will experience isolation, transformation, and Otherness during a quest for individuation. This often takes the form of an identity exploration with the ultimate goal of discovery and acceptance. This emphasis distinguishes Gothic for Girls from Children's Gothic or Female Gothic.

GOTHIC FOR GIRLS

Girlhood has been identified as a slippery category that contains a tension and lack of stability, as it changes and is interpreted differently across generations (Gibson 2008). Fairy tales can also shift to suit their time, and the modern form is described as "contemporary in setting, direct in style, allegorical in intent" (Teverson 2013, 81). With these points in mind, I suggest that *Misty* is an exemplar of a type of Gothic designed for young girls that is also present in other contemporary Gothic girls' stories stretching over the cusp of the millennium. As Reynolds et al. (2001), Crawford (2014), and Buckley (2018) all identify, these narratives are heavily intertextual, creating fear and ambivalence by gesturing toward security and safety even as they often undercut this. They draw on the Female Gothic but use fairy-tale ideas to modify its tone and its themes to suit a younger audience, as follows:

Gothic for Girls explores and enacts identity. It focuses on a young female protagonist who is usually isolated or trapped in some way. It takes place in a magical realist world, which juxtaposes the mundane and the supernatural. Time, place, and character are abstract and often symbolic. The genre confronts readers with the unknown or the Other, as protagonists are initially unaware of magical potential and the narrative enacts and mediates their wakening awareness. The narrative is driven by simultaneous fear and attraction, generally in the form of terror, and often relating to incarceration, transformation (physical or mental), and doubt. It may use symbols that bring these tropes together, such as the feminine carceral (where the female body becomes a prison, e.g., through uncontrolled transformation) or the spectral woman (unheard and unseen, where isolation and solipsism dominate). Luxury (objects, property, desires) and traditional fairy-tale sins (greed, pride, laziness) are common sources of conflict. When established Gothic archetypes appear, they are often handled knowingly or subverted in some way. Temptation and transgression provide the catalysts for the narrative, creating a clear moral or lesson. While traps, curses, and other magical dangers abound, they are seldom effective alone, and personal responsibility plays a large part. Self-control or self-acceptance provides the means of escape, although escape is not always possible. Gothic for Girls constructs and acknowledges girlhood as an uncanny experience, interrogating expectations and reimagining its fears.

CHAPTER 13

MAKE *MISTY* FOR ME

Gothic has always appealed to female readers, despite historically problematic gender politics. Its tendencies toward subversion speak to the disempowered, and it perhaps comes as no surprise that in recent decades Gothic's attraction to young audiences has become more visible. Peter Hunt (1991) argues that nonadult readers are much more competent than has been assumed, and a number of critics have tried to redress the feeling that scholarship on children's literature is the exclusive domain of adults.[1] Reynolds et al. (2001, 9) note that children read for agency, and in particular suggest that, for some girls, reading horror "offers ways of negotiating current constructions of the 'right' way to grow up female" (10). This research follows critics such as Sarland (1991), who argues that, for girls in particular, reading certain types of fiction has the potential to intensify feelings of agency and control. Without offering value judgments, Sarland also finds that girls and boys may read the same text in different ways owing to sociosexual differences (drawing on data from a study of *Rambo* readers).

Despite this, young readers' opinions are often ignored, and the interests and tastes of female audiences in particular are trivialized and maligned. As noted, Crawford (2014) exposes the ways in which critical discourse systematically undermines *Twilight* readers. He explores the three main theories mobilized against the series' appeal (fans are too stupid to understand its message or are blinded by Edward; fans are sucked in by marketing; and fans are already ideologically brainwashed into accepting abuse as romance) and argues that all these positions denigrate the series' readership (203). He thus aligns moral panics over *Twilight* with previous responses to horror, claiming that "while it often camouflaged itself as a debate over literary quality and/or ideology, the *Twilight* debate was, at base, primarily a debate over the legitimacy of different reading strategies" (221). He also follows Ormrod (2011) in noting the role of gender in this debate. In this discourse, Romantic vampires are critiqued for weakening the archetype, which previously held heteronormative masculine values. Similarly, male audiences are assumed to be able to deal with problematic elements and distinguish fantasy from reality, whereas female readers are not, despite clear evidence to the contrary (Crawford 2014, 200). Critics such as Hills (2002) and Busse (2013) note that such gendered "regimes of truth" are often constructed around fandoms, enabling a moral dualism that is "created and sustained by systems of cultural value" (Hills 2002, 21). This dichotomizes "good," masculine fandom ("intellectual, aggressive and objective") against "bad" feminine idolatry ("passive, emotional, sensitive and subjective") (Busse 2013, 74). Proctor (2016) further explores how narratives of freakishness are often attached to the tastes of female fans, arguing that the movement of fandom from the margins to the mainstream "has not yet redressed the gender politics at work in the representational spaces of the media, fan communities and academia."

By exploring critically overlooked texts such as *Misty*, I hope to have contributed to the illumination of the reading material and practices of these silenced audiences. Spooner (2017, 101) argues that "reading happy Gothic can enable the marginalized culture of girlhood to be restored to the academic frame," and that its texts are complex and often wildly inventive spaces that challenge and subvert expectations of femininity, childhood, and Romance. This chapter looks more closely at the uses that *Misty*'s readers made of the comic's content, and their responses to its themes and ideas. I draw attention to the diverse readership of the comic, whose critical and active responses problematize the notion of a singular "real" reader (rather than ideal/implied), thus acknowledging Buckley's claim that the subject positions of Children's Gothic are best understood as constructed, multiple, mobile, and nomadic.

My approach to this "active audience" follows Hermes' discussion of the emergence and use of this term. Hermes points out that to label the audience as "active" suggests an implicit passivity in media audiences more generally. We see this also in scholarly work that treats popular audiences as "dupes" (Schrøder 2000) or relies solely on text-based analysis (Modleski [1982] 1990). Instead, I draw on the *Misty* letters page to complement my previous discussions by exploring the ways that readers "made meaning" from *Misty*. In so doing, I also follow the work of Ang (1985) by taking the feelings expressed in readers' letters as the basis for my analysis, rather than applying an interpretative framework. Although the *Misty* letters were not produced in response to research questions, their content overwhelmingly deals with the pleasures and responses of the comic's fans. My goal is to investigate the ways in which *Misty*'s readers used and responded to the comic, and to reflect on these findings within the wider contexts of scholarship on female magazine reading and comics letters pages. Tinkler (1995), Hermes (1995), and Tebbutt (2016) have all argued that periodicals and the responses of their readers can tell us a great deal about the constructed and assigned nature of gender roles and social expectations.

The "Write to Misty" letters page appears in nearly every issue from #8 onward and offered £5 for the Star Letter and £2 for every letter printed.[2] It covers either a double or single page and includes a picture of Misty and a selection of letters. It contains a voting coupon that encourages critical response by asking readers to vote for their favorite three serials and also their least favorite. But much of the discussion throughout also centers on readers' lives and Misty herself—readers display an overwhelming desire to know who she is. She responds to both compliments and complaints, deflects requests for her life story, and gives mysterious fragments of information about herself.

Reading the printed selection reveals an active, empowered, and diverse audience. The letters show a readership that spans ages nine to eighty-five, although Misty claims that her readers are as young as seven (#10) and spread across the globe. Readers comment critically on what they do and do not like, send in creative work, and share anecdotes about how *Misty*'s stories reflect them and their lives. This community feeling is emphasized as readers also respond to each other's praise and complaints, offer to swap and sell back issues, and talk about setting up comics clubs of their own.

Few critics have analyzed comics letters pages in any depth, and those who have tend to focus on historical American comics, arguing that the collaborative nature of these spaces enables creativity and community. Gordon (2012) points out that letter writing provides a means for fans to engage actively and through interpretative activity become creators in their own right (sometimes even literally, as fresh talent is drawn from this fan base). Stein (2013) looks at American comics and calls their letters pages "serial paratexts" that foster collaboration between creator and readers. Coman (2012) and Pustz (2007) also claim that open-ended discussion in letter writing is part of a process of community formation, and Gordon (2012, 130) describes the comics letters writers as "a social network and a discursive community." Turning to British comics, Gibson (2015, 170) also argues that letters pages create a sense of connection and allow readers to feel part of "a mature and expansive international community."

The limited scholarship may be due to an aura of suspicion around letters pages, especially historically, where it often seems possible that content was dictated or simply made up by the publishers. This does not seem to be the case here; Misty claims at one point that she receives five hundred letters per week (#90), and this vast number is confirmed by both Wilf Prigmore and Brenda Ellis, who stresses that the *Misty* mail "was never made up, they didn't have to. It was coming out their ears." She continues: "They got an incredible mail bag every week.... They were absolutely devotees the *Misty* lot.... Thousands of letters would come, thousands." In addition, while many British comics printed sample letters in their early issues or asked for particular types of letters, *Misty* offered no guidance. For example, *Spellbound* initially printed sample letters in its "Spookyspot" (#1–7) and requested that readers "write and tell us about any 'out of this world,' fantastic or fascinating adventures" (#4), or "If anything strange or spine-chilling has happened to you or anyone you know, we are d-d-dying to hear about it!" (#9). By contrast, Misty's requests for letters are simply phrased: "I want to hear from you . . . to know what you think of the stories, and to hear your news and views about anything and everything" (#1), and "Don't forget to write to me at the address on this page" (#2). Barker (1989, 47) nonetheless points out that the selected (if not solicited) nature of letters creates a constructed narrative, and we can thus usefully consider the letters page as part of the self-projected image of the comic. This chapter explores what self-image the "Write to Misty" page constructs and whether it is consistent with (1) the dominant discourses of the horror genre, (2) the reputation and readership of British girls' comics, and (3) the use (and abuse) of comics letters pages more generally.

Rather than devising and then hunting for a particular set of criteria to answer these questions, I instead made cumulative notes on the content of the letters pages and used them to see if any patterns emerged. When I had finished, I tested my conclusions against pages selected from random issues. I discovered that the self-image constructed by *Misty*'s letters page is built on the following six ideas: creativity, curiosity, connection, community and conversation, comment and criticism, and compass. In fact, the very first letters page (#8, fig. 13.1) contains the seeds of nearly all the different themes that would appear in the remaining ninety-two issues.[3] Creativity comes out through the "Riddle" and the "Spooktacular!" poem; curiosity can be seen in "True or Not?" (asking who makes up the stories); and a connection with the comic is claimed via the shared names of readers ("Maggie and Marcella"), the reader's dog's behavior ("Fright of the Dog"), and its role in cheering up the two readers who are ill ("Misty Medicine" and "Misty Fever"). We see nothing that supports community/conversation, but as this is the first letters page and a dialogue has yet to begin, this is not surprising. Comment and criticism are present in the discussion of telekinesis ("The STAR Letter") and the praise for particular stories ("Best Ever," "Misty Fever"). Finally, the page demonstrates a wide compass of both age and location through the male readers ("Is He a Cissy?" and "Best Ever") and the reader in Dublin ("Misty Fever").

CREATIVITY

Misty's readers are imaginative, and creative work features in almost every issue. Poems are the most common, particularly acrostic poems, rhyming verse, and blank verse, though a limerick features in #26. Almost all are about Misty

Write to Misty

King's Reach Tower Stamford Street London SE1 9LS

☆☆☆☆☆ The STAR Letter ☆☆☆☆☆

The story I enjoy most is 'Moonchild' perhaps because telekinesis is a true thing. I've often tried moving things across the room just by staring at them and concentrating but for me it's easier to pick them up and carry them. I bet I could stare at this letter all week and still have to post it to get it to you.

MARY BARNES, LONDON SE12

MISTY MEDICINE
I am nearly 9 years old but get miserable sometimes because I have an over active thyroid gland which makes me gain weight. Having no friends at home and being on a special diet upsets me but your comic is the one thing that cheers me up and I look forward to it every week.
Jasmin Foster, Berkhamstead, Herts.

IS HE A CISSY?
Yesterday my sister bought 'Misty'. I read it through twice and thought it was great. In fact I like it so much I want to order it, but one small problem is I'm a boy and I'll feel a cissy. Can you help me?
Sean Newton, Penzance, Cornwall.

★★★★★

MISTY FEVER
I'd been in bed ill for a few days and was bored stiff till my mother brought home 'Misty'. When my friends read just the first story they were down at the newsagents like a shot to order it. The comic really cheered me up. 'Paint it Black' and 'The Sentinels' had me shaking so much my mother thought I was getting a fever but when she realised I'd just read 'Misty' she understood.
Una Fitzpatrick, Dublin.

RIDDLE
Here is a riddle for you and your readers to try:
My first is in Mystery
But not in Storey,
My second is in Giving
But not in Glory,
My third is in Slot
But not in Machine,
My fourth is in Dirty
But not in Clean,
My fifth is in Yellow
And Also in Grey
My whole is a comic which I read today
(ANSWER) MISTY
**"MISTY FAN"
Bolton, Lancs**

★★★★★

MAGGIE & MARCELLA
I think your stories are very good and it is a coincidence that Maggie is the story 'Paint it Black' has the same initials as me. Each week when I get my 'Misty' everything that happens to Maggie I shall pretend is happening to me. It will be very thrilling to see what Maggie and I get up to.
Marcella Cox, South Harrow, Middx

DON'T FORGET NOW — I WANT TO HEAR FROM YOU!

FRIGHT OF THE DOG
My dog 'Cindy' is a cocker spaniel and frightened of cats. One day while walking we came to two monuments of wild cats and all of a sudden she started barking and yelping. When my Mum lifted her she got even worse. She was barking and crying because of the stone monuments of the cats. I don't think she'd be much good in 'The Cult of the Cat'
Diane Morrison, Inverness

★★★★★

TOPS
I think your comic is really fabulous. I read it from cover to cover and I agree with you, it certainly is NOT to be read at night. I can't think of a better way to spend 8p. How much more for so little money! I'll be one of hundreds, I'm sure, to place a regular order for my favourite comic. All my pals agree with me when I say it's really TOPS
Yvonne Coll, Letterkenny, Co. Donegal, Ireland

TRUE OR NOT?
I would like to know whether you make up your own stories? And I think you're pretty, too but I bet you're prettier than they make you look in the comic.
Alison Whitford, Newmarket, Suffolk

Some of the stories I have known for years. Others are told me by my friends of the mists. Misty.

★★★★★

BEST EVER
I think Misty is a super mag. full of exciting stories which I enjoyed. One of my favourites was 'The Cult of the Cat' which was very exciting and I'd like to see more of those kinds of stories in the future. The opening page has a lovely message from you which would just make anyone want to read on. I even caught my younger brother reading it and when I told him it was a girl's comic he didn't put it down which just goes to show how interesting it must be. I know I'm going to get 'Misty' every week and enjoy everything in it. Everyone who's enjoyed it ought to recommend it to their friends. Misty's the best magazine I have ever read.
Joanne D'Arcy, Billingham, Cleveland

SPOOKTACULAR!
Here is a poem I wrote about your comic. Hope you like it:—
I bought your comic last week
And it was without a doubt
The best and most spooktacular Comic that is out.
Moonchild is my favourite
And if you print my rhyme,
I'll buy a years supply of Misty
and read it all the time.
Jacky Insole, Barking Essex.

Figure 13.1. "Write to Misty" (*Misty* #8). Reproduced with permission of Misty™ Rebellion Publishing IP Ltd.; copyright © Rebellion Publishing IP Ltd., all rights reserved.

herself and are sometimes addressed directly to her ("Your beauty is beyond compare, / Your round dark eyes, your long, black hair" [Suzanne Ware, #46]). Readers engage with the comic's tone and language and bring in suitable mythic references; the following offers a good example:

> She comes in the fog
> pushed on by the seas,
> Her hair caressed by
> the nymphs of the breeze.
> The mermaids come and
> watch from the streams
> This beautiful maid from
> the Cavern of Dreams.
> Her dress is made from
> the crest of a wave
> And lined with moonbeams
> Diana will save.
> She sits in the mist
> and tells of her land,
> A place no mortal could
> ever have planned.
> (Beverley Moses, #44)

A more irreverent tone is also apparent in later work ("Dear Misty, do you sleep at night / With slime-muck on your bed?" [Tanya Rhodes, #74], to which Misty responds, "*The Cavern of Dreams is rather more comfortable than you imagine*"). Other subjects do feature in verse, such as "What is an image?" (Deborah Matthews, #47), spiders (Arlene Russo, #45), Miss T (Sarah Moolla, #70), nightmares (Amanda Neai, #76), and a reprimand for those who do not reserve their copies (Joanne Darkins, #94). However, they always revolve around the themes and aesthetic of *Misty*. For example:

> Black is the colour of the misty dark night.
> Black is the blankness when out goes the light.
> Black is the feeling when receiving a fright.
> Black is the colour of the raven taking flight.
> . . .
> Black is the colour. Black is nigh.
> (Helen Jones, #57)

Just as readers mimic the style and tone of Misty's introductions, so this piece inspired a response a few months later in a submission from a different reader ("Red is the colour of the demon king, / Red is the colour of his blood red ring, / . . . Red is an inferno, blazing and bright, / Red is the colour that will put the world right" [Angela Roberts, #69]).

As well as rhyming verse, we find prose poems and epistles, also written in the mythic style of Misty's own introductions to each issue. For example:

> Nothing but silent, swirling mists, then as they part you catch a glimpse of a world where no mortal dare tread . . . (A. Shannon, #47)

> A child was found in the Forest of Darkness, born at midnight then abandoned, she was carried away by Mika, god of the Wind to the Castle of the Mist. The child grew up to dance with the wind and play with the darkness. Her eyes were of stars and her skin as pale as the moon . . . (Christine Fortune, #46)

Some letters also use more innovative formats to try to capture what *Misty* means to its readers. One reader describes *Misty* as a cake recipe: "Add 2 ounces of terror to 1 ounce of horror, bind together with 1 teaspn of fright and beat in 2 teaspns queasiness. . . . Ice with colour after baking in a cold, creepy dungeon and decorate with animals, e.g. cats, bats, spiders, snakes" (Misty Fan, #27). *Misty* also inspires creativity beyond written work, such as from sisters Yvonne and Adele, who "taped some of your stories, complete with sound effects, on our tape recorder . . . so on cold, dark nights we can listen" (Adele Appleby, #53). A mother also writes in to say that "the stories are so good and my two children wrote a play based on one of them. The school performed it and raised £124.50p for charity I am very proud to say" (Mrs. Jane Guffick, #27).

Readers share other forms of less dramatic (but nonetheless creative) responses. In #29 Kaye Shirley sends in her "Misty comic review," which sums up what has happened so far in all the serialized stories, suggesting that this should be included once a month to help new readers catch up. Although the review is unprinted, Misty describes it as "a splendid and artistic piece of work." In #26 J. F. D. Wood works out the cost of each word in *Misty* based on its 8p cover price ("Each copy has 32 sides of paper. If you divide 8 between 32 you get the cost of one side") and combines this with the average number of words per page (200) to get the average price of one word ("0.25 ÷ 200 = 0.00125 or 1/800 if you prefer fractions"). S/he concludes that one word of *Misty* costs just 1/800 of a penny and that readers should consider "the time and effort put into the production of the magazine, the cost of the paper, the work put in by the illustrator and the writer on behalf of Misty herself" before complaining about the cover price, ending with the direct challenge "So, all you misers, who's going to say 8 pence is expensive to you now?" Jokes also appear, starting in the same issue, under headings such as "Ghastly Ghosts," "Ghostly Gags," and "Ghastly Gags."

Finally, the letters page demonstrates readers' use of critical and intertextual thinking to navigate the comic. Claudette Young writes in to point out the similarities between a character in "Mr. Walenski's Secret" (#64) and Anne Frank, asking, "Is the story somehow connected with her?" (#74). Susan Collinge links the story "Welcome Home" (#68) to the Greek myths about Hades and Cerberus (#76). Joanne Harrison provides information about children who have been brought up by wolves, asking, "Has your story of the Wolf Girl anything to do with this?" (Misty responds by citing the legend of Romulus and Remus, and some more contemporary cases, clarifying, "*Most Misty stories are based on facts though sometimes details are altered*" [#78]). In the same issue, the star letter is one that notes the coincidences between the Kennedy and Lincoln assassinations (Fiona Hamilton, #78). Misty's responses reward this sort of critical acuity and encourage critical and intertextual thinking.

CURIOSITY

As the creative work shows, Misty herself is the focus for many readers. Their interest in her ranges from the curious to the obsessive, and doubtless she was the subject of many teenage crushes. Gibson's study of comics readers' memories draws on several interviews with lesbian participants to demonstrate their resistive readings of heterosexual comics stories, and it includes a mention of *Misty* from Elsa, who says, "I fancied Misty like mad" (2015, 133). Numerous letter writers compliment Misty on her beauty and speak about their connection with her, such as Carol Robinson's letter about Misty's appearance to her in a dream (#45), Tracey Moss's comment "I think you are very pretty but I am not" (#33), or Lisa Wilder's letter (#45), which gushes, "I think your comic is the most breathtaking, most frightening, most enchanting comic out and every time I go to bed I think of you." Eighteen-year-old Tom Gill (#83) takes a more direct approach and, after saying how much he enjoys the comic for its unifying supernatural theme, hard-hitting moral line, and psychological realism, concludes: "And most important of all because of you yourself, Misty. Which other magazine can boast of a goddess like yourself running it? Someone with the beauty of youth but the wisdom of age. The prattling schoolgirls or rival comics just aren't in the same league." He says he will be ordering Misty for himself when he goes to university, and "I won't be ashamed of it."

Many letters contain direct questions about Misty's background and origins, and readers show an overwhelming desire throughout to know who she is and for more information about her. Misty generally answers and signs her name to all these responses but seldom gives much away. For example, Linda Okiwe's (#18) letter says, "I make lots of guesses about where you come from. One is that you were found as a baby in the pool of life by the mother of the mists and she brought you up to become a sister of the mists," to which Misty replies, "*Very close to the truth, Linda.*"

In #19 three readers write asking for more information on Misty's appearance, requesting a poster (Marie-Louise Kerr), a photograph (Deborah Holness, because "are the drawings good?"), and clarification of her hair and eye color (Karen King, because the picture is "always in black and white"). Misty responds to them all that a color poster will appear in the Summer Special. In #26 Jane Rooney writes on behalf of herself and friends to ask how old Misty is, with a request to "please answer the question." Misty replies, "*Child of the mists, born on the very first midnight hour, I am as old as time itself, Jane.*" Mandy Wheeler (#47) wonders, "Have you got a zodiac sign or not?" and receives the response "*Though I am in this world I am not of it and being as old as time I live outside zodiacal influences.*" Tracy Young (#57) asks, "Who taught you to read and write because you're a child of the mists so I don't expect you went to a normal school when you were small," and is told that this was done by "*the Lords of the Mists who now, alas, are no more.*" Michelle Casson (#72) queries why Misty's eyes keep changing color on the front cover (from blue to green or yellow), and Misty responds that in "*certain lights*" they appear green and can "*flash*" yellow in the dark. Julie Ferguson (#59) asks, "What is that star round your neck? A star from your world or a charm for energy?" and Misty replies, "*It is a charm of real stardust conferring many special powers on the wearer.*" Similar questions continue throughout the entire run. Some are confrontational in pointing out inconsistencies or improbabilities and testing the boundaries of fiction and reality. For example, Alice Higgins (#29) states, "I began to wonder. If you're in a world of your own how do the publishers get the stories off you? Also how do you get our letters? Or do you live in London?" Misty replies, "*The publishers send their very bravest men to collect the stories and deliver your letters to me, Alice.*"

Effectively, readers want to know Misty's story while also being aware that this can never be possible, and the tantalizing pieces of information offered become moves in a game between writer and reader. Molly Adesigbin (#40) points out that telling her story would make Misty "not mysterious or mystic any more," and A. Twiselton (#22) summarizes this perfectly: "A girl wrote to 'Misty' saying she thinks you live in a house. *I* think you don't live anywhere but blow across the moon's face like the wind and I don't think you were born anywhere but just happened. I hope you *don't* tell us your story because I like to think of you as something strange with no story to tell."

The questions range from those that treat Misty as real and want more information about her age, appearance, and powers, to more interrogative points about where she lives and how she writes the comic. In this way, *Misty*'s readers help to construct the character's identity, shaping it by the questions they ask, and by putting forward their own ideas. They draw exhaustively on intertextual knowledge and engage with the lexis and themes of the text to do so.

CONNECTION

Misty readers are keen to point out connections between their lives and the stories and to share ways in which these have helped them navigate problems and fears. Many letters tell a ghost story or supernatural encounter from the reader's own life, such as Laura Rogers, who writes about her father's haunted clock (#62). Perhaps these readers are trying to match Misty's tales with their own spooky story or are following the pattern set by previous comics like *Spellbound* that explicitly invited these types of submissions.

Readers also find echoes of the stories in their daily lives, as in Ellen Ward's letter (#11) that parallels her experiences while wearing *Misty*'s cat ring with the events of the serial "The Cult of the Cat," or Michelle Hawkes's (#23) corroboration of the superstitions attached to bees (referring to "Honey's Bees," #13). After reading "The Haunting of Hazel Brown" (#41–42), Lesley Mouncer (#53) writes, "I kept looking over my shoulder to make sure my glove wasn't following me and then one day . . . it WAS! I ran downstairs to try and get rid of it but it followed me. . . . I've never been so scared in my life"—she then explains that, after she tidied up her sewing kit, both glove and foot got caught up in some loose black cotton. More movingly, Gwen Howard (#57) shares her experience: "I read a story in *Misty* about a girl called Goldie ["Spend, Spend, Spend," #45] who came to a bad end. . . . After reading that story over breakfast I went out to feed my guinea-pig who was also called Goldie and found her dead. . . . You will probably think I am silly writing this letter to you but somehow it's as if you knew and told me in a story." Michelle Findlay (#55) writes that she understood "Whistle and I'll Come . . ." only after her rabbit died, and shares her sadness. Deaf reader Vickie (#70) writes in praise of "The Choice of Silence." There are also examples where the stories have directly affected readers, such as Carmen Barrett and Donna Carroll (#85), who both write to say that after reading "Sweet Tooth" (#78) they will be eating fewer sweets, and Kaeti Edridge (#85) has a similar response to "Fancy Another Jelly Baby?" (#71).

This type of identification with the *Misty* stories is common and often based on names or scenarios. Readers such as Tula Roman (#35) and Nicola Dixon (#66) identify with their counterparts in "The Black Widow" and "The Cult of the Cat" on the basis of shared names. Deirdre Marris (#27) identifies with the latter in more self-conscious terms: "I am very embarrassed to tell you every so often I have a 'whisker' growing out of my cheek. I pull it out so nobody will notice but I do wonder whether I have been chosen to take the place of Nicola to be a servant of Bast." Tabitha Modica (#76) also writes to say, "Sometimes I feel like the girl in your story 'Wolf Girl' but instead of a wolf I feel like a horse." A trend for sharing unusual names takes over from #67, where Effie identifies with the use of her name, peaking when Saffron, Salaudh, Tinuriel, Mhairi, and Nimue all have letters printed in #73. The "odd names" discussion trickles on into later issues, with names such as Carolan and Luna (#74), Genovefa (#82), and Oania (#83) and also extends to surnames (such as Notwithit, #75; and Kitcat, #76).

Readers also share phobias and fears (such as Janet Palmer's claustrophobia, #11), and the cathartic value of *Misty*'s stories is clear from numerous letters. Simone Matthews (#31) says that "*Misty* has helped me a lot because I used to be scared of ghosts and darkness. But when I started reading your comic I got less scared. Now every night I just look out for ghosts. And the darkness does not frighten me any more." Stephanie Moss (#23) dreams Misty as "lingering around looking after scared people and they're never harmed," and Misty replies, "*Right, Stephanie. Nothing to be scared of when I'm around.*" As in her introductions to the issues, so Misty is a reassuring presence on the letters page, which perhaps explains why readers share problems that worry them, for example, Fiona Ware's (#54) concerns about the "queer feeling" of déjà vu she experiences (continued by other readers in #63).

It seems that *Misty* has a big impact on its readers' lives and attitudes and that they are as keen to find themselves in its pages as they are to learn more about Misty. Gail Hunter (#48) writes, "I was born on Halloween. So does this make me some sort of relative of yours?" to which Misty replies, "*I like to think all readers of my paper are part of the great Misty family, Gail.*"

As Tabitha Troughton concludes her poem (#55):

> Misty is a mystery.
> Who is Misty? Who?
> Could the lovely Misty be
> In some strange reality—you?

COMMUNITY AND CONVERSATION

The *Misty* letters page reflects a strong sense of community and conversation, and when subjects are raised, other readers often continue them. For example, after Fiona's letter about her déjà vu (#54, quoted earlier), five readers' letters responding to her are printed in #63, sharing similar experiences and possible explanations, both spiritual and scientific. Interestingly Misty supports a scientific (rather than supernatural) conclusion: "*I believe it is nothing to do with reincarnation but the mysterious workings of the human brain of which so little is known.*" She also comments, "*There's been more post on this subject than anything we've ever mentioned and practically everyone claims some experience of it.*"

As well as telling Misty about the comics societies and *Misty* fan clubs they have set up (#59, #96), readers also talk to one another through the letters page, inviting others to join these groups (Kathleen Pittaway, #95; Edmund Marmse [Harmse], #96), sharing or selling previous issues, or responding to letters and opinions. Sometimes their letters are not even addressed to Misty, for example, Jane Allen Maerdy's letter (#74) "to thank all the girls who sent me their instructions for the Wheel of Fortune after I'd asked for them on your letter page [#62]," or Julie Hudson's letter, which begins, "If anyone is interested I am selling my Misty Annual" (#74). There are even direct challenges: "I've noticed one thing. It's only ever girls who write in and get their letters published. So, come on, boys, get writing or don't you like to admit you read Misty?" (Rachel Perren, #62). Although letters from boys have appeared from the very first letters page, this provokes response from male readers in #68 and #71.

The sharing and selling of back issues and the much-coveted annuals (many examples appear in #74) begin with Misty's response in #60 to Aileen McMahon, who received four Christmas annuals; Misty suggests that Aileen write again so that she can put her in touch with readers who could not get an annual. There is also debate about previous opinions, for example, "I noticed Clare Harris's letter about bringing back Miss Nocturne and I fully agree with her" ("Countess" Kathleen Pittaway, #95), or "Your reader was wrong when she said there were only two other ways of killing vampires other than a stake through the heart" (Nichola Layzell, #95). Sally Pratt and Caroline Nicholson write, "We think you are putting vampires and monsters in your comic too often. We prefer mystery stories" (#67), and R. McInnes responds (poetically) to say, "I disagree with the two girls who suggested less monsters and more mystery. . . . An element of mystery's all right but overdoses would make Misty commonplace.... I prefer a comic that puts tingles in my back, not tangles in my book" (#76).

Across periods of many months, readers enter into dialogue with one another, lending or selling annuals and back issues, setting up independent comics clubs and reading groups and inviting their peers to join, responding directly to other letters, and debating the opinions and preferences expressed. The *Misty* community thrives on both conversation and challenge.

COMMENT AND CRITICISM

Misty encourages critical comment, as the voting coupon included on each letters page demonstrates. Participation is encouraged; for example, Miss T exhorts readers, "Come on, now, Misty and me want you to fill in this coupon!" (#16), and Misty namechecks those who have sent in voting slips for their favorite stories (#48). The letters too contain lots of praise, but I will also consider the negative and controversial comments put forward.

Particular admiration for the Nightmare stories appears in #12 and #17, as well as for Misty's "letter of introduction" (#10) and the "distinguished look" of the cover (#98), and readers often write in about their favorite stories. They disagree on the types of content preferred, though: Wendy Ashton praises the "complete stories" for their morals and variation (#10), whereas Patricia Daniel criticizes them in the same issue ("Why don't you ever finish your stories? I was looking forward to reading the end of "Red Knee—White Terror!"). *Misty* is not shy about printing negative comments or encouraging dissent, especially if these help demonstrate the comic's popularity (complaints about not being able to get the annuals, for example, feature throughout the run). A debate as to whether *Misty* was better at its start begins in #40, and more letters on this subject are printed in #51, where Misty claims that opinion is divided equally. Various aspects of the comic come under fire, such as Wendy the Witch, who is "too babyish" for Jennifer Watts (#65), the comic's layout (the Star Days horoscopes and splash pages are deemed a "waste of space" and "disgraceful" by Lorraine Forbes, #97), specific details or errors made in stories (#75) and some of the endings (#99, where Polly Phillips complains that the protagonist in "Take the Money" was too severely punished). The tone of *Misty* is something readers are conscious of and anxious to protect from any perceived damage, such as Elisabeth Kendall's letter (#93), which praises the magazine but then complains about the pop culture content of the "Magic Circle" game. Her admonishment is not just critical but also promises creativity, saying: "Not what we expect from you at all. I will have to rewrite the cards."

As in all enthusiastic debate, though, readers are passionate when they disagree, and things sometimes get personal. The letter from "Jennifer" (#34) is the most controversial:

> I don't suppose you'll print this, you're probably too cowardly, but I want to tell you I think your comic is appalling, really awful and makes me want to be sick. Your comic should be banned. I expected the comic to be about witches and spooky but nice stories. But no. Take for instance your 15th July issue [#24] with the pet shop story. It upset me—the poor mouse—and I know many girls feel the same way so make the comic better and print this letter.
> P.S. Get this printed!

Misty responds that she has printed this letter because it is "the only" one like it she has received since *Misty* started, pointing out that justice was done in the story to the children who killed the mouse, and asking what other readers think. And they tell her. Lucy Hadland (#36) gives a more positive appraisal of "The Pet Shop," saying she was pleased the children came to a "sticky end." In #41 Misty dedicates nearly the entire letters page to a "small selection" of readers' responses, saying she has been overwhelmed with letters in a ratio of thirty to one against Jennifer's opinions. These letters range from the pragmatic to the "disgusted" and "appalled" and attack Jennifer's "childish" notions of ghost stories and lack of imagination. Interestingly, the subject then comes up again in #50, where Misty is then critiqued for printing so many letters against Jennifer ("Even if her letter was a bit nasty weren't you also nasty to print so many letters criticising her," writes Linda Mansfield) and reminded that readers are invited to give their opinions (Ann Heron). Similar arguments continue to crop up when a strongly negative opinion is offered. Tina Pym complains about Misty in #81, calling the comic "awful" and saying that its "eerie" stories are "nearly all the same," and three readers respond in #94, suggesting that she is a "simple" person with no imagination (Tracey Schavenen) and should return to the other "normal cissy girl comics" (Rachel Creamer). A spirited defense of Miss T takes place after a letter from Amanda Starling says, "I think she's STUPID and ought to be in stupid comics, not yours" (#79). This dominates the letters page for three issues (#89–91), with poems and lively letters both for and against. In the final count, Misty claims that 270 people support Miss T with just twenty-six against: "*a victory for the little witch of more than ten to one.*"

The letters page itself even comes under attack, in terms of both its authenticity and its content. Concerns about its honesty crop up periodically (#13, #59, #61)—and, ironically, the same letter is printed twice from Christine Lord, asking, "Can it be PROVED these are real letters from readers?" (#59, #61). The letters themselves also come under fire: Tania Hill writes in #56 that the page "gets a bit boring when everyone writes in to say how great your comic is" and appealing to "girls, grans, mums and dads (and boys)" for some more interesting letters. She receives no comment from Misty and an abrupt response from Nadia Romanelli (#65): "Tania Hill can speak for herself. I *enjoy* reading the letter page and other people's opinions and experiences." This brief analysis shows that, as well as containing many compliments, "Write to Misty" does not shy away from printing negative comments and even personal abuse directed at Misty and her readers. Misty could even be accused of stirring up controversy by inviting argument, but she does not exercise unilateral power, preferring to appeal to readers to respond to and defend her position. However, she does justify and explain herself when directly confronted.

COMPASS

Finally, the letters page demonstrates that the compass of *Misty*'s readership covers diverse ages, genders, and locations. Nicola Thompson (#27) writes that, in response to a survey suggested by their English teacher, "throughout the school *Misty* was by far the favourite comic among the girls." Although the average reader seems to be a preteen or early teenage girl, the age range is stretched in both directions. Misty claims that, based on her post, she has fans aged seven to twenty-one (#10), but readers complain throughout that their parents, teachers, and brothers steal the comic (Miryam Hosker and Pamela Kundnani, #21), and Anita Hosker names it "the Great Mystery Paper for Girls and Nosey Mums" (#21). Responses flood in from readers who fall outside this bracket, such as "I'm a married Mum with two girls aged 13 and 12 and I get *Misty* every week and we *all* read it" (Mrs. Jane Guffick, #27), and Ms. J. Broadley writes (#29):

> My daughter at the age of nine
> Thinks your comic is just fine
> Her Nan now at the age of fifty
> First introduced the comic Misty
> I never thought I'd be on the hook
> For any comic or any book.
> Which go to show it suits all ages
> And excites us when we turn the pages.

There is also seventy-year-old reader Mrs. Beatrice Woodman (#37), and Karen Cunningham's eighty-five-year-old gran, who has started putting in her own order (#52). When complaining about "Wendy the Witch," Jennifer Watts argues that she is only suitable for "8 and under and I think most of your readers must be 10 and over" (#65). Although probably true of the majority, there are letters from ten-year-old Nicola Jackson (praising "Miss T") and nine-year-old Elizabeth Tring asking if Misty could "put the most scary stories at the beginning and the less scary ones at the end so's I can get to sleep at night" (#84).

Readers also come from different demographics, such as second-year university student Patricia Tierney, who thinks that "*Misty* is a good weekly for *anyone* to read" (#22), and Ross M. W. Wallace writes that he and his university friends all read the comic and "the youngest is 21" (#71). Male readers of *Misty* also come in all ages, from fourteen-year-old Paul Sothern (#78) and eighteen-year-old Tom Gill (#83) to Fionvala Ni Chiosain's uncle, who is "too embarrassed to write himself" but claims *Misty* is "the first really original spook comic he ever read" (#28). A collection of boys' letters is printed in #71: Darren Hood says, "I'm fourteen and I have not missed one copy since No. 1.... It's the most exciting comic I've ever read"; and Robert Green also calls it "better than most boys' comics." Male fandom is also dedicated: Catrina Binky exposes her dad as "a real Misty fan.... He buys the comic for me but then reads it himself. He even cuts up the mag, and is making a great scrapbook of all the stories stuck together to make full-length picture strips" (#72); and Edmund Harmse (#96) writes from his home in South Africa that he has set up a *Misty* fan club.[4]

The global reach of *Misty* is also obvious. When Geraldine Forrestall, in Ireland, criticizes the comic for not printing letters from other countries (#89), Misty claims readers in "France [#35, #75], Holland, Australia, New Zealand, United Arab Emirates [#46], United States [#32, #45, #86] and Germany." Moreover, letters come in from Bolivia (#58), Mallorca (#59), and Romania (#73). These readers mostly write to praise *Misty* and complain they have nothing like it in their own countries. Misty even responds in French to "Martine la Bordellerie de Souvant," who writes from La Châtaigneraie in France. There may even be a slightly knowing exchange happening here, as although Misty's reply is innocuous enough and in basic French (saying simply that she is delighted to meet the reader and happy she likes the comic), the reader's name is likely to be a joke (in the manner of "Lady Martine Fancy Pants"), as it literally translates as "From the Brothel of Souvant."[5] The compass of Misty's readership thus covers a wide spread of ages, genders, and locations, demonstrating active, amusing, and creative engagement. *Misty*'s range is summed up best, perhaps, in her response to Chantal Clarkson (#45), who asks, "Can you tell me why adults like Misty so much?" and is told, "*Everybody loves a good story.*"

This analysis of "Write to Misty" shows that readers engage with the comic in many different ways, and all demonstrate creative, critical, and collegial reader response. Given *Misty*'s genre and audience, this seems particularly apt. Much of the appeal of horror and Gothic literature comes from its challenge to our bravery and imagination; its innate conservatism and morality; and (paradoxically) its challenge to social norms and notions of acceptability. The foregoing subheadings cover all these aspects. Creativity and curiosity stimulate our imagination and test our bravery; connection, community and conversation, and compass allow us to feel that we belong and confirm our own normality; and comment and criticism sustain our subversive and challenging streak.

The categories align with the landscape of girls' comics and story papers at the widest level: for example, *Girls' Realm* (1898–1915), one of the first story papers for girls, encourages its readers to know their editor, Miss Corkran; puts them in contact with one another; sustains their diversity of nationality, class, age, and experience; and includes their challenges and criticisms of the publication (Rodgers 2012). As such, these classifications address the comic's target readership and social context as much as they suit its themes. Horror and Gothic have historically appealed to middle-class female readers, providing escapism from restricted choices and limited lives. *Misty* gives its readers space to respond to its content creatively and critically and to engage with one another on these terms. Gibson's (2015) study of remembered reading similarly argues that 1970s girl readers used their comics to negotiate patriarchy both as a community and individually. They read widely and sometimes resistively (i.e., creatively and critically) and shared their experiences and the comics themselves with each other. Her interviews also reveal a depth of emotional experience and detailed knowledge about these lost and devalued texts that is apparent on the *Misty* letters page and also in its fan base today, as shown by the websites and social media groups campaigning for the comic's return.

Gibson's work additionally mentions American comics letters pages. In contrast to the problem pages and competitions more commonly found in British periodicals, the letters pages in American comics were filled with readers "commenting directly on the stories and the issues raised in the text . . . spotting continuity errors and demanding costume changes," demonstrating a wide spread of age and gender, and encouraging readers to feel "they were part of a mature and expansive international community" (2015, 170).[6] Stein (2013, 167) also looks at the letters pages of superhero comics in the 1950s and 1960s, claiming that these spaces transform readers into authors of letters and even implied coauthors of future stories, and turn editors into readers (of mail), fostering collaboration. Although the type of authorship discourse that Stein discusses (where readers use expert knowledge to speculate about various writers' and artists' input) is not present in *Misty*, "Write to Misty" otherwise supports the claims of both critics. It is strongly egalitarian, offering a community and collaborative spirit, and Misty (like the editors Stein discusses) "play[s] the role of the moderator always at the service of [her] audience" (168) and encourages creative and critical opinion. While Misty doesn't explicitly shape the letters page by inviting particular types of submissions, the letters that are printed are selected from a large quantity and thus form a mediated and constructed narrative. Misty claims that she tries for "*a balance of poems, true strange experiences, original thoughts, criticisms and jokes*" (#53), but the personal nature and passion of the "Write to Misty" page go far beyond this as creative and critical opinions are shared and debated by a vibrant and diverse community.

CHAPTER 14

LEAVING THESE MISTY ISLES

Despite its popularity, *Misty* had a relatively short life of just 101 weekly issues. This chapter discusses the material produced after the original run ended. I open by considering the possible reasons for the comic's demise and look closely at the process of merging *Misty* into *Tammy*, demonstrating how Misty was quickly sidelined as her role was significantly altered and weakened. I examine the material included in the annuals and reprints and draw attention to how they shaped *Misty*'s legacy. Finally, I note the postmillennial reemergence of *Misty* in fan websites and tribute publications and reprints and new material from Egmont and Rebellion Publishing.

It's hard to find out why *Misty* ended. Artist John Armstrong says that *Misty* "was cancelled by Maxwell after a strike" (Lillyman 2009), but I have been unable to confirm this, and it seems likely that Armstrong is thinking of the 1984 strike that resulted in the sudden end of *Tammy*.[1] *Misty*'s editorial team do not remember any clear reason for its termination; Jack Cunningham (2017) says, "It just stopped, almost as quietly as it had started. . . . They just sort of pulled the rug away from under it." Wilf Prigmore (2017b) also has "no idea why it ended—I'd moved on by then. It could well be falling sales—*June* folded on a circulation of 200,000, but they still said it wasn't making enough profit." John Sanders (2019) confirms that high sales (over 200,000 copies per week) were required at IPC to keep titles going, saying: "We were into a slogging war with the opposition, we had to match their cover prices and that meant high circulation sales. You know, when a title goes on the downward slide, your worst enemy can be your own sales department, telling you not to bother with that one, no one wants it." Reader Helen Fay (2016) says she wrote to IPC in 1981 after *Misty* was canceled, and received a reply from Bill Harrington, with the title of editor, saying that *Misty* had been merged to "shore up the falling sales of *Tammy*." Falling profit margins of one or both titles are therefore the most likely reason for *Misty*'s cancellation, especially considering the "cost center" policy discussed in chapter 1, which meant that every weekly issue had to make money (Prigmore 2017b, 2018b).

Prigmore (2017b) adds, "Or maybe the enthusiasm had gone—the stories seemed less dramatic at the end." *Misty*'s final editor, Norman Worker, was one of the previous generation of Fleetway staffers and had been editor of *Sally* (1969–71). Both Prigmore and Pat Mills describe Worker as "old school": "He always had a pipe on the go and a shirt and tie and jacket.... He really looked very much like the Storyteller" (Prigmore 2016a). Mills (2011, 2016a) claims that Worker was "not suitable" and "didn't adapt," describing a change in later issues of *Misty* toward more single stories and an increased historical focus: "The old wishy-washy story about a haunted coach in the seventeenth century or eighteenth century, it's not really going to compel you to come back next week and buy the next issue of *Misty*" (2016a). Based on a random sampling of ten issues, the ratio of historical stories does indeed increase from midway through *Misty*'s run and reaches a high toward the end,[2] although (as noted in chap. 5) the ratio of serial to single stories is more or less even at the end of its run.

But although *Misty* ceased weekly publication, it was not forgotten. In the United Kingdom, a holiday special appeared in 1980, the annuals continued publication until 1986, and the comic received a brief revival after this as *The Best of Misty Monthly*, composed of reprints from the weekly issues and running for eight issues (February–September 1986). A French Canadian *Misty* was launched in 1980 and was published fortnightly, although I have been unable to find out how long this lasted (Bradley 2016). *Misty* material was also used in Canada as part of a larger series of mystery-horror anthologies called Collection Kaléidoscope (PAF Loisirs, 1976–80) (Méon 2016).[3] These are softcover collections printed in black and white on low-grade paper, with the text quite clumsily hand-lettered in French. The series is a mix of IPC material from comics such as *Misty* and *2000AD*, alongside reprints of Franco-Belgian comics such as *Timour* and *Tounga*. Titles such as *Sortilèges* (Spells), *Fantômes et vampires* (Ghosts and vampires), *Cauchemars* (Nightmares), and *Histoires de bêtes insolites* (Stories of unusual beasts) are anthologies of single *Misty* stories, and there are also collections of the serials *Les sentinelles* ("The Sentinels"), *L'enfant de la lune* ("Moonchild") and *Le Culte du Chat* ("The Cult of the Cat").

As the 1980s progressed, *Misty* reprints continued to appear in the United Kingdom in IPC's *Barbie* comic (licensed from Mattel, 1985–87) (Helsbels 2009), which combined old stories from *Misty* and other IPC comics with original colored strips such as "Around the World with Barbie" and features on *Top of the Pops* and pop groups like Wham! The *Barbie* comic's Swedish translation (Pandora Press, 1986–89) also contained numerous IPC reprints, and other Swedish comics used *Misty* material, such as "Kattdyrkarna" ("The Cult of the Cat"), which featured in the shortlived "semiannual" *Date* (Hemmets Journal, 1983–85) (Holm 2018). Other countries also reprinted *Misty* stories, often in combination with other IPC and DC Thomson content. Holm (2017a,

2017b) notes that the German comic *Vanessa—Freundin der Geister* (Friend of the spirits) (Bastei-Verlag, 1982–90) reprints a number of *Misty* serials and single stories in full color across its 215 issues. These include "The Cult of the Cat" and "Nightmare Academy," alongside "Roots," "The Family," and "The Pet Shop." Miss T also makes repeated appearances renamed as "Scharlotte Schock" (Scharlotte Shock). She is complemented by other British girls' comics strips such as "The Ghosts of St. Gildas" (see, e.g., *June and Pixie*, February–June 1974; also Holiday Special 1974), retitled as "Scharlotte Schock's Gespenster-Schule" (Scharlotte Shock's spook school). This original run was followed by a larger reprint magazine *Vanessa—Ein schönes Mädchen im Land der Geister und Gespenster* (A beautiful girl in the land of spirits and spooks) (1990–91) and anthologies that collected previous issues (e.g., Sammelband [anthology] #1037 collects *Vanessa* #175–77 and has the same cover as the *Misty* Annual 1982).[4] *Vanessa* was a successful franchise and also produced two specials, forty paperbacks, and twelve audio dramas (Holm 2018).

While all this reprinting was going on, in 1987 the IPC Youth Group was sold (under the name of Fleetway) to Robert Maxwell, and IPC later became IPC Media, then Time Inc. In 1992 Fleetway was purchased by Egmont, forming Fleetway-Egmont. Things were officially quiet in the Cavern of Dreams for a while (although the fan sites and publications were not, as will be discussed), until in 2009 and 2012 Egmont released a hard copy and e-book *Best of Misty* collection as part of the company's "Classic Comics" digital imprint. Then in 2016 Rebellion Publishing bought the complete Fleetway/IPC Youth Group archive from Egmont. They have since released two collections reprinting *Misty* serials (2016 and 2017), and one *Scream! & Misty* Halloween Special of new material (2017). In France, a high-quality hardback *Anthologie Misty* has just been published by Delirium (2018), collecting the serials "Moonchild," "The Four Faces of Eve," and "The Sentinels," alongside the single stories "Roots" and "Shadow of a Doubt."

Much of the material in the *Misty* holiday specials and annuals is analyzed in other chapters alongside the main run of stories, but from the start they included reprints from older comics. British comics' holiday specials and annuals had always reprinted material in this way and sometimes did not look too far afield for this. For example, the story "Friends and Neighbours" (Summer Special 1978) is the start of a longer serial taken from the same run of *Sandie* issues (ca. April 1972) that provided "Wendy the Witch" material for the *Misty* comics and annuals. But further changes took place in the annuals once the *Misty* weekly was no more. First, the number of pages dropped consistently, from 144 pages (Annuals 1979, 1980, 1981) to 128 pages (Annual 1982), then down to 112 pages (Annuals 1983, 1984, 1985), and finally to just 96 pages (Annual 1986). The early annuals (1979–81) include a welcome from Misty, which reused versions of Bellwood artwork from early inside covers with the Cunningham calligraphy. However, the picture of Misty on the inside cover of Annual 1982 seems to be by Mario Capaldi, artist for its first story, and her spoken introduction here refers only to this tale. After this point there is no image or message from Misty inside the cover of the later annuals.

The proportion of original stories or non-*Misty* reprints also drops considerably at this time. Whereas the bulk of the early annuals combined new material with reprints from other titles, by 1983 reprinted *Misty* stories appear frequently. For example, the *Misty* Annual 1983 is dominated by a reprint of "Moonchild" and contains only two additional comic strip stories, plus three pages of comedy ("Miss T" and "Cilla the Chiller") and three text stories. The rest of the annual is made up of features, recipes, craft ideas, and the like. This pattern continues in the following annuals, which reprint "The Cult of the Cat," "Grandfather's Clock" (originally "The Clock of Cluny Jones," *Tammy*), and "The Ghost of Golightly Towers," respectively. Included in this increase in familiar material are other, more surprising, reworkings. A redrawn story appears: "The Evil Garden" (Annual 1981), which was previously published as "Garden of Evil" in *Misty* #53. The script is the same with only minor tweaks, but the story has been redrawn entirely with the addition of two-tone color. Even more surprising is the text story "The Snow Girl," which appears in *Misty* Annual 1982 (credited as "A Reader's Story . . . by Nicola Ogden") but comes originally from DC Thomson's *Spellbound* #17. The two tales are identical except for new illustrations and very minor edits made to the wording (e.g., the final sentence "And I'm alone. And I'm helpless" becomes "And I'm alone—helpless!"). While reprinted material is usual in these collections, it is extremely odd for it not to come from the publisher's own back catalog, and it is unclear what has happened here—did this writer submit the same story to DC Thomson and IPC? Or did an enterprising reader copy a *Spellbound* story and claim it as her own? Or did IPC simply reuse Thomson's story?

This mystery aside, the reuse of material is characteristic of British comics' publishing practices. A cycle of a few years was felt to be appropriate for reprinting old content, the reasoning being that the original audience would have moved on by then. However, the memories of *Misty* readers of the time do not support this practice. In particular, Debbie Thompson (2017) remembers, "It was great to see and read 'The School of No Escape.' . . . I did not get the first seven or eight issues of *Sandie* so it was good to read it from the very start." This serial began in *Sandie* #1 (February 12, 1972) and is reprinted in *Misty* Annual 1979, so it is clear that the turnover of readers was much slower than publishers assumed. While some fans continued to buy the annuals based on loyalty to the comic, others did not: Chris Lillyman (2016) says, "I'm not even sure if I bought the last few annuals.... I just sort of parted ways with it." Others such as Jon Bishop (2017) came to know *Misty* through the annuals alone, having missed the original run. Those who stuck with *Misty* remember feeling that she was vanishing: Lorraine Douglas (2017) recalls "the sense that the annuals were becoming thinner and less original as the years went by," a memory that is shared by others, and borne out by closer analysis of the content.

Although the features and articles in each annual are new to *Misty*, they often revisit old subjects: palmistry is covered in the 1979 and the 1984 annuals, and a quiz to test readers' bravery appears in both the 1983 and 1985 books. While the majority of features stick to a spooky theme, some do seem an odd fit, for example, "Find a Future Boy-Friend" in Annual 1982. In general there is an increased emphasis on text pieces over comics strips in the annuals (not least due to the increasing number of articles and features), and the number of text fiction stories varies between three and seven in each annual. There is also a trend in the later annuals to have Misty herself appear in a text story (1982, 1983, 1985, 1986). These are all high-fantasy tales set in fictitious worlds, where Misty appears as a supporting or advising character to help solve a problem or outwit a dangerous foe. The stories themselves are not very well written: the fantasy worlds lack conviction and are sometimes incongruous. For example, "When the Sky Falls" (1983) gives its antagonist a distinctly contemporary voice and love for pudding, and in "When the Earth Caught Fire" (1985) Misty's amulet saves the princess from a hungry monster by turning the roof of his cave into crisps that he eats instead. However, these stories are clearly seeking to address the original comic's perceived lack of stories about Misty herself while still attempting to preserve some of her distance and mystery, as they keep her slightly removed from the action in a helper role. As the first of them establishes: "This is not Misty's story. None but she can tell that, though she was there—unseen!"

While the annuals tried to simultaneously maintain Misty's presence and distance in a variety of ways, the merger of *Misty* and *Tammy* followed a trajectory in which Misty was quickly excluded. The final issue of *Misty* (#101) was published on January 12, 1980, and while the cover uses the upbeat tone that was typical of mergers (announcing "IMPORTANT NEWS For All Readers—INSIDE!"), Misty's final greeting to her readers is more gloomy:

> My heart is heavy for today we come to a parting of the ways. I must return to the misty lands where I shall spend much of my time helping to quell the dark forces of evil which are rising there. But I could not leave you, my Misty readers, without your spine-chilling tales, so I have arranged with my friend, The Mystery Storyteller, in TAMMY to pass on my tales to you. I shall appear in Tammy myself from time to time, and I will be there to greet you next

week. You may read more about all this on page eleven. Meanwhile, the call comes from the mists and I must be gone, but do not be sad . . .
WE SHALL MEET AGAIN NEXT WEEK!
Misty

Page 11 reassures readers that they will be able to continue reading their favorite stories in *Tammy*, promising the return of "The Black Widow," the appearance of "Miss T," and a new "Strange Story from the Mists." This summary of the merger shares much of its text with an equivalent page in *Tammy* (January 12, 1980); however, the *Tammy* announcement has no sense of finality or sadness. *Tammy*'s cover features the comic's devil character with a sandwich board, stating that there is "EXCITING NEWS," and its interior explanation frames the merger as an opportunity for "an even greater variety of reading" and more "strange and mysterious stories." The page stresses to readers that their "regular favourites" will remain and mentions the return of "Bella" in a new story, ahead of the "Black Widow" and "Strange Story" namechecks. As Scott (2017a) points out, there wasn't much room for *Misty* in this comic, and *Tammy* makes it clear here that it will not be sacrificing any of its regulars to make space for *Misty*. The first issue of *Tammy and Misty* (January 19, 1980) bears this out and seems very much slanted in the former's favor in both appearance and content. The Misty title is around a quarter of the size of Tammy's and is positioned centrally underneath it, on its moon-and-bat logo. The cover image shows *Tammy*'s usual cover girls (previously named as older Tammy and pigtailed June, who graced *Tammy*'s covers from around 1974 to 1980), looking startled with a white-haired woman standing guardian-like behind them. Drawn by John Richardson, if this is Misty, then her ethereal, vampish beauty (not to mention her raven black hair) departed with Shirley Bellwood.

Misty appears just once in this merger issue, in the first panel of "Friend Pepi" (this week's "Strange Story from the Mists," the new byline for this section). She explains here: "Regular 'Misty' readers will know that I have been called away on an urgent mission. But I shall always be with you in spirit—and sometimes in person, to bring you stories from the mists. When I am away I shall be sending my stories to my friend, 'The Storyteller.'" Her image is cropped from a Bellwood drawing, but the capitalized lettering and tone are less authentic, lacking the mystic quality of her previous welcomes. The story is drawn by Juan Ariza, providing some continuity with the old *Misty*, but it is condensed to the more standard three-page length and lacks any bite. Although it doesn't name Misty explicitly, "Spider Woman" also starts: a four-page installment of a new serial featuring Mrs. Webb from "The Black Widow." The opening page is dramatic, with a large half-page opening panel of Mrs. Webb's lair and a close-up inset panel of spiders, and the thrilling tone continues in Paula's discovery of skeletons and spiders aboard a deserted ship. There is also a page of "Edie and Miss T," where the two chaotic cartoon characters meet for the first time (characteristically, Miss T's spell to make herself pretty has gone wrong, and she appears in Edie's mirror). The horoscope section is renamed "Starry Eyed," and Misty no longer appears on the letters page, which is called "Noticeboard" and filled with more generic fare: a recipe, a poem about the weather, and two funny anecdotes from readers.

Overall, there is little in the comic of *Misty*, and she is swiftly edged out over the following weeks. A blonde approximation of her appears again on the following week's cover (January 26, 1980), but the *Tammy* cover girls continue without her after this. The byline "Strange Story from the Mists" remains, but only her silent image appears to introduce "The Witch at the Window" (this issue's Strange Story), and this too lacks the usual bite of a *Misty* tale. The Storyteller hosts the Strange Stories for the next two issues, and by February 16, 1980, Misty's image has shrunk to a tiny box of just 1" x 1.5," inset into the opening panel of the "Strange Story from the Mists." While the weekly Strange Stories continue, her appearances become less and less frequent throughout the following months and years, and as the current *Tammy* serials end, they are not replaced with *Misty* ones. Misty appears approximately once a month from March to May 1980, whereas the Storyteller is in almost every issue, sometimes with more than one tale.

The *Misty* title and moon-and-bat logo remain in the center of the cover for the first six months, but on October 11, 1980, the moon-and-bat logo vanishes, and the title's lettering shrinks considerably (to approximately one-eighth of *Tammy*'s size) and moves to an offset position on the right. As the Strange Stories continue, Misty's presence becomes still less frequent, although she has a brief revival in July and August 1981, when she appears weekly for a time. However, these are her final few appearances, and the *Misty* title features for the last time on the cover on September 26, 1981. It is removed without comment in the following week's issue (October 3, 1981), along with the "From the Mists" byline to the Strange Stories. The Storyteller has the Strange Stories slot all to himself for a few weeks, even though some of these tales seem better suited to Misty as Actions Backfire on the protagonist through some magical means. For example, in "Playing Truant" (November 21, 1981), absentee Sheila's school, house, and surroundings all repay her bad behavior by "playing truant" and vanishing without trace.

The removal of Misty references is in readiness for the *Tammy and Jinty* merger on November 28, 1981, which combines Miss T, Edie, and Snoopa into "The Crayzees." On December 12, 1981, Gypsy Rose arrives to introduce the Strange Story "Fire of the Fey Folk." Rose appears again the following week in "Pretty as a Picture," with the Storyteller also introducing "Lady with the Lamp" in the same issue (December 19, 1981), and the two share the Strange Stories slot after this. All that remains of Misty is a small image of her face within the "Starry Eyed" horoscopes. Her last appearance in a story in *Tammy and Jinty* comes nearly six months later, when she bookends "The Mists of Time" (May 15, 1982). This follows a long hiatus and is captioned "Back by popular demand, Misty takes a rare trip away from the Cavern of Dreams, to bring you a story about a topic close to her heart . . ." The story is set in Roman-occupied Britain around AD 200 and is about a Roman girl who follows her brother's regiment and is encountered as a ghost by a group of modern schoolchildren. In this, the story looks back to the "Misty-erious" feature in the first *Misty* annual (1979), which includes the legend of a Roman legion swallowed up by the mists whose ghosts are still sighted in Dorset, and there is a pleasing circularity to this (Lillyman 2002). In this final tale, Misty escapes from her tiny introductory box and appears in three full-sized panels, extolling the power of the mists at its opening, interjecting a comment before the story's denouement, and concluding by mentioning more sightings of ghostly Roman regiments in Britain. However, she is drawn by the story's artist rather than Bellwood, and her tone is uneven, mixing the casual and classical ("Well, there you are. . . . I must return to the mists whence I came. I hope we shall meet again, ere long").

The story is not one of her most dramatic, and in general her stories in *Tammy and Misty* lack the bite and extremity of the usual *Misty* one-shots. For example, in "Friend Pepi" (January 19, 1980), Rosa tells the simple retrospective story of her father, a toymaker beloved by the children but despised as poor by the townsfolk. When he dies, nobody comes to the funeral (the children have all forgotten him), but that night all the toys he has made steal out of their houses and gather at his graveside, his "true friends." The tale ends here with a large final tableau and in general has dynamic (if somewhat crowded) page layouts. Its ending is more melancholy than dramatic, though—a true *Misty* story might have included a final page in which the toys leave entirely or seek some other revenge to pay back the adults and children who rejected their maker. By contrast, "Accidents will Happen" (March 1, 1980) is more in keeping with *Misty*'s usual style: Ann's friend Julie is hit by a vehicle and dies after being moved by a crowd of people who suddenly appear, but Ann sees her on television that evening at the site of another accident. When Ann herself is then run over the same crowd appear, with Julie among them, and Ann dies and joins them (the final panel shows them crowding forward with the ghoulish refrain "An accident . . . ! An accident!") The serial "The Take-Over" (April 12, 1980) also begins with Misty's introduction and opens with the suggested body swap of star athlete Jenny and jealous Sandra after a coach crash. These stories have more of a *Misty* tone, as they feature unhappy and undeserved ends for their protagonists, dramatic visuals, and supernatural themes.

But despite the end of the comic's run and Misty's slow demise in both her annuals and the pages of *Tammy*, readers did not forget her. After the European reprints, the 1990s were a quiet time, but as internet blogs and sites began to gain greater traction around the millennium, in December 2002 Chris Lillyman set up Mistycomic.co.uk. He remembered *Misty* from his childhood, and creating the website was a labor of love and a cathartic task. Lillyman's aim was "to create a comprehensive record of one of the great British comics" (2016), and he went on to publish two Mistycomic.co.uk fanzines in 2005 and 2009. These glossy magazine-style collections are most reminiscent of the *Misty* holiday specials in their size and scope and include comics and prose stories, poems, interviews, posters, and suchlike created by *Misty* fans.

Mistycomic.co.uk and other British girls' comics websites evidence the dedication of fans and ongoing interest in a neglected genre and use the internet to continue the active engagement of the letters pages. In general they are a combination of archives, blogs, newsletters, and magazine features. In particular, sites such as *Girls Comics of Yesterday: All about Girls Comics* (http://girlscomicsofyesterday.com, launched by Lorraine Nolan ca. 2011), *A Resource on Jinty: Artists, Writers, Stories* (http://jintycomic.wordpress.com, launched by Jenni Scott in April 2014), and *Great News for All Readers* (http://greatnewsforallreaders.com, launched by David Moloney on August 31, 2015) all contain invaluable resources such as creator interviews, scanned pages, and summaries of issues and stories. Other comics sites and blogs such as *Blimey!* (Lew Stringer, launched 2006), *Down the Tubes* (John Freeman, launched 1998), and *The Bronze Age of Blogs* (Pete Doree, launched 2009) are also invaluable repositories for articles and reflections on girls' comics. Older sites such as *Blupoblog* (https://blupoblog.wordpress.com) and *The Tammy Project* (http://tammycomic.blogspot.co.uk) and the numerous forum threads devoted to British girls' comics (such as www.comicsuk.co.uk) also contain a wealth of information.

The "Get MISTY Back in Print!" Facebook page was launched by Lee Grice and Nic Wilkinson in August 2012. Although the idea was to campaign for Misty's return, this never really materialized, since shortly after the group was set up, Egmont announced its forthcoming *Misty* reprints. Egmont's first *Misty* publication was a "Special Souvenir" issue (2009), one of four "Classic Comics" specials the company produced that year (the others were *Battle*, *Roy of the Rovers*, and *Buster*), followed in 2012 by the e-book *Tales from the Mist 1: The Best of Misty* (2012), edited by John Richardson, Carlos Guirado, and Jesús Redondo. It was a shorter version of the printed 2009 collection, and although Pat Mills (2016b) was not impressed by the content (all single stories), these are definitely tales with stings in their tails. Most have unhappy or ambivalent endings for their protagonists, and there are plenty of twists and misdirections.

The two Rebellion collections that followed took a different direction and to date have focused entirely on the serials (though vol. 3, 2018, will include both serial and single stories). This decision, of course, gives a different impression of *Misty* than a weekly reader might find by emphasizing its bildungsroman stories of personal development, adventure, and acceptance. However, Rebellion's third release was arguably the most exciting yet: a Halloween anthology of new material titled *Scream! & Misty* (2017). This brought together four stories reviving various serials from these (and other) comics. Overall the anthology is a great read and doesn't suffer unduly from nostalgia; glossy pages and smooth coloring make it visually more reminiscent of new *2000AD* than classic British comics.

In addition, it is notable that the *Scream! & Misty* collection attempts to mediate the gender divide in traditional British comics and to present a diverse range of characters. As well as using stories from both girls' and boys' comics, and some female creators, the new collection brings characters of different ages, ethnicities, and genders together in many stories. In "The Sentinels" Jen is accompanied (at first) by her boyfriend Omar. "The Dracula File" takes place at a dinner party, focalizing through its hostess Rajani. "Black Max" follows schoolgirl protagonist Maxine into the adventure. But despite this, questions of age and gender have dominated critical discussion of the new collections. Barnett (2016) and Banville (Freeman 2017b) both query whether the reprinted stories have any appeal beyond an older, nostalgic audience, although Pat Mills (2014b) argues that younger readers enjoyed these tales, based on "a straw poll of local kids aged 8–11."

This debate forms part of a wider set of contradictions in the discussions of gender and audience surrounding contemporary comics. On the one hand, we are told that female readers are a valuable potential new market; on the other hand, it is claimed that they already make up nearly half of the audience (Freeman 2017b; Khan 2017). Female audiences have (varied) needs that must be addressed and attracted, but texts and brands cannot simultaneously speak to all aspects of this readership. Comics must attract new readers, but their publishing practices (serialization, disposability) run counter to this imperative. Visual storytelling is still felt to be the domain of children, yet this audience is not sufficiently catered to today.

These tensions can be read as examples of a larger set of paradoxes that underlie comics, which critics such as Pizzino (2016) and Beaty and Woo (2016) have ably explored. Comics exist in tension, both on the page (Hatfield 2005) and off, as the medium seems engaged in a perpetual and ongoing struggle against its own perceived illegitimacy and against definitions and analyses that privilege the literary over the artistic. Pizzino critiques the bildungsroman metanarrative attached to comics, arguing that the repeated claims in the press that comics have now "grown up" with the arrival of the graphic novel have, ironically, kept them in stasis. He argues that by attempting to promote particular "exceptional" comics, scholarly and critical discourse around the medium has devalued the bulk of its publications as worthless ephemera. Beaty and Woo also draw attention to the ways in which definitions, exhibitions, and pedagogies of comics privilege literariness, which can be seen in the creation of a scholarly canon based on authorship (rather than artistry) and the use of concepts such as auteur theory and formats such as the graphic novel to sustain this.

The reprints and reissues of *Misty* over the past four decades demonstrate that such comics have more than nostalgic value to their aging readership. Gibson (2015) has explored the way in which girls' comics helped young readers negotiate their identities, and Moloney (2017) and Lillyman (2016) extend this process to adulthood. Moloney says: "These comics meant so much to me—they were *my* publications, while my parents had their newspapers.... I do believe that these favorite artifacts of our childhood are important to us at a very personal level. They're like religious relics—they hold something within them, or trigger something within us, that help us to explore ourselves and get perspective on who we were and who we are today." Critics such as Hague (2014) have explored the multisensory impact of comics (visual, audible, tactile, olfactory, and gustatory), but my analysis demonstrates that this process of identity negotiation goes beyond materiality and nostalgia, as the numerous ways in which the *Misty* readers sought to find themselves in the comic have already been noted.

In this light, the mergers that spelled the end for so many British girls' comics take on a more sinister light: as destructive acts attacking readers' identities, as well as dismissing the emotional investment they had put into a comic. Lillyman (2016) emphasizes the disrespect that mergers showed to both titles and readers. For example, *Tammy* "was at the top of the tree and how did they reward them? It just ended.... Stories like 'Cora Can't Lose' never finished." As a reader, the merger announcement "fills you with dread," alongside worries about what will be done to "your" comic—a poor payoff for readers' devotion and emotional commitment: "You invest time and effort and sometimes merchandise, and that's how you get treated."

The nature of fandom is to use its artifacts to carve out a distinct identity for oneself. In this light, a merger is deeply damaging, as it forces readers to engage with something that they have previously defined their tastes against ("That's not MY comic"). The construction of the British girls' comics around female names, bolstered by their cover girl characters and the direct messages that would appear inside from them, were all efforts to give each comic a distinct identity of its own. It is therefore no surprise that mergers were completely incompatible with the unique personality of each.

It is easy to blame the demise of *Misty* on its lack of recurring characters and thus perceived lack of identity, as Mistyfan points out: "This became telling when *Misty* merged with *Tammy* because it is the regulars who keep going in a merger and carry on after the comic they came from disappears" (Mills 2012). But, taken as a whole, *Misty* had a clear brand and enough bite to stand out: Lillyman (2016) describes it as the "odd one out" among the other "girly girly" comics, and this unique character was enhanced by the comic's visual distinction through Bellwood's images of Misty. However, as a section in a bigger paper, this distinctiveness was swiftly lost, and the elements that made *Misty* so memorable were quickly diluted. Its seductive host and otherworldly feel vanished, and readers no longer felt welcomed into another realm. The dramatic layouts were toned down to fit with *Tammy*'s look, and the terrifying story endings were reduced not just in quantity but also in quality, as payoffs became less excessive and spectacular. As I have demonstrated, Misty's brief bookended introductions were not enough to sustain her identity, which had always remained vague due to the means of its construction. Readers knew so little about her beyond metaphor, tone, and allusion that there was nothing to carry forward without Bellwood's visuals and Shaw's poetic greetings, and her voice quietly vanished into the mists.

REFLECTIONS

Finishing a book feels a little like standing on a precipice—or perhaps I would just like to imagine myself as this sort of Gothic heroine. I look back over my shoulder and worry about what I have left undone, what I have not included, what I have not been able to uncover. My aims were to shed light on an era and genre of the British comics industry that has received limited critical attention to date. I desperately wanted to unearth more information about the people and processes that brought us a comic like *Misty* and to address some of the myths and assumptions about British girls' comics. I also wanted to explore and define the particular type of mystery and fear that *Misty* offered and develop existing Gothic theory by reflecting on what Gothic for Girls might mean in the context of wider critical work on this area and related genres.

I'm extremely happy to share the extensive primary research that I've done for this book (both in print and in my online database) and to bring to light the names, words, and images of so many involved writers, artists, and editors. As the first full-length study of any single British girls' comic, I hope this book paves the way for many more. By bringing together close reading and empirical research, I also hope I have demonstrated how these methodologies can work together. The potential impact of this research lies both in its primary data and in my suggestions as to how we might better understand and create comics and Gothic for children.

Although I'm not sure if my definition of Gothic for Girls will endure, I remain convinced of the value of such an attempt. At this point in time, in March 2018, my online searches around "Gothic" and "Girls" bring up a series of pages on the theme "How to Dress Goth," adverts for clothing brands such as Hot Topic, a YouTube video (from saphire190) entitled "Hottest Gothic Girls," similar collected images of "Sexy Gothic Girls," a number of Pinterest pages (typically "25 Best Looks for Gothic Girls"), and the Wikihow page "How to Attract a Goth Girl" (in twelve steps, with pictures). These sites dominate over the handful of artistic and literary links that appear, which include a music video for the song "Gothic Girl" by the 69 Eyes, Chris Riddell's *Goth Girl* series of children's books, and "Gothic for Girls," a 2016 touring performance by History Wardrobe composed of readings of classic texts in historical costume. I am unsurprised (but still saddened) by the dominance of superficial and sexualized images associated with both Gothic and girls.

Childhood is a liminal state, a moment of Otherness and uncertainty. Its fairy tales and dark fantasy stories have psychological, cultural, communicative, and intertextual value. They offer multiple subject positions that help real readers to name and face their fears, to understand the world around them and their place in it, and to begin to actively interpret metaphor, allegory, citation, and symbolism. Story outcomes must be negotiated and their impact understood. Gothic for Girls challenges and instructs its readers in a number of ways: offering warnings and moral lessons, and exposing societal expectations and limitations. The active reading and engagement required by the comics medium only enhances its power.

The value that *Misty* readers placed on "their" comic was apparent from all the people I spoke to and the level of active engagement in its letters page. These feelings of ownership and the emotional resonance of childhood artifacts indicate the ways in which readers use such texts to shape their identities. *Misty*'s history also demonstrates the power of fandom (if made visible and granted a platform) to contribute to its own stories (e.g., shaping the Misty character and voting on material) and to keep them alive. Key strategies of adaptation and collaboration are apparent as social themes and other media texts informed the comic's content from the start and then kept it going through fan sites and campaigns.

My research also revealed the extensive collaboration that went into these publications. The comic that became *Misty* was woven from numerous different ideas, and what I would consider its most memorable elements (e.g., longer stories, dramatic visuals, host character, mystery theme, and ambivalent or shock endings) came from many different people. *Misty*'s identity clearly evolved as the comic continued, and I was struck by the scope and extent of the editorial duties. My research into *Misty* demonstrated the power of commercial competition, as the rivalry between DC Thomson and IPC produced exciting and innovative work across numerous titles. Somewhat paradoxically, it also exposed the way in which profit-driven production can damage and diminish creativity as publishers cannibalized their own titles in search of bigger sales.

The demise of the British comics industry is a sad result of the lack of value placed not just on its creators but also on childhood agency. These comics had a vast readership, and the medium as a whole has a subversive strength and a visual power that has often been overlooked or undermined. My examination of the intertwined histories of children's literature and Gothic is a fitting backdrop for the concerns that have dogged the history of comics. Historically the medium has been felt to be not fit for study, not appropriate to be read by adults, arrested in its development, and relegated to the subcultural and juvenilia. We are just starting to recognize and allow comics' return from this confinement and their potential to be much more to many readers. But (like the heroine of a *Misty* story) we must proceed with caution, and with responsibility.

My research into the Female Gothic revealed that many of the historical critical discourses around this genre framed their chosen texts as anomalies. This allowed critics and contemporaries to acknowledge the artistry of a writer such as Radcliffe without having to reevaluate the contribution made by women authors in the emerging Gothic. Academia all too often treats our chosen texts as exceptions to the norm, and comics studies has frequently claimed value for individual titles in this way and by making comparisons with more established disciplines. While this book has looked closely at *Misty*, I do not wish to make similar claims for its exceptional brilliance. Although this comic has a special place in my heart, speaking objectively, I can see many of its strengths in other publications of the time, and I have traced many of its influences from previous titles and surrounding media.

The anonymous authors, invisible artists, and overlooked editors of *Misty* made something extraordinary—as did all the unsung creators of British comics. As publishers seek to revitalize the industry and comics studies moves toward the creation of its own canons (both academic and fan based), we must tread carefully. Our aim should be to take a more inclusive approach than has been the case previously in literature, art, and society.

Figure 15.1. "The End." *Misty* logo designed by Jack Cunningham. Reproduced with permission of Misty™ Rebellion Publishing IP Ltd.; copyright © Rebellion Publishing IP Ltd., all rights reserved.

NOTES

FOREWORD

1. Inspired by Mel, and generously supported by Inkpot Studios, this story is included here as fig. 0.1, written by Julia Round with art by Letty Wilson.

INTRODUCTION

1. "Mirror . . . Mirror" is included in its entirety as fig. 8.6 (chap. 8).
2. "Shadow of a Doubt" (#58; see figs. 8.4b and 11.2) and "Happy Birthday Spooky Sue" (#50) are particular favorites.
3. This is the total number of stories published, comprising serials, series, and single stories in both prose and comics formats. The myths and legends told in features such as "These Misty Isles . . ." are not included.

CHAPTER 1. THE RISE AND FALL OF BRITISH GIRLS' COMICS

1. There was only one missed week: *Misty* did not appear on January 6, 1979, owing to a printers strike. Pete Wrobel (union rep at IPC from 1978 to 1992) talks a little about industrial action at IPC in Scott 2015a.
2. *Scream!* (IPC, 1984) was a weekly anthology comic with a horror theme (and a mysterious host-editor named Ghastly McNasty), which lasted fifteen issues before merging with *Eagle*. This was perhaps due to fallout from industrial action, although IPC managing editor Gil Page claims that "the settle down sales figures never justified the company's confidence in it," and group editor Barrie Tomlinson confirms that the comic was difficult to produce: the issues were always late, as they received intense scrutiny from management (McDonald 2016). *Scream!* can be read online at http://www.backfromthedepths.co.uk/gallery.htm.
3. See, e.g., http://readcomiconline.to/Comic/Misty.
4. Comments taken from Mel Gibson's keynote address at the "Transitions" conference (Birkbeck London, October 31, 2016) and Paul Gravett's introduction to "Draw Misty for Me" (a Comica event at the British Library, August 17, 2014).
5. See, e.g., the work of Martin Barker, Mary Cadogan, Patricia Craig, Mel Gibson, Angela McRobbie, Joan Ormrod, Penny Tinkler, Melanie Tebbutt, and Valerie Walkerdine.
6. Murray (2017, 183) points out that this references both the Beatles and the Fantastic Four.
7. Reader Helen Fay (2016) received a reply from Bill Harrington in late 1981 when she wrote to the *Misty* editor to complain about its cancellation.

8. While other names such as Gerry Finley-Day and John Wagner have been mentioned in association with *Misty*, I have found no evidence of this; in fact, Wagner (2018) confirms he only submitted one story to *Misty*, and it was rejected.

9. Due to the lack of creator credit, these lists are entirely inductive, and many artists and writers have likely been forgotten; please contact me via my website if you have further suggestions.

10. This develops the thematic strategy adopted by 2000AD, which notoriously rebranded a red Frisbee as a "Space Spinner" for its #1 free gift in 1977.

11. A snapshot survey of the children's comics shelves at WHSmith on April 10, 2018, demonstrates that, of the twenty-five titles available for girls, fifteen come from branded franchises (such as *My Little Pony*, *Hello Kitty*, *Barbie*, *Disney's Cinderella*, *Shopkins*, and *Sylvanian Families*); six are strongly coded pop or fashion titles (*Go Girl*, *Girl Talk*, *Top of the Pops*); and just four are not obviously affiliated with particular brands or themes (*Sweet*, *Cuddles*, *The Phoenix*). All except *The Phoenix* are strongly coded as female (pink covers), display branded toys or accessories of some type on the cover, and the vast majority include free gifts. There are often multiple titles promoting the same brand, for example, four different *My Little Pony* magazines and three *Shopkins* publications.

12. Pat Mills (2015, 2017a) has claimed that writers Alan Davidson and Anne Digby left IPC to work on the Dutch version of *Tina* because editor Wilf Prigmore refused to give them story credit. However, Anne Digby (2017) and Wilf Prigmore (2017b) both dispute this story, and we should note that Prigmore was the editor who first included story credits in *Tammy*. Anne Digby (2017) states categorically: "The only reason Alan [Davidson] quit writing for IPC was because a mass market in paperback for children's books had opened up in the 1970s."

CHAPTER 2. ANONYMOUS AUTHORS

1. A useful resource to accompany this and the following chapter is my database of *Misty* stories hosted at www.juliaround.com/misty, which can be searched by contributor name, issue, story title, and story content, to show who wrote or drew each story (where known), what it is about, and where it appears and is reprinted. This is a work in progress, and I always welcome further information.

2. Some titles from smaller publishers, such as Dez Skinn's *House of Hammer* (Top Shelf, 1976–78), did include creator credits.

3. Aimed at John Wagner, Kelvin Gosnell, and Wilf Prigmore, respectively. Pat Mills also inserts "Professor Mills" into his story "Red Knee—White Terror!" (see figs. 2.1, 2.2).

4. "A Horse Called September" had previously appeared as a thirteen-part text serial in *June and Pixie* (March 16, 1974–June 15, 1974), credited to Anne Digby.

5. A text adaptation of "Into the Fourth at Trebizon" began on February 5, 1983, and a comics adaptation of "First Term at Trebizon" (drawn by Phil Gascoine) ran from November 19, 1983, to February 3, 1984.

6. Actual rates for three-page scripts (from Terence Magee, personal email, taken directly from *Battle Picture Weekly* detail books):

>*Battle Picture Weekly* (1975):
>John Wagner: £32.60
>Pat Mills: £32.30
>Gerry Finley-Day: £30.00
>Writers such as Terry Magee, Ken Mennell, Eric Hebden, Alan Hebden,
>   R. Carpenter: £28.05

Battle Picture Weekly (1976):
John Wagner: £38.25
Scott Goodall, Alan Hebden, Eric Hebden, Tom Tully: £36.00
Gerry Finley-Day: £34.00

7. Terence Magee worked as both a staff and freelance writer at Fleetway/IPC from 1960 to 1991. He never wrote for *Misty* but worked on a number of boys' and girls' comics. He was subeditor for *June and School Friend* (1966–70) and later editor of *Battle Picture Weekly* and *Battle Action*.

8. Quantitative analysis of a random sample of ten issues reveals that four-page stories contain a mean average of 26.995 panels; five-page stories contain 32.0 panels; and six-page stories contain 33.875 panels. The mode average (most common) number of panels is 25 panels (across four pages), 32 panels (across five pages), and 26 panels (across six pages).

9. Ted Andrews (2017a, 2017b) has alternatively claimed that this story was scripted by Bill Harrington based on an idea they had discussed.

10. *Mirabelle* had previously run from 1956, absorbing competitor titles *New Glamour* in 1958, *Marty* in 1963, and *Valentine* in 1974.

11. Other writers whose names appear in *Tammy* in the 1980s and who worked on IPC's girls' comics in the 1970s include Benita Brown, Jenny McDade, Ian Mennell, Jay Over, and Roy Preston, but I have not been able to link them directly to any *Misty* stories.

12. Tinkler (1995) cites Rosemary Mary Story, who wrote under the names Desmond Reid, Ross Wood, and Richard Jenkins; Ceciley Hamilton, who wrote as Max Hamilton; and Gertrude Ken Olivers, who wrote under the name of Kent Carr.

13. In the original quotation, Mills refers here to the real name of prolific children's writer Anne Digby. Ironically, his remarks are tied to the groundbreaking "Cinderella" strip "Little Miss Nothing" (*Tammy*), which was actually written by her husband Alan Davidson.

CHAPTER 3. ASTONISHING ARTISTS

1. For examples, see figs. 11.1, 4.1, and 3.3.

2. The biographical summaries in this chapter are necessarily brief. For readers interested in finding out more about these extremely talented people, David Roach's *Masters of Spanish Comic Book Art* (2017) and websites such as www.tebeosfera.com and www.lambiek.net are the most useful sources.

3. A similar logo appears in the *Jinty* story "Dance into the Darkness," first published June 17, 1978 (some six months after *Misty*'s launch).

4. Original text reads: "Era yo que lo organizaba así, Fué posterior a la primera época Warren y teníamos total libertad en compaginar las páginas. Para mí era una forma de ir en dirección contraria a la aburrida compaginación de la llamada 'línea clara' europea. En ocasiones me pasaba, y la lectura de la página era confusa. El manga ha mantenido este estilo hasta hoy mismo." Trans. Julia Round.

5. For more information on the various Spanish publishing houses, see McGlade 2016; Roach 2013, 2017.

6. Guiral (2010) quotes Macabich as saying he arrived at the time of an engravers' strike and fulfilled an urgent demand for art.

7. Original text reads: "Bardon Art fue no sólo una correa de transmisión entre la oferta y la demanda de editores extranjeros y profesionales españoles, sino un campo de pruebas, un digno método de supervivencia y una escuela para muchos dibujantes jóvenes." Trans. Julia Round.

8. Original text reads: "La historia de nuestra historieta les debe un espacio y un reconocimiento, a Macabich y a todos los agentes, técnicos, guionistas y dibujantes de agencia, profesionales que han trabajado en silencio y con dignidad." Trans. Julia Round.

9. See http://isidremonesart.blogspot.co.uk/2014/10/drawings-bizarres.html or http://www.ilustradores.com/component/content/article/14-isidre-mones/24-isidre-mones.html.

10. Original text reads: "Siempre tuve una sospecha existe una franja de féminas británicasentre 40 y 45 años traumatizadas por aquellos cómics que ilustré? Yo las solapé con mi trayectoria de Warren, y poco disimulé el aspecto terrorífico. Recuerdo el gato /comeniñas malas. La niña atrapada en el ambar / la casa embrujada./ Los monstruos del circo, /el de la Peste medieval." Trans. Julia Round.

11. Original text reads: "UF!!! Es horripilante!! Como puede hacer esas historietas para niñas!! Lo permitio la Thatcher?" (Did Thatcher allow it?). Trans. Julia Round.

12. For more information, see http://www.badiaromero.com.

13. My grateful thanks to María and her son David Gesalí for our email conversations.

14. For more information, see http://www.blasgallego.com. My thanks also to Blas for our email conversations.

15. See https://jesusredondo.carbonmade.com.

16. See *A Resource on Jinty* for a full list of his girls' comics work. https://jintycomic.wordpress.com/2016/01/24/jose-casanovas.

17. Her niece remembers Shirley speaking of living opposite Joan Collins in London, saying that they used to try to out-glam each other (Gaunt 2017).

18. The posters that appeared in the holiday specials can be viewed at http://mistycomic.co.uk/Misty/Pull_Outs/Pages/Super_Misty_Posters.html, and the annual covers can be found at http://mistycomic.co.uk/Annuals.html. It is not certain if Bellwood also painted the other two covers (for the *Misty* Summer Special 1978 and Annual 1979), but this seems likely.

19. The first cover to feature Misty herself is *Misty* #27 (August 5, 1978), shown on the cover of this book, and it seems surprising that it took her a little over six months to make it to this position.

CHAPTER 4. VISCERAL VISUALS

1. While this quantitative analysis aims to be objective, I should note that having just one individual doing the tagging is necessarily subjective. Such subjectivity is an ongoing problem with any attempt to quantify comics material, which by its nature is not made up of discrete minimum units.

2. The selection and organization of these tags and categories are credited entirely to Paul Fisher Davies.

CHAPTER 5. SHOCKING STORIES

1. "The Cult of the Cat," "Day of the Dragon," "Don't Look Twice," "The Four Faces of Eve," "Hush, Hush, Sweet Rachel," "The Loving Cup," "Moonchild," "The Nine Lives of Nicola," "The Salamander Girl," "The Secret World of Sally Maxwell," and "Wolf Girl."

2. "The Black Widow" is also continued as "The Spider Woman" in *Tammy and Misty*, January 19, 1980.

3. "The Body Snatchers," "The Cats of Carey Street," "End of the Line," "The Ghost of Golightly Towers," "Hangman's Alley," "The Haunting of Hazel Brown," "House of Horror," "Journey into Fear," "A Leap through Time," "Long Way from Home," "Midnight Masquerader," "Nightmare Academy," "Paint It Black," "The School of the Lost . . . ," "Screaming Point," "The Sentinels," "The Silver Racer-Back," "Whistle and I'll Come . . . ," and "Winner Loses All!"

4. "The Black Widow," "Danger in the Depths," "The Haunting of Hazel Brown," "Journey into Fear," "The Ring of Confidence," and "The Silver Racer-Back."

5. For full discussion of this history, see Barker 1984 on the United Kingdom, and Nyberg 1998 and Hajdu 2008 on the United States. See also relevant chapters in Sabin 1996; Chapman 2011; and Round 2014a.

CHAPTER 6. HORROR AND GOTHIC IN THE 1970S

1. *Scarred For Life* (Brotherstone and Lawrence 2017) contains an exhaustive catalog of the dominant British media of the 1970s from this angle.

2. *Becoming Unbecoming* (Una 2015) reflects on the era's violence and misogyny by situating the author's own experiences of sexual assault against this backdrop.

3. Edited by Herbert van Thal, this series became a cult classic, although to date it has received limited critical attention. A full-length study is being produced by Johnny Mains, who has also edited a number of new anthologies.

4. I still remember watching a film called *Robbie* (British Transport Films, 1979) in primary school, in which a boy has both feet amputated after an accident playing on a railway line. It ends on the harrowing image of his defunct football boots (a similar image of an unworn coat is used in *Play Safe—Frisbee*), with the haunting narration: "Robbie still keeps his boots. Nobody knows why, not even Robbie. After all, they'll never be any use to him."

CHAPTER 7. OUR FRIEND OF THE MISTS

1. For further discussion of *The Witch's Tale*, see Hand 2012.

2. This is altered to "Gypsy Rose's Tales of Mystery and Magic" from the next issue onward.

3. Dates where known: "Madame Marlova Remembers," *Debbie* #186–211 (September 4, 1976–February 26, 1977). "Cremond Hall," *Spellbound* #21 (September 12, 1977), continued as "Cremond Castle," *Spellbound* #38–52 (June 11, 1977–September 17, 1977) and *Spellbound* #67–69 (December 31, 1977–January 14, 1978). Subsequently reprinted as "Blackwell Hall" in *Nikki* #212–18 (March 11, 1989–April 22, 1989). "Dolwyn's Dolls," *Bunty* #1287–91 (September 11, 1982–October 9, 1982), *Bunty* Annuals 1983 and 1984, and subsequent issues of *Bunty Picture Story Library*. "A Tale from the Toy Museum," *Bunty* #1493–n.d. (August 23, 1986–n.d.) and *Bunty* Annuals 1988 and 1989. "The Button Box," *Tammy* (n.d.). Jade Jenkins (various titles), *M&J* #115–221 (July 24, 1993–August 5, 1995). www.girlscomicsofyesterday.com.

4. Please see my online database at www.juliaround.com/misty for the sources of these reprints where known.

5. In the late 1970s, Goth music was inaugurated with the release of Bauhaus's "Bela Lugosi's Dead" (1979), and powerful women (in music and otherwise) were on the rise in the 1980s (O'Shea 2015a discusses possible influences in more detail).

6. In addition to this, one unpublished drawing of Misty was found damaged after being used as a cutting board. It was completed by David Roach and included in the *Mistycomic.co.uk* fan publication (2009) (see chap. 14).

7. The pull-outs and giveaways can be viewed at http://www.mistycomic.co.uk/Misty/Pull_Outs/Pull_Outs.html.

8. I am indebted to Paul Fisher Davies for the quantitative data provided here using NVivo.

9. I am indebted to Paul Fisher Davies for the quantitative data provided here using Voyant Tools.

10. The issues containing passive greetings are #60, #64, #78, #81, and #100.

11. Four issues had no words on the inside cover, and one is from Miss T rather than Misty.

CHAPTER 8. A TAXONOMY OF TERROR

1. This quotation has mistakenly been attributed to Will Brooker in the past.
2. My thanks to Mark Round for outstanding numerical wizardry with spreadsheets.
3. As before, I should note that the analysis still has the potential to be subjective because the coding has been done by one person.
4. Figure produced by subtracting 22 (the positive final installments) from the 341 serial episodes to produce 317 ambivalent and 2 negative "endings," and adding this to the data on the singles and reprints.
5. My thanks to the audience member who used this phrase in the Q&A session after my paper "Gothic and Comics" (presented at the "Comics: The Politics of Form" seminar series, Oxford University, February 15, 2018).
6. Although the term "formula" has negative connotations, Mills (2011) stresses: "When I say 'formula' I don't mean to imply that the story lacks any passion because it follows guidelines.... The formula on girls' comics was actually quite good, you had a lot of freedom but you still had some guidelines."
7. In keeping with the first three categories, it would be logical for this to also have a positive and negative manifestation (B+/B−); however, the links between good deeds and positive outcomes are often less direct, and so these stories (such as "The Swarm," #9) are coded under "Redemption."

CHAPTER 10. DEEP CUTS: GOTHIC CONCEPTS AND IDENTITIES

1. For reasons of space, I cannot offer a full critical review of this work, but the critics cited here are useful starting points.
2. Also claimed as written by Bill Harrington with input from Ted Andrews (Andrews 2017a, 2017b).

CHAPTER 11. SURFACE REFLECTIONS: GOTHIC SYMBOLS, SETTINGS, AND ARCHETYPES

1. The total number of graphic and text story installments of all three story types, across all the *Misty* weeklies, annuals, and specials.
2. These calculations recognize that some tales (such as "The Simple Job," #56; or "Dark Secrets . . . Dark Night," #13) contain more than one archetype.
3. These charts revise the figures given in my 2017 article "*Misty*, *Spellbound*, and the Lost Gothic of British Girls' Comics," which considers only the comic strip stories in the *Misty* weeklies (omitting text stories and those in the annuals, specials, etc.) and uses an estimated number of total story episodes rather than an exact count.
4. Both are preempted by *The Silver Kiss* (Annette Curtis Klause, 1992), which follows in the footsteps of Anne Rice's sympathetic vampires, reframed as a teenage love story.
5. This relatively low number does not include the stories that deal with a magical item or anonymous curse, which I explore in chapter 8.

CHAPTER 12. GOTHIC FOR GIRLS

1. See Tehrani 2013 for discussion of the many interlinked versions of this story, dating back to the first century.
2. A *Dramarama* adaptation of this that we watched in primary school terrified me (Thames TV, 1987).

3. Stine's *Goodnight Kiss* (1992, 1996), Pike's *The Last Vampire* (1994–96, resumed 2010), and Hoh's *The Vampire's Kiss* (1995).

CHAPTER 13. MAKE *MISTY* FOR ME

1. See, e.g., Chambers 1977; Rudd 1992; Benton 1999 (which surveys the development of such criticism); and numerous small-scale studies such as Pope and Round 2014.

2. No letters page appears in #1–7, #15, #20, and #25.

3. This is perhaps unsurprising, as their selection may have encouraged more of the same type.

4. Harmse also writes directly to IPC on February 19, 1980, after the comic has ended, enclosing a copy of his proposed fan club newsletter and asking for permission to use images from the comic (fig. 3.5a).

5. Thanks to Jean-Christian Dumas for this explanation.

6. Gibson contrasts these points about American comics letters pages to British ones; however, it seems to me that "Write to Misty" combines both.

CHAPTER 14. LEAVING THESE MISTY ISLES

1. A major NUJ strike that led to redundancies took place in 1984 and was responsible for the sudden demise of many comics such as *Tammy* and *Scream!* (Scott 2016b).

2. From analyzing a randomly generated sample of every tenth issue: within the first thirty issues of *Misty*, virtually no historical stories appear. Between issues #30 and #70, this figure rises to an average of two historical stories per issue, then drops back to an average of no historical stories per issue between #70 and #90, and then rises to a high of averaging three stories per issue for the remainder of the comic's run.

3. For a partial list of titles in this series, see https://www.bedetheque.com/search/albums?RechCollection=Kaléidoscope&RechEO=1.

4. Thanks to Irmi Bowley and Martina Taylor for help with German translation.

REFERENCES

Alderson, Connie. 1968. *Magazines Teenagers Read*. London: Pergamon Press.
Andrews, Ted. 2017a. Personal interview with Julia Round. Conducted by telephone, January 23, 2017.
Andrews, Ted. 2017b. Personal interview with Julia Round. Conducted by telephone, October 19, 2017.
Ang, Ien. 1985. *Watching Dallas*. London: Methuen.
Appleyard, J. A. 1991. *Becoming a Reader: The Experience of Fiction from Childhood to Adulthood*. Cambridge: Cambridge University Press.
Ariès, Philippe. 1973. *Centuries of Childhood*. Harmondsworth: Penguin.
Armitt, Lucie. 2012. "The Magical Realism of the Contemporary Gothic." In *A New Companion to the Gothic*, ed. David Punter, 510–22. Oxford: Blackwell.
Armitt, Lucie. 2017. "The Gothic Girl Child." In *Women and the Gothic*, ed. Avril Horner and Sue Zlosnik, 60–73. Edinburgh: Edinburgh University Press.
Ashliman, D. L. 1997. "Incest in Indo-European Folktales." https://www.furorteutonicus.eu/germanic/ashliman/mirror/incest.html. Accessed October 12, 2017.
Auerbach, Nina. 1995. *Our Vampires Ourselves*. Chicago: University of Chicago Press.
Austen, Jane. (1817) 1992. *Northanger Abbey*. Ware, Hertfordshire: Wordsworth Editions.
Austin, Sara. 2013. "Performative Metafiction: Lemony Snicket, Daniel Handler and the End of *A Series of Unfortunate Events*." *The Looking Glass: New Perspectives on Children's Literature* 17 (1). https://www.lib.latrobe.edu.au/ojs/index.php/tlg/article/view/387/381. Accessed November 18, 2017.
Baddeley, Gavin. 2002. *Gothic Chic: A Connoisseur's Guide to Dark Culture*. London: Plexus Publishing.
Baker, Tom. 1999. *The Boy Who Kicked Pigs*. London: Faber and Faber.
Bakhtin, Mikhail. 1984. *Rabelais and His World*. Trans. Hélène Iswolsky. Bloomington: Indiana University Press.
Baldick, Chris, ed. 1992. *The Oxford Book of Gothic Tales*. Oxford: Oxford University Press.
Baldick, Chris, and Robert Mighall. 2012. "Gothic Criticism." In *A New Companion to the Gothic*, ed. David Punter. Oxford: Blackwell.
Barker, Martin. 1984. *A Haunt of Fears*. Jackson: University Press of Mississippi.
Barker, Martin. 1989. *Comics: Ideology, Power and the Critics*. Manchester: Manchester University Press.
Barnett, David. 2016. "*Misty*: The 'Girls' Comic' Returning from the 70s to a New Age of Children." *Guardian*, October 3, 2016. https://www.theguardian.com/books/booksblog/2016/oct/03/misty-the-girls-comic-returning-from-the-70s-to-a-new-age-of-children. Accessed October 9, 2017.
Barthes, Roland. 1973. *The Pleasure of the Text*. Trans. Richard Miller. https://emberilmu.files.wordpress.com/2011/08/roland-barthes-the-pleasure-of-the-text.pdf. Accessed February 15, 2018.

BBC. 2014. "Number of UK Homes with TVs Falls for First Time." *BBC*, December 9, 2014. https://www.bbc.com/news/entertainment-arts-30392654. Accessed August 11, 2017.

Beard, Mary R. 1946. *Woman as Force in History*. New York: Macmillan.

Beattie, James. 1783. *Dissertations Moral and Critical*. London: Printed for W. Strahan and T. Cadell. Edinburgh: W. Creech.

Beaty, Bart, and Benjamin Woo. 2016. *The Greatest Comic Book of All Time*. London: Palgrave Pivot.

Becker, Ernest. 1973. *The Denial of Death*. New York: Simon and Schuster.

Becker, Suzanne. 1999. *Gothic Forms of Feminine Fictions*. Manchester: Manchester University Press.

Bennett, Lucy, and Paul Booth, eds. 2016. *Seeing Fans: Representations of Fandom in Media and Popular Culture*. London: Bloomsbury.

Benton, Mike. 1999. "Readers, Texts, Contents: Reader-Response Criticism." In *Understanding Children's Literature*, ed. Peter Hunt, 86–102. Abingdon: Taylor and Francis.

Berry, Hannah. 2018. "Bumping the Lamp: An Interview with Graphic Novelist Hannah Berry." Interview with Alex Fitch. *Studies in Comics* 8 (2): 227–43.

Bettelheim, Bruno. 1975. *The Uses of Enchantment*. London: Penguin Books.

Bewell, Alan. 1988. "'An Issue of Monstrous Desire': Frankenstein and Obstetrics." *Yale Journal of Criticism* 2 (1): 105–28.

Beville, Maria. 2009. *Gothic-Postmodernism: Voicing the Terrors of Postmodernity*. New York: Rodopi.

Birkhead, Edith. 1921. *The Tale of Terror: A Study of the Gothic Romance*. http://www.gutenberg.org/ebooks/14154. Accessed October 24, 2017.

Bishop, Jon. 2017. Comment on "Get MISTY Back in Print!" Facebook. https://www.facebook.com/groups/getmisty/permalink/1592651360757228. Accessed October 26, 2017.

Blair, Shirley. 2018. Personal correspondence with Julia Round. Conducted by email, February 14, 2018.

Boodman, S. 2002. *Children's Literature Review* 79:185.

Boon, Kevin. 2011. "The Zombie as Other: Mortality and the Monstrous in the Post-nuclear Age." In *Better Off Dead: The Evolution of the Zombie as Post-Human*, ed. Deborah Christie and Sarah Juliet Lauro, 50–60. New York: Fordham University Press.

Botting, Fred. 1994. "*Dracula*, Romance and the Radcliffean Gothic." *Women's Writing* 1 (2): 181–202.

Botting, Fred. 1996. *Gothic*. London: Routledge.

Botting, Fred, ed. 2001. *The Gothic*. Cambridge: D. S. Brewer.

Botting, Fred. 2008. *Gothic Romanced: Consumption, Gender and Technology in Contemporary Fictions*. London: Routledge.

Bourdieu, Pierre. 1984. *Distinction: A Social Critique of the Judgement of Taste*. London: Routledge and Kegan Paul.

Bowers, Maggie Ann. 2004. *Magic(al) Realism*. New York: Routledge.

Bradley, Darren. 2016. Social media post. Facebook, March 2, 2016. https://www.facebook.com/groups/getmisty/permalink/1076842249004811. Accessed October 24, 2017.

Braidotti, Rosa. 2011. *Nomadic Subjects: Embodiment and Sexual Difference in Contemporary Feminist Theory*. 2nd ed. New York: Columbia University Press.

Braude, Anne. 1998. "Women Who Run with the Werewolves: The Evolution of the Post-feminist Gothic Heroine." *Niekas*, July 1998, 103–12.

Breton, André. (1936) 1971. "Limits Not Frontiers of Surrealism." In *Surrealism*, ed. Herbert Read, 93–116. London: Faber and Faber.

Brett, Bernard. 1983. *The Hamlyn Book of Mysteries*. London: Hamlyn.

The British Critic. 1818. Review of *Frankenstein* from *The British Critic*, n.s., 9 (April 1818): 432–38. Also reprinted in *Port Folio* (Philadelphia) 6 (September 1818): 200–207. Available online at

Romantic Circles, https://www.rc.umd.edu/reference/chronologies/mschronology/reviews/bcrev.html. Accessed February 27, 2018.

Brophy, Bridget. 1965. "The Rights of Animals." *Sunday Times*, October 10, 1965.

Brotherstone, Stephen, and Dave Lawrence. 2017. *Scarred for Life Volume One: The 1970s*. Lonely Water Books.

Bruhm, Steven. 1994. *Gothic Bodies: The Politics of Pain in Romantic Fiction*. Philadelphia: University of Pennsylvania Press.

Bruhm, Steven. 2006. "Nightmare on Sesame Street; or, The Self-Possessed Child." *Gothic Studies* 8 (2): 98–113.

Buckley, Chloé. 2014. "Gothic and the Child Reader, 1850–Present." In *The Gothic World*, ed. Glennis Byron and Dale Townshend, 254–63. London: Routledge.

Buckley, Chloé. 2018. *Twenty-first Century Children's Gothic*. Edinburgh: Edinburgh University Press.

Busch, Wilhelm. 1865. "Max and Moritz: A Juvenile History in Seven Tricks." *German Stories*. https://germanstories.vcu.edu/mm/mmengvor.html. Accessed October 18, 2017.

Busse, Kristin. 2013. "Geek Hierarchies: Boundary Policing and the Gendering of the Good Fan." *Participations: Journal of Audience and Reception Studies* 10 (2): 73–91.

Butler, David. 2008. Review. *Gothic Television*. *Screen* 49 (2): 250–54.

Cadogan, Mary, and Patricia Craig. 1976. *You're a Brick, Angela: The Girls' Story, 1839–1985*. London: Victor Gollancz.

Capaldi, Vanda. 2012. *Mario: A Biography in Poetry*. Vanda Capaldi.

Carrington, Victoria. 2011. "The Contemporary Gothic: Literacy and Childhood in Unsettled Times." *Journal of Early Childhood Literacy* 12 (3): 293–310.

Carroll, Lewis. (1865, 1872) 1998. *Alice's Adventures in Wonderland and Through the Looking Glass*. Penguin Classics edition. London: Penguin.

Carter, Angela. (1979) 1998. *The Bloody Chamber and Other Stories*. London: Vintage.

Cavallero, Dani. 2002. *The Gothic Vision: Three Centuries of Horror, Terror and Fear*. London: Continuum.

Chambers, Aidan. 1977. "The Reader in the Book." *Signal* 23:64–87.

Chapman, James. 2011. *British Comics: A Cultural History*. London: Reaktion Books.

Chatterjee, Ranita. 2004. "Sapphic Subjectivity and Gothic Desires in Eliza Fenwick's *Secresy* (1795)." *Gothic Studies* 6 (1): 45–56.

Chavanne, Renaud. 2010. *Composition de la bande dessinée* [The composition of comics]. Montrouge: PLG.

Christie, Alison. 2015. "Alison Christie: Interview." Posted by Comixminx. *A Resource on Jinty: Artists, Writers, Stories*. https://jintycomic.wordpress.com/2015/01/11/alison-christie-interview. Accessed February 14, 2018.

Clery, E. J. 1994. "Ann Radcliffe and D. A. F. de Sade: Thoughts on Heroinism." *Women's Writing* 1 (2): 203–14.

Clery, E. J. 1995. *The Rise of Supernatural Fiction, 1762–1800*. Cambridge: Cambridge University Press.

Clover, Carol J. 1992. *Men, Women and Chainsaws: Gender in the Modern Horror Film*. London: British Film Institute.

Coats, Karen. 2008. "Between Horror, Humour and Hope: Neil Gaiman and the Psychic Work of the Gothic." In *The Gothic in Children's Literature: Haunting the Borders*, ed. Anna Jackson, Karen Coats, and Roderick McGillis, 77–92. London: Routledge.

Cohen, Stanley. (1972) 1987. *Folk Devils and Moral Panics*. Oxford: Blackwell.

Cohn, Neil. 2014. "The Architecture of Visual Narrative Comprehension: The Interaction of Narrative Structure and Page Layout in Understanding Comics." *Frontiers in Psychology*. https://doi.org/10.3389/fpsyg.2014.00680. Accessed October 17, 2017.

Collings, Angela. 2012. "Bunty, Twinkle Then the Devil Arrived with Misty: My Love of Girls' Comics." Blog post. *Angelacollings*, November 24, 2012. https://angelacollings.wordpress.com/tag/misty-comic. Accessed February 29, 2016.

Coman, Anthony. 2012. "Profaning the Serial Comic: Letters Columns in Fiction Traumics." Paper presented at "Monster in the Margins: The Ninth Annual Conference on Comics and Graphic Novels," University of Florida, April 13–15, 2012.

Comics UK. 2012. "Non-white Protagonists." Comics UK. http://comicsuk.co.uk/forum/viewtopic.php?f=140&t=7380. Accessed April 20, 2018.

Comics UK. 2015. "GNFAR post on *Misty*." Comics UK. http://comicsuk.co.uk/forum/viewtopic.php?f=140&t=6786. Accessed October 9, 2017.

Cooke, Lez. 2003. *British Television Drama: A History*. London: BFI.

Coote, Briony. n.d. "The Button Box." *Books Monthly*. http://www.booksmonthly.co.uk/button.html. Accessed July 15, 2016.

Coote, Briony. n.d. "Common Categories for Serials in Girls' Comics." *Books Monthly*. http://www.booksmonthly.co.uk/common.html. Accessed February 14, 2018.

Corson, Jamie T. 2010. "The Modernization of the Gothic Heroine: From Ann Radcliffe to Stephenie Meyer, a Feminist Perspective." MA thesis, Rutgers University. https://rucore.libraries.rutgers.edu/rutgers-lib/26492/PDF/1/play. Accessed January 18, 2018.

Crandall, Nadia. 2008. "Cyberfiction and the Gothic Novel." In *The Gothic in Children's Literature: Haunting the Borders*, ed. Anna Jackson, Karen Coats, and Roderick McGillis, 39–56. London: Routledge.

Crawford, Joseph. 2014. *The Twilight of the Gothic: Vampire Fiction and the Rise of the Paranormal Romance*. Cardiff: University of Wales Press.

Creed, Barbara. 1993. *The Monstrous Feminine*. London: Routledge.

Cross, Julie. 2008. "Frightening and Funny: Humour in Children's Gothic Fiction." In *The Gothic in Children's Literature: Haunting the Borders*, ed. Anna Jackson, Karen Coats, and Roderick McGillis, 57–76. London: Routledge.

Cummins, June. 2008. "Hermione in the Bathroom: The Gothic, Menarche, and Female Development in the Harry Potter Series." In *The Gothic in Children's Literature: Haunting the Borders*, ed. Anna Jackson, Karen Coats, and Roderick McGillis, 177–94. London: Routledge.

Cunningham, Jack. 2017. Personal interview with Julia Round. Conducted by telephone, April 5, 2017.

Daffron, Eric. 1999. "Male Bonding: Sympathy and Shelley's *Frankenstein*." *Nineteenth-Century Contexts* 21 (3): 415–35.

Daly, Mary. 1978. *Gyn/Ecology: The Metaethics of Radical Feminism*. Boston: Beacon Press.

Damon-Moore, Helen. 1994. *Magazines for the Millions: Gender and Commerce in the* Ladies' Home Journal *and the* Saturday Evening Post, *1880–1910*. New York: State University of New York Press.

Davenport-Hines, Richard. 1998. *Gothic: Four Hundred Years of Excess, Horror, Evil and Ruin*. New York: North Point Press.

Davis, James P. 1992. "*Frankenstein* and the Subversion of the Masculine Voice." *Women's Studies* 21 (3): 307–22.

Davison, Carol Margaret. 2004. "Haunted House/Haunted Heroine: Female Gothic Closets in 'The Yellow Wallpaper.'" *Women's Studies* 33:47–75.

Davison, Carol Margaret. 2009. "Monstrous Regiments of Women and Brides of Frankenstein: Gendered Body Politics in Scottish Female Gothic Fiction." In *The Female Gothic: New Directions*, ed. Diana Wallace and Andrew Smith, 196–214. London: Palgrave Macmillan.

DeLamotte, Eugenia. 2004. "'Collusions of the Mystery': Ideology and the Gothic in *Hagar's Daughter*." *Gothic Studies* 6 (1): 69–79.

De Lauretis, Teresa, ed. 1986. *Feminist Studies/Critical Studies*. Bloomington: Indiana University Press.

Dendle, Peter. 2011. "Zombie Movies and the Millennial Generation." In *Better Off Dead: The Evolution of the Zombie as Post-Human*, ed. Deborah Christie and Sarah Juliet Lauro. New York: Fordham University Press.

Diehl, Digby. 1996. *Tales from the Crypt*. New York: St. Martin's Press.

Digby, Anne. 2015. "Pat Davidson Writes to the Blog." *A Resource on Jinty: Artists, Writers, Stories*. https://jintycomic.wordpress.com/2015/12/06/pat-davidson-writes-to-the-blog. Accessed April 20, 2016.

Digby, Anne. 2016. "Pat Davidson Writes." *A Resource on Jinty: Artists, Writers, Stories*. https://jintycomic.wordpress.com/2016/03/15/pat-davidson-writes/comment-page-1/#comment-3352. Accessed April 20, 2016.

Digby, Anne. 2017. Personal correspondence with Julia Round. Conducted by email, August 11, 2017.

Doane, Mary Ann. 1982. "Film and Masquerade: Theorising the Female Spectator." *Screen* 23 (3–4): 74–87.

Doane, Mary Ann. 1987. *The Desire to Desire: The Woman's Film of the 1940s*. Bloomington and Indianapolis: Indiana University Press.

Doane, Mary Ann. 1991. *Femmes Fatales: Feminism, Film Theory, Psychoanalysis*. London: Routledge.

Douglas, Lorraine. 2017. Comment on "Get MISTY Back in Print!" Facebook. https://www.facebook.com/groups/getmisty/permalink/1592651360757228. Accessed October 26, 2017.

Edwards, Justin D. 2013. "The Abyss." In *The Encyclopedia of the Gothic*, ed. William Hughes, David Punter, and Andrew Smith, 4–5. Oxford: Wiley-Blackwell.

Ellis, Brenda. 2016. Personal interview with Julia Round. Conducted in person, August 15, 2016.

Ellis, Kate Ferguson. 1989. *The Contested Castle*. Chicago: University of Illinois Press.

Ellis, Kate Ferguson. 1994. "Ann Radcliffe and the Perils of Catholicism." *Women's Writing* 1 (2): 161–70.

Ellis, Kate Ferguson. 2012. "Can You Forgive Her? The Gothic Heroine and Her Critics." In *A New Companion to the Gothic*, ed. David Punter, 457–68. Oxford: Blackwell.

Enki, Yanki. 2008. "The Modern and the Types of Gothic Ambivalence: The Theory of the Gothic from the Modern to the Postmodern." MA thesis, Istanbul Bilgi University. http://openaccess.bilgi.edu.tr:8080/xmlui/bitstream/handle/11411/607/The%20modern%20and%20the%20types%20of%20gothic%20ambivalence%20The%20theory%20of%20the%20gothic%20from%20the%20modern%20to%20the%20postmodern.pdf?sequence=1. Accessed March 3, 2018.

Farber, Stephen. 1972. "The New American Gothic." In *Focus on the Horror Film*, ed. Roy Huss and Theodore J. Ross, 94–102. Englewood Cliffs, NJ: Prentice Hall. http://www.jstor.org/stable/1211159?seq=1#page_scan_tab_contents. Accessed May 9, 2016.

Farson, Daniel. 1978. *The Hamlyn Book of Ghosts in Fact and Fiction*. London: Hamlyn.

Farson, Daniel. 1979. *The Hamlyn Book of Horror*. London: Hamlyn.

Farson, Daniel. 1984. *The Hamlyn Book of Monsters*. London: Hamlyn.

Fay, Helen. 2016. Comment on "Get MISTY Back in Print!" Facebook. https://www.facebook.com/groups/getmisty/permalink/1203811176307917/?comment_id=1203820119640356&comment_tracking=%7B%22tn%22%3A%22R1%22%7D. Accessed October 18, 2017.

Fay, Helen. 2017. Comment on "Get MISTY Back in Print!" Facebook. https://www.facebook.com/groups/getmisty/permalink/1592651360757228. Accessed October 26, 2017.
Fenwick, L. 1953. "Periodicals and Adolescent Girls." *Studies in Education* 2 (1): 27–45.
Fitzgerald, Lauren. 2004. "Female Gothic and the Institutionalisation of Gothic Studies." *Gothic Studies* 6 (1): 8–18.
Fleenor, Juliann E., ed. 1983. *The Female Gothic*. Montreal: Eden Press.
Frank, Alan. 1974. *Horror Movies*. London: Octopus.
Frank, Alan. 1976. *Monsters and Vampires*. London: Octopus.
Fraser, Josie. 2009. "Interesting 09." Blog post. *Socialtech*, September 14, 2009. http://fraser.typepad.com/socialtech/2009/09. Accessed March 1, 2016.
Freeman, John. n.d. "Let's Here It for the Girls." Mistycomic.co.uk. http://www.mistycomic.co.uk/Lets_Here_It_For_The_Girls.html. Accessed February 3, 2016.
Freeman, John. 2016. "In Memoriam: Illustrator and Comic Artist Shirley Bellwood." *Down the Tubes*. https://downthetubes.net/?p=30937. Accessed February 14, 2018.
Freeman, John. 2017a. "Scream and Misty Reunited for an All-New Hallowe'en Special!" Facebook, July 20, 2017. https://www.facebook.com/groups/getmisty/permalink/1507755889246776. Accessed October 21, 2017.
Freeman, John. 2017b. "Scream Misty for Me—Cover Controversy over New 'Hallowe'en Special' Continues." *Down the Tubes*. http://downthetubes.net/?p=39514. Accessed October 21, 2017.
Freeman, Nick. 2016. "Witchcraft." In *The Encyclopaedia of the Gothic*, ed. William Hughes, David Punter, and Andrew Smith, 745–47. Oxford: Wiley-Blackwell.
Freud, Sigmund. 1919. "The Uncanny." http://web.mit.edu/allanmc/www/freud1.pdf. Accessed January 21, 2016.
Friedan, Betty. 1963. *The Feminine Mystique*. New York: W. W. Norton.
Frye, Northrop. 1957. *Anatomy of Criticism: Four Essays*. Princeton, NJ: Princeton University Press.
Gaiman, Neil. 2002. *Coraline*. London: Bloomsbury.
Gallagher, Stephen. 2000. *Journeyman: The Art of Chris Moore*. London: Paper Tiger.
Gallego, Blas. 2016. Personal correspondence with Julia Round. Conducted by email, July 9, 2016.
Gaunt, Elizabeth. 2017. Personal correspondence with Julia Round. Conducted by email, November 16, 2017.
Georgieva, Margarita. 2013. *The Gothic Child*. London: Palgrave Macmillan.
Germanà, Monica. 2013. *Scottish Women's Gothic and Fantastic Writing*. Edinburgh: Edinburgh University Press.
Gesalí, David. 2017. Personal correspondence with Julia Round. Conducted by email, September–October 2017.
Gibbs, David, ed. 1993. *Nova, 1965–1975*. London: Pavilion.
Gibson, Mel. 2003. "What Became of *Bunty*? The Emergence, Evolution and Disappearance of the Girls' Comic in Post-war Britain." In *Art, Narrative and Childhood*, ed. Morag Styles and Eve Bearne. Stoke on Trent: Trentham Books.
Gibson, Mel. 2008. "Nobody, Somebody, Everybody: Ballet, Girlhood, Class, Femininity and Comics in 1950s Britain." *Girlhood Studies* 2:108–28.
Gibson, Mel. 2010. "What Bunty Did Next: Exploring Some of the Ways in Which the British Girls' Comic Protagonists Were Revisited and Revised in Late Twentieth-Century Comics and Graphic Novels." *Journal of Graphic Novels and Comics* 1 (2): 121–35.
Gibson, Mel. 2015. *Remembered Reading*. Leuven, Belgium: Leuven University Press.
Gifford, Denis. 1976. *A Pictorial History of Horror Movies*. London: Hamlyn.
Gilbert, Sandra M., and Susan Gubar. 1979. *The Madwoman in the Attic: The Woman Writer and the Nineteenth-Century Literary Imagination*. New Haven, CT: Yale University Press.

Gleeson-White, Sarah. 2001. "Revisiting the Southern Grotesque: Mikhail Bakhtin and the Case of Carson McCullers." *Southern Literary Journal* 33 (2): 108–23.

Gooderham, David. 2003. "Fantasizing It as It Is: Religious Language in Philip Pullman's Trilogy, *His Dark Materials*." *Children's Literature* 31:155–75.

Goodman, Sam. 2014. "'This Time It's Personal': Reliving and Rewriting History in 1970s Fiction." In *The 1970s: A Decade of Contemporary British Fiction*, ed. Nick Hubble, John McLeod, and Philip Tew, 117–44. London: Bloomsbury.

Gordon, Ian. 2012. "Writing to Superman: Towards an Understanding of the Social Networks of Comic-Book Fans." *Participations* 9 (2): 120–32. http://www.participations.org/Volume%209/Issue%202/9%20Gordon.pdf. Accessed January 18, 2018.

Gosnell, Kelvin. 2017. Personal interview with Julia Round. Conducted in person, April 26, 2017.

Gravett, Paul. 2008. "Gianni De Luca and *Hamlet*: Thinking outside the Box." *European Comic Art* 1 (1): 21–35. http://www.paulgravett.com/articles/article/gianni_de_luca_hamlet. Accessed February 15, 2018.

Great News for All Readers. 2018. "#OTD 18 February 1978." Facebook, February 18, 2018. https://www.facebook.com/GREATNEWSFORALLREADERS/posts/1616595155100626. Accessed February 27, 2018.

Grenby, Matthew O. 2014. "Gothic and the Child Reader, 1764–1850." In *The Gothic World*, ed. Glennis Byron and Dale Townshend, 243–53. London: Routledge.

Groensteen, Thierry. 2009. *The System of Comics*. Jackson: University Press of Mississippi.

Groensteen, Thierry. 2012. "Definitions." In *The French Comics Theory Reader*, ed. Ann Miller and Bart Beaty, 93–114. Leuven, Belgium: Leuven University Press.

Gross, Louis S. 1989. *Redefining the American Gothic: From* Wieland *to* Day of the Dead. Ann Arbor: UMI Research Press.

Guiral, Antoni. 2010. "Bardon Art: Un adiós silencioso." *Cómic Tecla* 33:1–5. http://www.l-h.cat/gdocs/d7531562.pdf. Accessed August 25, 2017.

Haefele-Thomas, Ardel. 2017. "Queering the Female Gothic." In *Women and the Gothic*, ed. Avril Horner and Sue Zlosnik, 169–83. Edinburgh: Edinburgh University Press.

Hague, Ian. 2014. *Comics and the Senses: A Multisensory Approach to Comics and Graphic Novels*. London: Routledge.

Hajdu, David. 2008. *The Ten-Cent Plague*. New York: Picador.

Halberstam, Judith. 1995. *Skin Shows: Gothic Horror and the Technology of Monsters*. Durham: Duke University Press.

Hand, Richard J. 2012. *Terror on the Air! Horror Radio in America, 1931–1952*. Jefferson, NC: McFarland.

Hatfield, Charles. 2005. *Alternative Comics*. Jackson: University Press of Mississippi.

Heiland, Donna. 2004. *Gothic and Gender*. Oxford: Wiley-Blackwell.

Helsbels. 2009. "IPC Barbie Comics from the 1980s." *Comics UK*. http://www.comicsuk.co.uk/forum/viewtopic.php?f=14&t=3034#p27404. Accessed January 14, 2018.

Hemming, James. 1960. *Problems of Adolescent Girls*. London: Heinemann.

Hendrix, Grady. 2017. *Paperbacks from Hell*. Philadelphia: Quirk Books.

Hermes, Joke. 1995. *Reading Women's Magazines*. Cambridge: Polity Press.

Hermes, Joke. (1998) 2013. "Active Audiences." In *The Media: An Introduction*, ed. Daniele Albertazzim and Paul Cobley. London: Routledge.

Hills, Matt. 2002. *Fan Cultures*. London: Routledge.

Hoad, Phil. 2015. "How We Made 2000AD." *Guardian*, December 8, 2015. https://www.theguardian.com/books/2015/dec/08/how-we-made-2000-ad-judge-dredd-comics-interview. Accessed March 7, 2018.

Hoeveler, Diane Long. 1998. *Gothic Feminism: The Professionalisation of Gender from Charlotte Smith to the Brontës*. Liverpool: Liverpool University Press.
Hoeveler, Diane Long. 2017. "American Female Gothic." In *The Cambridge Companion to American Gothic*, ed. Jeffrey Andrew Weinstock, 99–114. Cambridge: Cambridge University Press.
Hoffmann, Heinrich. (1844) 1848. *Struwwelpeter: Merry Tales and Funny Pictures*. http://www.gutenberg.org/files/12116/12116-h/12116-h.htm. Accessed October 18, 2017.
Hogle, Jerrold E. 1994. "The Ghost of the Counterfeit in the Genesis of the Gothic." In *Gothick Origins and Innovations*, ed. Allan Lloyd Smith and Victor Sage. Amsterdam: Rodopi.
Hogle, Jerrold E. 2002. "Introduction: The Gothic in Western Culture." In *The Cambridge Companion to Gothic Fiction*. Cambridge: Cambridge University Press.
Holland, Steve. 2007. "The Professionals." *Bear Alley*, October 13, 2007. https://bearalley.blogspot.co.uk/2007/10/professionals.html. Accessed August 25, 2017.
Holland, Steve. 2008. "Comic Cuts." *Bear Alley*, June 26, 2008. https://bearalley.blogspot.co.uk/2008/06/comic-cuts_26.html. Accessed August 25, 2017.
Holm, Hans. 2017a. Personal correspondence with Julia Round. Conducted by email, January–April 2017.
Holm, Hans. 2017b. "Serier vi inte minns: Skräckserier för tjejer" [Series we do not remember: Horror series for girls]. Unpublished lecture. Rum för Serier, Malmö, November 8, 2017. http://portal.research.lu.se/portal/en/publications/serier-vi-inte-minns(ea0e946e-5afa-4135-9f12-98aea5842a6c).html. Accessed March 1, 2018.
Holm, Hans. 2018. Personal correspondence with Julia Round. Conducted by email, February 21, 2018.
Horner, Avril. 2010. "Women, Power and Conflict: The Gothic Heroine and "Chocolate-Box Gothic." *Caliban: French Journal of English Studies* 27:319–30.
Horner, Avril, and Sue Zlosnik. 2004. "Skin Chairs and Other Domestic Horrors: Barbara Comyns and the Female Gothic Tradition." *Gothic Studies* 6 (1): 90–102.
Horner, Avril, and Sue Zlosnik. 2005. *Gothic and the Comic Turn*. London: Palgrave Macmillan.
Horner, Avril, and Sue Zlosnik. 2017. "No Country for Old Women: Gender, Age and the Gothic." In *Women and the Gothic*, ed. Avril Horner and Sue Zlosnik, 184–98. Edinburgh: Edinburgh University Press.
Horner, Avril, and Sue, Zlosnik, eds. 2017. *Women and the Gothic*. Edinburgh: Edinburgh University Press.
Howard, Jacqueline. 1994. *Reading Gothic Fiction: A Bakhtinian Approach*. Oxford: Clarendon Press.
Hubble, Nick, John McLeod, and Philip Tew, eds. 2014. *The 1970s: A Decade of Contemporary British Fiction*. London: Bloomsbury.
Hubner, Laura, Marcus Leaning, and Paul Manning, eds. 2015. *The Zombie Renaissance*. London: Palgrave Macmillan.
Hughes, William, David Punter, and Andrew Smith, eds. 2013. *The Encyclopedia of the Gothic*. Oxford: Wiley-Blackwell.
Hume, Robert. 1969. "Gothic versus Romantic: A Revaluation of the Gothic Novel." *PMLA* 84 (2): 282–90.
Hunt, Leon. 1998. *British Low Culture: From Safari Suits to Sexploitation*. London: Routledge.
Hunt, Peter. 1991. *Criticism, Theory and Children's Literature*. Oxford: Blackwell.
Hunt, Peter. 1994. *An Introduction to Children's Literature*. Oxford: Oxford University Press.
Hunt, Peter, ed. 1999. *Understanding Children's Literature*. Abingdon: Taylor and Francis.
Hutchings, Peter. 1993. *Hammer and Beyond: The British Horror Film*. New York: Manchester University Press.
Ingram, Tony. 2008. "Supercats and Orphan Brats—DCT's Spellbinding Girls' Comic." *Crikey!—The Great British Comics Magazine!* 6:4–7.

IPC. 1977. *IPC Magazines Bulletin*, no. 427 (August 9, 1977). Copy provided by Wilf Prigmore.

IPC. 1979. *International Publishing Corporation Directory of Publications and Services*. April 1979. Copy provided by Wilf Prigmore.

Irigaray, Luce. 1985. *This Sex Which Is Not One*. Trans. Catherine Porter and Carolyn Burke. Ithaca, NY: Cornell University Press.

Irigaray, Luce. 1987. *Sexes and Genealogies*. Trans. Gillian C. Gill. New York: Columbia University Press.

Jachimiak, Peter Hughes. 2014. *Remembering the Cultural Geographies of a Childhood Home*. London: Routledge.

Jackson, Anna. 2008. "Uncanny Hauntings, Canny Children." In *The Gothic in Children's Literature: Haunting the Borders*, ed. Anna Jackson, Karen Coats, and Roderick McGillis, 157–76. London: Routledge.

Jackson, Anna, ed. 2017. *New Directions in Children's Gothic: Debatable Lands*. London: Routledge.

Jackson, Anna. 2017. "New Directions in Children's Gothic: Debatable Lands." In *New Directions in Children's Gothic: Debatable Lands*, ed. Anna Jackson, 1–15. London: Routledge.

Jackson, Anna, Karen Coats, and Roderick McGillis, eds. 2008. *The Gothic in Children's Literature: Haunting the Borders*. Oxford: Taylor and Francis.

Jackson, Rosemary. 1981. *Fantasy: The Literature of Subversion*. London: Routledge.

Jacobs, Jason. 2000. *The Intimate Screen: Early British Television Drama*. Oxford: Oxford University Press.

James, Kathryn. 2009. *Death, Gender and Sexuality in Contemporary Adolescent Literature*. New York: Routledge.

Jameson, Fredric. 2000. *Postmodernism, or The Cultural Logic of Late Capitalism*. Durham, NC: Duke University Press.

Jenkinson, Augustus John. 1940. *What Do Boys and Girls Read? An Investigation into Reading Habits with Some Suggestions about the Teaching of Literature in Secondary and Senior Schools*. London: Methuen.

Jephcott, Pearl. 1942. *Girls Growing Up*. London: Faber and Faber.

Jephcott, Pearl. 1948. *Rising Twenty: Notes on Some Ordinary Girls*. London: Faber.

Jones, Timothy. 2009. "The Canniness of the Gothic: Genre as Practice." *Gothic Studies* 11 (1): 124–34.

Jones, Timothy Graham Stanford. 2010. "The Gothic as Practice: Gothic Studies, Genre and the Twentieth-Century Gothic." PhD thesis. Wellington: Victoria University of Wellington. http://researcharchive.vuw.ac.nz/xmlui/bitstream/handle/10063/1357/thesis.pdf?sequence=2. Accessed April 19, 2018.

Jones, Timothy. 2015. *Gothic and the Carnivalesque*. Cardiff: University of Wales Press.

Joshi, S. T. 2001. *The Modern Weird Tale*. Jefferson, NC: McFarland.

Joshi, S. T. 2004. *The Evolution of the Weird Tale*. New York: Hippocampus Press.

Kaplan, Deborah. 1983. "Proper Ladies and Heroines." *Novel: A Forum on Fiction* 17 (1): 81–84.

Kayser, Wolfgang. (1957) 1981. *The Grotesque in Art and Literature*. Trans. Ulrich Weisstein. New York: Columbia University Press.

Khair, Tabish. 2014. "Gothic Remains in South Asian English Fiction." In *The Gothic and the Everyday*, ed. Lorna Piatti-Farnell and Maria Beville, 215–24. Houndmills: Palgrave Macmillan.

Khan, Omar. 2017. "Who Runs the World? Forbidden Planet's Omar Khan Talks *Doctor Who*'s New Casting." *Licensing.biz*, August 3, 2017. http://www.licensing.biz/opinion/read/who-runs-the-world-forbidden-planet-s-omar-khan-talks-doctor-who-s-new-casting/046348. Accessed October 14, 2017.

Kilgour, Maggie. 1995. *The Rise of the Gothic Novel*. New York: Routledge.

Kilpeckhall. 2016. Comment on "About" page. *A Resource on Jinty: Artists, Writers, Stories*, August 23, 2016. https://jintycomic.wordpress.com/about/#comment-2177. Accessed September 12, 2016.

King, Stephen. 1981. *Danse Macabre*. New York: Berkley Publishing.
Klaehn, Jeffrey, ed. 2007. *Inside the World of Comic Books*. Montreal: Black Rose Books.
Kristeva, Julia. 1982. *Powers of Horror*. New York: Columbia University Press.
Lacan, Jacques. 1982. *Feminine Sexuality: Jacques Lacan and the "Ecole Freudienne."* Ed. Juliet Mitchell and Jacqueline Rose. Trans. Jacqueline Rose. New York: W. W. Norton.
Laing, R. D. 1960. *The Divided Self: An Existential Study in Sanity and Madness*. Harmondsworth: Penguin.
Laycock, Joseph. 2009. *Vampires Today: The Truth about Modern Vampirism*. Westport, CT: Praeger.
Lecigne, Bruno. 1982. "Une esthétique de la jouissance." *Les Cahiers de la Bande Dessinée* 52. Special issue on Guido Crepax. Grenoble: Glénat, 1st quarter, 1982.
Ledoux, Ellen. 2017. "Was There Ever a 'Female Gothic'?" *Palgrave Communications* 3, article no. 17042. doi:10.1057/palcomms.2017.42. Open access, https://www.nature.com/articles/palcomms201742. Accessed December 17, 2017.
Ledwon, Lenora. 1993. "*Twin Peaks* and the Television Gothic." *Literature/Film Quarterly* 21 (4): 260–70.
Lesnik-Oberstein, Karín. 1994. *Children's Literature: Criticism and the Fictional Child*. Oxford: Clarendon Press.
Lesnik-Oberstein, Karín. 2000. "The Psychopathology of Everyday Children's Literature Criticism." *Cultural Critique* 45:222–42.
Lesnik-Oberstein, Karín, ed. 2004. *Children's Literature: New Approaches*. New York: Palgrave Macmillan.
Lévi-Strauss, Claude. 1984. "Structure and Form: Reflections on a Work by Vladimir Propp." Trans. Monique Layton. In *Theory and History of Folklore*, by Vladimir Propp, ed. Anatoly Liberman, 167–88. Minneapolis: University of Minnesota Press.
Lillyman, Chris. 2002. "*Misty*: The Publication." Mistycomic.co.uk. http://mistycomic.co.uk/Misty.html. Accessed October 1, 2017.
Lillyman, Chris. 2007. "Welcome." Mistycomic.co.uk. http://mistycomic.co.uk/Welcome.html. Accessed October 24, 2017.
Lillyman, Chris. 2009. "Interview with John Armstrong." In *Mistycomic.co.uk Special*. Nottingham: Consumable Café Limited.
Lillyman, Chris. 2016. Personal interview with Julia Round. Conducted by Skype, September 15, 2016.
Lippe, Anya Heise-von der. 2009. "Others, Monsters, Ghosts: Representations of the Female Gothic Body in Toni Morrison's *Beloved* and *Love*." In *The Female Gothic: New Directions*, ed. Diana Wallace and Andrew Smith, 166–79. London: Palgrave Macmillan.
The Literary Panorama, and National Register. 1818. "Review of Frankenstein." *Literary Panorama, and National Register*, n.s., 8 (June 1, 1818): 411–14. Republished at the website *Romantic Circles*. https://www.rc.umd.edu/reference/chronologies/mschronology/reviews/lprev.html. Accessed February 27, 2018.
Lloyd, Chris. 2018. Personal interview with Julia Round. Conducted by telephone, June 14, 2018.
Locke, John. (1693) 1989. *Some Thoughts concerning Education*. Ed. J. W. Yolton and J. S. Yolton. Oxford: Clarendon.
Lofts, William O. G. 1978. "Why Did Men Write for Girls?" *Collectors Digest Annual*, Christmas 1978, 61–63. http://www.friardale.co.uk/Collectors%20Digest/1978-Xmas-CollectorsDigest-ChristmasAnnual-32.pdf. Accessed January 18, 2018.
London, Bette. 1993. "Mary Shelley, *Frankenstein*, and the Spectacle of Masculinity." *PMLA* 108 (2): 253–67.
Loo, Oliver. 2014. Introduction to *The Original 1812 Grimm Fairy Tales*. Raleigh, NC: Lulu.com.

Lorrsadmin. 2014. "Nothing Ever Goes Right!" *Girls Comics of Yesterday: All about Girls Comics*, July 28, 2014. http://girlscomicsofyesterday.com/2014/07/nothing-ever-goes-right. Accessed August 18, 2017.

Lovecraft, H. P. 1927. "Supernatural Horror in Literature." The H. P. Lovecraft Archive. http://www.hplovecraft.com/writings/texts/essays/shil.aspx. Accessed March 3, 2017.

Lüthi, Max. 1986. *The European Folktale: Form and Nature*. Trans. John D. Niles. Bloomington: Indiana University Press.

Magee, Terence. 2014. "Terence Magee: Interview." *A Resource on Jinty: Artists, Writers, Stories*, May 13, 2014. https://jintycomic.wordpress.com/2014/05/13/terence-magee-interview. Accessed September 20, 2017.

Magee, Terence. 2017. Personal correspondence with Julia Round. Conducted by email, April 2017.

Mains, Johnny. 2017. Introduction to *Scarred for Life Volume One: The 1970s*, by Stephen Brotherstone and Dave Lawrence, 8–9. Lonely Water Books.

Maple, Eric, Lynn Myring, and Eliot Humberstone. 1977. *The Usborne Guide to the Supernatural World*. London: Usborne.

Marriott, James, and Kim Newman. 2006. *Horror. The Definitive Guide to the Cinema of Fear*. London: André Deutsch.

Marsh, Ian, and Gaynor Melville. 2011. "Moral Panics and the British Media: A Look at Some Contemporary 'Folk Devils.'" *Internet Journal of Criminology*. http://www.internetjournalofcriminology.com/marsh_melville_moral_panics_and_the_british_media_march_2011.pdf. Accessed May 9, 2016.

Martín, Antonio. 2000. *Apuntes para uni historia de los tebeos* [Notes for a history of the comics]. Barcelona: Glénat. Originally published in 1967–68 as a series of four articles in *Revista de Educación*. Madrid: El Ministerio de Educación, Cultura y Deporte de España.

Martin, Robert K., and Eric Savoy. 2008. *American Gothic: New Interventions in a National Narrative*. Iowa City: University of Iowa Press.

Martin, Sara. 2002. "Gothic Scholars Don't Wear Black: Gothic Studies and Gothic Subcultures." *Gothic Studies* 4 (1): 28–43.

Marwick, Arthur. 1982. *British Society since 1945*. Harmondsworth: Penguin.

Masschelein, Anneleen. 2013. "The Uncanny." In *The Encyclopedia of the Gothic*, ed. William Hughes, David Punter, and Andrew Smith, 699–702. Oxford: Wiley-Blackwell.

McDonald, David. 2016. *It's Ghastly! The Untimely Demise of Scream!* Castlebar, County Mayo, Ireland: David McDonald T/A Hibernia.

McDonald, David. 2018. "When Comics Ruled the Earth: An Interview with Gil Page." In *The Fleetway Files*, by David McDonald, 10–15. Castlebar, County Mayo, Ireland: David McDonald T/A Hibernia.

McGavran, James Holt. 2000. "'Insurmountable Barriers to Our Union': Homosocial Male Bonding, Homosexual Panic, and Death on the Ice in *Frankenstein*." *European Romantic Review* 11 (1): 46–67.

McGillis, Roderick. 2008. "The Night Side of Nature: Gothic Spaces, Fearful Times." In *The Gothic in Children's Literature: Haunting the Borders*, ed. Anna Jackson, Karen Coats, and Roderick McGillis, 227–42. London: Routledge.

McGlade, Rhiannon. 2016. *Catalan Cartoons: A Cultural and Political History*. Cardiff: University of Wales Press.

McGrath, Patrick. 1997. "Transgression and Decay." In *Gothic: Transmutations of Horror in Late Twentieth-Century Art*, ed. Christoph Grunenberg, 153–58. Cambridge, MA: MIT Press.

McIntyre, Clara F. 1921. "Were the 'Gothic Novels' Gothic?" *PMLA* 36:652–64.

McMillan, G. 2017. "'2000AD' Publishers Reviving 2 Classic British Horror Comics This Halloween." *Hollywood Reporter*, August 2, 2017. http://www.hollywoodreporter.com/

heat-vision/2000-ad-publishers-revive-two-classic-british-horror-comics-halloween-1025958. Accessed August 9, 2017.

McRobbie, Angela. 1978a. "*Jackie*: An Ideology of Adolescent Femininity." Occasional paper. Centre for Cultural Studies. University of Birmingham.

McRobbie, Angela. 1978b. "Working Class Girls and the Culture of Femininity." In *Women Take Issue: Aspects of Women's Subordination*, ed. Women's Studies Group, Centre for Contemporary Cultural Studies, 96–108. London: Hutchinson.

McRobbie, Angela. (1981) 2013. "Just like a *Jackie* Story." In *Feminism for Girls: An Adventure Story*, ed. Angela McRobbie and Trisha McCabe, 113–28. London: Routledge.

McRobbie, Angela. 1991. *Feminism and Youth Culture: From Jackie to Just Seventeen*, London: Macmillan.

Méon, Jean-Matthieu. 2016. Personal correspondence with Julia Round. Conducted by email, October 25, 2016.

Meyers, Helene. 2001. *Femicidal Fears: Narratives of the Female Gothic Experience*. Albany: State University of New York Press.

Mighall, Robert. 1999. *A Geography of Victorian Gothic Fiction: Mapping History's Nightmares*. Oxford: Oxford University Press.

Milbank, Alison. 1994. "Milton, Melancholy and the Sublime in the 'Female' Gothic from Radcliffe to Le Fanu." *Women's Writing* 1 (2): 143–60.

Milbank, Alison. 2009. "Bleeding Nuns: A Genealogy of the Female Gothic Grotesque." In *The Female Gothic: New Directions*, ed. Diana Wallace and Andrew Smith, 76–97. London: Palgrave Macmillan.

Miles, Robert. 1994. "Introduction." *Women's Writing* 1 (2): 131–42.

Miles, Robert. 1995. *Ann Radcliffe: The Great Enchantress*. Manchester: Manchester University Press.

Miles, Robert. 2002. *Gothic Writing, 1750–1820: A Genealogy*. 2nd ed. Manchester: Manchester University Press.

Miles, Robert. 2009. "'Mother Radcliff': Ann Radcliffe and the Female Gothic." In *The Female Gothic: New Directions*, ed. Diana Wallace and Andrew Smith, 42–59. London: Palgrave Macmillan.

Miller, Rhoda. 2017a. "Rhoda Miller—Interview." *A Resource on Jinty: Artists, Writers, Stories*, February 3, 2017. https://jintycomic.wordpress.com/2017/02/03/rhoda-miller-interview. Accessed October 21, 2017.

Miller, Rhoda. 2017b. "Women in Comics Roundtable." Remarks made at the Dundee Literary Festival, October 18, 2017. Dundee University, UK.

Mills, Pat. 2011. "Interview with Jenni Scott." *FA - The Comiczine*. http://comiczine-fa.com/interviews/pat-mills. Accessed October 26, 2017.

Mills, Pat. 2012. Misty: The Female *2000AD*. Blog post, *Pat Mills*. https://patmills.wordpress.com/2016/09/06/misty-lives. Accessed July 7, 2014.

Mills, Pat. 2014a. "THE FORMULA Part 1—Inspiration." Blog post. *Millsverse*, October 20, 2014. https://www.millsverse.com/formula1-inspiration. Accessed February 29, 2016.

Mills, Pat. 2014b. "THE FORMULA Part 4—Steps and Straw Polls." Blog post. *Millsverse*, October 30, 2014. https://www.millsverse.com/home-welcome-to-the-millsverse-home-of-pat-mills-45. Accessed April 10, 2018.

Mills, Pat. 2015. Personal correspondence with Julia Round. Conducted by email, September 11, 2015.

Mills, Pat. 2016a. Personal interview with Julia Round. Conducted by Skype, July 28, 2016. https://www.juliaround.com.

Mills, Pat. 2016b. "Misty Lives!" https://patmills.wordpress.com/2016/09/06/misty-lives. Accessed October 28, 2017.

Mills, Pat. 2017a. *Be Pure! Be Vigilant! Behave!* Estepona: Millsverse Books.

Mills, Pat. 2017b. Personal correspondence with Julia Round. Conducted by email, August 16, 2017.

Mills, Pat. 2017c. Personal correspondence with Julia Round. Conducted by email, October 3, 2017.

Mills, Pat. 2017d. Personal correspondence with Julia Round. Conducted by email, October 4, 2017.

Mills, Pat. 2017e. Personal correspondence with Julia Round. Conducted by email, November 3, 2017.

Mills, Pat, Malcolm Shaw, John Armstrong, Brian Delaney, and Shirley Bellwood. 2016. *Misty Volume One*. Oxford: Rebellion Publishing.

Mills, Pat, Malcolm Shaw, Juan Ariza, María Barrera Castell, Mario Capaldi, and Brian Delaney. 2018. *Anthologie Misty*. Trans. Jean-Paul Jennequin and François Peneaud. Selected by Laurent Lerner. Nogent-sur-Marne: Delirium.

Millsverse. 2017. Social media post. Facebook, August 6, 2017. https://www.facebook.com/millsverse/photos/a.343918609148444.1073741828.342276845979287/766550923551875/?type=3. Accessed October 21, 2017.

Misty. #1–101. London: IPC.

Mistyfan. 2014a. "Gypsy Rose's Tales of Mystery and Magic." *A Resource on Jinty: Artists, Writers, Stories*, April 20, 2014. https://jintycomic.wordpress.com/2014/04/20/gypsy-roses-tales-of-mystery-and-magic. Accessed June 3, 2016.

Mistyfan. 2014b. "The Slave Story Theme." *A Resource on Jinty: Artists, Writers, Stories*, August 31, 2014. https://jintycomic.wordpress.com/2014/08/31/the-slave-story-theme. Accessed August 11, 2017.

Modleski, Tania. (1982) 1990. *Loving with a Vengeance: Mass-Produced Fantasies for Women*. New York: Routledge.

Moers, Ellen. (1976) 1978. *Literary Women: The Great Writers*. London: Women's Press.

Moloney, David. 2016. Social media post. Facebook, January 19, 2016. https://www.facebook.com/groups/getmisty/permalink/1054816821207354. Accessed October 24, 2017.

Moloney, David. 2017. Personal correspondence with Julia Round. Conducted by Facebook Messenger and email, October 24, 2017.

Monés Pons, Isidre. 2014. "Drawings Bizarres 2." *Isidre Monés*, October 16, 2014. http://isidremonesart.blogspot.co.uk/2014/10/drawings-bizarres.html. Accessed March 8, 2018.

Monés Pons, Isidre. 2018. Personal correspondence with Julia Round. Conducted by Facebook Messenger and email, March–August 2018.

Morgan, Robin. 1970. *Sisterhood Is Powerful: An Anthology of Writings from the Women's Liberation Movement*. New York: Random House.

Mulvey-Roberts, Marie. 2009. "From Bluebeard's Bloody Chamber to Demonic Stigmatic." In *The Female Gothic: New Directions*, ed. Diana Wallace and Andrew Smith, 98–114. London: Palgrave Macmillan.

Munford, Rebecca. 2013. "Family." In *The Encyclopedia of the Gothic*, ed. William Hughes, David Punter, and Andrew Smith, 225–27. Oxford: Wiley-Blackwell.

Murray, Chris. 2017. *The British Superhero*. Jackson: University Press of Mississippi.

Nairn, Tom. 1977. *The Break-Up of Britain: Crisis and Neonationalism*. London: NLB.

Novak, Maximillian E. 1979. "Gothic Fiction and the Grotesque." *Novel: A Forum on Fiction* 13 (1): 50–67.

Nyberg, Amy Kiste. 1998. *Seal of Approval*. Jackson: University Press of Mississippi.

O'Brien, Brad. 2008. "Vita, Amore, e Morte—and Lots of Gore: The Italian Zombie Film." In *Zombie Culture: Autopsies of the Living Dead*, ed. Shawn McIntosh and Marc Leverette, 55–70. Lanham, MD: Scarecrow Press.

Olson, Danel. 2011. "The Longest Gothic Goodbye in the World: Lemony Snicket's *A Series of Unfortunate Events*." In *20th Century Gothic: Great Gothic Novels since 2000*, ed. Danel Olson, 506–26. Lanham, MD: Scarecrow Press.

Olson, Danel, ed. 2011. *20th Century Gothic: Great Gothic Novels since 2000*. Lanham, MD: Scarecrow Press. 506–26.

Orenstein, Peggy. 2011. *Cinderella Ate My Daughter*. New York: HarperCollins.

Ormrod, Joan. 2011. "Pa/trolling the Borders of the Federal Vampire and Zombie Agency Website." In *Fanpires: Audience Consumption of the Modern Vampire*, ed. Gareth Schott and Kirstine Moffat, 33–54. Washington, DC: New Academia Publishing.

O'Shea, Keri. 2015a. "Childhood Terrors—'Sugar and Spice and All Things Nice': Misty Comics and Horror for Girls (Part 1 of 2)." *Warped Perspective*. http://warped-perspective.com/index.php/2015/01/23/sugar-and-spice-and-all-things-nice-misty-comics-and-horror-for-girls-part-1-of-2. Accessed February 29, 2016.

O'Shea, Keri. 2015b. "Childhood Terrors—'Sugar and Spice and All Things Nice': Misty Comics and Horror for Girls (Part 2 of 2)." *Warped Perspective*. http://warped-perspective.com/index.php/2015/01/25/sugar-and-spice-and-all-things-nice-misty-comics-and-horror-for-girls-part-2-of-2. Accessed February 29, 2016.

Otto, Peter. 2013. "Gothic Echoes / Gothic Labyrinths," sec. 9 of "Introduction." Gothic Fiction: Rare Printed Works from the Sadleir-Black Collection of Gothic Fiction at the Alderman Library, University of Virginia. http://www.ampltd.co.uk/digital_guides/gothic_fiction/introduction9.aspx. Accessed April 18, 2013.

Paddon, Lee. 1987. "Drawing on Inspiration." *Crash Online*, no. 37. http://www.crashonline.org.uk/37/richrdsn.htm. Accessed August 25, 2017.

Palmer, Paulina. 2004. "Lesbian Gothic: Genre, Transformation, Transgression." *Gothic Studies* 6 (1): 118–30.

Payne, Winn. 2016. Comment on "Get MISTY Back in Print!" Facebook, January 19, 2016. https://www.facebook.com/groups/getmisty/permalink/1054816821207354/. Accessed June 2, 2019.

Peeters, Benoît. 1991. *Case, planche, récit* [Panel, page, story]. Tournai, Belgium: Casterman.

Peirse, A. 2010. "A Broken Tradition: British Telefantasy and Children's Television in the 1980s and 1990s." *Visual Culture in Britain* 11 (1): 109–24.

Pepetone, Gregory. 2012. *Hogwarts and All: Gothic Perspectives on Children's Literature*. Oxford: Peter Lang.

Pfifer, Lynn. 2011. "Slacker Bites Back: *Shaun of the Dead* Finds New Life for Deadbeats." In *Better Off Dead: The Evolution of the Zombie as Post-Human*, ed. Deborah Christie and Sarah Juliet Lauro, 163–74. New York: Fordham University Press.

Piatti-Farnell, Lorna, and Maria Beville. 2014. "Introduction: Living Gothic." In *The Gothic and the Everyday*, ed. Lorna Piatti-Farnell and Maria Beville, 1–14. Houndmills: Palgrave Macmillan.

Piatti-Farnell, Lorna, and Maria Beville, eds. 2014. *The Gothic and the Everyday*. Houndmills: Palgrave Macmillan.

Pirie, David. 1973. *A Heritage of Horror: The English Gothic Cinema, 1946–1972*. London: Gordon Fraser.

Pizzino, Christopher. 2016. *Arresting Development*. Austin: University of Texas Press.

Pope, James, and Julia Round. 2014. "Children's Responses to Heroines in Roald Dahl's *Matilda*." *Children's Literature in Education* 46 (3): 257–77.

Priest, Hannah. 2011. "What's Wrong with Sparkly Vampires?" *The Gothic Imagination*, July 20, 2011. http://www.gothic.stir.ac.uk/guestblog/whats-wrong-with-sparkly-vampires. Accessed February 27, 2018.

Prigmore, Wilf. 2016a. Personal interview with Julia Round. Conducted by telephone, November 3, 2016. https://www.juliaround.com.

Prigmore, Wilf. 2016b. Personal correspondence with Julia Round. Conducted by email, November 22, 2016.

Prigmore, Wilf. 2017a. Personal correspondence with Julia Round. Conducted by email, March 23, 2017.

Prigmore, Wilf. 2017b. Personal interview with Julia Round. Conducted in person, British Library, London, October 25, 2017.

Prigmore, Wilf. 2017c. Personal correspondence with Julia Round. Conducted by email, October 26, 2017.

Prigmore, Wilf. 2018a. Personal correspondence with Julia Round. Conducted by email, February 25, 2018.

Prigmore, Wilf. 2018b. Personal correspondence with Julia Round. Conducted by email, February 28, 2018.

Prigmore, Wilf. 2018c. Personal correspondence with Julia Round. Conducted by email, March 9, 2018.

Proctor, William. 2016. "A New Breed of Fan? Regimes of Truth, One Direction Fans, and Representations of Enfreakment." In *Seeing Fans: Representations of Fandom in Media and Popular Culture*, ed. Lucy Bennett and Paul Booth, 67–78. London: Bloomsbury.

Propp, Vladimir. (1928) 1968. *Morphology of the Folktale*. 2nd ed. Austin: University of Texas Press.

Punchard, Grant. 2016. Personal correspondence with Julia Round. Conducted by email, October 2016.

Punter, David. 1980. *The Literature of Terror*. Oxford: Blackwell.

Punter, David. 1994. "Death, Femininity and Identification: A Recourse to *Ligeia*." *Women's Writing* 1 (2): 215–28.

Punter, David. 1998. *Gothic Pathologies: The Text, the Body and the Law*. Houndmills: Macmillan.

Punter, David. 2013a. "Theory." In *The Encyclopedia of the Gothic*, ed. William Hughes, David Punter, and Andrew Smith, 686–93. Oxford: Wiley-Blackwell.

Punter, David. 2013b. "Gothic Poetry, 1700–1900." In *The Gothic World*, ed. Glennis Byron and Dale Townshend, 210–20. London: Routledge.

Punter, David. 2017. "Figuring the Witch." In *New Directions in Children's Gothic: Debatable Lands*, ed. Anna Jackson, 67–80. London: Routledge.

Pustz, Matthew. 2007. "'Let's Rap with Cap': Fan Interaction in Comic Book Letters." In *Inside the World of Comic Books*, ed. Jeffrey Klaehn, 163–84. Montreal: Black Rose Books.

Radcliffe, Ann. 1826. "On the Supernatural in Poetry." *New Monthly Magazine and Literary Journal* 16 (1): 145–52. http://academic.brooklyn.cuny.edu/english/melani/gothic/radcliffe1.html. Accessed October 16, 2016.

Rank, Otto. 1971. *The Double: A Psychoanalytic Study* [*Der Doppelganger*, 1914, revised 1925]. Chapel Hill: University of North Carolina Press.

Rayner, Jacqueline. 2012. "Jinty, Tammy, Misty and the Golden Age of Girls' Comics." *Guardian*, August 18, 2012. https://www.theguardian.com/books/2012/aug/18/jinty-misty-girls-comics-dandy. Accessed May 17, 2017.

Rayner, Jacqueline. 2014. "Paper Worlds: Why Girls' Comics Were Wonderful." *BBC*. http://www.bbc.co.uk/cult/comics/features/girls_comics.shtml. Accessed October 21, 2017.

Reynolds, Kimberley, Geraldine Brennan, and Kevin McCarron. 2001. *Frightening Fiction*. London: Continuum.

Richardson, John, Carlos Guirado, and Jesus Redondo, eds. 2012. *Misty 1: Tales from the Mist*. Amazon Kindle e-book.

Richardson, Keith. 2018. Social media post. Facebook, October 1, 2018. https://www.facebook.com/groups/getmisty/permalink/1987456864610007. Accessed October 24, 2018.

Rivière, Joan. (1929) 1991. "Womanliness as a Masquerade." In *Joan Rivière: Collected Papers, 1920–1958*. London: Karnac Books.

Roach, David. 2013. "The Spanish Invasion." *Comic Book Artist*, no. 4, 64–65. https://issuu.com/twomorrows/docs/cba4preview/17. Accessed October 4, 2017.

Roach, David. 2016. Personal interview with Julia Round. Conducted in person, September 20, 2016.
Roach, David. 2017. *Masters of Spanish Comic Book Art*. Mount Laurel, NJ: Dynamite.
Roche, David. 2014. *Making and Remaking Horror in the 1970s and 2000s: Why Don't They Do It Like They Used To?* Jackson: University Press of Mississippi.
Rodgers, Beth. 2012. "Competing Girlhoods: Competition, Community, and Reader Contribution in *The Girl's Own Paper* and *The Girl's Realm*." *Victorian Periodicals Review* 45 (3): 277–300.
Róheim, Géza. 1992. *Fire in the Dragon and Other Psychoanalytic Essays on Folklore*. Ed. Alan Dundes. Princeton, NJ: Princeton University Press.
Röhrich, Lutz. 1991. *Folktales and Reality*. Trans. Peter Tokofsky. Bloomington: Indiana University Press.
Roper, Lyndal. 2012. *The Witch in the Western Imagination*. Charlottesville: University of Virginia Press.
Rousseau, Jean-Jacques. (1762) 1979. *Emile, or On Education*. Trans. A. Bloom. London: Penguin.
Round, Julia. 2013. "Apocatastasis: Redefining Tropes of the Apocalypse in Neil Gaiman and Dave McKean's *Signal to Noise*." *International Journal of Comic Art* 15 (2): 453–64.
Round, Julia. 2014a. *Gothic in Comics and Graphic Novels: A Critical Approach*. Jefferson, NC: McFarland.
Round, Julia. 2014b. "We Share Our Mother's Health." In *Comic Book Geographies*, ed. Jason Dittmer, 127–40. Stuttgart: Franz Steiner.
Round, Julia. 2015. "Revenant Landscapes in *The Walking Dead*." *International Journal of Comic Art* 17 (2): 295–308.
Round, Julia. 2017. "*Misty, Spellbound* and the Lost Gothic of British Girls' Comics." *Palgrave Communications* 3, article no. 17037 (2017). doi:10.1057/palcomms.2017.37. Open access, https://www.nature.com/articles/palcomms201737. Accessed November 14, 2017.
Round, Julia. 2019. "Comics and Gothic: From *A Haunt of Fears* to a Haunted Medium." In *Gothic and the Arts*, ed. David Punter. Edinburgh: Edinburgh University Press.
Rubenstein, Marc A. 1976. "'My Accursed Origin': The Search for the Mother in *Frankenstein*." *Studies in Romanticism* 15 (2): 165–94.
Rudd, David. 1992. *A Communication Studies Approach to Children's Literature*. Sheffield: Pavic/Sheffield Hallam University Press.
Rudd, David. 2008. "An Eye for an I: Neil Gaiman's *Coraline* and Questions of Identity." *Children's Literature in Education* 39 (3): 159–68.
Ruskin, John. 1851–53. *The Stones of Venice* I–III. London: J. M. Dent and Sons.
Russell, Jamie. 2005. *Book of the Dead: The Complete History of Zombie Movies; The Complete History of Zombie Cinema*. Godalming: FAB Press.
Russo, Mary. 1986. "Female Grotesques: Carnival and Theory." In *Feminist Studies/Critical Studies*, ed. Teresa de Lauretis, 213–29. Bloomington: Indiana University Press.
Russo, Mary. 1994. *The Female Grotesque*. London: Routledge.
RuthB. 2010. "Douglas Perry (Girls' Comics 1970s–1990s?)." *Comics UK*. http://comicsuk.co.uk/forum/viewtopic.php?f=127&t=3770&start=15. Accessed August 1, 2016.
Sabin, Roger. 1996. *Comics, Comix and Graphic Novels*. London: Phaidon Press.
Sadenwasser, Tim. 2014. *The Gothic Fairy Tale in Young Adult Literature*. Ed. Joseph Abbruscato and Tanya Jones. Jefferson, NC: McFarland.
Sage, Victor. 1988. *Horror Fiction in the Protestant Tradition*. New York: St. Martin's Press.
Sanders, John. 2018a. Personal correspondence with Julia Round. Conducted by email, June 27, 2018.
Sanders, John. 2018b. Personal correspondence with Julia Round. Conducted by email, July 2, 2018.
Sanders, John. 2019. Personal correspondence with Julia Round. Conducted by email, March 25, 2019.

Sanjek, David. 1994. "Twilight of the Monsters: The English Horror Film, 1968–1975." In *Reviewing British Cinema, 1900–1992*, ed. Wheeler Winston Dixon. Albany: State University of New York Press.

Sarland, Charles. 1991. *Young People Reading: Culture and Response*. Milton Keynes: Open University Press.

Schott, Gareth, and Kirstine Moffat, eds. 2011. *Fanpires: Audience Consumption of the Modern Vampire*. Washington DC: New Academic Publishing.

Schrøder, Kim Christian. 2000. "Making Sense of Audience Discourses: Towards a Multidimensional Model of Mass Media Reception." *European Journal of Cultural Studies* 3 (2): 233–58.

Scott, Jenni. 2014a. "Jinty 16 December 1978." *A Resource on Jinty: Artists, Writers, Stories*. https://jintycomic.wordpress.com/2014/06/11/jinty-16-september-1978. Accessed April 21, 2018.

Scott, Jenni. 2014b. "Jinty and Lindy 25 December 1976." *A Resource on Jinty: Artists, Writers, Stories*. https://jintycomic.wordpress.com/2014/07/11/jinty-and-lindy-25-december-1976. Accessed April 21, 2018.

Scott, Jenni. 2015a. "IPC/Fleetway and the NUJ: Interview with Pete Wrobel." *A Resource on Jinty: Artists, Writers, Stories*. https://jintycomic.wordpress.com/2015/09/01/ipcfleetway-and-the-nuj-interview-with-pete-wrobel. Accessed March 1, 2016.

Scott, Jenni. 2015b. "Female Writers in a Girls' Genre." *A Resource on Jinty: Artists, Writers, Stories*. https://jintycomic.wordpress.com/2015/02/28/female-writers-in-a-girls-genre. Accessed September 12, 2016.

Scott, Jenni. 2016a. "Douglas Perry." *A Resource on Jinty: Artists, Writers, Stories*. https://jintycomic.wordpress.com/2016/02/15/douglas-perry. Accessed August 25, 2017.

Scott, Jenni. 2016b. "Last *Tammy* Ever Published: 23 June 1984." *A Resource on Jinty: Artists, Writers, Stories*. https://jintycomic.wordpress.com/2016/03/29/last-tammy-ever-published-23-june-1984. Accessed August 21, 2018.

Scott, Jenni. 2017a. "Pre-Misty Merger: Tammy January 12, 1980." https://jintycomic.wordpress.com/2017/01/07/pre-misty-merger-tammy-12-january-1980. Accessed October 20, 2017.

Scott, Jenni. 2017b. "Alice in a Strange Land (1979)." *A Resource on Jinty: Artists, Writers, Stories*. https://jintycomic.wordpress.com/2017/03/19/alice-in-a-strange-land-1979. Accessed April 21, 2018.

Sedgwick, Eve Kosofsky. 1986. *The Coherence of Gothic Conventions*. London: Methuen.

Serrato, Phillip. 2017. "'These Are Troubling, Confusing Times': Darren Shan's *Cirque du Freak* as Post-9/11 Gothic." In *New Directions in Children's Gothic: Debatable Lands*, ed. Anna Jackson, 51–66. London: Routledge.

Sharpe, Sue. 1976. *Just like a Girl: How Girls Learn to Be Women*. Harmondsworth: Penguin.

Shavit, Zohar. 1986. *Poetics of Children's Literature*. Athens: University of Georgia Press.

Shaw, Malcolm, Mario Capaldi, John Richardson, and Shirley Bellwood. 2017. *Misty Volume Two*. Oxford: Rebellion Publishing.

Shaw, Malcolm, Bill Harrington, Jack Cunningham, Ted Andrews, Wilf Prigmore, and Norman Worker, eds. *Misty #1–101*. London: IPC. http://readcomiconline.to/Comic/Misty. Accessed October 31, 2017.

Sherwood, Mary Martha. 1818. *The Fairchild Family*. https://www.gutenberg.org/files/29725/29725-h/29725-h.htm. Accessed October 17, 2017.

Smith, Andrew. 2004. "Love, Freud, and the Female Gothic: Bram Stoker's *The Jewel of Seven Stars*." *Gothic Studies* 6 (1): 80–89.

Smith, Andrew, and Diana Wallace. 2004. "The Female Gothic: Then and Now." *Gothic Studies* 6 (1): 1–7.

Smith, Andy W. 2013. "Magazines." In *The Encyclopedia of the Gothic*, ed. William Hughes, David Punter, and Andrew Smith, 414–17. Oxford: Wiley-Blackwell.

Smith, Anna. 2008. "The Scary Tale Looks for a Family: Gary Crew's *Gothic Hospital* and Sonya Hartnett's *The Devil Latch*." In *The Gothic in Children's Literature: Haunting the Borders*, ed. Anna Jackson, Karen Coats, and Roderick McGillis, 131–44. London: Routledge.

Smith, Orianne. 2013. *Romantic Women Writers, Revolution, and Prophecy: Rebellious Daughters, 1786–1826*. Cambridge: Cambridge University Press.

Smith, Michelle J., and Kristine Moruzi. 2018. "Vampires and Witches Go to School: Contemporary Young Adult Fiction, Gender, and the Gothic." *Children's Literature in Education* 49 (1): 6–18.

Sowerby, Robert. 2012. "The Goths in History and Pre-Gothic Gothic." In *A New Companion to the Gothic*, ed. David Punter, 25–37. Oxford: Blackwell.

Spiegel, Alan. 1972. "A Theory of the Grotesque in Southern Fiction." *Georgia Review* 26 (4): 426–37.

Spooner, Catherine. 2004. *Fashioning Gothic Bodies*. Manchester: Manchester University Press.

Spooner, Catherine. 2007. *Contemporary Gothic*. Manchester: Manchester University Press.

Spooner, Catherine. 2013. "Masks, Veils, and Disguises." In *The Encyclopedia of the Gothic*, ed. William Hughes, David Punter, and Andrew Smith, 421–24. Oxford: Wiley-Blackwell.

Spooner, Catherine. 2017. *Post-millennial Gothic: Comedy, Romance and the Rise of Happy Gothic*. London: Bloomsbury.

Stein, Daniel. 2013. "Superhero Comics and the Authorizing Functions of the Comic Book Paratext." In *From Comic Strips to Graphic Novels*, ed. Daniel Stein and Jan-Noel Thön, 155–90. Boston: Walter de Gruyter.

Stein, Daniel, and Jan-Noel Thön, eds. 2013. *From Comic Strips to Graphic Novels*. Boston: Walter de Gruyter.

Stein, Karen F. 1983. "Monsters and Madwomen: Changing Female Gothic." In *The Female Gothic*, ed. Juliann E. Fleenor, 123–37. Montreal: Eden Press.

Summers, Montague. 1938. *The Gothic Quest: A History of the Gothic Novel*. London: Fortune Press.

Sweetman, Tom. 2007a. "Play Misty for Me." *Crikey!—The Great British Comics Magazine!* 1:30–34.

Sweetman, Tom. 2007b. "The Devil in the Shop." *Crikey!—The Great British Comics Magazine!* 1:41–43.

Tammyfan. 2013. Comment on "Slaves of 'War Orphan Farm.'" *Tammy Project*, June 25, 2103. http://tammycomic.blogspot.co.uk/2013/06/slaves-of-war-orphan-farm.html. Accessed August 1, 2017.

Tantimedh, Adi. 2014. "My Search for a Lost British Girl's Comic Series—Look! It Moves!" *Bleeding Cool*. http://www.bleedingcool.com/2014/04/14/my-search-for-a-lost-british-girls-comic-series-look-it-moves-by-adi-tantimedh. Accessed September 12, 2016.

Tatar, Maria. (1987) 1993. *Off with Their Heads! Fairy Tales and the Culture of Childhood*. Princeton, NJ: Princeton University Press.

Tatar, Maria, ed. 1999. *The Classic Fairy Tales*. New York: Norton.

Tavinjer. 2015. "Artist Spotlight: Isidre Monés." Blog post. *Tavinjer*, August 21, 2015. https://tavinjer.wordpress.com/2015/08/21/artist-spotlight-isidre-mones. Accessed March 9, 2018.

Taylor, Laurie N. 2008. "Making Nightmares into New Fairytales: Goth Comics as Children's Literature." In *The Gothic in Children's Literature: Haunting the Borders*, ed. Anna Jackson, Karen Coats, and Roderick McGillis, 195–208. London: Routledge.

Tebbutt, Melanie. 2016. *Making Youth: A History of Youth in Modern Britain*. London: Palgrave.

Tehrani, Jamshid J. 2013. "The Phylogeny of Little Red Riding Hood." *PLoS ONE* 8 (11): e78871. https://doi.org/10.1371/journal.pone.0078871. Accessed March 18, 2018.

Teverson, Andrew. 2013. *Fairy Tale*. London: Routledge.

Thompson, Debbie. 2017. Comment on "Get MISTY Back in Print!" Facebook, October 23, 2017. https://www.facebook.com/groups/getmisty/permalink/1592651360757228. Accessed October 26, 2017.

Thomson, Stephen. 2004. "The Child, the Family, the Relationship: Family, Storytelling, and Ideology in Philip Pullman's *His Dark Materials*." In *Children's Literature: New Approaches*, ed. Karín Lesnik-Oberstein, 144–67. New York: Palgrave Macmillan.

Tinkler, Penny. 1995. *Constructing Girlhood: Popular Magazines for Girls Growing Up in England, 1920–1950*. Oxford: Taylor and Francis.

Todorov, Tzvetan. 1975. *The Fantastic*. Trans. Richard Howard. Ithaca, NY: Cornell University Press.

Tomlinson, Barrie, Ian Rimmer, and Simon Furman, eds. 1984. *Scream!* #1–16. London: IPC Publishing. http://www.backfromthedepths.co.uk/gallery.htm. Accessed October 31, 2017.

Tóth, Reka. 2010. "The Plight of the Gothic Heroine: Female Development and Relationships in Eighteenth Century Female Gothic Fiction." *Eger Journal of English Studies* 10:21–37.

Townshend, Dale. 2008. "The Haunted Nursery: 1764–1830." In *The Gothic in Children's Literature: Haunting the Borders*, ed. Anna Jackson, Karen Coats, and Roderick McGillis, 15–38. London: Routledge.

Townshend, Dale. 2013. "Doubles." In *The Encyclopedia of the Gothic*, ed. William Hughes, David Punter, and Andrew Smith, 189–95. Oxford: Wiley-Blackwell.

Townshend, Dale. 2016. "Gothic and the Cultural Sources of Horror, 1740–1820." In *Horror: A Literary History*, ed. Xavier Aldana Reyes, 19–52. London: British Library.

Trease, Geoffrey. 1948. *Tales out of School*. Surrey: Windmill Press.

Trombetta, Jim. 2010. *The Horror! The Horror!* New York: Abrams ComicArts.

Truffin, Sherry R. 2008. *Schoolhouse Gothic*. Newcastle-upon-Tyne: Cambridge Scholars Publishing.

Tuchman, Gaye. 1978. "Introduction: The Symbolic Annihilation of Women by the Mass Media." In *Hearth and Home: Images of Women in the Mass Media*, ed. Gaye Tuchman, Arlene Kaplan Daniels, and James Benet, 3–38. New York: Oxford University Press.

Tuchman, Gaye, Arlene Kaplan Daniels, and James Benet, eds. 1978. *Hearth and Home: Images of Women in the Mass Media*. New York: Oxford University Press.

Turney, Jo. 2010. "Sex in the Sitting Room." In *British Culture and Society in the 1970s: The Lost Decade*, ed. Laurel Forster and Sue Harper, 263–74. Newcastle: Cambridge Scholars Publishing.

Twitchell, James B. 1985. *Dreadful Pleasures: An Anatomy of Modern Horror*. Oxford: Oxford University Press.

TV Times. https://radiosoundsfamiliar.com/complete-tv-times-july2nd-1977.php. Accessed August 14, 2017.

Una. 2015. *Becoming Unbecoming*. Brighton: Myriad Editions.

Varma, Devendra P. 1957. *The Gothic Flame: Being a History of the Gothic Novel in England*. London: Arthur Baker.

Veeder, William. 1998. "The Nurture of the Gothic, or How Can a Text Be Both Popular and Subversive?" In *American Gothic: New Interventions in a National Narrative*, ed. Robert K. Martin and Eric Savoy, 20–39. Iowa City: University of Iowa Press.

Vitruvius [Marcus Vitruvius Pollio]. Ca. 27 BC. "The Decadence of Fresco Painting." In *De Architectura*. http://www.artandpopularculture.com/De_Architectura#CHAPTER_V_THE_DECADENCE_OF_FRESCO_PAINTING. Accessed April 18, 2018.

Wagner, John. 2016. "John Wagner: Interview." Posted by Comixminx. *A Resource on Jinty: Artists, Writers, Stories*. https://jintycomic.wordpress.com/2016/11/30/john-wagner-interview. Accessed February 18, 2018.

Wagner, John. 2018. Social media post. Facebook, February 3, 2018. https://www.facebook.com/helen.fay64/posts/1775970839088155?comment_id=1776010779084161&reply_comment_id=1778219005530005&notif_id=1517828332644073&notif_t=feed_comment_reply&ref=notif&hc_location=ufi. Accessed February 14, 2018.

Walkerdine, Valerie. 1984. "Some Day My Prince Will Come: Young Girls and the Preparation for Adolescent Sexuality." In *Gender and Generation*, ed. Angela McRobbie and Mica Nava, 162–84. London: Macmillan.

Wallace, Diana. 2004. "Uncanny Stories: The Ghost Story as Female Gothic." *Gothic Studies* 6 (1): 57–68.

Wallace, Diana. 2009. "'The Haunting Idea': Female Gothic Metaphors and Feminist Theory." In *The Female Gothic: New Directions*, ed. Diana Wallace and Andrew Smith, 26–41. London: Palgrave Macmillan.

Wallace, Diana, and Andrew Smith, eds. 2009. *The Female Gothic: New Directions*. London: Palgrave Macmillan.

Walpole, Horace. 1764. *The Castle of Otranto*. http://www.gutenberg.org/files/696/696-h/696-h.htm. Accessed May 17, 2017.

Warwick, Alexandra. 2007. "Feeling Gothicky?" *Gothic Studies* 9 (1): 5–15.

Wasson, Ellis. 2016. *A History of Modern Britain: 1714 to the Present*. Oxford: John Wiley and Sons.

Weinstock, Jeffrey, ed. 2013. *The Works of Tim Burton: Margins to Mainstream*. New York: Palgrave.

Weinstock, Jeffrey, ed. 2017. *The Cambridge Companion to American Gothic*. Cambridge: Cambridge University Press.

Wellington, Jan. 2008. "Learning to Transgress: Embedded Pedagogies of the Gothic." *Pedagogy* 8 (1): 170–76.

Wheatley, Helen. 2006. *Gothic Television*. Manchester: Manchester University Press.

Wheatley, Helen. 2013. "Television." In *The Encyclopedia of the Gothic*, ed. William Hughes, David Punter, and Andrew Smith, 677–82. Oxford: Wiley-Blackwell.

Wheeler, I. 2017. "Why Pat Mills Is Right about *Scream! and Misty*." Facebook, August 6, 2017. https://www.facebook.com/millsverse/photos/p.766552903551677/766552903551677/?type=3&theater. Accessed August 10, 2017.

Williams, Anne. 1995. *Art of Darkness: A Poetics of Gothic*. Chicago: University of Chicago Press.

Williams, Gilda. 2014. "Defining a Gothic Aesthetic in Modern and Contemporary Art." In *The Gothic World*, ed. Glennis Byron and Dale Townshend, 412–26. London: Routledge.

Williams, Raymond. 1977. *Marxism and Literature*. Oxford: Oxford University Press.

Winnett, Susan. 1990. "Coming Unstrung: Women, Men, Narrative, and Principles of Pleasure." *PMLA* 105 (3): 505–18.

Winnicott, Donald W. 1982. *Playing and Reality*. London: Routledge.

Winship, Janice. 1987. *Inside Women's Magazines*. London: Pandora.

Wisker, Gina. 2004. "Viciousness in the Kitchen: Sylvia Plath's Gothic." *Gothic Studies* 6 (1): 103–17.

Wisker, Gina. 2005. *Horror Fiction: An Introduction*. London: Continuum.

Wolf, Naomi. 1991. *The Beauty Myth: How Images of Beauty Are Used against Women*. London: Vintage.

Wolfreys, Julian. 2008. *Transgression: Identity, Space, Time*. London: Palgrave.

Wollstonecraft, Mary. 1792. *A Vindication of the Rights of Women*. http://www.earlymoderntexts.com/assets/pdfs/wollstonecraft1792.pdf. Accessed April 18, 2018.

Wood, Henrietta Rix. 2016. *Praising Girls: The Rhetoric of Young Women, 1895–1930*. Carbondale: South Illinois University Press.

Wood, Robin. 1979. "An Introduction to the American Horror Film." In *The American Nightmare: Essays on the Horror Film*, ed. Robin Wood and Richard Lippe, 7–28. Toronto: Festival of Festivals.

Wood, Robin. (1983) 2003. *Hollywood from Vietnam to Reagan . . . and Beyond*. New York: Columbia University Press.

Worker, Norman. 1984. Correspondence with Shirley Bellwood, by post, dated October 10, 1984. Copy provided by Basil and Sue Sellwood.

Wright, Angela. 2004. "'To live the life of hopeless recollection': Mourning and Melancholia in Female Gothic, 1780–1800." *Gothic Studies* 6 (1): 19–29.

Wright, Angela. 2017. "Heroines in Flight: Narrating Invisibility and Maturity in Women's Gothic Writing of the Romantic Period." In *Women and the Gothic*, ed. Avril Horner and Sue Zlosnik, 15–30. Edinburgh: Edinburgh University Press.

Yang, Sharon Rose, and Katherine Healey, eds. 2016. *Gothic Landscapes: Changing Eras, Changing Cultures, Changing Anxieties*. London: Palgrave.

Zipes, Jack, ed. (1986) 1993. *Don't Bet on the Prince: Contemporary Feminist Fairy Tales in North America and England*. Aldershot: Gower.

Zipes, Jack. 1995. *Fairy Tales and the Art of Subversion*. London: Routledge.

Zipes, Jack. 2014. "Introduction: Rediscovering the Original Tales of the Brothers Grimm." In *The Original Folk and Fairy Tales of the Brothers Grimm*, by Jacob and Wilhelm Grimm, trans. and ed. Jack Zipes. Princeton, NJ: Princeton University Press.

Zlosnik, Sue, and Avril Horner. 2013. "Comic Gothic." In *The Encyclopedia of the Gothic*, ed. William Hughes, David Punter, and Andrew Smith, 122–26. Oxford: Wiley-Blackwell.

INDEX

Page numbers in **bold** indicate illustrations.

abject, the, 12, 200, 206, 208–10, 212–14, 218, 224–26
Abominable Snowman, 239, 240
abstraction, 12, 187, 250, 251, 254–57, 263
abuse, 31, 100, 114, 122, 158, 224, 249, 264, 267, 278
Ace of Wands, 122
Action, 22, 30, 39, 124
adaptation, 36, 77, 101, 105, 118, 124, 125, 136, 161, 235, 241, 258, 260–62, 295, 298nn4–5, 302n2 (chap. 12)
adolescence, 16, 216, 222, 245, 246, 250, 259, 261; puberty, 125, 212, 218, 219, 250, 251, 259; teenage, 12, 16, 116, 117, 179, 181, 218, 219, 221, 241, 245, 250, 257, 261, 271, 278, 302n4 (chap. 11)
Aesop, 251
aesthetic, 6–11, 28, 31, 60, 84, 88, 91, 104, 150, 199, 208, 209, 213, 249, 269, 296
Aiken, Joan, 120
Ailey, Paul, **33**
Alderson, Connie, 16, 17
Alfred Hitchcock Presents, 127
ALI, 64, 65
Alice in Wonderland, 260, 261
alien, 94, 112, 113, 163, 196, 201, 245, 257
Almond, David, 261
alterity, 234, 235, 259
Amalgamated Press, 18–20, 36, 37, 44, 64
ambiguity, 86, 88, 89, 117, 126, 134, 153, 179, 242, 250, 258, 259
ambivalence, 7, 10, 100, 112, 153–56, 159, 182, 201, 203, 215, 221, 224, 225, 246, 249, 254, 259, 261, 263, 290, 295, 302n4 (chap. 8)
Amicus, 117

Andersen, Hans Christian, 252, 253, 258
Anderson, M. T., 250
Andrews, Ted, 4, 24, 26, 29, **33**, 35, 60, 61, 299n9, 302n2 (chap. 10)
Ang, Ien, 265
animal, 19, 68, 110, 112–14, 116, 126, 159, 187, 214, 219, 221, 234, 241, 243, 253, 270; animal rights, 110, 113, 116, 234, 241, 243
Appleyard, J. A., 221
archetype, 6, 12, 23, 74, 119, 167, 202, 208, 226, 237–43, 245, 246, 250, 254, 256, 257, 263, 264, 302n2 (chap. 11)
Ariès, Philippe, 252
Ariza, Juan/José, 28, 67, 75, 110, **111**, **171**, **176**, **178**, **191**, 228, **230**, 287
Armitt, Lucie, 247, 248, 256
Armstrong, John, 28, 36, 60, 67, 68, 71–72, **73**, 115, 125, **172**, 234, 282
asymmetry, 91, 92
Atlas, 105
audience, xiii, 12, 13, 15, 17–19, 22, 24, 28, 46, 105, 116, 122, 203, 207, 208, 218, 245–47, 261–66, 279, 280, 285, 291; readers, xii, 13, 15, 17, 18, 28–31, 34, 44, 46, 47, 59, 89, 90, 92, 101, 102, 114, 126, 128, 134, 142, 144, 151, 170, **175–78**, 181, 182, 203, 210, 218, 226, 231, 235, 247, 250, 252–54, 257, 259, 264–67, **268**, 269, 278–80, 291, 292, 295. *See also* male readers
Audrey Rose, 24, 125
Auerbach, Nina, 6, 226
Austen, Jane, 46
Austin, Sara, 261
authority, 12, 65, 82, 129, 200, 208, 216, 224, 225, 246

Baddeley, Gavin, 8
Badía Romero, Enric, 65, 75, 300n12

325

Badía Romero, Jorge, 64, 67, 75, **189**
Baker, Tom, 6
Bakhtin, Mikhail, 213
Baldick, Chris, 7, 8, 204, 206, 234
ballet, 19, 21, 130, 158, 252
Barbie, 283, 298n11
Bardon Art, 63–65, 77, 299n7 (chap. 3)
Barker, Martin, 15–17, 267, 297n5, 301n5 (chap. 5)
Barnett, David, 291
baroque, 90–93
Barrera Castell, María, 28, 64, 67, 75, **76**, 85, 110, **188**, **217**, 300n13
Barthes, Roland, 168
Bartholomew, Bob, 23
Báthory, Elizabeth, 235
Battle Action, 299n7 (chap. 2)
Battle Picture Weekly, 22, 36, 39, 78, 290, 298n6, 299nn6–7 (chap. 2)
Bauhaus (band), 301n5 (chap. 7)
Bauman, Jill, 118
Baxendale, Leo, 79, 102, 104
BBC, 41, 42, 119, 121, 122, 124
Beano, The, 102, 105
Beard, Mary, 241
Beatles (band), 66, 297n6
Beattie, James, 8
Beaty, Bart, 291, 292
Becker, Ernest, 250
Becker, Suzanne, 204
Becoming Unbecoming, 301n2 (chap. 6)
BEEB, 41
Bellamy, Frank, 72, 83
Bellwood, Shirley, 4, 15, 28, **33**, 65, 79, **81**, 82, 132, 133, 135, 136, 285, 287, 289, 293, 300nn17–18
Benton, Mike, 303n1 (chap. 13)
Bernard, Catherine, 258
Best of Misty Monthly, The, 14, 136, **137**, 283, 284
Bettelheim, Bruno, 250, 252
Beville, Maria, 8, 46
Bewell, Alan, 207
Bielsa, José, 64
bildungsroman, 100, 225, 291
Birds, The, 117
Birkhead, Edith, 6
Bishop, Jon, 286
Black Christmas, 117

"Black Widow, The," 42, 71, 84, 153, 273, 287, 300n2, 301n4 (chap. 5)
Blair, Shirley, 79
"Bluebeard," 203, 215, 218, 251, 258
Blyton, Enid, 72
bodging, 60, 63, 83, 84
body, 11, 16, 82, 106, 127, 134, 139, 141, 143, 146, 150, 168, 201, 202, 205, 209, 210, 212, 213, 216, 222, 224, 245–48, 263, 289
"Body Snatchers, The," 75, **76**, 88, 112, 122, 217, 224, 300n3
Bones (host), 130
Boodman, S., 249
Boris Karloff's Thriller, 127
Botting, Fred, 6, 46, 82, 92, 104, 203, 207
Bourdieu, Pierre, 7
Bowers, Maggie Ann, 256
Boyfriend, 72
Boy Who Kicked Pigs, The, 6
Bradley, Darren, 283
Braidotti, Rosa, 252
Braude, Anne, 200
Brennan, Paddy, 151
Brontë, Charlotte, 247
Brontë, Emily, 235
Brophy, Brigid, 113
Brotherstone, Stephen, 109, 301n1 (chap. 6)
Brown, Benita, 299n11
Brown, Mike, 28, 79, **103**, 124
Brown, Rosemary, 235
Bruguera, Francisco, 64
Bruhm, Steven, 248
Buckley, Chloe, 7, 46, 205, 247, 249, 251, 252, 258, 260, 261, 263, 265
Buddy, 71
Buffy the Vampire Slayer, 262
Bullet, 22, 74
bullying, 102, 105, 115, 116, 125, 126, 151, 158, 159, 161, 162, 181, 219, 243, 255
Bunty, xiii, 17–20, 22, 25, 31, 43, 44, 72, 78, 115, 130, 301n2 (chap. 7)
Bunty Picture Story Library, 301n2 (chap. 7)
burial, 123, 151, 155, 202, 204, 209, 210, 214, 215, 218, 235, 241, 246; feminine carceral, 209, 218, 221, 258, 263; incarceration, 97, 100, 208, 210, 225, 261, 263
Burton, Tim, 91, 104, 261, 262
Busch, Wilhelm, 251
Busom, Rafael, 41, 83, **173**

Busse, Kristin, 265
Buster, 123, 124, 290
Butler, David, 122

Cadogan, Mary, 16, 297n5
camp, 104, 209
Campbell, Ramsey, 118
Candy Floss, 78
canon, 46, 247, 292, 296
Cánovas, José, 28, 41, 64, 67, 78, **233**
Capaldi, Mario, 28, 67, 68, 72, 97, **99**, 124, 159, 214, 285
Capaldi, Vanda, 68
carnivalesque, 213, 231, 249
Carpenter, R., 298n6
Carrie, 24, 38, 117, 118, 125, 126
Carrington, Victoria, 8, 248
Carroll, Lewis, 260, 261
Carter, Angela, 200, 247
Casanovas, José, 78, 300n16
"Cats of Carey Street, The," 68, 97, 112, 114, 153, 164, 300n3
Cavallero, Dani, 168
Chamber of Darkness, 128
Chambers, Aidan, 303n1 (chap. 13)
Chapman, James, 16–20, 22, 34, 301n5 (chap. 5)
Charlton Comics, 128
Chatterjee, Ranita, 206
Cherie, 71
chiaroscuro, 91, 92
child, xii, xiv, 3–5, 12, 29, 32, 38, 104, 105, 107, 108, 114, 116, 119–123, 125, 126, 128, 142, 146, 205, 224, 227, 247–53, 255, 256, 258–61, 264, 265, 271, 277, 290–92, 294, 295; Children's Gothic, 122, 252–54, 256, 259, 262, 265; children's literature, xiii, 5, 6, 12, 20, 31, 36, 37, 43, 44, 74, 77, 114, 134, 247–52, 256, 260, 261, 264, 295; children's television, 34, 121, 122
Chisholm, Ian, 102
Christie, Agatha, 119
Christie, Alison, 28, 37, 43, 45, 151
Church, Doug, 28, 83, 84
"Cilla the Chiller," 94, 102, 105, 124, 152, 285
Cinderella, 258, 259, 298n11
Cinderella story. *See* formula
cinema, 10, 19, 25, 26, 29, 74, 91, 108–9, 116–18, 120–22, 124, 126, 134, 243
civil rights, 118
Cixous, Hélène, 213

class, 15, 19, 35, 46, 47, 59, 66, 114, 115, 118, 248, 258, 280
Clery, E. J., 200, 203
clothing. *See* fashion
Clover, Carol, 118
Coats, Karen, 249, 250, 253
Cohen, Stanley, 115
Cohn, Neil, 89
Coker, Barry, 64, 65
collaboration, 38, 63, 75, 266, 280, 295
Collection Kaléidoscope, 283, 303n3 (chap. 14)
Collings, Angela, 187
Collins, Joan, 300n17
Collins, Joe, 21, 28, 40, 42, 67–68, **69**, 102, 146
Collins, Wilkie, 235
Coman, Anthony, 266
comedy, 11, 26, 42, 68, 79, 84, 94, 102, 104–7, 123, 124, 128, 131, 152, 168, 182, 238, 242, 254, 256, 285; humor, 6, 23, **33**, 68, 79, 101, 104–7, 120, 128, 133, 250; irony, 6, 43, 91, 102, 105, 113, 121, 133, 168, 203, 213, 218, 277; parody, 6, 8, 47, 78, 104, 105, 113, 216, 238, 254, 256, 261; whimsical macabre, 11, 94, 102, 104, 105, 107
Comics Code, 105
Commando, 74
competitions, 26, 40, 43, 106, 132, 168, 280
computing, 38, 109; computer games, 34, 38, 72
conservatism, 7, 12, 14, 18, 34, 66, 108, 168, 202, 205–7, 246, 258, 280
consumerism, 16, 20, 47, 117, 203, 218, 247
Conti, Carlos, 64
Cook, Oscar, 120
Cooke, Lez, 120
Cooper, Susan, 260
Coote, Briony, 131, 156
Cor, 123
Coraline, 250, 261
Corson, Jamie T., 155, 200, 209
Country Life, 61
cover, 4, 9, 12, **27**, 29, 61, 62, 65, 77, 79, 82–83, 101, 118, 123, 127, 131, 133, 135–36, **137–38**, 139, **140**, 141, 143, 148, 187, **188–95**, 196, 212, 231, 272, 276, 284, 286–88, 298n11, 300nn18–19; inside cover, **27**, 28, 42, 61, 79, 127, 133, 136, **137–38**, 139, **140**, 148, 285, 301n11
cover girls, 83, 101, 127, 131, 133, 150, 287–88, 292
craft features, 79, 132, 285

Craig, Patricia, 16, 297n5
Crandall, Nadia, 250
Crawford, Joseph, 5, 7, 17, 261–65
Creaciones Editoriales, 63–65, 71, 75
Creed, Barbara, 118, 204
Creepy, 64, 74, 78, 128
Crepax, Guido, 90
Cross, Gillian, 260
Cross, Julie, 249, 250, 256
Crunch, The, 74
crypt, 10, 146, 147, 214; encryption, 9, 202, 215
Cuddles, 298n11
"Cult of the Cat, The," 27, 29, 42, 71, 83, 95, 96, **98**, 100, **194**, 222, 231, 234, 273, 283–85, 300n1
Cummins, June, 256
Cunningham, Jack, 4, 21, 25, 26, **33**, 35, 37, 39, 45, 46, 60–63, 67, 79, 86, 132, 134, 142, 282, 285, **296**

D'Adderio, Hugo, 28
Daffron, Eric, 207
Dahl, Roald, 120, 127, 250, 260
Daly, Mary, 242
Damian Darke (host), 23, 129, 135
Damon-Moore, Helen, 16
Dance of the Vampires, 117
"Danger in the Depths," 78, **177**, 301n4 (chap. 5)
Date, 283
d'Aulnoy, Marie-Catherine, 258
Davenport-Hines, Richard, 234
Davidson, Alan, 28, 31, 37, 45, 116, 159, 161, 298n12, 299n13
Davies, Anita, 44
Davies, Paul Fisher, 83, 84, 136, 140, **180**, 300n2 (chap. 4), 301nn8–9 (chap. 7)
Davies, Roy, 123
Davis, James P., 207
Davison, Carol Margaret, 97, 100, 209
Day of the Triffids, The, 19
DC Comics, 128
DC Thomson, xiii, 14, 18–24, 29, 32, 36, 39, 40, 42–44, 65, 68, 71, 72, 74, 75, 77, 78, 83, 129, 132, 196, 283, 285, 295
Dead of Night, 119
death, 6, 19, 47, 100, 105, 106, 110, 113, 114, 121, 123–26, 129, 130, 151–53, 155, 156, 158, 159, 163, 164, 196, 213, 214, 216, 218, 222, 227, 228, 232, 242, 249, 251, 252, 273, 289
Death Line, 124
Debbie, 23, 31, 43, 130, 301n3 (chap. 7)
decay, 91, 92, 141
De Felitta, Frank, 125
DeLamotte, Eugenia, 204
Delaney, Brian, 28, 60, 67, 71, **85**
delinquency, 110, 115, 116, 164, 234
Delirium, 284
del Toro, Guillermo, 91
De Luca effect, 86, 97, 179, 243, 253
demon, 106, 122, 156, 196, 237, 239, 240, 270
De Palma, Brian, 118
devil, the, 122, 151, 161, 237, 239, 240, 242, 287
Diana, xiii, 19, 20, 23, 31, 72, 77, 114, 115, 128–30
diegesis, 87, 131; storyworld, 92, 129, 131, 216, 234, 259
Diehl, Digby, 105
Digby, Anne, 18, 31, 34, 36, 37, 39, 45, 298n12, 298n5, 299n13
Disney, 61, 259, 260, 298n11
Dixon, Jeanne, 235
Doane, Mary Ann, 232
domesticity, 12, 16, 110, 114, 120, 200, 201, 204, 205, 207, 210, 225, 232, 245, 246, 261
Dominguez, Manel, 66
"Don't Look Twice," 68, 100, 167, 222, 300n1
double, 12, 97, 143, 144, 181, 201, 203, 205, 206, 210, 215, 221, 226–28, 231, 232, 245, 246, 250, 261; doppelgänger, 158, 226, 227, 261
Douglas, Lorraine, 286
Downer, Peter, **33**
Dracul, Vlad, 235
Dramarama, 122, 302n2 (chap. 12)
Dr. Jekyll and Mr. Hyde, 227, 228
Dr. Terror's House of Horrors, 117
du Maurier, Daphne, 247

Eagle, 18, 22, **33**, 35, 72, 77, 83, 297n2; *New Eagle*, 61
Eastwood, Clint, 26
EC Comics, 47, 105, 119, 127, 128, 130, 131, 133, 150, 168, 238
Edgewood, Maria, 248
Editorial Bruguera, 64. *See also* Creaciones Editoriales
editorial practices, 37, 38, 44, 60–63, 83, 84, 86, 91, 101, 135, 142, 143, 294–96, 298n12

education, 23, 72, 249, 251. *See also* pedagogy
Edwards, Justin D., 10
Edward Scissorhands, 91
Eerie, 64, 74, 78, 128
Egmont, 13, 14, 282, 284, 290
Eliot, George Fielding, 119
Eliot, T.S., 40
Ellis, Brenda, **33**, 40, 41, 45, 116, 266
Ellis, Kate Ferguson, 110, 202, 207, 209, 219
emanata, 47, 68
Emily the Strange, 91
Emmanuelle, 117
"End of the Line," 40, 41, 72, 124, 300n3
Enki, Yanki, 153
Enlightenment, 7, 8
environmentalism, 40, 109, 110, 112, 113, 116, 126, 234
Escolano, Ramon, 64, 65
Esin, 77
ethnicity, 109, 114, 115, 118, 291
excess, 9, 10, 75, 83, 92–94, 104, 107, 118, 146, 147, 150, 158, 181, 213, 251, 293
Exorcist, The, 116, 118

fairy, 110, 155, 239, 240, 257
fairy tale, xiii, 12, 123, 215, 247, 248, 250–54, 256, 258–60, 262, 263, 295; fable, 248, 251; folklore, 134, 237, 248, 251
fandom, xiii, 13, 25, 28, 32, 60, **80**, 100, 114, 235, 264–66, 275, 278–80, 282, 284, 285, 290, 292, 295, 296, 301n6, 303n4 (chap. 13)
fantastic, the, 153, 249, 256
Fantastic Four, the, 297n6
fantasy, 31, 77, 122, 134, 167, 222, 261, 265, 286, 295
Farber, Stephen, 91
fashion, 16, 17, 34, 44, 66, 77, 106, 108, 218, 298n11; clothing/style, 115, 234, 294
father, 97, 110, 112, 114, 120, 124, 129, 151–53, 161, 216, 217, 222, 224, 228, 257, 261, 273, 289. *See also* paternity
Fay, Helen, 35, 42, 282, 297n7
fear, 6–10, 12, 59, 68, 74, 78, 95–97, 104, 106, 110, 113, 115, 125, 128, 142, 147, 148, 153, 155, **169**, 170, 182, 187, 196, 199, 205, 209, 210, 213, 215, 217, 224, 228, 231–32, **233**, 237, 238, 242, 243, 245, 246, 248–50, 253, 255, 256, 259–61, 263, 273, 274, 294, 295
Fearnley, John, **33**

Feito, Eduardo, 28, 36, 67, 72, 125, **220**, 234
Feldstein, Al, 105
Female Gothic, 12, 47, 97, 187, 199–206, 208–10, 215, 218, 227, 238, 241, 246, 247, 254, 260, 263, 296
feminism, 16, 40, 82, 133, 134, 200–202, 204, 213, 242, 258
Fenwick, L., 18
Fight Club, 227
film. *See* cinema
Finley-Day, Gerry, 21, 22, 36, 37, 40, 151, 158, 298n8, 299n6 (chap. 2)
Finney, Jack, 119
Fleenor, Juliann E., 202, 219
Fleetway, 14, 20, 22, **33**, 36, 40–42, 66, 71, 75, 283, 284, 299n7. *See also* IPC
focalization, 112, 125, 181, 182, 203, 205, 207, 210, 231, 246, 291
formalism. *See* page layout
formula, 11, 22, 28, 41, 94, 106, 151, 156, 158–62, 182, 302n6 (chap. 9); Cinderella story, 158–62, 179, 182, 256, 299n13; Friend story, 158–62, 182; Mystery story, 158–62, 179, 182; Slave story, 151, 158, 160, 162
"Four Faces of Eve, The," 41, 71, 124, 161, 167, 222, 225, 284, 300n1
Franch, Jordi, 75, 77
Franco, Francisco, 66, 67, 78
Frank, Alan, 122
Frank, Anne, 271
Frankenstein, 46, 131, 207, 218, 226
Frankenstein's creature, 167, 234, 237, 243
Frankenweenie, 261
free gifts, 26, 28, 29, 61, 79, 298, 301n7 (chap. 7)
Freeman, John, 28, 34, 79, 290, 291
Freeman, Nick, 134
Freixas, Carlos, 64, 75, 78
Freud, Sigmund, 10, 153, 204, 206, 209, 215, 226, 227
Friedan, Betty, 16
Friend story. *See* formula
Frye, Northrop, 6

Gaiman, Neil, 250, 261, 262
Gaines, Bill, 105. *See also* EC Comics
Gallagher, Stephen, 71
Gallego, Blas, 28, 41, 64, 66, 67, 77, 300n14
Garner, Alan, 260
Gascoine, Phil, 116, 298n5

Gaskell, Elizabeth, 247
Gaunt, Elizabeth, 115, 300n17
gender, 6, 10, 12, 13, 15, 17, 19, 35, 45–47, 118, 187, 199, 200, 202–8, 232, 238, 254, 259, 262, 264, 265, 278–80, 291
genie, 43, 239, 240
Georgieva, Margarita, 247, 248
Germanà, Monica, 8, 82, 134, 227
Gesalí, David, 75, 300n13
Gesalí, Guillermo, 75
Gesalí, María. *See* Barrera Castell, María
Ghastly McNasty (host), 297n2
ghost, xiii, 9, 12, 19, 23, 26, 44, 71, 82, 94, 102, 106, 119, 121–24, 129, 130, 134, 135, 151, 156, 159, 161, 167, **178**, 196, 199, 204, 205, 212, 225–27, 235, 237–41, 243, 248, 249, 252, 257, 260, 261, 271, 273, 274, 277, 283–85, 289. *See also* haunting
"Ghost of Golightly Towers, The," 71, 159, 241, 285, 300n3
Ghoulunatics (host), 128, 133, 134
Gibbs, David, 108
Gibson, Mel, 4, 15–17, 19, 187, 263, 266, 271, 280, 292, 297n1, 297nn4–5, 303n6 (chap. 13)
Gifford, Denis, 122
Gilbert, Sandra, 200, 245, 258
Ginger Snaps, 250
Girl, xiii, 18, 22, 42, 45
Girls' Crystal, 18
Girls' Realm, 280
Girl's Own Paper, The, 18
Girl Talk, 298n11
Glamour Library, 79
Gleeson-White, Sarah, 212, 213, 222, 245
Go Girl, 298n11
Gonzalez Martinez, Rafael, 64
Goodall, Scott, 299n6 (chap. 2)
Gooderham, David, 249
Goodman, Sam, 109
Goosebumps, 260
Gordon, Ian, 266
gorgon, **173**, 196. *See also* Medusa
Gosnell, Kelvin, **33**, 36, 39, 298n3
Gothic cusp, 12, 234, 245, 254. *See also* historicism
Gothic for Girls, xiii, 5, 12, 13, 187, 205, 207, 209, 246, 247, 254, 260, 262, 263, 294, 295
Gothic heroine, 7, 11, 17, 31, 46, 47, 68, 94, 96, 97, 100, 107, 114, 123, 126, 151–53, 155, 158, 159, 161, 182, 199–204, 209, 215, 218, 219, 222, 231, 234, 241, 253, 258, 262, 294, 296
Goth music, 301n5 (chap. 7)
Goth subculture, 8, 153, 294
Goudon, Jacques, **157**
Grange Hill, 71
Gravett, Paul, 4, 86, 297n4
Gray, Fraser, **33**
Grice, Lee, 290
Griffith, Bill, 90
Grimm, Brothers, 251, 253, 254, 260
Groensteen, Thierry, 89–92, 170
Gross, Louis S., 8
Gross, Philip, 261
grotesque, the, 9, 10, 12, 74, 104, 170, 181, 196, 199, 205, 206, 208, 212–15, 218, 222, 250, 251, 254
Gual, Josép/José, 28, 65, 77, **177**, **190**, 196, **197**
Gubar, Susan, 200, 245, 258
Guirado, Carlos, 28, 66, 67, 77, 83, 290
Guiral, Antoni, 64, 65, 299n6 (chap. 3)
Gypsy Rose (host), 130, 135, 288, 301n2 (chap. 7)

Haefele-Thomas, Ardel, 46
Hague, Ian, 292
Hajdu, David, 301n5 (chap. 5)
Halberstam, J., 118
Halloween, 116, 117
Hallucinations, 78
Hamilton, Ceciley, 299n12
Hammer, 117
Hand, Richard J., 301n1 (chap. 7)
"Hangman's Alley," 77, 234, 300n3
Harrington, Bill, 24, 26, 28, 35, 42, 43, 45, 84, 95, 96, **98**, 132, 142, 282, 297n7, 299n9, 302n2 (chap. 10)
Harris, Charlaine, 241, 262
Harris, Max and Sue, **33**
Hartley, L. P., 120
Hartley, Maureen, 151
Hatfield, Charles, 291
haunting, 6, 8–10, 74, 102, 112, 130, 146, 163, 196, 219, 237, 238, 241, 248, 250, 252, 254, 273, 283. *See also* ghost
"Haunting of Hazel Brown, The," 71, 159, 273, 301n4 (chap. 5)
Haunt of Fear, The, 128, 238
Hebden, Alan, 298n6, 299n6 (chap. 2)

Hebden, Eric, 298n6, 299n6 (chap. 2)
Heiland, Donna, 9, 199
Hello Kitty, 298n11
Hemming, James, 222
Hendrix, Grady, 118
Herbert, James, 118
Hermes, Joke, 16, 17, 265
Hernandez, Santiago, 41
heroine. *See* Gothic heroine
Hidalgo, Francisco, 63
Hills, Matt, 265
historicism, 11, 42, 66, 92, 127, 141, 150, 228, 234, 235, 245, 283, 295, 303n2 (chap. 14). *See also* Gothic cusp
Hoad, Phil, 36
Hodgson Burnett, Frances, 260, 261
Hoeveler, Diane Long, 200, 204, 209, 241, 245
Hoffmann, Heinrich, 107, 251
Hogle, Jerrold, 8, 235, 237
Hoh, Diane, 261, 303n3 (chap. 12)
Holland, Steve, 71
Holm, Hans, 283, 284
homelessness, 114
Homero, 28, 67, 70, 71, 84, 85, 95, 96, **98**, **192**, **194**
Horner, Avril, 100, 104, 106, 199, 200, 204, 205, 209, 241
Hornet, 22
horror, xiii, 3, 5, 8–13, 19, 24, 25, 28, 34, 35, 38, 47, 59, 74, 75, 78, 82, 94, 97, 104, 105, 108, 116–24, 126–28, 132, 133, 147, 150, 151, 156, 158, 167, **171–74**, 187, **192–95**, 196, 199, 203, 206, 207, 214, 215, 221, 231, 235, 237, 238, 243, 245, 248–51, 254, 255, 257, 261, 264, 267, 270, 280, 297n2, 300n1 (chap. 6)
host, 4, 11, 23, 28, 40, 82, 94, 105, 127–33, 150, 288, 293, 295, 297n2; Abel, 128; Bones, 130; Cain, 128; Cousin Eerie, 128; Damian Darke, 23, 129, 135; Ghastly McNasty, 297n2; Ghoulunatics, 128, 133, 134; Gypsy Rose, 130, 135, 288, 301n2 (chap. 7); Headstone P. Gravely, 128; Man in Black, 19, 129, 135; Misty (host), 15, 25, 61, **80**, 82, 102, 126, 127, 132–50, 187, 196, 231, 266–82, 285–90, 293, 295, 300n19, 301nn6, 301nn10–11; Roderick "Digger" Krupp, 128; She of the Shadows, 130; Storyteller, 128–32, 135, 283, 286–88; Tharg the Mighty One, 133; Uncle Creepy, 128; Vampirella, 128

Houghton, Ken, 28, 60, 78, **229**
House of Hammer, 77, 298n2
"House of Horror," 74, 97, 158, 243, 300n3
House of Mystery, 128
House of Secrets, 128
House of Whipcord, 117
Howard, Jacqueline, 204, 205, 252
Howarth, Lesley, 261
Hubbard, Mike, 129
Hulton Press, xiii, 18, 20
Hume, Robert, 9
humor. *See* comedy
Hunt, Leon, 108, 109, 117
Hunt, Peter, 264
Hush . . . Hush, Sweet Charlotte, 124
"Hush, Hush, Sweet Rachel," 40, 72, 88, 101, 124, 125, 136, 210, 221, 228, 300n1
Hutchings, Peter, 118

identity, 12, 14, 30, 31, 47, 92, 96, 100–102, 107, 115, 118, 124, 128, 131, 132, 199, 202, 208–10, 212, 217–19, 222, 224, 226–28, 231, 232, 243, 245, 246, 248, 250, 254, 258–63, 273, 292, 293, 295
ideology, 6, 15–18, 201–3, 264
inheritance, 8, 96, 106, 156, 207, 231, 257
Invasion of the Body Snatchers, 122, 232
IPC, 14, 18, 20–24, 26, 29, 30, 32, 35–40, 42–44, 46, 47, 61, 65, 67, 68, 72, 77–79, 123, 132, 134, 282–85, 295, 297nn1–2, 298n12, 299n7 (chap. 2), 299n11, 303n4 (chap. 13). *See also* Fleetway
IRA, 109
Irigaray, Luce, 209, 232, 241
isolation, 12, 105, 127, 139, 150, 158, 159, 161, 181, 199, 202, 209, 210, 219, 241, 246, 247, 254, 258–63
ITV, 26, 118, 120, 122, 127
I Was a Teenage Werewolf, 117

Jackie, xiii, 17, 20, 22, 31, 71, 77
Jackson, Anna, 5, 248, 250, 251
Jackson, Rosemary, 222
Jacobs, Jason, 120
James, Henry, 247
James, Kathryn, 5
James, M. R., 124
James Bond, 42
Jameson, Fredric, 7

Jana, 75
Jane Eyre, 201, 227
Jaws, 116, 124
Jenkinson, Augustus John, 18
Jephcott, Pearl, 18
Jinty, xiii, 3, 18, 22, 24, 31, 32, 38, 39, 41, 43, 45, 46, 75, 78, 79, 94, 114, 116, 130–32, 151, 155, 288–90, 299n3, 300n16. See also *Tammy and Jinty*
Jinty and Lindy, 130
Jinty and Penny, 42, 115. See also *Penny*
Jones, Jeffrey Catherine, 118
Jones, Timothy, 7, 128, 131, 133
Joshi, S. T., 46
jouissance, 168, 182
journey, 100, 113, 127, 134, 142, 143, 146, 218, 222, 226, 247, 254, 260
"Journey into Fear," 68, 95, 153, 217, 255, 300n3, 301n4 (chap. 5)
Judy, 17, 19, 20, 22, 25, 72, 90, 130, 151
June, 3, 22, 31, 41, 94, 130, 131, 282, 287
June and Pixie, 123, 284, 298n4
June and School Friend, 23, 31, 71, 129, 299n7. See also *School Friend*
Jung, Carl, 226
Jungman, Ann, 261
juxtaposition, 12, 93, 105, 110, 113, 141, 150, 196, 205, 207, 212, 221, 227, 234, 253, 254, 256, 257, 263

Kaplan, Deborah, 100
Kayser, Wolfgang, 212–14
Kemp, Gene, 261
Kerry Drake, 71
Khair, Tabish, 6
Khan, Omar, 291
Kilgour, Maggie, 234
Kilpeckhall, 32
Kincaid, Angela, 28
King, Cecil Harmsworth, 20
King, Stephen, 9, 101, 118, 247
Kiss Kiss, 120
Klause, Annette Curtis, 261, 302n4 (chap. 11)
Krazy, 79
Kristeva, Julia, 210, 212

Lacan, Jacques, 226, 232
Laing, R. D., 227
Langelaan, George, 119

Last House on the Left, The, 117
Last Tango in Paris, 117
Law, David, 102
Lawrence, Dave, 109, 301n1 (chap. 6)
layout. See page layout
Laycock, Joseph, 242
"Leap through Time, A," 72, 97, 153, 222, 234, 255, 300n3
Lecigne, Bruno, 90, 91
Lecturas, 78
Ledoux, Ellen, 201, 205
Lee, Christopher, 235
legend, 23, 26, 41, 122, 123, 235, 271, 289, 297n3. See also myth
Lesnik-Oberstein, Karín, 252
lettering, 38, 237, 287, 288
Levin, Ira, 118
Lewis, Brian, 129
Lewis, Matthew, 199, 207, 235
L'Héritier, Marie-Jeanne, 258
Lichtenstein, Roy, 135
Lights Out, 118
Lillyman, Chris, 72, 282, 286, 289, 290, 292, 293
liminality, 5, 46, 59, 93, 96, 130, 131, 134, 135, 212, 242, 248, 250, 295
Lindy, 31, 132. See also *Jinty and Lindy*
Lippe, Anya Heise-von der, 205
Lively, Penelope, 260
Lloyd, Chris, 21, 29, 79
Locke, John, 249
Lofts, William O. G., 44
logo: cover logo, 61, 287, 288, **296**; story logo, 27, 28, 60–61, 88, 221
London, Bette, 207
"Long Way from Home," 77, 300n3
Loo, Oliver, 251
Look and Learn, 42, 78, 79
Lorente, Louis, 65
Lorrsadmin, 151
Lovecraft, H. P., 8, 9
Love Story Picture Library, 79
"Loving Cup, The," 71, 88, 161, 231, 235, 300n1
Lugosi, Bela, 301n5 (chap. 7)
Lüthi, Max, 254, 255
Lynch, Tony, **33**

Macabich, Jordi, 64, 65, 299, 300n8
MacAdory, Roy, **33**
Magee, Terence, 36, 37, 46, 298n6, 299n6 (chap. 3)

magic, xiii, 3, 7, 11, 12, 43, 82, 95, 97, 102, 106, 113, 116, 130, 135, 155, 158, 162–68, 179, 181, 182, 196, 199, 209, 210, 217, 245, 253, 257, 258, 276, 288, 301n2 (chap. 7), 302n5 (chap. 11)
magical realism, 234, 254, 256, 261, 263
magician, 122, 128, 239, 240
Mains, Johnny, 109, 301n3 (chap. 6)
male characters, 12, 129, 207, 208, 216, 224, 225, 246, 261
Maleficent, 262
Male Gothic, 203, 204, 206, 207, 213
male readers, 264, 267, 275, 279
M&J, 130, 301n3. See also *Mandy*; *Judy*
Man in Black (host), 19, 129, 135
Mandy, 17, 19, 90, 115. See also *M&J*
Marilyn, 19, 22, 66
marriage, 19, 100, 201–3, 209, 210, 225, 242
Marriott, James, 116, 117
Marsh, Ian, 115
Martín, Antonio, 65
Martin, Sara, 8
Marty, 299n10
Marvel, 68, 105, 128
Marwick, Arthur, 109
Marxism, 40, 110, 202
Masefield, John, 260
mask, 12, 78, 106, 167, 226, 231–32, **233**, 245, 246, 250; unmask, 218
Masschelein, Anneleen, 153, 215
Masterton, Graham, 118
maternity, 202, 207, 213, 247, 258. See also motherhood
Matysiak, David Cuzik, 129
Max and Moritz, 251
Maxwell, Robert, 282, 284
McDade, Jenny, 299n11
McDonald, David, 22, 31, 32, 297n2
McGavran, James Holt, 207
McGeary, David, 119
McGillis, Roderick, 250
McGillivray, Dave, 117
McGlade, Rhiannon, 299n5
McIntyre, Clara F., 234
McKean, Dave, 250
McRobbie, Angela, 16, 17, 297n5
Medusa, 156, 239, 240. See also gorgon
Melanie, 77
melodrama, 6, 107, 214
Melville, Gaynor, 115

memory, xiii–xiv, 3, 4, 13, 59, 87, 108, 156, 159, 167, 221, 228, 250, 255, 271, 285, 286. See also nostalgia
Mennell, Ian, 299n11
Mennell, Ken, 298n6
Méon, Jean-Matthieu, 283
mermaid, 167, 239, 240, 269
metamorphosis. See transformation
metaphor, 12, 32, 82, 134, 142, 143, 201–4, 218, 219, 221, 222, 227, 232, 245, 247, 259, 293, 295. See also symbolism
Meyer, Stephanie, 241, 262
Meyers, Helen, 155, 200
Micron, 77
"Midnight Masquerader," 71, **85**, 95, 224, 225, 300n3
Mighall, Robert, 6–8, 204, 206, 234
Miller, Mavis, 38, 41, 46
Miller, Rhoda, 23, 29, 44
Mills, Pat, 4, 10, 11, 17, 18, 21, 22, 24, 25, 28, 31–32, **33**, 34, 36–42, 44, 45, 47, **48–58**, 65–67, **73**, 82–84, 100, 101, 108, 115, 119, 124, 125, 132, 151, 158–62, 182, 216, **217**, 224, 283, 290, 291, 293, 298n12 (chap. 1), 298n3 (chap. 2), 298n6 (chap. 2), 299n13, 302n6 (chap. 9)
Mirabelle, 20, 26, 41, 66, 75, 77, 79, 299n10
mirror, 3, 4, 43, 74, 78, 95, 179, 181, **183–86**, 212, 214, 218, 227–28, **229**, 232, 288, 297n1
Mirror Group, 20
Mirrormask, 250
"Miss T," 26, 28, 40, 42, 43, 68, **69**, 84, 94, 101, 102, 104, 105, 124, 136, 145, 146, 152, 238, 242, 269, 276, 277, 279, 284, 285, 287, 288, 301n11
Misty (host), 15, 25, 61, **80**, 82, 102, 126, 127, 132–50, 187, 196, 231, 266–82, 285–90, 293, 295, 300n19, 301n6, 301nn10–11
Mistyfan, 158, 293
Modleski, Tania, 201, 215, 265
Moers, Ellen, 8, 155, 199–201, 206, 207, 245
Moloney, David, 32, 290, 292
Monés, Isidre, 4, 28, 63, 64, 67, 74, **169**, **180**, **183–86**, 210, **211**, **223**, 299n7 (chap. 3), 300nn9–11
Monk, The, 235
Monster Fun, 123
monstrosity, 5, 6, 74, 82, 102, 106, 110, 118, 119, 122, 123, 145–47, 156, 167, 187, 196, 201, 202, 204, 208, 214, 217, 222, 224, 232, 234, 237, 238, 245, 250, 253, 254, 257, 275, 286
monstrous-feminine, the, 204

"Moonchild," 26, 40, 72, **73**, 100, 101, 115, 125, 153, 161, 221, 234, 255, 283–85, 300n1
Moondial, 122
Moonie, George, 102
Moore, Chris, 71
Moore, Steve, 45
moral panic, 115, 264
More, Hannah, 248
Morgan, Robin, 242
Moruzi, Kristine, 5, 161
motherhood, 19, 44, 100, 112, 115, 120, 125, 133, 135, 151, 159, 181, 201, 202, 204, 205, 207, 212, 214, 221, 222, 231, 261, 272. See also maternity
movie. *See* cinema
Mulvey-Roberts, Marie, 218
mummy, 23, 123, 133, 237, 239, 240
Munford, Rebecca, 216
Murray, Chris, 297n6
My Little Pony, 298n11
mystery, xii–xiii, 5, 10–12, 14, 19, 22–25, 28, 31, 34, 35, 40, 41, 45, 47, 59, 82, 94, 95, 97, 101, 108, 119, 124, 129, 130, 132, 142, 143, 145–48, 150, 158–63, 166, 179, 182, 187, 196, 199, 215, 216, 225, 227, 231, 238, 255, 266, 272, 274, 275, 278, 283, 285–87, 294, 295, 297n2, 301n2 (chap. 7)
Mystery and Imagination, 118
Mystery story. *See* formula
myth, 6, 23, 26, 41, 61, 96, 122, 133, 167, 207, 241, 242, 269–71, 297n3. See also legend

Nairn, Tom, 109
narratology. *See* page layout
nature (natural world), 11, 110, **111**, 112, 127, 134–36, 139, 141, 143, 149, 150, 159
Newbery, John, 248
New Eagle, 61. See also *Eagle*
New Glamour, 299n10
Newman, Kim, 116, 117
New Mirabelle, 26, 41. See also *Mirabelle*
Newnes, George, 20
Newnes and Pearson, 20, 61
New Yorker, 120
Night Gallery, 119
"Nightmare Academy," 71, 95, 160, 161, 224, 284, 300n3
Nikki, 78, 130, 301n3 (chap. 7)

"Nine Lives of Nicola, The," 42, 71, 78, 95, 96, 300n1
Northanger Abbey, 46
nostalgia, 108, 112, 234, 256, 260, 291, 292. *See also* memory
Novak, Maximillian E., 212
Nyberg, Amy Kiste, 301n5 (chap. 5)

Odhams Press, 20, 79
Oliphant, Margaret, 247
Olivers, Gertrude Ken, 299n12
Olson, Danel, 261
Once Upon a Time, 262
O'Neill, Kevin, 36
Orenstein, Peggy, 259
Ormrod, Joan, 4, 264, 297n5
Ortega, Francisco, 64
O'Shea, Keri, 234, 235, 301n5 (chap. 7)
Other, the, 7, 12, 22, 24, 37, 63, 83, 118, 142, 144, 146, 147, 150, 196, 207, 226, 227, 231, 232, 246, 254, 261, 263, 286
Over, Jay, 299n11

Paddon, Lee, 74
Page, Gil, 22, 31, 32, 77, 297n2
page layout, 4, 11, 22, 23, 28, 37, 60, 63, 72, 78, 83–86, 88–92, 97, 110, 146, 170, 179, 196, 210, 215, 228, 237, 276, 289, 293; arthrology, 90; blockage, 89, 90; grid, 23, 84, 86, 89, 90, 151, 179, 228; panel border, 23, 68, 72, 78, 84–90, 92, 93, 97, 110, 129, 131, 179, 210, 216, 228; spatio-topia, 90–92, 170, 214; splash page, 28, 62, 84, 88, 89, 91, 92, 96, 97, 276; tier, 84–86, 88–90, 92, 179; tilting, 89, 90, 141, 179
"Paint It Black," 26, 37, 71, 88, 95, 97, 161, 163, 217, 300n3
Palahniuk, Chuck, 227
Palmer, Pauline, 204, 242
Pan Book of Horror, The, 119
Pandora's Box, 218
paranoia, 201, 202, 222, 225, 261
paratext, 88, 131, 266
Partlett, Reg, 104
paternity, 130, 201, 207, 224. *See also* father
patriarchy, 12, 15, 82, 129, 134, 155, 200–205, 208, 216, 217, 219, 224, 225, 242, 246, 259, 280
Payne, Winn, 32
Paynter, Robert, 23

Pearce, Philippa, 260, 261
Pearson, 20, 61, 77, 79
pedagogy, 247–50, 252, 253, 292. *See also* education
Peeters, Benoît, 89
Peirse, A., 122
Penny, 24, 31, 42, 78, 79. See also *Jinty and Penny*
People's Friend, 65, 79
Pepetone, Gregory, 250, 251
Perrault, Charles, 215, 250, 251, 258
Perry, Douglas, 28, 78
Phantasms, 78
Phillips, Sean, 78
Phoenix, The, 298n11
Piatti-Farnell, Lorna, 8
Picture of Dorian Gray, The, 129, 218, 227, 235
Pierson, Derek, **33**
Pike, Christopher, 260, 261, 303n3 (chap. 12)
Pink, 26, 41, 42, 77
Pirie, David, 118
Pitman Publishers, 72
Pizzino, Christopher, 291
plaisir, 168, 170, 182
Play Misty for Me, 25, 26
Pleasance, Donald, 121
Pocket Chiller Library, 123
Poe, Edgar Allan, 119, 235, 247
Point Horror, 260, 261
Polanski, Roman, 118
Pope, James, 303n1 (chap. 13)
postmodernism, 7, 104, 215, 243
Pow!, 79
Pow and Wham!, 79. See also *Wham!*
Preston, Roy, 299n11
Priest, Hannah, 46, 205, 247
Prigmore, Wilf, 4, 18, 21, 22, 24–26, **27**, 28–30, 32, **33**, 35–40, 42, 44, 46, 47, 61–63, 67, 101, 116, 132, 134, 135, 142, **157**, 266, 282, 283, 298n12 (chap. 1), 298n3 (chap. 2)
Princess, 79. See also *Tammy and Princess*
Princess Tina, 102, 124. See also *Princess Tina and Penelope*; *Tina*
Princess Tina and Penelope, 78. See also *Princess Tina*; *Tina*
Proctor, William, 265
progress, 110, 112, 114, 256
psychoanalysis, 6, 118, 200–202, 204, 205, 207, 215, 226, 250, 252

puberty. *See* adolescence
public information films, 107, 108, 120, 121, 126, 164
Puigaget, Martin, 66, 77
Pulgarcito, 75
pulp fiction, 46, 118
Punch, 115
Punchard, Kitty, 43
Punter, David, 6–8, 134, 203, 209, 218, 237, 242
Purdie, John, 21–25, 36
Pustz, Matthew, 266

Quesada, Miguel, 159, 161
Quinn, Seabury, 119

Rabelais, François, 213
racism, 109, 114, 115, 126
Radcliffe, Ann, 8–10, 96, 199–201, 204, 206, 207, 209, 216, 226, 296
Rambo, 264
Rank, Otto, 227
Rayner, Jacqueline, 105, 151–53, 156, 187, 238
readers. *See* audience
Reader's Digest, 41
Rebellion Publishing, 4, 13, 14, 282, 284, 291
Redondo, Jesús, 28, 75, 77, 234, 290, 300n15
"Red Riding Hood," 250, 254, 302n1 (chap. 12)
"Red Shoes, The," 252, 258
Reynolds, Kimberley, 5, 221, 245, 261, 263, 264
Rice, Anne, 226, 302n4 (chap. 11)
Richardson, John, 11, 28, 35, 55, 67, 72, 124, **174–75**, **236**, 287, 290
Richardson, Keith, 75
Riddell, Chris, 91, 294
Rivière, Joan, 232
Roach, David, 4, 28, 60, 63–66, 75, 83, 299n2, 301n6 (chap. 7)
Rodgers, Beth, 280
Rollerball, 124
Romance, 40
Romance (genre), 5, 7, 201, 203, 205, 207, 224, 248, 264, 265
romance comics, 15–17, 19, 20, 22, 35, 60, 61, 64, 66, 71, 75, 77, 79
Romeo, 20, 22, 71, 79
Romeo and Juliet, 262
Romero, Enric. *See* Badía Romero, Enric
Romero, George A., 116, 243
Romero, Jorge. *See* Badía Romero, Jorge

Roper, Lyndal, 134
Rosemary's Baby, 117, 118
Round, Julia, 88, 92, 110, 131, 146, 152, 196, 238, 242, 297n1, 299n4, 299n7 (chap. 3), 300n8, 300nn10–11, 301n4 (chap. 7), 303n1 (chap. 13)
Rousseau, Jean-Jacques, 249
Rowling, J. K., 250
Roxy, 20, 66, 79
Rubenstein, Marc A., 207
Rudd, David, 260, 303n1 (chap. 13)
Rumeu, Jaime. *See* Homero
Ruskin, John, 212, 213
Russo, Mary, 212, 213, 269

Sabin, Roger, 15, 17, 19, 20, 301n5 (chap. 5)
Sadenwasser, Tim, 261
Sage, Victor, 226
"Salamander Girl, The," 62, 77, 100, 114, 231, 232, 300n1
Sally, 25, 31, 34, 79, 283. See also *Tammy and Sally*
Sanders, John, 20, 21, 23–25, 30, 132, 282
Sandie, 31, 78, 79, 94, 102, **103**, 123, 284, 285
Sanjek, David, 118
Sansom, William, 119
Saporito, Alf, 123
Sarland, Charles, 264
School Friend, 18–20, 22, 31, 128, 132. See also *June and School Friend*
"School of the Lost . . . , The," 72, 97, 153, 158, 160–62, 224, 255, 300n3
school story, 19, 22, 36, 95, 97, 123, 158, 160–62, 217, 224, 234, 249, 255, 284, 285
Schrøder, Kim Christian, 15, 265
science fiction, 19, 28, 31, 41, 45, 71, 105, 124, 163, 165, 166, 168, 257
Scott, Jenni, 45, 78, 100, 114, 287, 290, 303n1 (chap. 14)
Scream!, 72, 77, 238, 297n2, 303n1 (chap. 14)
Scream! & Misty, 14, 284, 291
"Screaming Point," 75, 97, 210, 217, 224, 300n3
"Secret World of Sally Maxwell, The," 71, 161, 163, 167, 221, 225, 300n1
Sedgwick, Eve Kosofsky, 8, 202, 208, 209
Selecciones Ilustradas, 63–66, 74, 77
Semic Comics, 42
sensation literature, 9, 104, 123, 199, 202, 208, 248

Sentinel, The, 124
"Sentinels, The," 35, 40, 41, 68, 97, **99**, 124, 221, 231, 232, 255, 283, 284, 291, 300n3
serials, 11, 12, 18, 19, 22, 23, 26, 37, 40–44, 62, 67, 68, 71, 72, 74, 75, 77–79, 88, 94, 95, 97, 100, 101, 107, 112, 113, 115, 116, 118, 122, 124, 128, 130, 131, 144, 145, 152, 155, 156, 158, 161, 162, 165–67, 182, 199, 204, 208, 210, 215, 217, 221, 222, 225, 234, 235, 239, 240, 243, 255, 266, 270, 273, 283–85, 287–89, 291, 297n3, 298nn4–5
Serie-Magasinet, 71
series, 11, 26, 42, 68, 79, 84, 94, 95, 102, 105, 107, 124, 128–31, 152, 182, 238, 297n3
Serling, Rod, 127
Serrato, Phillip, 212, 216, 245
sexuality, 5, 47, 82, 115, 118, 125, 135, 200, 202, 232
sexualization, 25, 117, 118, 125, 259, 294, 295
shadow, 78, 91, 92, 97, 121, 122, 139, 142–49, **176**, **191**, 196, 199, 210, 216, 221, 226, 228, **230**, 260, 284, 297n2
Shadows, 122
sharawaggi. *See* asymmetry
Sharpe, Sue, 16, 17
Shavit, Zohar, 249
Shaw, Malcolm, 21, 24, 26, 28, **33**, 35, 40, 41, 43, 45, **99**, 116, 124, 142, 144, **223**, 293
She of the Shadows (host), 130
Shelley, Mary, 46, 200, 207, 226, 235
Sherwood, Mary Martha, 248
Shopkins, 298n11
"Silver Racer-Back, The," 72, 95, 160, 163, 196, 224, 300n3, 301n4 (chap. 5)
Silvester, Gaythorne, 23
single stories, 11, 23, 26, 40, 67, 68, 71, 72, 74, 75, 77, 78, 94, 95, 100, 101, 105–7, 116, 120, 121, 155, 158, 159, 162, 165–68, 170, 179, 182, 204, 208, 222, 225, 239, 240, 255, 283, 284, 290, 291, 297n3
Sissi, 75
Sixth Sense, 124
skeleton, 122, 130, 187, 196, 214, 237–40, 252, 288
Skinn, Dez, 298n2
Slave story. *See* formula
Smash!, 79
Smith, Andrew, 153, 201, 204–6
Smith, Anna, 250

Smith, Michelle J., 5, 161
Smith, Orianne, 96, 100
Snicket, Lemony, 261
Southern Vampire Mysteries, The, 241, 262
Sowerby, Robert, 8
Spellbound, xiii, 3, 10, 14, 23, 24, 28, 31, 59, 75, 77, 91, 129, 130, 132, 152, 196, 238, 266, 273, 285, 301n3 (chap. 7), 302n3 (chap. 11)
spider, 47, **48–54**, **55–58**, 170, 196, 199, 224, 239, 240, 269, 270, 287, 288, 300n2
Spiegel, Alan, 212
Spooner, Catherine, 5, 7, 8, 46, 91, 92, 104, 107, 205, 208, 231, 238, 247, 262, 265
Spurgeon, Maureen, 44
Starblazer, 74
Starlord, 39
Star Love Stories, 77
Stein, Daniel, 266, 280
Stein, Karen, 202
Stenning, John, 25, **33**
stereotype, 16, 17, 23, 66, 114, 237, 241–43, 246, 251, 257, 258
Stevens, Ray, 26
Stevenson, Robert Louis, 227, 235
Stine, R. L., 261, 303n3 (chap. 12)
Stoker, Bram, 119, 207
Story, Rosemary Mary, 299n12
Storyteller (host), 128–32, 135, 283, 286–88
storyworld. *See* diegesis
Strand, The, 61
Struwwelpeter, Der, 251
sublime, the, 7, 9, 199, 203, 205, 206, 213, 249
subversion, 7, 12, 59, 82, 117, 135, 150, 155, 168, 205–7, 226, 242, 245, 246, 253, 257, 258, 263, 264, 280, 295
Summers, Montague, 6
"Supercats," 23, 75, 132
Supergirl, 259
supernatural, the, 5, 6, 8–10, 12, 23, 24, 28, 31, 47, 94, 97, 118, 122, 123, 125, 126, 129, 130, 163, 164, 167, 203, 204, 206, 218, 235, 237, 245, 256, 257, 263, 271, 273, 275, 289
Sweetman, Tom, 28
Swindells, Robert, 260
Sylvanian Families, 298n11
symbolism, 6, 12, 13, 74, 88, 115, 127, 134, 139, 144, 150, 204–9, 215, 226, 227, 232, 242, 245, 250–54, 256, 258, 260, 261, 263, 295. *See also* metaphor

Tales from the Crypt, 117, 128, 130, 290
Tales from the Mist 1: The Best of Misty, 290
Tales of the British Isles, 41
Tales of the Unexpected, 119, 120, 127
Tammy, 13, 14, 17, 18, 22, 24, 25, 31–32, **33**, 36, 39, 40, 42–45, 71, 72, 75, 78, 79, 94, 102, 124, 129–32, 151, 158, 161, 162, 224, 282, 285–88, 290, 292, 293, 298n12, 299n11, 299n13, 301n3 (chap. 7), 303n1 (chap. 14)
Tammy and Jinty, 42, 43, 78, 288, 289. *See also Jinty*
Tammy and Misty, 42, 78, 133, 287, 289, 300n2
Tammy and Princess, 42. *See also Princess*
Tammy and Sally, 159. *See also Sally*
Tammyfan, 101, 162
Tantimedh, Adi, 45
Tarzan, 75
Tatar, Maria, 251
Tavinjer, 74
Tebbutt, Melanie, 15, 16, 115, 265, 297n5
technology, 14, 34, 109, 163
teen. *See* adolescence
Tehrani, Jamshid J., 302n1 (chap. 12)
television, xiii, 9, 26, 34, 41, 71, 108, 109, 116, 118, 120–22, 124, 127, 262, 289
Temple Rogers Artists Agents, 71
temporality, 10, 146, 150, 206, 227, 254. *See also* time
terror, xii, 6, 8–13, 35, 40, 47, **55–58**, 62, 113, 117, 119, 133, 146–48, 151, 170, 187, **188–91**, 196, 199, 202, 203, 206, 207, 219, 248, 250, 263, 270, 276, 300n10
Teverson, Andrew, 251, 258, 263
Texas Chainsaw Massacre, The, 116, 117
Tharg the Mighty One (host), 133
Thatcher, Ma, 151
Thatcher, Margaret, 300n11
Thompson, Debbie, 285
Thomson, Stephen, 249
Three Faces of Eve, The, 124
Tigon, 117
time, 8, 86, 123, 127, 141, 143, 144, 146–48, 181, 227, 228, 235, 254, 257, 263, 272. *See also* temporality
Timour, 283
Tina, 75, 298n12. *See also Princess Tina*
Tinkler, Penny, 15, 18, 44, 222, 224, 265, 297n5, 299n12
Todorov, Tzvetan, 153, 163, 256

Tomlinson, Barrie, 77, 297n2
Top of the Pops, 283, 298n11
Tops/TV Tops, 71
Tornado, 72
Tóth, Reka, 100, 155, 159, 200, 209, 216
Tounga, 283
Toutain, Josép, 63–65
Tower of Shadows, 128
Townsend, Phil, 151
Townshend, Dale, 9, 199, 226, 248, 249
transformation, 12, 47, 62, 91, 94, 97, 100, 110, 121, 122, 156, 159, 161, 179, 199, 208, 209, 213, 215, 218, 222, 225, 242, 243, 245, 246, 253, 259–63
transgression, 5, 7, 10–12, 47, 82, 83, 85, 88, 91–94, 100, 108, 118, 120, 126, 131, 146, 158, 202, 205–8, 210, 212, 213, 218, 225, 227, 228, 231, 235, 238, 246, 249, 251, 252, 255, 263
Trease, Geoffrey, 18
Trebizon school series, 36, 298n5
Trombetta, Jim, 105
Troya, 78
truancy, 114, 288
True Blood, 262
True Stories, 61
Truffin, Sherry R., 160, 249, 250
Tuchman, Gaye, 16
Tully, Tom, 299n6 (chap. 2)
Turney, Jo, 109
Twain, Mark, 235
Twilight, 17, 46, 241, 260, 262, 264
Twilight Zone, The, 118, 127
Twinkle, 31
Twitchell, James B., 9
2000AD, 17, 24, 28, **33**, 36, 39, 41, 45, 63, 65, 67, 72, 77–78, 83–84, 90, 108, 133, 283, 291, 298n10

Una, 301n2 (chap. 6)
uncanny, the, 4, 10, 12, 23, 47, 74, 88, 104, 107, 119, 120, 125, 153, 155, 159, 161, 167, 208–10, 213–19, 221, 222, 225–27, 232, 234, 241, 243, 246, 247, 250, 254–56, 261, 263
urban environment, 6, 16, 114, 122, 234, 256

Valentine, 20, 22, 61, 66, 79, 299n10
vampire, 6, 12, 68, 102, 117, 119, 122, 156, 196, 215, 226, 237–42, 245, 250, 253, 261, 262, 264, 275, 283, 302n4 (chap. 11), 303n3 (chap. 12); Dracula, 6, 102, 129, 235, 242, 243, 291

vandalism, 106, 115, 119, 121, 163, 257
Vanessa, 284
Vanity Fair, 116
van Thal, Herbert, 119, 301n3 (chap. 6)
Varma, Devendra, 6, 9
Vault of Horror, The, 117, 128, 133
Veeder, William, 249
Vicomte, Le, 78
Victor, 22
Vincent, Adrian, 23
Vitruvius, 212
Vlad the Drac, 261
voodoo, 78, 196, 243
Vosper, Ian, **33**

Walduck, Desmond, 151, 158
Walker, Pete, 117
Walkerdine, Valerie, 16, 297n5
Wallace, Diana, 204, 205, 209, 215, 238, 241
Walpole, Horace, 6, 92, 216, 226
warlock, 237
Warlord, 22, 83
Warren, Norman J., 117
Warren Publishing, 63, 64, 74, 75, 78, 128, 299n4, 300n10
Warwick, Alexandra, 7
Wasson, Ellis, 109
Watts, Isaac, 248
Weinstock, Jeffrey, 104
Weldon, Fay, 200
Wellington, Ian, 249
"Wendy the Witch," 28, 79, 84, 94, 102, **103**, 104–5, 123, 152, 238, 242, 276, 279, 284
Wenn, Len, 45
werewolf, 101, 117, 119, 122, 237, 239, 240, 243, **244**, 253
Wesson, Peter, **33**
Westell, Robert, 261
Wham!, 79, 123
Wham! (band), 283
Wheatley, Dennis, 118
Wheatley, Helen, 9, 91, 120, 122
Whedon, Joss, 262
When a Stranger Calls, 117
whimsical macabre. *See* comedy
"Whistle and I'll Come . . . ," 68, 97, 100, 114, 124, 152, 159, 241, 255, 273, 300n3
Whitehouse, Mary, 26
Whizzer and Chips, 79, 124

Whoopee!, 123, 124
Wilde, Oscar, 227, 235
Wilkes, Peter, 28, 78, **198**, 199, **244**
Wilkinson, Nic, 290
Williams, Anne, 6, 155, 203, 204, 206
Williams, Gilda, 8
Williams, Raymond, 249
Wilson, Letty, viii–xi, 297n1
"Winner Loses All!," 68, 153, 161, 300n3
Winnett, Susan, 207
Winnicott, Donald W., 249
Winship, Janice, 16
wishes, 43, 116, 149, 159, 163–65, 182, 250, 262
Wisker, Gina 9, 204
Wiskin, Chris. *See* Lloyd, Chris
witch, 12, 23, 28, 42–44, 68, 71, 79, 82, 84, 94, 102, **103**, 106, 112, 118, 121–23, 127, 128, 134, 135, 145, 146, 152, 167, 196, 199, 226, 231, 235, 237–40, 242, 243, 258, 260, 276, 277, 279, 284, 288, 301n1 (chap. 7)
Wizard of Oz, The, 62
Wolf, Naomi, 16, 258, 259
"Wolf Girl," 72, 113, 159, 219, **220**, 234, 243, 271, 274, 300n1
wolfman, 243. *See also* werewolf

Wolfreys, Julian, 92
Wollstonecraft, Mary, 209
Woman, 30
Woman in White, The, 235
Woman's Own, 30
Woman's Realm, 30, 77
Woman's Weekly, 30, 61, 77
Woo, Benjamin, 291, 292
Wood, Henrietta Rix, 16
Wood, Robin, 117, 118
Wordsworth, William, 235
Worker, Norman, 26, 32, 34, 45, 79, **80**, 135, 144, 283
Wow!, 123, 124
Wright, Angela, 100, 204, 209, 218
Wrobel, Pete, 297n1
Wuthering Heights, 235, 262

Yang, Sharon Rose, 110
young adult (YA) literature, xiii, 5, 161, 212, 216, 248, 250, 261, 262

Zipes, Jack, 251, 258
Zlosnik, Sue, 104, 106, 200, 204, 205, 209
zombie, 6, 74, 167, 196, 237–40, 243

ABOUT THE AUTHOR

© Clifton Photographic Company

Julia Round researches and writes about Gothic, comics, and children's literature. She is particularly interested in analyzing the unusual places that Gothic can be found in all its structural, thematic, and aesthetic forms.

Julia is one of the editors of the academic journal *Studies in Comics* (Intellect Books) and of the book series Encapsulations (University of Nebraska Press). She is co-organizer of IGNCC, the annual International Graphic Novel and Comics Conference (now in its tenth year). She holds a BA in English literature and MA in creative writing from Cardiff University, and a PhD in English literature from Bristol University. She is a principal lecturer in the Faculty of Media and Communication at Bournemouth University, where she is also programme leader for the University's MA English and Literary Media course, and the convenor of its Narrative Research Group.

In 2015 Julia received the Inge Award for Comics Scholarship for her work on *The Walking Dead*. She speaks at numerous international conferences each year and has published many peer-reviewed articles and chapters in multiple languages. Her critical books include the monograph *Gothic in Comics and Graphic Novels: A Critical Approach* (McFarland, 2014) and the coedited collection *Real*

Lives, Celebrity Stories (Bloomsbury, 2014). Recently she also published her first short comic, "Doll Parts," in the anthology *Wilma: Whatever Happened to Girls' Comics?* (Inkpot, 2017).

Julia lives in her beloved hometown of Bristol, England, with her partner Greg and their daughter Dana. You can find out more, read her articles and comics, and contact her directly at www.juliaround.com; she is always happy to talk!

SELECTED PUBLICATIONS

Gothic in Comics and Graphic Novels: A Critical Approach. Jefferson, NC: McFarland, 2014.

"Gothic and Comics: From *The Haunt of Fear* to a Haunted Medium." In *The Edinburgh Companion to Gothic and the Arts*, ed. David Punter. Edinburgh: Edinburgh University Press, 2019.

"Spaces of Horror in *Locke and Key*." In *Horror: A Reader*, ed. Simon Bacon. Oxford: Peter Lang, 2019.

"*Misty, Spellbound* and the Lost Gothic of British Girls' Comics." *Palgrave Communications* 3, article no. 17037 (2017). https://www.nature.com/articles/palcomms201737.

"Gothique et bande dessinée, des fantômes entre les cases." Trans. Benoît Glaude. In *Le statut culturel de la bande dessinée: Ambiguïtés et évolutions / The Cultural Standing of Comics: Ambiguities and Changes*, ed. Maaheen Ahmed, Stéphanie Delneste, and Jean-Louis Tilleuil. Louvain-la-Neuve: Academia-L'Harmattan, 2017.

"Revenant Landscapes in *The Walking Dead*." *International Journal of Comic Art* 17, no. 2 (Fall 2015).

"Children's Responses to Heroism in Roald Dahl's *Matilda*." By James Pope and Julia Round. *Children's Literature in Education* 46, no. 3 (October 2014).

"The Zombie Walk." In *Mythologies Today*, ed. Julian McDougall and Peter Bennett. London: Routledge, 2013.

"Gothic and the Graphic Novel." In *A New Companion to the Gothic*, ed. David Punter. London: Blackwell, 2012.

"Mutilation and Monsters: Transcending the Human in Garth Ennis/Steve Dillon's *Preacher*." In *The Human Body in Contemporary Literatures in English: Cultural and Political Implications*, ed. Sabine Coelsch-Foisner and Marta Fernández Morales. Frankfurt am Main: Peter Lang, 2009.

Lightning Source UK Ltd.
Milton Keynes UK
UKHW020643170120
357103UK00001B/5

9 781496 824462